Saadia Gaon: His Life and Works

Malter, Henry

BIBLIOLIFE

THE MORRIS LOEB SERIES

SAADIA GAON
HIS LIFE AND WORKS

BY

HENRY MALTER, Ph. D.

Professor of Rabbinical Literature at the Dropsie
College for Hebrew and Cognate learning

PHILADELPHIA
THE JEWISH PUBLICATION SOCIETY OF AMERICA
1921

אן אללה לא יכלّי אמّתה מן תלמיד פי כל עצר יעלّמה
ויבצّרה חתّי יפתיהא ויעלّמהא ותנצלח בה אחואלהא.

God does not leave His nation at any period without
a scholar whom He inspires and enlightens, so that he
in turn may so instruct and teach her, that thereby her
condition shall be bettered (Saadia, *Sefer ha-Galui*).

To
SOLOMON SOLIS COHEN, M.D.
in token of
high esteem and sincere friendship

PREFACE

The present book was originally designed to furnish a biography of Saadia Gaon for the biographical series of the Jewish Publication Society of America, at whose request the work was undertaken. At that time, about six years ago, there were already in existence (as will be seen from pp. 90 f.) a considerable number of sketches of Saadia's life, written in various languages (Hebrew, Latin, French, German, English, Russian, and Dutch); but all of them were based upon the epoch-making essay of Rapoport, who, writing nearly a century ago (1828)—long before the Genizah gave up its treasures—had at his disposal only the scanty material scattered in the mediæval sources. For the biographical part in particular, only the Report of Nathan ha-Babli, the Epistle of Sherira Gaon, and some additional remarks by Abraham Ibn Daud were available. All that could be gathered from these sources about Saadia's life was that he was born in Egypt in 892, that he was appointed Gaon of Sura in 928, was deposed by the Exilarch David b. Zakkai and later reinstated (the deposition and reinstallation being related with some detail), and that he died in 942. Rapoport's biography, if it may be so called, consists therefore, chiefly of learned notes dealing with Saadia's writings, so far as these were accessible to him or known from quotations. Subsequent writers on Saadia followed Rapoport's example, adding nothing to the Gaon's biography, but entering more fully upon the description and characterization of his teachings.

Even after the new material of the Genizah had come to light, scholars concerned themselves in the main with the identification of the various fragments of Saadia's works and the analysis of their contents. Incidentally attention was called also to new historical facts contained in some of the fragments, but no attempt was made to interrelate these facts and to combine the isolated data into a general picture of Saadia's life. Even the fragments relating to the Ben Meir controversy, so important for our knowledge concerning Saadia's movements in the East, have been considered more in their bearings upon the question of calendar, than in their relation to Saadia.

For the purpose of writing a biography this material was rather discouraging. It seemed that any attempt to draw a complete picture of Saadia's life on the basis of the few disconnected biographical data which had so far been utilized would prove fruitless, and that, instead, one should devote every effort to a full description of the Gaon's works and a systematic presentation of his doctrines. However, in order to get a more definite view of the subject it was necessary to submit the entire material of the old, as well as of the newly discovered, sources to a careful reexamination; to correlate the widely scattered details; and to try to interpret them in the light of already established facts. After repeated study of certain Genizah fragments, hitherto partly ignored and partly misinterpreted, new points of view gradually revealed themselves and fresh combinations appealed for consideration. Finally, after much sifting and analyzing, grouping and classifying of the collected details, the subject of our investigation stood out in relief. For here was Saadia, the *man*, with his human faults and virtues, his passions and convictions, his sufferings and rejoicings, victories and defeats. His entire life opened before us and we could follow his career almost without interruption. At times we were also granted a glimpse into his family affairs and his personal relations with his pupils.

At first the plan suggested itself, to use all this biographical material as external framework—as the convenient setting to what is after all the most important aspect of Saadia's life, namely, the scientific work which he bequeathed to

posterity. Such disposition of the material would have had
the advantage of enabling us to follow step by step the intellectual growth and development of Saadia, as he advanced
in years and maturity. Upon closer examination, however,
this arrangement did not appear feasible, since our knowledge
of the various writings of Saadia is not of a nature to warrant
definite conclusions regarding their chronological order.
Moreover, the combined treatment of Saadia's life and
works under such a plan would have required a volume
far exceeding the limits set for the biographical series of
the Jewish Publication Society.

I had therefore decided to treat of Saadia's life independently of his works, and to leave the presentation of his
literary activity for a separate volume. The Committee of
the Jewish Publication Society, however, upon receiving
the manuscript of the biography in the form in which it
appears in the present volume, did not deem it advisable to
issue a biography of Saadia without including between the
same covers an adequate appreciation of his writings. Moreover, it was desired to preserve the footnotes, which are not
exactly suited for a purely popular sketch. To solve the
difficulty it was considered best to have the two parts published together as the first volume in the scientific series of
the Morris Loeb Foundation.

This method had some drawbacks. By dividing the material into two distinct parts repetitions have in several instances become inevitable. Thus a work like the *'Agrōn,*
in itself of comparatively little importance, but of special
significance for our understanding of Saadia's earlier education, had to be discussed in more than one connection,
each time from a different viewpoint. Similarly, some of
the other works, as the Commentary * on the *Sefer Yeẓirah,*
the *Sefer ha-Galui,* and the *'Emūnōt we-Dēōt,* had to be
taken up for discussion in the biography. For no matter

* Throughout this volume commentary is spelt with a capital when,
as in the case before us, it forms part of the title of the Hebrew or
Arabic work referred to.

under what aspect the life of a scholar and author is viewed,
it cannot be entirely detached from his works. On the
whole, however, an earnest effort has been made to avoid
such repetitions as much as possible.

In an exhaustive work on Saadia it might further be
expected that the general characterization of his achievements in the various branches of learning would be illustrated by numerous details and quotations from the respective works. This would seem especially desirable in the
section dealing with Saadia's Bible exegesis, although the
most important features of his work in this line have been
repeatedly discussed by numerous modern authors. However, the field of Bible exegesis is so immense and Saadia's
contributions to it so manifold, that their elaborate discussion
would have required a special monograph. Here was a
case of *divide et impera!* The brief summarizing exposition
touches on the main features of Saadia's exegesis, and the
numerous references to old and new sources, as given in the
notes and the Bibliography, will do the rest.

Some inconsistencies will be noticed in the transliteration
of Hebrew and Arabic names, titles of books, etc. It was
not thought necessary in all instances to burden the print
with the devices used in technical works in the endeavor
to represent the exact sounds of the Oriental words. The
exceptions, however, are comparatively few and mostly in
common and frequently recurring words, as *Ibn, Tafsir, Ali,
Galui, Zikron, Genizah,* and the like. Proper names occurring in the Bible, as Anan, Berechiah, Hophni, Nahshon, etc.,
are reproduced without diacritical points, as they are found in
the English versions. Titles of books very frequently referred to are reproduced in full only when quoted for the
first time. In subsequent passages they are given in some
shortened form, as *Beiträge* (Dukes, Eppenstein, Jellinek),
Anfänge (Bacher), or in abbreviations, as *AL* (Steinschneider), and the like. In some instances the name of the
author was deemed sufficient, as Bornstein, Lazarus, etc., the

reader being expected to revert, in case of doubt, to the appended List of Abbreviated Titles (p. 429). In these matters, too, various inconsistencies came to my notice while revising the proofs, but it appeared too cumbersome to restore absolute uniformity in quotation.

A word must be added about the ' Bibliography.' The title is somewhat misleading and may needlessly frighten away the reader; but it has been adopted in the absence of a better short title equally convenient for repeated reference. This section of the work really represents an attempt at a critical history of the entire Saadia literature. I cherish the hope that any student who in the course of his reading has become interested in some of the branches of learning here presented, will welcome the help he may receive from it. The general reader, too, while not prepared to go into literary details, may find it gratifying to learn, by a glance through these pages, of the extraordinary attention the great Gaon has commanded throughout the ages, and the amazing amount of intellectual work that has been done by Jews and Christians in editing and translating, describing and elucidating his numerous writings.

In conclusion, I desire to express my profound gratitude to Miss Henrietta Szold, who, despite her manifold communal and literary activities, generously consented to go over the entire manuscript, to assist in putting it into final shape for publication. Apart from this general editorial work, which was no small task, she has made ever so many valuable suggestions in various directions, by which the work has greatly profited. I am under special obligation to my friend, Dr. Solomon Solis Cohen, who, in addition to many personal kindnesses, has taken the greatest interest in the present work. In a genuine spirit of friendliness he has given much of his precious time to a painstaking revision of the proofs, and, with his enviable mastery of English, removed, as by a touch of magic, many unevennesses in style and diction that had escaped my notice. He also was kind enough to furnish a translation of one of

Saadia's poems (see p. 337). My thanks are also due to my colleague and friend, Prof. Alexander Marx, of the Jewish Theological Seminary of America, who greatly assisted my efforts with his rare bibliographic knowledge and placed at my disposal a large number of books, some very rare, from his rich private library.

PHILADELPHIA,   HENRY MALTER.
        July, 1920.

INTRODUCTION

At the outset of his task the historian or biographer has to decide how he will envisage the broad problem presented. Shall he view the idea or the fact as the impelling force in human history? Are events born of ideas, or are ideas the necessary outcome of conditions? Do circumstances shape the individual, or does the individual compel circumstance? The first view may be designated as the genetic, or realistic, conception of history; the second, as the idealistic conception.

In a measure it is true that neither of the two factors, to the exclusion of the other, is the sole creative force in human history. The real point to be determined is as to which of them should be given the greater prominence in presenting and interpreting historical phenomena. The prevailing and, it would seem, correct view, is that the individual whose influence in shaping events may appear to be paramount at a certain period of the world's development, enters the arena as a genuine product of surrounding conditions, subject to all the laws of evolution by which other mortals are governed. Only gradually, the exceptional genius frees himself from the common shackles. He rises above his environment and takes the guidance of history into his own hands.

The first requirement, therefore, in presenting the life and work of such a genius, is to ascertain and depict the conditions that furnished the basis for the later developed individuality. It is the only way of accounting for what seems in the beginning to be entirely out of harmony with the general laws of causation.

Saadia Al-Fayyûmî is not to be classed among these highest geniuses of the world; but his greatness is so real, and so individual in its quality, that he cannot be fully explained as a necessary product of his time and surroundings. Nevertheless, it is needful to investigate the conditions of his earlier life, his education and his family relations, which

must have contributed importantly toward making him the
founder of a new epoch in Jewish history and literature.

Unfortunately there is not enough material at hand to
allow us to form a trustworthy opinion of the circumstances
of our hero's earlier life. Nor are the historical records of
the Jews in Egypt during the age of Saadia such that we
can with certainty establish the influences at play in the
shaping of that great individuality during the years of
growth and development. The period in question is represented in Jewish annals by an almost blank page, and there
is but little hope that the page will ever be written upon,
unless the Genizah furnishes new material.

Not even legend,[1] the graceful substitute for stern history, has shown itself kind enough to Saadia to crown his
personality with a wreath of poetry and beauty, such as it
fashioned for not a few of the great men of the Jewish people
before and after him. The man who was to inaugurate a
new era in Jewish learning and literature springs out of the
darkness to light the torch of reason in the gloom-encom-
passed camp of his brethren, and, his mission performed,
darkness again engulfs him; for according to the records
Saadia died "in melancholia." No poet is known to have
sung the praises of the departed leader; no elegist has given
expression to the grief and sorrow that must have overtaken
Babylonian Israel at the untimely death of the greatest Gaon;
no chronicler has left us even a prosaic account of the events
immediately before and after this turning-point in the
history of the ancient academy of Sura. The only fact
that has been preserved is that a successor was installed,
who failed to keep alive the orphaned institution; for with
the death of Saadia, *the* Gaon, the Gaonate virtually ceased
to be.[2]

---

[1] See below, chapter viii.

[2] It is true that about fifty years after the death of Saadia the Sura
academy was reopened under the presidency of R. Samuel b. Hophni,
but the institution never regained the rank it occupied under Saadia.
Its very existence was made possible only through the close family
relations that were established between Samuel b. Hophni and the
Gaon Hai of Pumbedita (see below, note 281). Almost no Responsa

But though no definite information can be obtained with regard to the beginning and the end of Saadia's career, we are much more fortunate when we approach the main period of his life, a period that covered only about twenty-five years. During that time he put out one book after the other—dealing sharp blows to Karaism and the other enemies of traditional Judaism; translating, commenting, and elucidating the Bible and the Talmud; collecting and composing hymns and prayers; and writing the first philosophical Commentary on one of the most puzzling mystical works in Jewish literature. It was while engaged in this fruitful literary work that he was unexpectedly called to the highest position in the gift of tenth century Jewry. Soon thereafter we see him in a bitter struggle with the mighty Exilarch, the temporal head of the Babylonian Jews. Deposition and retirement into private life; the appearance of his *magnum opus*, the first philosophical presentation of Judaism since Philo; reconciliation with his enemies and re-installation in the office of Gaon,—all these events follow in rapid succession, and reveal to our eyes a man of astounding force and untiring energy; a life short when measured in years, but crowded with occurrences of tremendous import for the subsequent history of the Jewish people.

Such is, in brief, the story of Saadia Gaon, the details of which occupy the following chapters.

As noted, the first twenty years and more of Saadia's life, the years most essential in shaping character and individuality, are wrapped in obscurity. A complete biography is therefore impossible. However, the manuscript material brought to light within the last two decades contains various details which, when properly correlated, enable us to fill some of the gaps in our knowledge of Saadia's career and to give an authentic account of certain important happenings hitherto unknown. For instance, on the basis of

---

exist of Samuel b. Hophni, who had otherwise written extensively on various subjects, which also indicates that under his Gaonate the Jews of the Diaspora did not turn to Sura for legal and religious advice, but to the more important academy of Pumbedita.

a new and, it would seem, plausible interpretation of some
Genizah documents, we gain valuable information about
Saadia's family relations, the causes that induced him to
leave his native country, his travels, and his connection with
the academy of Sura prior to his election as Gaon.

For full appreciation of Saadia's life and work we should
know the condition of the Egyptian Jews during the ninth
century; that is to say, the social and intellectual atmosphere
in which the future Gaon grew up. Here again the few
details at our command have not been derived from the
commonly known Jewish and general sources; it has been
necessary to cull them from recently unearthed, fragmentary
documents. And valuable as they are, they are not direct
information; they only afford a basis for certain inferences.
Therefore, so far as concerns Saadia's surroundings during
his formative period, we must confine ourselves to general remarks showing the points of contact between the culture and
learning which we later find represented in Saadia, and the
culture and learning of his immediate predecessors and contemporaries. An attempt at a more detailed description of
the various channels through which Saadia received the
many-sided education that made it possible for him to become the highest exponent of Jewish culture in the Orient
would lose itself in vague hypotheses, adventurous rather
than informative.

The facts about Saadia's early training and education,
and to some extent also the cause of his emigration from
Egypt, must thus remain a matter of speculation. Happily,
we are better informed about his life and activity during
the many years of his sojourn in the East, prior to his
installation as Gaon (928). This information likewise
comes to us through the documents that are continually
cropping up from the famous Egyptian Genizah. Nearly
all of these documents relate to what is called the Ben Meir
controversy,—a controversy in which Saadia played the most
important part, and which therefore forms an essential portion of his biography. But it is only when we approach the
last period of Saadia's life, beginning with his election to

the Gaonate, that the sources of information flow more abundantly, and our knowledge of the Gaon becomes more adequate. It is thus in keeping with the literary material at hand that the period covering Saadia's experiences in the Gaonate (the period which hitherto has constituted the whole of Saadia's biography) is treated here with more detail than the others.

Welcome, however, as a complete knowledge of the circumstances of Saadia's earlier life would be, both to the biographer and the student, the absence of such information is, in this case, less deplorable than in that of other eminent persons. Saadia's historical importance, as an official personage, as the religious head and representative of Babylonian Jewry and, in part, of the Jews in European countries, is undeniably great. But he appeals to our interest less through his powerful individuality as a public leader and uncompromising fighter for his cherished ideas and principles, than through his scholarly attainments—through the literary monuments left to posterity in nearly all branches of Jewish learning and literature. Our concern is therefore primarily with Saadia the scholar and investigator; the pioneer and pathfinder in the field of Jewish science; the linguist, grammarian, lexicographer and exegete; the Talmudist and the philosopher—in brief, the first scientific expounder of Biblical and traditional Judaism.

But is this not exactly what we should expect in a work on the life of a great man in the history of the Jewish people? History in its last analysis is mind materialized, thought transformed into action. In this sense the Jews of the Diaspora, taken as a whole, had no history; for they had little opportunity to act, they were everywhere acted upon. Their story is therefore not the account of a people's national and political activity, but that of human patience and endurance. From another point of view, too, the history of the Jews differs from that of any other nation. The history of a people revolves, for the most part, around its great men, who by their powerful individuality give direction to its destiny; the Jewish people, having been deprived of all temporal power, had no such career to offer to those of its sons who, by virtue of extraordinary natural gifts, were qualified for leadership in the great movements of national life. The gifted personalities among the Jews spent themselves, with few exceptions, in the effort to acquire learning, sacred and secular. Essentially, Jewish history is a record of scholars and their literary productions, with the emphasis laid on the latter. It is a history of learning more than of living, of literature rather than of affairs.

It is thus in keeping with the general character of Jewish history that the biography of Saadia should primarily be a record of his literary achievements and of his spiritual influence. Much space must therefore be devoted to the presentation of his teachings in the various departments of Jewish learning of which he was the founder. In the field of religious philosophy and ethics Saadia's theories are to be detached from all that is incidental or, from our point of view, unessential, so that his general attitude and his basic system of religion may come out clearly. A brief characterization of the Gaon's standing in the estimation of later ages and of the importance attributed to his works by Jewish medieval authors, concludes the presentation.

In order to give the student of Saadia all the information he may have occasion to look for in the course of his inquiries, an exhaustive bibliography is necessary, not only of the writings of the Gaon himself, but also of the vast literature, reaching down to the present time, in which Saadia or his writings form the main subject of discussion. Aside from this practical purpose, the immensity of this Saadia literature in the various fields of research will make the reader realize at a glance, perhaps better than any description, the great significance of the man whose life and works were the origin and source of so much scholarly activity in generations past and present, and may stimulate him to enter upon the same field and continue the chain of Saadia students for the furtherance and promotion of Jewish learning and literature.

CONTENTS

PART I
LIFE OF SAADIA GAON

THE FIRST PERIOD OF SAADIA'S LIFE
(4652-4675=892-915)

CHAPTER I

ORIGIN AND FAMILY RELATIONS

Saadia[3] was born, in the year 892, in the village of

[3] The Hebrew form of this name is, like that of similar names occurring in the Bible (*e. g.,* עֶזְרִיה, נְעַרְיָה, יְשַׁחְרִיה), סְעַדְיָה, or fuller סְעַדְיָהוּ, not סַעַדְיָהוּ, as Harkavy, זכרון לראשונים, etc. (hereafter quoted briefly: *Zikron*), V, 162, 164, and Bacher, *JE.,* X, 579, have it (but comp. מֶעַדְיָה). This form of the name is proved by rhymes found in MSS., where the metre positively requires it; comp. D. S. Margoliouth, *Lines of Defense of the Biblical Revelation,* London, 1900, p. 41, n. 1; Renan, *Les écrivains Juifs Français* (reprint from *Histoire littéraire de la France,* Vol. XXXI), p. 155 (501); Steinschneider, *Arabische Literatur,* p. 40. The correct transliteration is therefore *Se'adiah* which is, indeed, adopted by some recent scholars, as by Margoliouth, *l. c.;* comp. *JQR.,* XIII, 158, no. 6, and Cowley, *Catalogue of the Hebrew MSS. in the Bodleian Library,* II, *s. v.* I have preferred, however, to retain the old traditional form of transliteration, for after all the form employed for the sake of the metre may have been merely theoretical, and is no proof that the name was generally so pronounced. Grammatically סְעַדְיָה stands for יִסְעַדְיָה, being the (shortened) imperfect of the verb סַעַד, *to support,* and the noun יָה =God, meaning "may God support" (the bearer of the name). Sometimes the word יה is supplanted by אל = God, giving the same meaning (comp. חֲנַנְיָה=חֲנַנְאֵל). Thus the Gaon is called סַעְדָאֵל by Moses Ibn Ezra, *JQR.,* X, 224; *JE., s. v. Saadia.* This form, however, was used as a proper name mainly among the Ḳaraites. In Arabic Saadia called himself *Sa'īd* which means *fortunate.* A rhetorical description of the Hebrew language, representing a part of Saadia's earliest known work, the *'Agrōn* (Harkavy, *Zikron,* V, 52), gives the double acrostic סעיד בן יוסף, similarly in his hymn on the 613 precepts (ed. Joel Müller, in *Oeuvres complètes de Saadia,* IX, 67 ff.; comp. *ibidem,* p. xxi) and in his *'Azhārōt* (קובץ מעשי ידי גאונים קדמונים, Berlin, 1857, pp. 52 ff.), as well as in his Polemic against Ḥiwi, edited by Davidson, New York, 1915, pp. 34 f.; comp. Bacher, *RÉJ.,* XXXV, 291. Occa-

Dilâz,ʼ in the district of Fayyûm, Upper Egypt. He seems to

---

sionally Saadia is called also המצרי, the *Egyptian* (Dukes, *Beiträge*, II, 16), perhaps also בן הצפני with allusion to צפנת פענח (Gen., 41, 45), the name of his father being likewise Joseph; see Harkavy, *MWJ.*, V, 26.

According to Steinschneider, *JQR.*, XI, 327, the Hebrew name by which Saadia called himself in a later work, the *Sefer ha-Gâlui* (Harkavy, *Zikron*, V, p. 163, last line; 165, ll. 6, 10), was the original, of which the Arabic *Saʼid* was the translation. Bacher (*Rivista Israelitica*, II, 46; comp. *JE.*, X, 579), on the other hand, thinks that the Hebrew name is an artificial equivalent of the original Arabic *Saʼid*, which view seems to me the more probable. This is certainly the case with Saadia's Hebrew by-name הפיתומי, which was substituted for the original Al-Fayyûmi, *i. e.*, of Fayyûm (comp. Geiger *Wissenschaftliche Zeitschrift*, V, 314, note), perhaps because of the phonetic resemblance of the two words, or more probably because the Gaon himself (as also Muhammedan writers; comp. Steinschneider, *JQR.*, XI, 588, no. 580) in his Arabic translation of the Bible renders the Biblical פתם (Exod. 1, 11) by פיום, though modern research has proved that the Biblical *Pitom* is situated in Lower Egypt and therefore cannot be identical with the Fayyûm, which is in Upper Egypt. It is a well known fact that Saadia liked to render Hebrew words and proper names by Arabic equivalents of similar sound, even when he knew that they had nothing in common but the sound; see the references given by Taubeles, *Saadia Gaon*, Halle 1888, p. 27, n. 7, especially W. Engelkemper, *De Saadiac Gaonis Vita* etc., Münster, 1897, p. 7, n. 3. Frankl (*Monatsschrift*, 1871, p. 355) takes the untenable view that פיתומי is a derivation from פתה, meaning "deceiver," and was originally given to Saadia by his adversaries with the purpose of vilifying him. Were this true it would be highly improbable that all the Hebrew authors who quote the Gaon reverentially with the adjective Pitomi should have been unaware of its disparaging meaning. When the Karaite Sahl b. Maẓliaḥ (960) in an Epistle published by Pinsker (לקוטי קדמוניות, II, 36) refers to Saadia as "the *Pitomi* who deceived (*patah*) the people," he simply plays on the by-name Pitomi by which Saadia was already known.

For completeness' sake it may be added that the Arabic historian Al-Masʼûdi, quoted below, note 20, calls Saadia "Saʼid Ibn Jaʼkûb," which is, perhaps to be changed into Ibn *Abi* Jaʼkûb, in which form it is the by-name (*kunya*) of Joseph; see for this matter Steinschneider, *JQR.*, IX, 622, *Arab, Literatur*, p. 46.

ʼThe information that Saadia was born in Dilâz is found first in a controversial letter of Saadia's opponent known only under the

have been of humble parentage, his father, Joseph, probably
deriving his livelihood from some trade. If we are to put
credence in certain contemporary sources, Saadia's father
was successively or simultaneously a butcher, a barber, a
leech,[5] and a muezzin.[6] For some reason not stated in these
sources he was exiled from Egypt and died in Jaffa.[7] The
same documents assert that Saadia was not of Hebrew origin; that his parents were descendants of Egyptians of the
village of Dilâz who had been converted to Judaism. It
would in no wise be derogatory to Saadia if any of these assertions, or all of them, proved to be true. The employ-
ment of a man, if pursued honestly, detracts nothing from
his personal worth, nor would the fact that his ancestors
happened to be proselytes lessen in any degree our recogni-

name Ben Meir. The letter was written in the winter of 921-22, and
was published first by Harkavy, *Zikron*, V, 213-220; see particularly
ib., p. 216, line 1. Ben Meir repeats the same in a second letter written
in the summer of the same year and published first by Schechter,
JQR., XIV, 56 ff., and in *Saadyana*, Cambridge, 1903, p. 20; see *ib.*,
line 6. Both letters were republished with numerous corrections and
notes by H. J. Bornstein in the *Sefer ha-Jōbēl* in honor of N. Sokolow, later in a separate volume under the title מחלקת רב סעדיה גאון,
ובן מאיר Warsaw, 1904. In the following notes I shall refer to the
pages of this important work in its separate edition only. For the
matter under discussion see *ib.*, pp. 50, 90. Another opponent of
Saadia, Aaron Sarjâda, later Gaon of Pumbedita, also refers to
Saadia disparagingly as a " Dilâzian gentile "; see Harkavy, *l. c.*, p.
234, l. 15. About the place Dilâz see the references given by Harkavy,
l. c., p. 234, n. 9; comp. *ib.*, pp. 145, n. 2, 165, n. 11; Wüstenfeld,
Geschichte der Fatimiden Chalifen, Göttingen, 1881, p. 313. For the
year of Saadia's birth see also Buber, שערי ציון, Jaroslau, 1885,
p. 32, n. 420, and his Introduction to תנחומא, p. ר''מ. His contention, followed by Grünhut, הגן, 1899, p. 180, that Saadia was born
in 862 is without basis. [For the date 882, found recently in a
Genizah fragment, see *Postscript*.]

[5] See Bornstein, p. 90, n. 5; Harkavy, p. 230.

[6] Schechter, *Saadyana*, p. 20, n. 3; comp. Eppenstein, *Beiträge zur
Geschichte und Literatur im geonäischen Zeitalter* (reprint from
MGWJ., 1908-13), Berlin, 1913, pp. 127 f.; below, note 188.

[7] Schechter, *ib.*, n. 4. There is no reason to doubt the veracity of
the sources in this point. Saadia's father may have died in Jaffa on
his way East to join his son, see below, note 119.

tion of his character and greatness.[8] But coming, as these
reports do, from men known to have been the bitterest
enemies of Saadia, with the obvious intention of discrediting
and disqualifying the object of hatred, they must be put on a
level with the invectives and malicious charges against the
Gaon that are found in the same documents.[9] We may leave
such hostile testimony out of our calculation. On the other
hand, from the respectful tone in which a very prominent
and well-informed authority[10] refers to Saadia's father, we
may conclude that the latter, whatever his occupation may
have been, was a pious and learned Jew.

Moreover, I am inclined to think that the panegyric of
a Gaon and his family discovered some years ago in the
Genizah[11] has reference to none other than the Gaon Saadia

[8] The Talmud points with pride to several eminent teachers of
the Mishnah as descendants of non-Jews, and even R. 'Akiba, the
"father of rabbinical Judaism," was, according to an old tradition
(Nissim, פמתח, 18b), the descendant of proselytes. R. 'Akiba's
famous pupil, R. Meir, is said to have been the descendant of Nero
(b. Gittin, 56a); comp. Brüll, Jahrbücher, II, 154 ff.; Harkavy,
Zikron, V, 233, n. 3; see also Harkavy, Saadjah-Miscellen, Israelitische Monatsschrift (Beilage zur Jüdischen Presse), Berlin, 1890,
no. 12.

[9] Saadia is here accused of profaning the name of God, trans-
gressing in public the laws of the Sabbath, embezzling the funds
collected for the poor, and leading a debauched life; see Harkavy,
Zikron, V, 233. That there was not a shadow of truth in any of
these charges is evident from the fact that the same men who uttered
them, particularly the Exilarch David b. Zakkai, later reappointed
and recognized Saadia as Gaon, as the religious and spiritual head of
all Israel; comp. Harkavy, l. c., p. 223.

[10] R. Sherira, the Gaon of the sister-academy in Pumbedita (961-
998); see Sherira's Epistle, ed. Neubauer, I, 40, top; Bornstein, p. 90,
n. 5, end.

[11] Schechter, Saadyana, no. xxxv. The MS. was already out
of my hands, when another portion of this panegyric was published by Mr. Jacob Mann (JQR., N. S., vol. IX (1918-1919), pp.
153-160). Mr. Mann dismisses Schechter's tentative identification of
the hero of the poem with Saadia as out of the question, because in
the acrostic of the poem the author styles himself רבנו (our teacher)
which, had Saadia been the subject of the eulogy, he would certainly
not have done. Space forbids to enter here upon a detailed discussion
of the new portion of the panegyric. But it may be pointed out that

and his house. There we learn that he had three sons and two married daughters. There were also a brother and nephews, the sons of his sisters, who apparently were considered members of his family.[11] In two passages we are informed that Saadia's wife, "though advanced in years, was still fresh and vigorous and bearing fruit," and the writer expresses his wish that the child to which she was about to give birth should be a son.[12] Now it is known from historical sources that Rabbi Dosa, the only son of Saadia who acquired prominence as a scholar, was born during

---

no poet would properly refer to *himself* in the acrostic as "*Our Teacher*"! The title רבנו refers not to the author but, like the immediately following titles, to the subject of the poem. Without basis is also Mr. Mann's contention that this part of the panegyric is the continuation of the one published in Schechter's *Saadyana*, because there only three sons of the hero are alluded to (p. 68, l. 22), while here "already" four sons are mentioned, a fourth son having in the meantime been born. One may just as well reverse the order and say that when the part published in *Saadyana* was written one of the four sons had died. With such argumentation we get nowhere.

[11] Schechter, *Saadyana*, p. 64.

[12] I derive these details from the text in Schechter's *Saadyana*, p. 66, ll. 25-6; p. 67, ll. 18-19. My interpretation of the text will do away with the difficulty raised by Schechter, *l. c.*, p. 65, who opposes the identification of the Gaon, to whom the panegyric is dedicated, with Saadia on the ground that no reference is made therein to R. Dosa, the only son of Saadia known to history. At that time Dosa was not yet born. If, on the other hand, we assume that the Gaon referred to is Samuel b. Hophni, we are confronted not only with the difficulty, also pointed out by Schechter, *l. c.*, that Samuel's son-in-law, the Gaon Hai, is not mentioned, but also that his learned son, R. Israel, who is supposed to have assisted him in the Gaonate, is likewise disregarded; see for this matter Poznański, *RÉJ.*, LXII, 120-123, and *JQR.*, 1912-3, p. 403, bottom; Ginzberg, *Geonica*, I, 13, note. The author of the panegyric is most likely the same R. Abraham to whom Saadia in his letter to his pupils in Egypt (*Saadyana*, p. 25, l. 2, overlooked by Poznański, *Schechter's Saadyana*, p. 8) refers as "our friend," and perhaps identical with אברהם סגלת הישיבה mentioned in *Saadyana*, no. lvi, p. 148, l. 17; see Schechter, *Saadyana*, pp. vii, 147. It may also be noted that the eulogist refers to Yannai and Eleazar [Kalir] as the Gaon's models in the field of poetry (p. 73, l. 24) which is done also by Saadia in his אגרון

Saadia's first occupancy of the Gaonate (928-932)," the
period in which the panegyric under discussion must have
been written. If we bear in mind that we are dealing
with the Orient, where the women age at a very much
faster rate than with us, we shall concede that the author
of the eulogy might well describe Saadia's wife, who was
then about forty, in the terms quoted. That Saadia was
the father of several children besides the well-known Dosa
is borne out by two fragmentary letters which were likewise discovered in the Genizah.¹⁵ These were undoubtedly
written by Saadia, and in both he mentions his "beloved
children." The author of the eulogy, a certain Abraham
Kohen, who appears to have acted as the Gaon's secretary,
speaks with great veneration of his master's progenitors,¹⁶
perhaps including the father." The language is so vague
that it cannot be decided with certainty, whether in speaking
of Saadia's "forefathers" Abraham had in mind particular

(Harkavy, Zikron, V, 51) and in his Commentary on the Sefer
Yezirah, ed. Lambert. p. 23; see below, p. 44.

Recently A. Marmorstein (JQR., N. S., vol. VI (1915-1916), pp.
158 ff.) has put forth the view that "there are five different Abraham
Hakohen." However, as he has only four, he borows one from
Schechter's Saadyana, p. 64, n. 12. The passage in no way bears
out his contention.

¹⁴ See Poznański's article on Dosa, רב דוסא ברב סעדיה גאון (reprint from הגרן, vol. VI) Berdyczew, 1906, p. 9, who, approaching
the subject from another side, also arrives at the conclusion that
Dosa must have been born about 935. This, to my mind, is a little
too late, as in that year Saadia was already an exile, while our eulogy
refers to him as Gaon. That this eulogy, if it refers to Saadia, was
written after his reinstatement in the office (937) is quite improbable,
as in this case we should expect some explicit reference to the important events that took place during the years immediately preceding it.

¹⁵ Schechter, Saadyana, no. vii; Bornstein, p. 67; JQR., IX, 37,
reprinted by Epstein, RÉJ., XLII, 201, Bornstein, p. 69. The importance of these letters will be discussed later. Here I wish to state only
that the authorship of Saadia is established beyond doubt in spite of
the objections of Israel Lévi (RÉJ., XLI, 231); see Epstein, l. c., 202;
Bornstein, 71, and recently also S. Eppenstein, Beiträge, p. 91.

¹⁶ Schechter, Saadyana, pp. 66, l. 17; 68, l. 14 (?); 73, l. 28.

¹⁷ Schechter, Saadyana, p. 65, n. 5.

persons known to him, or used the word figuratively in a
general sense.[17a] In connection with this it should be noted
that Saadia himself claimed to be of the tribe of Judah. He
traced his pedigree directly to Shelah, the third son of
Judah,[18] while the historian Abraham Ibn Daûd (12th century) asserts that Saadia was a descendant of Ḥanina b.
Dosa, a teacher of the Mishnah in the first century.[19]

[17a] In the part published by J. Mann, however, the allusion to the
father is quite explicit; see Mann, *l. c.,* p. 159, n. 143.

[18] Harkavy, *Zikrōn,* V, 164, n. 10; 229, n. 5; comp. Bornstein,
pp. 72 f; below, note 230. We need not attach much importance
to this statement; it is repeated too often in the history of Jewish
celebrities to be true. Ben Meir (see below, note 150), Sherira (see
below, note 228), Rashi, Maimonides, Isaac Abarbanel, and many
others made similar assertions, or were put in such relationship by
generous Hebrew chroniclers; see Weiss, דור דור ודורשיו (Wilna,
1904), IV, 146; *idem,* בית תלמוד, I, 161, particularly Zunz in his
notes on the *Itinerary of Benjamin of Tudela* II, 6-9; see also below,
note 659.

[19] See Poznański, רב דוסא ברב סעדיה גאון, p. 7, n. 12.

CHAPTER II

SAADIA'S EARLY EDUCATION

The uncertainty that characterizes the first period of
Saadia's life is felt most strongly when we approach
the question of his early education. It is not merely a matter of the details needed for the completion of Saadia's
biography as an individual. We are concerned with the
beginning of a new epoch in the history of the Jewish
people, the immediate causes and surrounding circumstances of which, the Jewish historian is particularly desirous
of knowing. We should like to reach back to the very
roots of the thoroughgoing change in the intellectual development and literary activity of the Jews that coincides
with the appearance of Saadia on the scene. We should
like to know in how far Saadia's individual genius is responsible for the new era he inaugurated, or to what
extent we ought to feel indebted to his teacher or teachers,
Jewish or Muhammedan, and to the intellectual atmosphere
which he breathed during his formative period. Unfortunately, there is nothing in the available sources to clear up
these points, and the student must comfort himself with
the reflection that all beginnings are obscure.

The only positive reference to a teacher of Saadia is
found in the work of a contemporary Muhammedan writer,
the historian Al-Mas'ûdi [20] (died 957), who names as such a
certain Abû Kathir Yahya al-Kâtib of Tiberias. Mas'ûdi
reports that he had a religious disputation with Abû Kathir
in Palestine, and that the latter died in 320 of the Hegira
(= 932, C. E.). No further particulars are known about
this Abû Kathir, except that the famous Muhammedan

[20] In his *Kitâb at-Tanbih*, edited by J. M. De Goeje in *Bibl. Geogr.
Arabicorum*, vol. VIII, Leyden, 1894, p. 113. French translation by
Carra de Vaux, *Le Livre de l'Avertissement*, Paris, 1896, p. 169.

theologian Ibn Ḥazm (994-1064) quotes him together with Saadia and David Al-Muḳammiṣ (see p. 67) as one of the Jewish Mutakallimûn (theologians).[21] Modern Jewish investigators are inclined to identify him with Judah Abû 'Ali, or b. 'Alân, ha-Nazir of Tiberias,[22] an eminent grammarian, whom the Ḳaraites count as their own.[23]

[21] See below, note 33.

[22] The first to suggest this identification was L. Dukes in his קונטרס המסורת, Tübingen, 1846, p. 2. The suggestion was taken up by Steinschneider in his essay *Jüdische Literatur* in Ersch and Gruber's *Encyklopädie*, II, vol. 27, p. 414, n. 27 (1850; English edition, "Jewish Literature," London, 1857, p. 324, n. 27, Hebrew translation by H. Malter, Warsaw, 1897, p. 194, n. 4), also by Geiger in the Hebrew periodical *Ozar Neclmad*, II (1857), 158 (reprinted in Geiger's *Nachgelassene Schriften*, V, 32, and recently also by Poznański, קבוצת מאמרים, Warsaw, 1910, p. 233), and Pinsker, *Likkūtē* (1860), I, 5, 105. The Hebrew sources from which our knowledge of this grammarian is derived give his name as Judah b. 'Alân ha-Ṭabbarāni, *i. e.*, of Tiberias (so the Karaite Judah Hadassi, 12th century, in his *'Eshkōl*, Alphabet 257, letter מ: . . . יהודה בן עלן הטברני משכילי נ"ע; comp. *ibidem*, Alphabet 173, letter ט, where he mentions טברני המדקדק as the author of a work מאור עינים), and 'Ali b. Judah ha-Nazir (so David Ḳimḥi in מכלול, ed. Lyck, 1862, p. 81; comp. Dukes, *Beiträge*, II, 133; Bacher, *Die Anfänge der Hebr. Grammatik*, p. 44, n. 4). In the text I have given the name in accordance with Steinschneider, *Arab. Liter. der Juden*, § 23; comp. *ib.*, § 67, where the references to a considerable literature on the matter are given; see also *JQR.*, XIII, 315. Here it should only be mentioned that according to Pinsker, *l. c.*, 5 (accepted by Bacher in Winter and Wünsche's *Die jüdische Litteratur*, II, 141) this Judah is probably referred to by Abraham Ibn Ezra (מאזנים, beginning), who speaks of a "scholar of Jerusalem, whose name is unknown and who wrote eight valuable works on grammar in the Arabic language." He is mentioned also by the Karaite Lewi b. Jephet, 11th century (Pinsker, *l. c.*, II, 64; comp. *ib.*, p. 139, where a Hebrew elegy of Judah is quoted) and by Judah Ibn Bal'am, an eminent grammarian of the 11th century (Pinsker, *l. c.*, I, 5); comp. also Harkavy, *Zikron*, V, 115, and in לוח אחיאסף, Warsaw, 1894, pp. 279 f.; *Ha-Goren*, IV, 75 ff.

[23] See Harkavy, *l. c.* and *Zikron*, V, 115, who disputes this Ḳaraitic claim and, against Pinsker, concludes that he was a Rabbanite; comp. also Steinschneider, *AL.*, § 23.

3

The identity of this reported teacher of Saadia is of far-reaching importance, not only for his pupil's biography, but also for the general history of medieval Jewish literature. Ever since the question has been mooted as to when and by whom scientific methods of investigation were first introduced into the various fields of Jewish literature, particularly that of Hebrew philology and exegesis, scholars have been divided on that point. Jost,[24] Munk,[25] Geiger,[26] and particularly Pinsker[27] were of the opinion that the Karaites inaugurated the period of scientific activity, more especially as concerns grammatical and lexicographical works. From them the spirit of investigation spread to the Rabbanites. Pinsker, indeed, goes so far as to assert that "soon after the close of the Talmud there appeared a number of Karaite scholars who wrote on astronomy, philosophy, rhetoric, poetry, grammar, and lexicography," preparing thereby the new era of Jewish science, which is commonly considered Saadia's creation. It was Anan, the founder of Karaism (750), who originated the watchword, "Search well in the Bible!" and thus gave his followers the impetus to break with the Midrashic, allegorical interpretation of the Scriptures dominant among the Jews of his time, and to replace it by an exegesis based on grammatical and philological studies. On the other hand, Rapoport,[28] Steinschneider,[29] and more recently Bacher[30] and Harkavy,[31]

[24] Geschichte der Israeliten, II, 328.

[25] Notice sur Abou'l-Walid Merwan Ibn-Djanah, Paris, 1851, p. 4.

[26] Wissenschaftliche Zeitschrift für jüdische Theologie, V, 274; comp. also Poznański in Leben und Lebenswerk of Abraham Geiger, Berlin, 1910, p. 383.

[27] Likkute, I, 4 ff.; comp. his introduction to that work, p. iv, and Schorr's criticism of the same in He-Haluz, VI, 56 ff. For other references see Steinschneider, Jewish Literature, 326, n. 33; 327, n. 49; idem, Bibliographisches Handbuch, Leipzig, 1859, p. xii, n. 5.

[28] In his biography of Saadia in the Hebrew periodical Bikkure ha-'Ittim IX (1828), 20 ff.

[29] JQR., XIII, 314; XVII, 356; MWJ., XX, 236; comp. also ib., XIX, 260.

[30] Die Anfänge der hebräischen Grammatik, Leipzig, 1895, pp. 2, 38 f.

[31] Zikron, V, 36 f.; comp. MWJ., XX, 149, 236.

basing their views on the testimony of Abraham Ibn Ezra, who gives an historical enumeration of the first Hebrew grammarians, emphatically deny the claim of the Karaites, and assign priority to Saadia. Harkavy, the consistent opponent of Pinsker, even goes to the extreme of denying that the Karaites had any part at all in influencing the development of Hebrew philology; a view espoused, however, by no other scholar.

If, now, the above-mentioned Abû Kathir is identical with Judah b. 'Alân, supposedly referred to by Abraham Ibn Ezra as the author of eight works on grammar, and if he was a Karaite, as is claimed by Judah Hadassi and, following him, by Pinsker, we should have here not only the desired information on the nature and the sources of Saadia's early education, but also sufficient ground for the assumption that the Karaites had in fact taken the lead in bringing about the new era of learning and literature, of which Saadia was merely the first Rabbanite exponent. But such is not the case. There is no good reason to doubt the identification of Abû Kathir with Judah ben 'Alân, but it is altogether improbable that the latter was a Karaite. Many of the Karaite opponents of Saadia were his contemporaries, and could not have been ignorant of a circumstance so favorable to them. Had Saadia's teacher been a Karaite, and a scholar of such eminence that even a Muhammedan writer took notice of him, they would not have failed to advert to a fact that might seem to show both their own superiority and the ingratitude of their adversary.[32] On the other hand, there is excellent reason to believe that the teacher of Saadia was a Rabbanite. Al-Mas'ûdi makes an teacher of Saadia was a Rabbanite. Al-Mas'ûdi makes an explicit statement to this effect with reference to Abû Kathir,[33]

---

[32] This becomes the more certain when we remember that some Karaites accused Saadia of such ingratitude toward his Karaitic opponent Salmon b. Jeroham, whom they falsely declared as Saadia's teacher in order to base their accusation thereon; comp. Weiss, דור דור ודורשיו, Wilna, 1904, IV, 124, n. 1.

[33] That Abu Kathir was a Rabbanite may be concluded also from the fact that Ibn Ḥazm (see above, p. 33) mentions him as a Jewish

while in respect to Judah b. 'Alân the epithet *Tabbarānī
ha-Medakdek* (" the Tiberian grammarian ") renders it all
but certain that he belonged to the school of the Tiberian
Masorites, who were all adherents of traditional Judaism.

The information given by Al-Mas'ûdi enables us to
establish a relationship of pupil and master between Saadia
and one of the scholars of his time, whoever he may have
been. There is no evidence, however, that the relation existed during the first period of Saadia's life, while he was
still in Egypt. It may have fallen into the period of his
Palestinian sojourn. Saadia emigrated to Palestine in 915,
at the age of twenty-three.[33a] He was still young enough to
sit at the feet of a master; and Abû Kathir (who, according
to Al-Masûdi, died in 932) may have been sufficiently his
senior in years to take the part of his senior in learning.
From Arabic sources we know that Al-Mas'ûdi visited Palestine in 926,[34] probably the year of the religious disputation,[35]
mentioned before, carried on by him with Abû Kathir at
Tiberias. Here and on that occasion it may have been that
he made the acquaintance of Abû Kathir the master, and
Saadia the disciple. To be sure, in the year 926 Saadia
had settled permanently in Babylonia as a member of the

Mutakallim together with Saadia and Al-Mukammis (see Friedländer, *JQR.*, N. S., vol. I (1910-1911), p. 187, n. 6). It is not probable
that this Muhammedan polemist, who was familiar with Jewish matters (comp. Poznański, *JQR.*, XVI, 765-771) would have thus mixed
together Karaites and Rabbanites on the ground that they had theories
on the Kalâm in common. For Al-Mukammis see below, p. 67.

[33a] But see *Postscript*.

[34] See Brockelmann, *Geschichte der arab. Literatur*, I, 144; Steinschneider, *JQR.*, XII, 298.

[35] One of the disputed questions was whether the divine law was
intended for all times or was given with the view of being abrogated
at some future time when it will be replaced by a new law. This
problem greatly agitated the minds of Jewish and Muhammedan
theologians of the time, and Saadia himself has devoted much space
to its discussion in the third chapter of his *'Amânât;* comp. Steinschneider, *Polemische und apologetische Literatur*, p. 103; Guttmann,
Die Religionsphilosophie des Saadia, Göttingen, 1882, pp. 148 ff.;
Goldziher, *RÉJ.*, XLVII (1903), 41 f.

academy of Sura. This does not preclude, however, his having been in Tiberias the same year; he was in the habit of traveling.

Assuming all this to have been the case, nothing has been gained so far as concerns the first period of Saadia's life—the Egyptian period under consideration. We must again leave the safe ground of positive history and try to satisfy ourselves with conjectural indications. We shall have to set out, as it were, on a voyage of exploration to Egypt and the neighboring countries, or to countries known to have had some connection with ninth century Egypt, in order to discover the learned or otherwise prominent men living there shortly before and during the time of Saadia. Such men testify to an intellectual life and to literary activity in circles which, judging from particulars to be enumerated later, must have been accessible to Saadia, and must have determined his course.

In the first place, it must be pointed out that the language of the Jews of Egypt and the other Eastern countries under Muhammedan rule was, without doubt, chiefly Arabic. In all probability the language of the Korân had become the vernacular of most of the Jews and the Samaritans soon after the Heǵrah.[36] This being the case, it is obvious that Saadia could make use of the literature of the Arabs as well as the works of Judaeo-Arabic authors. That the Arabs, even previous to the time of Saadia, had developed a vast literature, covering all fields of human knowledge, is too well known to require detailed proof. Nor can there be any doubt that the literary productions of the Arabs living in the main seats of Arabic culture (Bagdad, Baṣra, etc.) were current also in Egypt, which until 972, when it was

---

[36] See A. E. Cowley, *JQR.*, VII, 565; *ib.*, XII, 495. The Arabic speaking Jews always attached a certain degree of sacredness to the Arabic language, which they considered as "corrupted Hebrew"; see for this matter Steinschneider, *JQR.*, XIII, 303-310; *idem AL.*, pp. xxiv, xxxiv; Bacher, *JE.*, V, 13. For quotations of the Korân in the works of Saadia see the references by Steinschneider, *JQR.*, XII, 499.

conquered by the Fâtimide Caliph Al-Mu'izz, was a de-
pendency of the 'Abbaside Caliphate that had its seat in
Bagdad. This political connection was re-enforced by constant migrations between the two countries, owing to the
pilgrimages to Mecca that were frequently undertaken by
the Muhammedans in large troops (caravans). Numerous
scholars in various fields of literature and science are known
to have lived in Egypt during the ninth and tenth centuries.[37] Still closer relations existed between Egypt and
the neighboring countries in northwestern Africa (Cyre-
naica, Tripoli, Algeria, and Morocco of today), especially

[37] For the many scholars who lived either their whole life or for
some period in Egypt before and during the time of Saadia, see
Brockelmann, Geschichte der arabischen Literatur, I, 91, 131, 142,
no. 4 (the great historian Al-Ṭabari), 148, 162c-d, 173 f., nos. 7-8,
176, 178 (the 'Imâm Al-Shâñ'i, founder of a school of Fuḳahâ', i. e.,
expounders of Muhammedan law, whose influence can be seen also
in Saadia's Halakic work; comp. Steinschneider, Hebräische Uebersetzungen, p. xxiii), 180, nos. 2-3, 198, no. 2 (a Ṣûfi), 221 (the astronomer Al-Fargâni; comp. Malter, Die Abhandlung des Abû Ḥâmid Al-
Gazzâli, Frankfurt a. M. 1896, pp. viii f.), 226 (the famous historian
Al-Ya'ḳûbi, died 891), 232, no. 5 (a teacher of Isaac Israëli, but see
Steinschneider, JQR., XIII (1901), 97); comp. also Steinschneider,
Orientalistische Litteratur-Zeitung, 1904, col. 431, no. 87A (probably
the same one who is mentioned in Wüstenfeld, Geschichte der
Fatimiden-Chalifen, p. 38, as living in the Maǵreb), ib., 1905, col.
213, no. 200 (where the date 1526-7 is to be corrected to 933, as in
Brockelmann, l. c., I, 173; see Steinschneider, ib., 1905, col. 489, l. 1),
col. 264, no. 234. For Judah b. Joseph of Raḳḳa in Egypt (or Meso-
potamia? see Steinschneider, Hebräische Übersetzungen, 378, n. 69;
p. 774; idem, JQR., XI, 328, top, and below, note 135), a physician and
philosopher (pupil of the famous astronomer Thabit b. Kurrah, who
died in 891), with whom Mas'ûdi reports he had a disputation at
Tiberias in 314 of the Heǵra (= 926, c. e.). see Steinschneider,
Arabische Literatur, § 24; comp. JQR., XIII, 298, and above, notes
21, 34. All the scholars mentioned in the passages referred to were
famous in the various fields of literature and science in which they
worked. It goes without saying that these scholars were not the
only ones in Egypt and the Maǵreb; that there were many more in
the various parts of both countries, who were not active as authors,
or whose works were lost during the following centuries. It is
therefore but reasonable to assume that there existed a compara-

after the rise of the Fâṭimide dynasty (909), which had established its seat in Ḳairwân,[71] a city subsequently famous in the history of the Jews.[72]

The question is to what extent did Saadia, prompted either by his own desire for learning, or other motives, familiarize himself with the works of Muhammedan authors before his emigration from Egypt to Palestine. We shall have occasion to show the influence of Arabic literature on Saadia in works of his, written beyond a doubt at a later period of his life. Here, only the following passage can be cited to prove that the Arabic influence had begun to show its traces at the time when he was preparing one of his earliest known literary productions, the Hebrew lexicon and rhyming dictionary '*Agrōn*. The very name of this book, written in his twentieth year,[73] is in imitation of titles used by Muhammedan authors for similar works.[74] It is not necessary, however, to draw conclusions from such technical details. Saadia expresses himself unreservedly about his indebtedness to Arabic authors, who served him as models in the composition of his work. "It is reported," he says, "that one of the worthies among the Ishmaelites, realizing to his sorrow that the people do not use the Arabic language correctly, wrote a short treatise for them, from which they might learn proper usages. Simi-

tively high standard of culture and civilization among the Egyptian Muhammedans of the eighth and ninth centuries, though their schools of learning, as Brockelmann (I. 131) avers, were entirely dependent upon those in the 'Irâḳ, the main country of the Caliphs and the seat of Arabic culture, which at that time had reached the highest mark in the history of the people.

[71] Comp. Wüstenfeld, *Geschichte der Fatimiden-Chalifen*, Göttingen, 1881, pp. 29 ff.

[72] See Poznański's אישׁ קורדּוא, Warsaw, 1909, where a full account is given of the Jewish scholars who are known to have lived in Ḳairwân from the beginning of the ninth to the middle of the eleventh century, when, owing to adverse political events, the Jewish community was disorganized and dispersed.

[73] See Harkavy, *Zikron*, V, 46, n. 6; 56, n. 40: comp. also *ib.*, p. 28, notes 8 and 9; Bacher, *REJ.*, XXIV, 308.

[74] Harkavy, *ib.*, 29 f.

larly, I have noticed that many of the Israelites do not observe even the common rules for the correct use of our
[Hebrew] language, much less the more difficult rules, so
that when they speak in prose most of it is faulty, and when
they write poetry only a few of the ancient rules are observed, and the majority of them are neglected. . . . This has
induced me to compose a work in two parts containing
most of the [Hebrew] words." [42] A few lines before
this passage he mentions having met numerous scholars who
spoke of the loss of many scientific works, two of which he
quotes by title. The rules of Hebrew grammar adverted
to in the fragments of this work possessed by us—only a
little more than the Introduction has been preserved—likewise reveal the influence of the school of Arabic grammarians.[43]

Great as the influence of Arabic culture on Saadia may
have been, his main teachers, even in the period under consideration, are to be looked for among his own brethren, and
the chief sources that inspired him in his youth with love
for knowledge and the ambition to follow a learned career
must be sought in the field of early Jewish literature. To
do justice to him we must take into account whatever is
known, either on the testimony of available sources or by
way of assumption, of his personal contact with learned
contemporaries or his acquaintance with the older writings.
The evidence thus secured will furnish us the background
against which Saadia's figure stands out prominently.

In the first place it must be taken into consideration that
Jewish life and some Jewish literary activity persisted in
Egypt long after the Alexandrian period. In the absence
of adequate historical records [44] its nature cannot be accu-

[42] Harkavy, ib., 45, lines 3 ff.; comp. Bacher, Die Anfänge der hebr.
Grammatik, p. 60.

[43] See Bacher, ib., p. 60, n. 3.

[44] Several interesting Greek documents, partly from the Fayyûm,
the birthplace of Saadia, and dating from the sixth and seventh
centuries are discussed by Théodore Reinach, Nouveaux documents
relatifs aux juifs d'Égypte, RÉJ., XXXVII, 218-225; see in particular p. 219, no. 3, and pp. 224 f., Post-scriptum.

rately defined. On the other hand, so far as the mediæval period is concerned, we can trace Jewish learning in various parts of Egypt as far back as two centuries before Saadia. This is sufficiently borne out by the various collections of Hebrew papyri found in Egypt, particularly in the district of Fayyûm, where Saadia was born.[45] A rather conservative estimate places the origin of the Fayyûm papyri in the first half of the eighth century. Most of the fragments contain remnants of liturgical hymns, one of them bearing, according to Zunz[46] and Steinschneider, close resemblance in style to a hymn by Eleazar Ḳalir. The existence of synagogue poets in the Fayyûm at so early a period, and no doubt also much later, down to the time of Saadia, may have inspired him with the idea of writing the *'Agrōn,* which was intended to teach the art of versification.[47]

The spread of Talmudic learning in Egypt long before Saadia is further attested by a document brought to light from the Genizah, in which a certain Abû 'Ali Ḥasan of Bagdad appears as "the Head of the Congregation" of Fostât (Old Cairo) in the year 750.[48] In another document one Nahum b. Abraham binds himself not to dispose of his share in a house, of which two others mentioned by name were joint owners with him, in such a way as to transfer his portion of the property to a certain Joseph Kohen. The agreement is drawn wholly on the basis of the Talmudic law governing the peculiar situation, and the phraseology used is also Talmudic. Mention is made of two synagogues situated in Fostât, for whose benefit the same Nahum was to pay a fine of twenty denarii in case of breach

---

[45] Steinschneider, *MWJ.,* VI, 250-254; *idem, Bibliotheca Mathematica,* Stockholm, 1895, p. 23; comp. Harkavy *Zikron,* V, 31; Th. Reinach, *l. c.; JE.,* V, 60, *s. v. Egypt.* For the origin of the Jewish community in the Fayyûm see in particular Blau, *Papyri und Talmud,* Leipzig, 1913, p. 10 and references.

[46] Quoted by Steinschneider, *MWJ.,* VI, 251.

[47] Harkavy, *Zikron,* V, 37.

[48] See *JQR.,* XVII, 426 ff.; Ginzberg, *Geonica,* I, p. 2, n. 1; p. 55, n. 1; p. 61, n. 1; p. 122, note, end; E. J. Worman, *JQR.,* XVIII, 1 ff.; comp. also Weiss, ודורשיו דור דור, Wilna, 1904, IV, 124.

of contract. Many other manuscript fragments discovered
in the Genizah, some of which belong to the ninth and tenth
centuries, contain references to the same two synagogues, and
make it otherwise certain that large Jewish settlements
existed in Egypt, particularly in Fostât, as early as the eighth
century, and probably even earlier, in the post-Alexandrian
period.[49] We may therefore take it for granted that a Saadia,
impelled by a keen desire for learning, early familiarized
himself with whatever knowledge existed among the Jews
of his own country.

That the Jews of Egypt before and during the time of
Saadia had been in possession of the literature and learning
emanating from the two academies of the Babylonian Geonim, the main seats of Jewish culture in those times, is likewise to be considered a matter of course. Indeed, there was
hardly any other country except Palestine, that was in such
frequent communication with Babylonia in the period under
consideration. The fact that, over and above a large
number of unclassifiable remnants of a diversified literature, so many fragments of the Babylonian and the
Palestinian Talmud,[50] as well as a very large collection of
Geonic Responsa[51] were among the treasures of the Genizah in Cairo, may be taken as proof that the study of the
Talmud in general and of the Geonic literature in particular

[49] See Worman, *JQR.*, XVIII, 12, top. 21, l. 5; 27, bottom; 38;
Bornstein, מחלקת רס"ג, p. 37, n. 2; 40, n. 2.

[50] שרידי הירושלמי, edited by Louis Ginzberg, New York, 1909.

[51] Forming the second volume of Ginzberg's *Geonica*, New York,
1909. This fact remains significant even if many of the manuscripts
were written at a period later than that of Saadia, for they may be
copies of much older originals, which were current in Egypt long
before. Most of the Responsa published by Ginzberg, so far as the
authorship can be ascertained, come from the Geonim Moses b.
Jacob, Sar Shalom, Natronai b. Hilai, Amram, Zemah b. Paltoi,
Nahshon (all of whom lived between 832-874), and others of the
pre-Saadianic period; comp. Ginzberg, *ib.*, pp. 19, 28, 88, 107, 143,
156, 176, 179, 186, 191, 210, 216, 237, nos. 10-13, 255, no. 2, 298, no.
26, 301 ff.; see also *Appendix* (*Sheëltot* and the *Halakot Gedolot*),
ib., 349 ff.

had had full sway among the Jews of Egypt at an early period. It goes without saying that the young and wide-awake Saadia followed the spirit of the time, and was a busy student of the entire range of Geonic writings. Possibly his acquaintance with this literature and his ardent desire to see with his own eyes the great spiritual leaders of the Jews of the Diaspora, were among the causes that subsequently induced him to emigrate to the land of the Geonim.

Another and a no less important factor that must be considered in the search for the sources of Saadia's early education is the relation between the Jews of Egypt and those of Palestine, especially the city of Tiberias. As early as the beginning of the eighth century Tiberias was the seat of a distinguished school of Masorites and punctuators of the Bible.[52] Palestine was also the soil from which sprang the Midrashim, the oldest collections of homiletical interpretations of Scripture. These originated between the sixth and tenth centuries and are as genuinely Jewish in spirit as the Talmud, next to which they rank in bulk in Jewish literature. Besides several works of Halakic content, belonging to the same period,[53] the mysterious *Sefer Yeẓirah* ("Book of Creation") is in all probability also the product of Palestine.

That Saadia, while yet in Egypt, at the door of Palestine, was thoroughly acquainted with the products of Palestinian authors can in many instances be substantiated by quotations in his own works. Thus, in his earliest surviving book (the *'Agron*), he mentions by name five "ancient Hebrew poets," whose compositions, he avers,

---

[52] The ספר תגין, published by J. J. L. Bargès, Paris, 1866, is probably also a product of the Tiberian Masorites. Sachs, in his introduction to the work, considers it still older. At any rate it was known also to Saadia, as he mentions it in his Commentary on the *Sefer Yeẓirah* (ed. Lambert, 94, top); comp. below, note 452.

[53] E. g. the *Sheëltot* (Halakic discussions) of R. Aḥa of Shabḥa (eighth century), the tractate *Soferim* (see the references in Bardowicz, *Die Abfassungszeit der Baraita der 32 Normen*, Berlin, 1913, p. 37, n. 2), and some of the מסכתות קטנות; see Bornstein, מחלקת, p. 111.

served him in some points as an example [54] Three of
these poets are the famous Payyetanim Jose b. Jose, Yannai,
and Eleazar Kalir, who, as is now ascertained, lived in Palestine during the seventh, and at the beginning of the eighth,
century. The identity of the two others, Joshua and Phinehas, is still doubtful, but in all probability both were Palestinians belonging to the school of Masorites [55] whose works
Saadia often used As to the *Sefer Yezirah*, we know that
Saadia wrote a philosophic commentary on it.[56] It is true
that this commentary belongs to a later period,[57] and it might
be assumed that he became acquainted with the *Sefer
Yezirah* during his sojourn in Palestine. Such an assumption, however, does not recommend itself. The book must
have been known in the East and also in Egypt some time
prior to Saadia's birth. It was probably the reputation of
the work that induced him to provide it with a commentary.[58]
At least two other authors, both contemporaries of Saadia,
but living in different countries, also wrote commentaries
on it, Isaac Israeli in Kairwân and Shabbetai Donnolo in

[54] Harkavy, *Zikron*, V, 51.

[55] Comp Bacher, *Anfange*, 42, 47, 50, n 2; for Phinehas see *ib.*
31, n. 1; Harkavy, *Zikron*, V, 112; comp. the list of Masorites, *HB.*,
XIV, 105; Brull, *Jahrbucher*, II, 174; for Joshua see Harkavy,
Zikron, V, 110

[56] *Commentaire sur Sefer Yesira* . . . *publié et traduit par Mayer
Lambert*, Paris, 1901.

[57] The year 242 *Contractuum* = 931 common era, is given by Saadia
himself (ed Lambert, p 52; French translation, p. 76) as that in
which the work was written, hence not in Egypt, as is generally
assumed. This matter will be discussed in detail later on, when the
work comes up for special consideration.

[58] Saadia himself at the end of his Introduction to the Commentary (Arabic text, p. 13, lines 5 f, French translation, p. 29) gives
as a reason for his writing the commentary " that the book is *not*
of frequent currency and that only few people are able to understand it " (אד׳ ליס הו כתאב כתיר אלוגראן ולא אלכתיר מן אלנאס
יקף עליה). This, however, seems to mean only that the book,
because of its unintelligibility, was not popular among the people in
general, and does not exclude its being well known and much studied
by scholars, who alone concern us here

Italy. Aside from these general considerations there is strong evidence that Saadia knew the *Sefer Yeṣirah* at the time he wrote the *'Agrōn* and was indeed influenced thereby as to certain grammatical doctrines. This is almost a certainty as regards Saadia's main grammatical work, the *Kitâb al-Luġah* ("Book on the Language"), which was probably written in Egypt soon after the *'Agrōn*. This book is no longer in existence,[59] but various particulars found in the works of later authors made it possible for Bacher [60] to give a full description of its original plan and arrangement, as well as of its contents. In his Commentary on the *Sefer Yeṣirah* [61] Saadia himself, in the course of his discussion of its grammatical features, not only quotes lengthy passages from his *Kitâb*, but also refers to the latter for a more elaborate treatment of certain points. If a more convincing fact is needed to prove that Saadia had the *Sefer Yeṣirah* before him when he wrote the grammar, it is furnished by the established circumstance that Saadia's grammatical theories coincide in many particulars [62] with those of his contemporary, the famous Masorite Moses b. Aaron b. Asher, concerning whom the *Sefer Yeṣirah's* influence has been proved beyond a doubt.[63] It should further be noted in this connection that Saadia was the one who first suggested [64] that the *Sefer Yeṣirah* originated in Palestine.

Finally, among the general promoters of intellectual life at about the time of Saadia, mention must be made of the Karaites. It is now the consensus of opinion among scholars that there is no foundation for the claim made by Karaite

[59] Some fragments were published by Harkavy in *Ha-Goren*, VI (1897), pp. 30-38.

[60] *Anfänge*, pp. 38-60.

[61] Ed. Lambert, p. 75, l. 3 from bottom, French part, p. 97; comp. Bacher, *Anfänge*, p. 40, n. 3; 45, n. 6, especially the *Bibliography*, below, p. 307, no. 2.

[62] Bacher, *Anfänge*, p. 44, n. 4; 47, n. 2; 48, no. 8.

[63] This was first shown by D. Rosin, *MGWJ.*, XXX (1881), 521; comp. Bacher, *ib.*, p. 21.

[64] At the end of his Introduction to the Commentary, p. 13, top, French, p. 29; comp. Bacher, *ib.*, p. 23, top.

authors and by some recent investigators, that the Karaites
were the first to enter the field of scientific reseach, particularly in Hebrew philology, which marks the beginning of a
new epoch.[63] Nevertheless, it would be futile to deny to the
Karaites before and during the time of Saadia the merit of
having been in some degree instrumental in bringing about
this new era in Jewish literature. They may not have
produced works in general comparable with Saadia's, but
their very existence as a schismatic sect, their negative
attitude toward traditional Judaism, and their active propaganda, in speech and in writing, for the new cause, could
not have failed to incite a counter-activity among the Rabbanites. Thus, they helped to prepare the intellectual ground
from which Saadia sprang, as the main defender of the
besieged fortress of Rabbinism. There is no need to
search for historical records to corroborate the course of
events as outlined. Saadia's own works, to whatever period
of his life they belong, are the clearest proof. That he
early felt the necessity of combatting the Karaite heresies is
obvious from the fact that in 915,[65a] when but in his twenty-
third year, he wrote a polemical work against Anan, the
founder of Karaism. This was followed by other polemical
writings against the teachings of eminent members of the
sect.[65] There is no room for doubt that, while yet in Egypt,
he knew besides the writings of Anan also those of Benjamin Nehâwendi, whom he mentions twice in a work belonging to a later period,[67] and Daniel Al-Kumisi,[68] though
both had probably lived in Babylonia or Palestine. The
Karaites, who were very active in their efforts to make con-
verts, early selected Egypt as a favorable place for mission-

[63] See above, notes 24-32.

[[65a] See *Postscript*].

[65] For a detailed account of Saadia's writings against the Karaites
see below, pp. 263 ff.

[67] *'Amânât*, ed. Landauer, Leyden, 1880, p. 201, ll. 2, 11; *'Emunot*,
ed. Cracow, p. 134.

[68] See Schechter, *Saadyana*, pp. 41 (comp. Poznański, *Schechter's
Saadyana*, Frankf. a/M., 1904, p. 4, *ad locum*), 144, no. lv; comp.
Poznański, *JQR.*, XIII, 681 ff.

ary work; [69] and in later years that country, especially Cairo, became their main seat. [70]

Thus far, the channels through which Saadia may have acquired his learning in his earlier years have been traced in a general way. We can now point out in particular a few scholars of eminence with whom, it is positively known, he came in contact in his formative period, and who undoubtedly influenced his career. In the first place, mention must be made of that famous physician and philosopher Isaac b. Sulaiman Israëli, whom the Christian scholastics style *eximius monarcha medicinae.* [71] Israëli died about 953, and, as he is reported to have lived over a hundred years, he was much older than Saadia. Like Saadia he was a native of Egypt, where he was a practising oculist for some years. Subsequently [72] he was called as physician to the court of Ziyâdat Allah, the third and last of the Aġlabite rulers of the Berber lands, who had established their seat in Kairwân. Whether Saadia, who was a young man when Israëli assumed his position in Kairwân, ever met him personally, is hard to say. It is known that the two men had a lively correspon-

[69] Comp. Pinsker, *Likkûtê*, II, 14, bottom; Steinschneider, *JQR.*, XVIII, 100, bottom; Geiger, *Ozar Nechmad,* IV, 34.

[70] Among the learned Karaites, who probably lived in Egypt and there disputed with Saadia, is Abû-'l-Surri Ben Zuṭa, frequently quoted by Abraham Ibn Ezra; comp. Poznański, *Karaite Literary Opponents of Saadiah Gaon,* London, 1908, p. 4; Gottheil, in Harkavy's *Festschrift,* German part, pp. 115 ff.

[71] For all details on Israëli see Steinschneider, *Arab. Liter.*, § 28, and recently Guttmann, *Die philosophischen Lehren des Isaak b. Salomon Israeli.* Münster, i/W., 1911.

[72] The date is not certain. Graetz gives the year 904, which is considered arbitrary by Steinschneider, *JQR.*, XIII, 96. The author of the article "Egypt" in the *JE.,* V, 61b, declares that Israëli "was recalled to Egypt from Kairwân, and entered the service of 'Ubaid Allah," and that he was still there, in royal service, at the death of Al-Manṣûr (952). He is evidently unaware of the fact that neither 'Ubaid Allah, the first, nor Al-Manṣûr, the third caliph of the Fâṭimide dynasty had ever ruled over Egypt, which was conquered only by Al-Mu'izz, the fourth Fâṭimide caliph, in 972. Israëli was thus never "recalled" to Egypt.

dence on scientific subjects for some time previous to Saadia's
departure from Egypt. This is explicitly stated by Dûnâsh
Ibn Tamim of Ḳairwân, a pupil of Israëli, in a commentary on the *Sefer Yeẓirah*,[73] written by Israëli and recast
by Dûnâsh, whose version alone has been preserved, in two
Hebrew translations from the Arabic. Dûnâsh informs the
reader at the beginning of his commentary that at the time
when this correspondence took place he was twenty years
old, and Israëli used to show him Saadia's letters, to test his
ability to understand and explain their scientific content. He
adds, not without self-complacency, that he was able to detect
the mistakes made by the writer, which pleased the teacher
greatly, because of Dûnâsh's youth at the time. Assuming
that the correspondence referred to was going on for some
time before Saadia's emigration to Palestine in 915, we come
to the conclusion that Dûnâsh was born at about the same
time as Saadia, in 892, not in 908, as has been hitherto
asserted.[74]

Dûnâsh does not show much admiration for Saadia. He
speaks of him rather disrespectfully,[75] though at the time
when this commentary was written, in 955-956, Saadia was
dead, and his fame was established, of which facts there is
no hint in the book. This is strange, but it is not the only
difficulty in connection with this commentary, which in
other respects too, which cannot be discussed here, is one
of the most complicated literary problems.[76] However, the
attitude of Dûnâsh toward Saadia is of little importance.

[73] Poorly edited, with irrelevant notes, by M. Grossberg, London,
1902. On the question of the authorship of this commentary see the
references given below, note 76.

[74] Comp. Poznański, אניֹשי קירואן, p. 18, top. [See *Postscript*.]

[75] I do not know on what ground Steinschneider bases his assertion
to the contrary (*Hebr. Übersetzungen*, p. 399, and *Bibliotheca Mathematica*, 1895, p. 25, bottom) ; comp. for instance the passages pp. 24,
46, 73. The main passage, p. 17, even contains clear allusions to
Saadia's conceit.

[76] These problems were treated exhaustively by Steinschneider,
Hebr. Übers., pp. 394-402; *Arab. Liter. der Juden*, pp. 44, 73.

We are here concerned merely to bring out the points that as early as the middle of the ninth century, when Israëli was born, Egypt was a fertile soil to produce men of the highest type of learning and that Saadia did not rise as a solitary palm in a desert, but grew up in an intellectual atmosphere created by scholars of various occupations and interests, though only a few of them are recorded in the available sources of our history.[77]

Besides Israëli and Dûnâsh numerous scholars are known to have lived in Kairwân with whom Saadia had relations, or whose literary productions he knew. There are references in one of his own works to the "men of Kairwân" and the "men of Africa," who "in our time" wrote a Hebrew work provided with accents and arranged in verses in the manner of the Biblical writings. This work, he says, served him as a model for his own.[78] It is true that these references to the scholars of Kairwân occur in a work written by Saadia long after his emigration from Egypt; but considering the facts that the Jewish community of Kairwân was very prominent during the ninth century, and that even the Babylonian Geonim had carried on correspondence with

[77] Comp. Guttmann, *Die philosophischen Lehren des Isaak ben Salomon Israëli*, Münster i/W., 1911, p. 2. Of the many Muhammedan scholars in Egypt before Saadia mention has been made above, note 37. Here the Jewish scholar Mashallah, should be pointed out, "one of the earliest and most eminent astrologers" (770-820), who, as Steinschneider assumes (*Arab. Liter.*, § 18; *Bibliotheca Mathematica*, 1894, p. 37), lived in Egypt. He is credited with thirty works on astronomy and astrology. Among the learned contemporaries of Saadia mentioned by Mas'ûdi (see above, notes 20, 37) is one Sa'id b. 'Ali Ibn אישׁלמיא of Rakka in Egypt, perhaps a Jew; comp. Steinschneider, *JQR.*, XI, 328. In Kairwân there lived at that time a Jewish scholar by the name Ziyâd b. Halfûn, who participated in the war waged by 'Ubaid Allah; see Wüstenfeld, *Geschichte der Fatimiden Chalifen*, 34, 59; Steinschneider, *Arab. Liter.*, p. 44, n. 4. For Judah b. Joseph al-Rakki see above, note 37.

[78] Harkavy, *Zikron*, V, 151, l. 19; 163, 8; 180, 10, especially pp. 209 f.; comp. Schechter, *JQR.*, XVI, 427; Poznański, *Anshe Kairwân*, p. 2.

4

some of its learned members as early as the eighth century,[79] it would be absurd to assume that Isaac Israëli was the only scholar of Ḳairwân whom Saadia knew while in Fayyûm, and that of all other " men of Africa " he learned only after he himself had left that continent and was travelling in Asia." No doubt the other early works which he mentions in connection with those of the Ḳairwân scholars were also known to him before he left Egypt.

Especial mention should be accorded to a passage in his Introduction to the *'Agrōn,* in which he informs us that to substantiate his views he cites parallels from the works of the ancient poets, as Jose b. Jose, Yannai, Eleazar Kalir, and others, whenever this is possible, and then adds, " As to the productions of more recent poets, I shall quote their authors by name only when I wish to praise them, but not when I criticize their words."[81] The passage shows that Saadia had a literature of considerable extent at his disposal when he wrote his first work. As the main part of the *'Agrōn* is lost, it is of course impossible to identify the authors or their works. Only the name of one poet, Nahra-wâni, is preserved in a passage quoted from the *'Agrōn* by a certain Mubashshir,[82] a contemporary of Saadia, who criti-

---

[79] Poznański, *Anshe Ḳairwân,* pp. 5 f.; comp. Ginzberg, *Geonica,* I. 32, 51, n. 2.

[80] Comp. Harkavy, *Zikron,* V, 35, n. 2. The words "in our time " (פי׳ עצרנא הרא) cited above do not necessarily mean the last, or the present year; they may as well denote a period of twenty-five years.

[81] Harkavy, *Zikron,* V, 51.

[82] Ginzberg, *Geonica,* I, 55, n. 1, tries to prove against Stein-schneider that the name is not the translation of the Arabic *Mu-bashshir,* but the Hebrew *Mebasser* (מבשׂר) which is an epithet of Elijah, meaning " Proclaimer of Good Tidings." It is strange, however, that of all the bearers of this name enumerated by Ginzberg, there is not one who lived outside of the Arabic-speaking countries. If the name was originally Hebrew, we might as well expect it to be used by Jews living elsewhere; for further details on this name see Steinschneider, *JQR.,* XII, 196, and Margoliouth, *JQR.,* XII, 708; XIII, 156, no. 2; comp. also below, p. 324, under *Lamentations.*

cized the views laid down in that work.[52] The identity of
this Nahrawâni is not fully assured.[54]

But high as the standard, whether of general civilization
or Jewish learning, would appear to have been in the Orient,
both from what has been said above and from what is generally known, it does not suffice to explain Saadia's greatness and many-sidedness. The great men whom we have
enumerated so far, were men of prominence in the circum-
scribed fields of literature and science to which they devoted
themselves. There were talmudists, philosophers, grammarians, and the like, previous to and contemporaneously
with Saadia. But with the exception of Israëli none of them
attained to distinction outside of his particular line of work.
Saadia is the first Jewish scholar whose universal mind
embraced all the branches of Jewish learning known in his
time. He acquired a mastery in each department that throws
into the shade the efforts of all his predecessors and contemporaries, and that has won for him the honorable title

[53] Harkavy, *Zikron*, V, 68-73; comp. Bacher, *Anfänge*, p. 41.

[54] See Harkavy's discussion of the matter, *ib.*, pp. 115 f.; comp. also
ib. p. 70, n. 4, and *Ha-Goren*, II 86; Epstein, *REJ.*, XLII (1901),
208. It may be added in this connection that the appearance in
Northern Africa of Eldad ha-Dani, shortly before the close of the
ninth century, which stirred up the Ḳairwân community and elicited
a responsum from the Gaon of Sura, produced some literature,
which must have become known to Saadia in Egypt (see for Eldad
the references in Steinschneider's *Geschichtsliteratur der Juden*,
§ 13). I also believe that Saadia knew and made use of the Book
Josipon, which will be proved in detail in my forthcoming edition of
Saadia's *'Amânât* in the Hebrew translation of Ibn Tibbon (*Emunôt
we-Deôt*, end of chapter 8). This was originally the opinion of
Zunz, but later, following Rapoport (in his biography of Ḳalir, note
7; see the collection יריעות שלמה, Warsaw, 1904, p. 30), he declared
his former opinion as "wholly groundless"; see Zunz, *Gottesdienstliche Vorträge* (1892), p. 159, n. d. For the present I wish to point
out that *Josipon* is referred to also in the Commentary on the *Sefer
Yeẓirah* by Dûnâsh (or Israëli), ed. Grossberg, p. 37; comp. also
Dukes, *Beiträge*, p. 99.

accorded to him by an admirer, " the chief spokesman in all
matters of learning " (ראש המדברים בכל מקום).[85]

[85] This title of honor was given first to R. Judah b. Ilai, one of the
most celebrated teachers of the Mishnah in the second century;
comp. b. Berākōt, 63b. There the phrase designates R. Judah as
the first speaker in the assembly of scholars, as the one who was
to open the learned discussions. Abraham Ibn Ezra was the first
to apply this Talmudic title to Saadia, but in a diverted sense, meaning to say, that "Saadia first introduced the cultivation of all
branches of Jewish knowledge, which was continued ever since
without noticeable interruption " (Steinschneider, *Bibliotheca Mathematica*, 1894, p. 102) ; comp. Steinschneider, *Arab. Literatur*, p. 46,
and Ewald-Dukes, *Beiträge*, II, 10.

THE SECOND PERIOD

CHAPTER III

SAADIA'S EMIGRATION TO THE EAST
(4675=915)[85a]

Dividing the life of a human being into periods marked by events carries with it the danger of arbitrariness. Man's life in reality is a continuous, though fluctuating, process of becoming and unfolding, which does not halt at any mental land-mark. Circumstances may step in one's way and prevent one from proceeding on a course as planned, but the life-energy of an individual is not paralyzed thereby. After many detours it asserts itself in its own way. This is especially true of men of genius and great mental energy of whatever kind.

In designating Saadia's emigration to the East as the beginning of the second period in his career, we do not mean to convey the idea that this external event was the cause or the effect of any radical change in Saadia's pursuits and aspirations, thus becoming essentially responsible for what we know of him from history. The chief aspect of Saadia's life as generally presented is that of a great scholar, and perhaps, to use a hackneyed modern phrase, of an " active worker " in the cause of traditional Judaism. He had begun his labors in both fields before he left Egypt. His first literary work (the *'Agrōn*) was issued in 913, and two years later, before departing from his native country,[85a] he wrote another to defend Rabbinism against the innovations of Anan. His work in the following period, though greater in scope and extent, was but a continuation of one or the other form of literary activity. Not even his appointment to the Gaonate of Sura, important as this incident

[85a See *Postscript*].

is from the viewpoint of his public career, was in any way instrumental in the making of Saadia, for by that time (928) he had passed the formative years. We have to think of Saadia simply as one who, from his early boyhood to the end of his days, was animated by two desires: to acquire and impart knowledge and to oppose the enemies of Talmudic Judaism. All the positions and relations into which he was brought during the period we are now to consider must be viewed merely as episodes in his life-history. They help us greatly to appreciate the man's character and disposition, but they do not represent a particular and significant phase in his intellectual development. It was not by virtue of these that he became the founder of a new epoch in Jewish history.

It is nevertheless useful, if only as a matter of form, to treat Saadia's arrival in the Holy Land as a turning-point in his career. It is at this juncture that Saadia, however slowly and dimly, emerges, as it were, from Egyptian darkness into the light of documentary history.

It has been generally assumed, hitherto, that Saadia lived in Egypt until the year 928, when, owing to his exceptional reputation as a scholar and to the lack of great men in Babylonia, he was called by the temporal head of Babylonian Jewry from his native country to occupy the seat of the Gaons of Sura.[56] It was also pointed out, with some pride and satisfaction, that the Babylonian authorities, for the first time disregarding a tacit rule or custom to appoint as Gaon only a native of Babylonia, had resorted to the importation of a foreign scholar.[57] The opening of the Genizah has changed the face of this chapter of Jewish history. Two little scraps of paper preserved among the numberless shreds of literature in the Cairene mausoleum for dilapidated books make it certain that Saadia had departed from Egypt not later than 915, and had sojourned for many years in various

---

[56] The source for this view is a passage in the סדר הקבלה of Abraham Ibn Daûd, who, as it seems, misunderstood his source, namely the Epistle of Sherira Gaon; see below, notes 125, 126.

[57] Graetz, *History of the Jews*, English translation, III, 193, and as late as 1902, S. Kraus in *Jewish Encycl.*, II, 413.

parts of Palestine, Syria, and Babylonia prior to his installation in the office of Gaon.

These fragments are parts of two letters written by him
somewhere in Babylonia, during the winter of the year
922 (January-March), and addressed to three of his former
pupils who had remained in Egypt.[83]. The master assures
his disciples that his "love and affection for [them][89]
has never waned, for educating the young leaves indelible
traces in the heart [of the teacher],[90] the more when it has
been undertaken for the sake of the fear of God and the
glorification of His name. As I have been desolate ever
since I left my wife[91] and children, so I have grieved over
my separation from you. May it be the will of the Almighty
that I see you[92] again in health and happiness. It is now
six and a half years that no word from you has reached me.
I even wrote to you condoling with you over the death of
the venerable old man,[92] blessed be his memory, but I saw no
answer. Only recently I was told by our friend R. David,
son of R. Abraham, that you had written to him and requested him to secure the opinions of the heads of the
academies regarding the fixation of the months Marḥeshwān

[83] The first letter, part of which is given here in English translation, was published first by Schechter in the *JQR.*, XIV (1901), 59,
also *Saadyana*, pp. 24 ff., while the second was published earlier by
Neubauer, *JQR.*, IX, 37 and, with a French translation, also by
Epstein, *RÉJ.*, XLII, 201 ff. Both were then re-edited with additional notes by Bornstein, מחלקת, pp. 67-71; see below, *Appendix*,
p. 412, nos. 4-5.

[89] The passage might also be translated, "your love and affection
for me," but the corresponding passage at the beginning of the
second letter supports the rendering as given in the text.

[90] The Hebrew here is rather obscure and none of the editors has
commented upon it. The wording suggests Is. 28, 16.

[91] Literally, "my tent," but the word אהל, like בית (house), is
used in a figurative sense to designate the mistress of the house;
comp. Moëd Ḳaṭan, 7b; *Bereshit rabbah*, section 41, § 4; Shabbat,
118b (the saying of R. Jose).

[92] The parallel passage in the second letter reads here "to make
me see *them* (i. e. his family) and you" (פניהם ופניכם).

[92] Probably the grandfather of the pupils.

and Kislew of the year 1233 [Seleucidan era = November
and December, 921, common era]. I presume that you wrote
to him, and not to me, only because, in accordance with
previous reports, you thought *that I was still in Palestine.*
He himself [R. David] suggested that you seem to have
thought so. He further requested me to write to you and
to inform you [regarding the state of affairs]." [84]

The rest of this letter, as well as nearly the whole of the
second letter, written two months later, deals with the question of the calendar, which does not concern us for the
present. But it should be mentioned that in both letters we
are informed incidentally that the writer had spent the preceding summer, or part of it (921), in Aleppo (Syria), and
from the second letter we learn that he *returned* thence
to Bagdad.

The important facts derived from these documents are
the following. Saadia had been married in Egypt, and left
a wife and children behind when he emigrated to the East.
He was recognized as a scholar and teacher in his native
country, and from his new home kept up a correspondence
with his former pupils. He left Egypt in June or July,
915, and lived for some time in Palestine,[85] then in Bagdad
and in Aleppo.[86] From Aleppo he returned to Bagdad, in
all likelihood before the Jewish New Year's festival
(autumn, 921). Incidentally we learn also of a certain
R. David, who, as the epithet " our friend " indicates, was
known to Saadia's pupils in Egypt, and like Saadia may have
been a former resident of that country, but now lived in
Babylonia. The father of this R. David is possibly identi-

[84] The Hebrew text suggests here the supplement "that it is not
so," meaning to say that he is no longer in Palestine. A comparison
with the corresponding passage in the second letter, however, proves
that he has reference to the matter discussed by him in the following
lines, the dispute with Ben Meir, which is the main burden of the
letter. The words supplied by me should therefore be taken in the
same sense.

[85] See below, pp. 64 f. [and especially *Postscript*].

[86] Comp. Poznański, *The Karaite Literary Opponents of Saadiah
Gaon*, p. 14.

cal with the R. Abraham who acted as the secretary of
Saadia several years later, and who is the author of the
panegyric which was discussed above.[97]
What induced Saadia to leave his birth-place, to separate from his kith and kin, and to wander about in foreign
lands, cannot be made out from these sources. The suggestion has been made that his thirst for knowledge, which, he
thought, was more readily obtainable in the East, and particularly his desire to come in closer contact with the main representatives of Jewish learning in the two Babylonian
academies, drove him from Africa to Asia.[98] Others think
that he started out originally with the pious intention of
settling on the holy soil of Palestine,[99] but that untoward
circumstances forced him to proceed further. In either
case his family was to follow at some later period.
Another suggestion may be derived from the history of his
time. He may have left Egypt because of the political
unrest and the perils of war that had troubled the country
since the new dynasty of caliphs, the Fâtimide, had pitched
its tent in Ḳairwân (909), the closest neighbor of Egypt.[100]
But these assumptions can serve at best only as explanations for Saadia's departure from Egypt and later from

[97] Pp. 28 ff. This possible identity has been overlooked, so far as I
can make out, by all who have dealt with the matter, also by
Poznański, *Schechter's Saadyana*, p. 8, *s. v.* Abraham ha-Kohen;
comp. above, note 13.

[98] Eppenstein, *MGWJ.*, 1910, p. 314 (*Beiträge*, p. 90) ; comp. above,
p. 43.

[99] Bacher, *JE.*, X, 579.

[100] In 914 a large army sent by the first Fâtimide caliph, 'Ubaidallah
Al-Mahdi, invaded northern Egypt under the leadership of his son,
Abu-'l-Ḳâsim, who later succeeded to the throne, conquering the city
of Alexandria and other parts of the country. After much fighting,
which must have lasted over a year, the Egyptians succeeded in
driving out the intruders, who are said to have left 7000 dead on the
field. In consequence an epidemic broke out in Egypt and the adjacent
countries, killing thousands of people, among them numerous well-
known scholars. The defeated caliph did not, however, give up the
fight but prepared for another invasion, though the plan was not
carried out until three years later, when Abu-'l-Ḳâsim actually took

Palestine to Babylonia. None of them explains why he did not return home when his attempts to establish himself elsewhere had failed, especially as he yearned to rejoin his family, and, as we shall see later, prayed for this consummation. It would be surprising in the extreme if, for no other reasons than those cited, a man like Saadia, who was to become the Gaon of Sura, the religious head of all Israel, should, for nearly seven years and perhaps longer, have accepted separation from his wife and children, and lived the life of an itinerant scholar. Travelling Jewish scholars are not, indeed, rare phenomena in later mediæval history. None of the more prominent instances, however, that might be thought of in this connection, is in any way similar to that of Saadia.

It would therefore appear that Saadia did not leave Egypt voluntarily, either because he was seeking knowledge, or because he wanted to live in the Holy Land. He was either banished by the authorities for some real or fancied offense, or he apprehended grave danger to his life, and decided to go into exile before it was too late. As we shall have occasion to observe later, Saadia was of a somewhat pugnacious disposition. He was a man of iron will and unbending determination, coupled with a keen sense of justice and uprightness. A man of this type may have a few friends and admirers, but certainly many more enemies and adversaries. We further know that Saadia began his battle with the Karaites by writing a book against Anan, the founder of the sect. It was written while Saadia was still in Egypt, and it was the first signal of a struggle that was to last all his life, and that made him the most hated and most feared

---

possession of the Fayyûm. Under such conditions it would appear very likely that Saadia and many others, of whom we do not know (comp. above, p. 56, with reference to David b. Abraham), thought it best to leave the troubled country and seek refuge among their brethren in the Holy Land; see for the content of this note Wüstenfeld, *Geschichte der Fatim. Chalifen*, pp. 50-55, and Aug. Müller, *Der Islam*, pp. 610 ff. [but see *Postscript*].

champion of Rabbinism against Ḳaraism.[101] Any one acquainted with social and political conditions in Muhammedan countries, and particularly with the administration of
justice by the Islamitic rulers of those days, knows how little
it took to bring death upon the most prominent men of the
country.[102] Slander and calumny were strong weapons in
the hands of revengeful and unscrupulous enemies such
as the Ḳaraites often proved to be, and where these failed,
bribery might prevail. It does not require a great stretch
of the imagination to assume that Saadia was the victim
of such persecution in youth, as he was in later life, because
he stood up unflinchingly for his religious convictions and for
the principles of right and justice. His emigration from
Egypt as well as his prolonged travels in the East were thus
against his will. Like Moses of old, he may have waited
for the message, " Go, return into Egypt, for all the men are
dead that sought thy life." [103] The message was never to
come. He was not to see Egypt again. This supposed
course of events lends especial significance to the repeated [104]
expression of his desire to return home. Otherwise it would
have to be taken as a mere phrase, since no other obstacle
is imaginable that would satisfactorily explain why he did
not carry his heart's desire into effect.

I do not advance this theory on account of its plausibility,
or because it helps us out of a difficulty. It is again a fragment from the Genizah [105] that suggests the thought and
throws new light upon this very important period in Saadia's
life. The nature of the work, of which the fragment
in question originally formed a part, cannot be defined

---

[101] For a detailed account of this matter see the learned study of
Poznański, *The Karaite Literary Opponents of Saadiah Gaon,* London, 1908. For the book against Anan see below, pp. 263, 379.

[102] Comp. for instance Brockelmann, *Geschichte der arab. Literatur,*
I, 232, no. 5, and Steinschneider, *JQR.,* XIII, 97.

[103] Exodus, 4, 19.

[104] So in the two fragmentary letters discussed above (pp. 55 f.) and
in another fragment translated in the following pages.

[105] Schechter, *Saadyana,* pp. 133-135.

with certainty. What we have consists of two disconnected leaves, containing together fifty lines, written in
Biblical style and provided with vowels and accents, a
method observable in other writings of Saadia.[106] Unfortunately, just where our interest grows keenest, several lines
are mutilated beyond repair. From what remains legible
it appears that it formed part of some sort of a diary, evidently written by Saadia on his journey from Babylonia to
Aleppo,[107] and thus preceding the two letters discussed above,

[106] Schechter, l. c., p. 133, n. 2.

[107] The exact time of this journey is not stated, but circumstances
point to the winter of the year 920/21. The fact that it was winter
is mentioned explicitly in the second leaf of the fragment (*Saadyana*,
p. 135, l. 2), which contains also the information that the goal of
the journey was the city of Aleppo, giving the route as follows:
Babylon (probably Bagdad, see Bornstein, p. 71, n. 2), Arbela (see
Rapoport, *'Erek Millin*, p. 192, s. v. ארבילי), Mosul (see Bornstein,
p. 71, n. 3). In the last city he met a "caravan of Arabs" coming
from Aleppo, who described the hardships they had experienced on
the road, adding that "many people died on the way on account of
the heavy snow and the severe cold." This induced him to interrupt
his travel and to remain for some time in Mosul, where he was
asked to set down the genealogy of R. Judah the Patriarch, the
compiler of the Mishnah, which he did (see below, p. 173, no. 3).
Now we have seen above that he subsequently carried out his desire
and actually visited Aleppo in the summer of 921. This makes it
more than probable that he stayed in Mosul only during the preceding winter, taking up his interrupted journey as soon as the
winter was over. Bornstein (p. 71), and Eppenstein (*Beiträge*,
p. 90, n. 4) take the altogether untenable view, according to which
the beginning of the fragment under discussion (*fol. 2 recto*) has
reference to the time when Saadia was about to leave Egypt. The
passage reads: כי נער אתה לא תדע צאת ובוא כי בן עשרים . . . .
("Thou art young, knowest not how to go out or come in, for thou
art twenty . . . .") and obviously represents part of the argument
of those who tried to keep him back from the proposed journey. In
the dotted space after the word עשרים (twenty) the aforementioned
authors supply the word ושלש (three), because at the time of
Saadia's departure from Egypt (915) he was 23 years old. This
interpretation is entirely out of the question, for Saadia immediately
goes on to say that all the persuasions notwithstanding he left Bagdad (see above) for Arbela. This, as we have shown above, must
have taken place during the winter 920/21, when Saadia was already

which were written subsequent to Saadia's stay in Aleppo.
The first leaf, which contains a prayer for protection on
the way, seems to have been written at the outset of the
journey. With a few words added in some places where
the original shows a lacuna, it runs as follows:

". . . . and now look down from Thy holy tabernacle [108]
and be jealous for Thy Torah; [for excellent is] [109] her
teaching. Not for the sake of [Thy servant, O God], but for
the sake of Thy great name by which he is called, [110] [guide
me in] [111] Thy holy Torah, which Thou hast given to us; truly,
Thou hast tried my heart and known me, hast searched me
and found that [I am innocent]. [112] Now Thy servant has
set his face to go into the land of Canaan and the land of
[Babylonia], for he heard that . . . ."

Here, where we expect to hear his reason for having emigrated to the land of Canaan, our curiosity is baffled by a
blank of about two lines, and we remain as wise as before.
From the last three words, however, it may be concluded with
some degree of probability that it was something new and

28, or 29 years of age, and the Hebrew text should be supplied
accordingly. That a man of that age should be described as נער
(youth) is not surprising. Saadia imitates throughout the style of
the Bible, where the word is often applied to men of mature age;
comp. e. g. Genesis, 41, 12, where Joseph, who according to Gen. 41,
1 and 41, 46, was at the time referred to by the chief butler 28
years old, is called נער. In the passage before us in particular
Saadia makes use of the verse I Kings, 3, 7. It may be added in
this connection that in the Midrash on Proverbs, 1, 4, the rabbis of
the Mishnah dispute the question how long one may be considered a
נער, R. Meir setting the limit at 25, and R. 'Aḳiba at 30. [See regarding this note *Postscript*, pp. 422 f.].

[108] Deuteronomy, 26, 15. As the following references will show, the
author uses whole phrases of the Bible throughout.

[109] The passage seems to have read as follows: וקנא לתורת[ך] כי
[נג]ידים הגיונה; comp. Proverbs, 8, 6; Ps. 19, 15; 49, 4. The last
word might perhaps be better translated by meditation. There is,
however, the difficulty that in the Bible the suffix in all passages
refers to the individual, while here it is made to refer to the Torah.

[110] Comp. Deut., 28, 10. Saadia uses the same phrase also in the
Sefer ha-Gālui (*Saadyana*, 6, ll. 11-12).

[111] Comp. Ps., 5, 9; 139, 24.

[112] Comp. Ps., 139, 1, 23.

unexpected that had happened and made him feel insecure
at home. The following lines seem to support this view:

"And now, O Lord, that Thou hast taken me out of my
city, mayest Thou lead me to my desire, and bring me back
in peace to the house of my father. Turn me not away
empty from before Thee,[113] for in the shadow of Thy mercy
I take refuge."[114] O prosper the way which I go,[115] save me
from the hands of the enemy and the ambush,[116] and provide
all my needs as those were provided who went forth out of
Egypt[117] . . . so that my persecutors may be confounded,
and my enemies be put to shame and say not in their heart,
Aha . . . . Hear, O God, the supplications of Thy servant
and let not his enemies say, Our hand is exalted . . . ."[118]

While much of this language may be accounted for by the
desire of the author to imitate the Biblical style, it is highly
improbable that this was the sole motive of the whole composition. At any rate we see here not only that the writer
had bitter enemies, but also that he was desirous of returning to his father's house and prayed for the opportunity to do
so. This surely indicates that his stay in Asia was an enforced one.

How long Saadia was separated from his family subsequent to the writing of the quoted letters to his pupils cannot

[113] Comp. 2 Sam., 1, 22; Is., 55, 11.

[114] Comp. Ps. 57, 2; 61, 5.

[115] Gen., 24, 42.

[116] This line is part of the prayer prescribed in the Talmud *Berakōt*,
29b for one who sets out on a journey (תפלת הדרך).

[117] In these words Saadia evidently alludes to his departure from
Egypt, comparing himself to the Israelites in the narration of the
Bible, whose needs were provided for in the desert.

[118] The text is here badly mutilated. I would suggest the following reading: והשיגני כל ת[קותי רוד]פי למען יכלמו[נצח]
ואויבי[חנם יבושו. החפר]פני שוטני ואל יאמרו בלבם האח
בלעגוהו]פנה אל השקי[ואל]תפן אל קשיי אל תבן]יש[ני]. For the
phrases here used by Saadia see Jeremiah, 17. 18; 20, 11; Psalms,
35, 4; 34, 6; 71,13; 35, 25; 69. 17; Deuteronomy, 9, 27; Psalms, 119,
31, 116. The word זקף (l. 7) does not belong to the text, but is
probably a gloss referring to the placing of an accent known under
this name.

be learned from the available sources. I am tempted to believe that his reunion with his family took place on Babylonian soil only a few months after the date of the letters, that is, in the summer of the year 922. In a letter of the Palestinian Ben Meir, whose bitter quarrel with Saadia will occupy us in the next chapter, the writer, in an effort to belittle his opponent, informs his friends, among other things of a very discreditable nature, that Saadia's father was "*thrust* out of Egypt and died in Jaffa." [119] It is quite possible that Saadia's father undertook the journey to his son with all the members of the latter's family, but, being advanced in age, could not endure the hardships of the long journey, and died on the way. Ben Meir's letter was written toward the end of the summer 922. [120] There was then about half a year's interval between this date and that of Saadia's correspondence with his pupils in Egypt (January-March, 922), during which time his family may have moved to the East. This view commends itself for several reasons. The year 922 was of decisive importance in Saadia's career. In the bitter war waged at that time between Ben Meir on the one side and the Babylonian Geonim on the other, regarding the right of fixing the Jewish calendar, it was Saadia's energetic support of the latter that brought about their ultimate victory. That his participation could be of such consequence is proof that he had already gained great influence among the Jews of the Orient. The Babylonian authorities no doubt had by that time recognized his resolute character and his great intellectual power, and they probably prevailed upon him to abandon forever his plan of returning to Egypt. Thereupon, having decided to make his permanent abode in Babylonia, it was natural to have his family follow him thither. It is also more than probable that he was then offered a position of honor and income within the academic circle, which he accepted.

[119] Schechter, *Saadyana*, p. 20, n. 4; Bornstein, p. 90, n. 5; above, note 7.

[120] A few days before the Jewish New Year; see Bornstein, pp. 12 f.

In a letter dated Fifth day, *19th of Tammuz, 1233, Seleucidan Era* (= July, 922), of which only the closing lines and
the signature have been preserved among the fragments of
the Genizah, Saadia adds to his name, so far as known for
the first time, the title *'Allūf Yeshū'āh* (= Master of Salvation).[121] The title *'Allūf* was usually accorded in the Babylonian colleges to the scholars who were third in rank after
the Gaon. Besides, it was sometimes granted as a special
distinction to foreign scholars, particularly Palestinians.[122]
The addition *Yeshū'āh* would indicate that the title was given
to Saadia as a distinction, in appreciation of his services in
the controversy with Ben Meir.[123] I am inclined to believe
that Saadia was actually made one of the *'Allūfim* of the
Sura academy, and thus became a regular member of the
institution about six years prior to his installation as
Gaon The statement of R Sherira, Gaon of Pumbedita
(968-987), that Saadia " was not one of the scholars of the
college, but from Egypt,"[124] does not mean that previous
to his installation he did not belong to the rank and
file of the academic body, but only, as we might say to-day,
that he was not a graduate of the college; while the asser-

---

[121] Schechter, *Saadyana*, p. 15, especially Bornstein, p. 72, n 2;
comp Müller, Introduction to Saadia's תרי"ג מצות (in *Oeuvres
complètes*, vol IX, p. xxi) , below, note 332 I do not know on what
ground Bornstein, p 12, asserts that when the Exilarch turned to
Saadia for assistance against Ben Meir Saadia had already been
bearing the title *'Allūf.*

[122] Comp. Ginzberg, *JE.*, s v. *'Alluf;* Epstein, *RÉJ*, XLII, 192, n 4;
Bornstein, p. 48, n 11, Poznański, עניני□ שונים, pp. 50, 62, 67;
Eppenstein, *Beitrage*, p 103 It is therefore not necessary to assume
with Harkavy, *Oeuvres complètes*, vol IX, p xli (see also Schechter,
Saadyana, p 15, n 1) that *'Allūf* was the title of Saadia's father,
comp. also Harkavy תשובות הגאונים, p. 377.

[123] Bornstein, p 72, n 2, thinks that the title was given to him in
recognition of his successful defense of traditional Judaism against
Karaism So far as the available historical records go, Saadia's
assumption of the title coincides with the time of the Ben Meir
controversy

[124] *Epistle of R. Sherira,* toward the end (Neubauer, *MJC.*, I, 40,
top).

tion of Abraham b. David (1160), according to which
Saadia was brought directly from Egypt and installed as
Gaon, is based upon a misinterpretation of R. Sherira's
statement, and does not deserve credence.[125] It is altogether
improbable that Saadia was living in Egypt when called to
the Gaonate[126]; far more credible is it that he was made
'Allūf during the Ben Meir controversy, and six years later
rose from this position to that of Head of the Academy.

The foregoing discussion has carried us a little beyond the
point with which we are immediately concerned. It was
necessary to anticipate somewhat, in order to show that during the years of his sojourn in the East, Saadia maintained the same high standard of learning and literary pro-
ductivity that had made him a conspicuous figure in his
native country. Thus he became early an eminent factor in
the intellectual and religious life of the Jews of the Orient.

There is evidence that some of his works were written during this period, though no definite dates can be
given.[127] The first few years he probably spent in Palestine,
perhaps in Tiberias, where he made the acquaintance of

[125] Comp. Poznański, *RÉJ.*, XLVIII (1904), 149, n. 3; Bornstein,
p. 72; Ginzberg, *Geonica*, I, 69, note.

[126] This is the view also of A. Epstein in *RÉJ.*, XLII (1901), 201,
who thinks that Saadia returned to Egypt after the struggle with
Ben Meir was over; comp. also recently Eppenstein, *Beiträge*, pp.
103, 116 f. As said above, there is no sufficient basis for this view.
Eppenstein seems to base his view on the fact that the *Kitâb Al-
Tamyîz*, one of Saadia's polemical works, was written in 926, which,
he says, probably following Poznański (*JQR.*, X, 244, bottom), was
"at *all events* done in Egypt." But Poznański wrote in 1898 before
the letters of the Genizah came to light, and the passage from a
work of Abraham b. Ḥiyya which he quotes there (p. 245) as proof,
only gives the year (926), not the country of the composition. If
our assumption, that Al-Mas'ûdi met Saadia in Tiberias is correct
(see above, p. 36) we should have additional proof that in 926, the
year in which the work mentioned above was written, Saadia was
in the East; for it was in that year that Mas'ûdi is known to have
visited Tiberias; comp. above, note 34.

[127] Regarding the chronological order of Saadia's writings see
below, note 293.

5

'Abû Kathir, who became his teacher.[128] In Tiberias, Saadia must have come in close contact with the School of Masorites,[129] especially with Ben Asher,[130] the last and most distinguished member of this school, of whose grammatical views Saadia wrote a refutation.[131] In all probability it was there that he made the personal acquaintance of Ben Meir,[132] with whom he was subsequently engaged in a bitter literary feud. There he may have met also some Muhammedan writers as well as learned Karaites, whose writings he refuted in special works.[133] All these men must have served as a stimulus to Saadia in his literary pursuits, and thus, directly or indirectly have furthered his scholarly career.

Special mention should be made of an eminent scholar whose name is well known in the history of Jewish philosophy, and whose works and personality had a decided influence on Saadia—the philosopher and controversialist

[128] See above, pp 36 f.

[129] Comp. Bacher, *Anfänge*, p 50 Possibly Abû Kathir himself, as the identification with Judah b 'Alân would indicate, was a member of the Masoretic school, though to judge from the nature of the questions that were disputed between him and Al-Mas'ûdi (comp Goldziher, *RÉJ.*, XLVII, 41) he appears to have been a philosopher, see above, note 35

[130] Comp. Graetz, *Geschichte*, V, 4th edition, p 324 (English version, III, 207) ; Bacher, *JE*, X, 582.

[131] Bacher, *l. c*, doubts, however, that it was done in a separate work, see below, *Bibliography*, section VIII, p 399

[132] Comp Bornstein, p 60, n 3, see also Poznański, *RÉJ*, XLVIII (1904), 149, n. 2

[133] Comp. Poznański, *JQR.*, X (1898), 238 ff. The Arabic historian Hamza al-'Isfâhâni (beginning of the tenth century) tells in his *Chronicles* (ed Gottwald, St Petersburg-Leipsic, 1844-1848), the fifth chapter of which is devoted to the history of the Jews, and was translated into German by Steinschneider (*MGWJ*, 1845, p, 271 ff.), that in 920-921 he met, at Bagdad, a celebrated Jewish scholar, named Zedekiah, "who communicated to him a short synopsis of the old Jewish chronology", see *JQR*, XIII, 299 Many other Jewish scholars may have lived at that time in Bagdad with whom Saadia probably came in contact.

David Ibn Merwân Al-Mukammiṣ,[134] of Raḳḳa, in Meso-
potamia.[135] Al-Mukammiṣ is the first known Jewish writer
on metaphysics in the Orient. Various philosophic theories
of his that have recently become known through lengthy
extracts from his works, show a striking resemblance to
theories propounded by Saadia.[136] This may not be absolute
proof of an interdependence of the two authors, as both may
have drawn upon common Arabic sources; but in addition
to this identity of doctrines, which makes a personal or literary relationship very probable, there is also the testimony of
Judah b. Barzillai, a noted scholar of the eleventh century, and author of an important commentary on the *Sefer
Yezirah.*[137] Judah incorporated several chapters of one of
Mukammiṣ's works into his own, and in introducing him to
his readers he says: " I do not know, whether he [Mukam-
miṣ] was one of the Geonim, but I have heard that R.
Saadia, of blessed memory, having been his contemporary,
knew him personally and *was instructed by him* "(ולמד ממנו).
Judah adds that he is " not quite sure about it," which, if the
Hebrew style is interpreted strictly, seems to refer, not only

[134] For details on Mukammiṣ see Steinschneider, *JQR.*, XIII,
450 and *Arabische Literatur*, pp. 37, 338, bottom; Poznański, *Zur
jüdisch-arabischen Literatur*, pp. 39 f.; Hirschfeld, *JQR.*, XV, 682,
688; XVI, 411; comp. also above, note 33, the quotation from Ibn
Ḥazm. A synopsis of Al-Mukammiṣ's philosophy was given by
Schreiner, *Der Kalâm in der jüdischen Literatur*, Berlin, 1895, pp.
22 ff.; comp. also Grätz, *Geschichte*, V (4), 322, note 5; Harkavy,
לקורות הכתות בישראל, in the Hebrew translation of Graetz's History, vol. III, pp. 498 f.

[135] See Harkavy, as quoted in the preceding note. A place by the
name of Raḳḳa is, according to some, also in Egypt, so that Mu-
ḳammiṣ, too, might be a native of that country, and an emigrant to
Palestine and Babylonia; see, however, Steinschneider, *Arabische
Literatur*, p. 37, n. 1, and § 25; *idem, Hebräische Uebersetzungen*, p.
378, n. 69; for other references see above, note 37. In the short fragment of a work of Mukammiṣ published by Hirschfeld, *JQR.*, XV,
682, Mukammiṣ is called אלשיראזי, *i. e.* of Shirâz, in Persia.

[136] Schreiner, *Der Kalâm*, pp. 22 ff.

[137] Published by Halberstam, Berlin, 1885. The passage referred
to in the text is on p. 77; comp. Goldziher, *RÉJ.*, XLII (1903), 184,
n. 2, where 178 is a misprint for 78.

to the last words, but to the whole statement. Because of
this we may accept the report as true, especially as the con-
temporaneity of the two authors has in the meantime been
established from other sources.[138] Whether Saadia met
Mukammus while traveling through the cities of Syria and
Babylonia, or at a later period, when he had settled in Sura,
cannot be decided, and it is irrelevant The former view
seems more probable, and for that reason the relation between
the two has been discussed in this place.

[138] From a work of the Karaite Abu Jùsuf Ja'kùb al-Ķirkısànı (10th
century), see Harkavy's additions to the Hebrew edition of Graetz's
History, III, 499; Poznański, *The Karaite Literary Opponents of
Saadiah Gaon*, pp. 8-11.

CHAPTER IV

SAADIA'S CONTROVERSY WITH BEN MEIR
(4681-82=921-922)

The subject of Saadia's controversy with Ben Meir forms
an entirely new chapter in the history of the Jews in the
Orient; for it is only half a century since the very name of
Ben Meir appeared on the scene for the first time, while the
literature on the controversy was brought to light only within the last two decades.[139] In connection with the present
work the material on this topic, which came from the
Genizah, is of the greatest importance from many points of
view. It was through the discovery of this material that
we first learned of the movements and activities of Saadia
prior to his appointment as Gaon. For nearly all the details
about his life and work following his departure from Egypt,
discussed in the preceding chapter, we depend on these
finds as the only source. Aside from the historical facts,
which we incidentally learn from these singular documents
on a remarkable political and religious struggle between the
Palestinian and Babylonian authorities of the tenth century,
we are granted a more complete picture of Saadia's character and personality than was obtainable before. Though

---

[139] The first notice of the existence of a man by the name of Ben
Meir was brought to light by the noted Karaite scholar Abraham
Firkovich in an article on his discovery of fragments of Saadia's
'Agrōn and the *Sēfer ha-Gālui*, published in the Hebrew periodical
המליץ, St. Petersburg, 1868, nos. 26, 27, also separately under the
peculiar title אר'ן .... ממצרים .... מבוא להקדמות רמות העולות
הרם"ג .... של מולדתו, Odessa, 1868; see Harkavy, *Zikron*, V,
12, 136; Bornstein, p. 41. Firkovich quotes the passage from the
Sefer ha-Gālui (now in Harkavy, *l. c.*, p. 151, last line) in which the
name Ben Meir occurs, but nothing could be learned from that
passage about his identity and his relations to Saadia, until, a
quarter of a century later, the literature on his controversy with the
latter was unearthed. For the details of that literature see below,
pp. 409-419.

we cannot possibly accept as true the immoderate charges
made against Saadia by the writers of some of these documents, they are nevertheless of value, inasmuch as they
present him to us in the light in which he was seen by some
of his contemporaries,[140] thus enabling us to make up our
account of him after a careful consideration of the facts on
both sides.

Before the two opposing parties are arrayed in their prolonged contest, an explanation of the historical causes
that led to the struggle is unavoidable. Otherwise I should
prefer to escape discussion of a subject that ranks as one
of the obscurest and most complicated in Jewish literature.
Besides, the origin and history of the Jewish calendar does
not readily lend itself to a popular presentation. Our purpose here will be served best by a brief summary of principles, avoiding as far as possible the details of computation.

It is generally accepted that the Jewish festivals were,
in Biblical times, fixed by observation of both the sun
and the moon. Gradually, certain astronomical rules were
also brought into requisition, primarily as a test, corroborating or refuting the testimony of observation. Such rules
are mentioned for the first time in the Book of Enoch,
in the Book of Jubilees, in the Mishnah, and later in
the two Talmudim. It has been authoritatively proved that
in spite of a more advanced knowledge of astronomy the
practice of fixing the new moon and the festivals by observation was in force as late as the latter part of the fifth
century.[141] The right to announce the new moon after re-

---

[140] Though the aspersions and denunciations of Saadia are contained only in the letters of his chief opponent Ben Meir, it is a
matter of course that the latter was not the only one who entertained such opinions of Saadia, but was the mouthpiece of a large
following, especially in Palestine, where Saadia had lived for several
years.

[141] See for the whole matter Bornstein's learned Introduction
to his work, pp. 15 ff., and the important work of F. K. Ginzel, *Handbuch der mathematischen und technischen Chronologie*, II, Leipzig,
1911, pp. 63 ff.

ceiving and testing the witnesses who had observed its appearance was the prerogative of the Palestinian Patriarchs, and the repeated attempts of the authorities in Babylonia to arrogate this right unto themselves were promptly frustrated by interdicts from Palestine.[142] With the beginning of the fourth century, however, Palestine, owing to the terrible persecutions suffered at the hands of the Romans, gradually ceased to be the spiritual center of Jewry. Babylonia, where better conditions prevailed under the Persian rule, took its place, and the religious right to fix the calendar likewise passed over to the heads of its flourishing academies, though not without protests from Palestine.[148] In Babylonia also, the practice of observation was continued until the time of the last Amoraim, although a practical system of reckoning had been known to scholars for more than a century. It was only after the close of the Babylonian Talmud, in the sixth or perhaps later, in the seventh century, that the observation of the moon was entirely given up, and a complete and final system of calendation introduced. This was adopted by all the Jews of the Diaspora, and has been accepted as binding down to the present day.[144]

The real originators of this calendar as well as the circumstances under which it was enforced are lost in the general obscurity of the history of the Oriental Jews during the first two centuries after the completion of the Talmud. It is certain, however, that the whole system of calendation, although promulgated in Babylonia, originated in Palestine.[145] There are indications that the Palestinian Jews felt sore at heart that they had to bow to the Babylonian authorities, whom they must have considered as usurpers of their inherited rights, and from time to time they must have tried to re-establish their lost authority, but in vain.[146]

[142] Bornstein, pp. 8 ff.

[143] Bornstein, p. 10; comp. Poznański, *JQR.*, X, 158.

[144] Bornstein, pp. 17-19; Ginzel, II, 70 f.

[145] For a full account see Epstein, *Ha-Goren*, V, 120 ff.; see, however, Ginzel, II, 78.

[146] Bornstein, p. 10.

With the beginning of the tenth century the situation was
again changed. The once flourishing Babylonian academies
of Sura and Pumbedita, especially the former, owing to general conditions and to the lack of strong leaders, began to
show a marked decline, so that the Sura academy was on the
point of closing its doors, and the sister-academy in Pumbedita was greatly reduced in strength by a bitter struggle between its leading scholars and a pugnacious exilarch.[147] At
this juncture a man of marked ability arose in Palestine, who,
recognizing the propitious moment, sought to take advantage of the situation in order to restore its former prerogatives to his country.[148] This man was [Aaron?] [149] Ben Meir,
a Palestinian by birth and the head of a school in his native
land. He claimed to be a descendant of the Patriarchs
of the house of Hillel, mentioning particularly R Gamliel
and R. Judah Hanasi as his progenitors.[150] With genuine
scholarly attainments and considerable facility in writing he
combined strong will and determined character; all of which
gained for him great influence even outside of Palestine

[147] The reports of Sherira Gaon and of Nathan the Babylonian
regarding the quarrel in Pumbedita differ very essentially in many
points Various attempts at reconciling the two sources have been
made. This is not the place to discuss the matter. See below,
chapter V, and in particular Ginzberg, *Geonica*, I, 55.

[148] A. Epstein in *Ha-Goren*, V, 125 ff. (comp. *ZfhB.*, X, 67), presents the matter as if Ben Meir's motives in starting the conflict were
purely scientific, that he tried to rectify what he considered erroneous
in the established calendar. This view can be accepted only with
great reservation. For whatever the merits of Ben Meir's calculation may have been, there is no doubt that his personal ambition and
perhaps still more, his desire to reassert the authority of the Holy
Land, played, consciously or unconsciously, a very important part
in his contention More than once in his letters he emphatically
denies to the Babylonians the right to fix the calendar, which, he
constantly reiterates, is the exclusive prerogative of his country,
comp. below, note 158

[149] The name Aaron in reference to Ben Meir occurs in a fragment
of Saadia's *Sefer ha-Mō'adim* The context, however, is rather
unclear; comp Bornstein, p. 58, n. 2, 111, bottom; Poznański, *RÉJ.*,
LXVII (1914), 291, n. 1, and below, note 175

[150] Bornstein, p 58, n. 2; above, note 18

In order to bring out Ben Meir's point of view it is necessary to explain some of the elementary rules of the Jewish calendar:

The Jewish lunar year consists of twelve alternating months, of 29 or 30 days, respectively. Such a year, counting 354 days, is called normal or *regular*. For certain reasons, to be explained presently, the year is sometimes made to count only 353 days, in which case it is designated as *deficient;* or a day is added, making 355, and then it is called *full*. To make a year full or deficient, the months of *Ḥeshwān* and *Kislēw* (approximately November and December) were selected for the necessary addition or subtraction. In a regular year *Ḥeshwān* always counts 29 and *Kislēw* 30 days ($=59$); in a full year a day is added to *Ḥeshwān* ($=60$), and in a deficient year a day is subtracted from *Kislēw* ($=58$). Whether a year is to be declared regular, full, or deficient depends upon four rules, called " Postponements," (רחיות) or the " Four Gates," [161] These must be observed in the appointment of every Jewish New

[161] The Four Rules, for which see Ginzel, II, 91 f., are found together in a writing called ארבעה שערים, the Four Gates, because it treats of the four days of the week (Monday, Tuesday, Thursday, and Saturday), on which alone *Rosh ha-Shanah* is allowed to fall, the days forming thus, as it were, the gates through which we enter into the respective new year. The original work of which the Four Gates formed a part, is lost. Nor can it be ascertained when and where or by whom it was composed. From the Ben Meir controversy we can see that as early as the beginning of the tenth century its authority was generally recognized. A certain Jose Al-Nahrawâni, probably a contemporary of Saadia, versified that part of the work which dealt with the Four Rules, and his versification also bears the name ארבעה שערים. Steinschneider discovered the work of Jose in a MS. at the Bodleian library, written in 1203, and published it in the periodical *Kerem Chemed,* IX (1856), 41. A. Epstein re-edited the same with copious notes in the *RÉJ.,* XLII (1901), 204-210. At the same time a commentary on Genesis and Exodus by Menahem b. Solomon (12th century) under the title מדרש שכל טוב was published by S. Buber (Berlin, 1901), wherein a different recension, of Palestinian origin, is found in connection with the verse Exod., 12, 2 (vol. II, 90-92). This recension was

Year's day (first of *Tishri*, approximately September). We
shall here mention only the two rules necessary for the
understanding of Ben Meir's attempted reform.

The first of these rules is that New Year's day should
never be appointed on either a Sunday, or Wednesday, or
Friday. Sunday is considered unfit, because with *Rosh ha-
Shanah* falling thereon, the seventh day of the Feast of
Tabernacles (*Hosha'na Rabbah*), on which the ceremony of
" beating the willow-twigs " is an important part of the service, would fall on the Sabbath, and the observance of the
ceremony could not be permitted. Wednesday and Friday
are likewise inadmissible, because the Day of Atonement
would then, to the great inconvenience of the people, fall on
either Friday or Sunday immediately before or after the
Sabbath. If, therefore, the new moon of the month of Tishri
was observed in the night preceding one of these three days
(Sunday, Wednesday, Friday). New-Year was proclaimed
on the day following; a custom still in force now that calculation has been substituted for observation, the calendar
having been fixed in agreement with this rule of Talmudic
origin.[152]

republished and fully discussed by Bornstein, pp. 26. 103-107 : comp.
also Epstein, *RÉJ.*, XLIV, 230-236, and *Ha-Goren*, V, 131. The
same recension in a more concise form was published by Marx
in his *Untersuchungen zum Siddur des Gaon R. Amram*, Berlin,
1908, pp. 18 f., from a MS. belonging to Sulzberger (originally
Halberstam). In a fragment from the Genizah published by
Schechter, *JQR.*, XIV, 498 (*Saadyana*, p. 128), which contains an
ancient list of books. Saadia is credited with a book by the name of
ארבעה שערים. This is not identical with the fragment published
by Schechter (*ib.*, pp. 128-130), which, though likewise discussing
the Four Gates, is of a polemical character and forms part of the
Sefer Zikkaron; see below, p. 415, no. 9; comp. below, pp. 168 f., nos.
1-2, and *Bibliography*, *IV*, p. 352, no. 2. Saadia mentions the
ארבעה שערים also in his Arabic Commentary on the *Sefer Yezirah*
(ed. Lambert, p. 80) ; comp. Bornstein, p. 25, n. 2.

A short but clear exposition of the Four Rules was given also in
Hebrew, by L. Steinitz, *Bikkūrē ha-Ittim*, 1822, pp. 236-240, and
recently by Ch. Tschernowitz, קצור התלמוד, Lausanne, 1919, pp. 283-
288.

[152] *Rosh ha-Shanah*, 20a; comp. Bornstein, pp. 119-21; Ginzel, II, 67.

The second rule is that in order to proclaim a New-Year's Day it is necessary, that the new moon be seen *before noon* of this day. If the new moon is not observed until exact noon, or later, no matter on what day of the week, the New Year has to be postponed to the following day. If that happens to be one of the three days declared inadmissible for *Rosh ha-Shanah,* the festival is of course postponed for two days. The supposed reason for this rule is that it takes fully six hours from the moment the new moon is caught sight of from some place of vantage until it becomes again visible. Now if the conjunction (*Mōlād*), that is, the meeting of the moon and the sun in the same degree of the zodiac, takes place at 12 (noon) sharp, or still later, there is no chance for the moon to become visible until sunset (six o'clock), when the Jewish astronomical day is considered over. In strictness, this rule (which is also Talmudic),[138] has pertinence only to a system depending on observation; but, as stated before, the rules of calendric calculation were made to agree with the original rules of practice, though the reasons given may have lost their value.

It will be readily understood from the above that whenever New Year is postponed, the year is made shorter, being reduced to 353 days and thus turned into a deficient year. The month of *Tishri,* however, is not made to suffer by this reduction. As stated before, the two days are taken off from the next following months, *Ḥeshwān* and *Kislēw,* which are made to count only twenty-nine days each. To use the technical term, they are both made *deficient.* It may be added to complete our survey that to bring the solar year and the lunar year into coincidence in a certain cycle (19 years), an intercalary month is inserted into the Jewish year at necessary periods, making a *leap* year of 383 to 385 days.

---

[138] *Rosh ha-Shanah,* 20b: נולד קודם חצות בידוע שנראה סמוך לשקיעת החמה לא נולד קודם חצות בידוע שלא נראה סמוך לשקיעת החמה. The meaning of this passage, however, is not clear, which gave rise to differing interpretations; see Epstein, *Ha-Goren,* V, 129 f.; below, note 164.

When observation was replaced by calculation, the calendar did not, indeed, have to be fixed by the authorities from year to year. Anybody familiar with the rules on which it was based could determine many years ahead on what day of the week New Year or any other festival would fall in a given year. In fact it was most essential to know, in order to arrange the calendar for any year, on what day *Rosh ha-Shanah* would fall two years later.

In the year 4681 of the Jewish era ($=921$ common era) it was anticipated that in the year 4684 (September, 923) the rule of two days' postponement, described above, would come into operation. Calculation showed that if observation had been still in practice, the new moon of *Tishri* could not be observed till about thirteen or fourteen minutes after meridian on the Sabbath. Consequently the accepted rules required, observation or no observation, that New Year be postponed to Monday. Now, it must be borne in mind that there is a difference of four, occasionally of five, or even of six days (leaving fractions out of consideration) between two successive years. That is to say, the festivals of a given year fall from four to six days *later in the week* than those of the preceding year. This is due to the fact that fifty weeks of the regular common year and fifty-four weeks of the regular leap year contain, the first only 350, and the second 378 days, while a complete year of twelve regular months counting alternately twenty-nine and thirty days, contains 354 days, and thirteen such months make a year of 384 days. If, therefore, in 923, the year under consideration, New Year was to fall on Monday, *Rosh ha-Shanah* of the previous year (922) must take place four days earlier, *i. e.,* on Thursday. Again, in 922 New Year had to be approximately six days later than in 921, because the year 921 happened to be a leap year. This would bring New Year of 921 on Friday; but as Friday had been declared unfit, Thursday had to be substituted. To sum up: the accepted order of the calendar in those three years was as follows: In 4682 (921/22) New Year on Thursday, the year *full* (385 days),* that is, *Hesh-*

---

* Because it was leap year, 355 + 30

wān and Kislēw containing each thirty days, and Passover
(which is also to be mentioned for reasons that will become
obvious later), falling on a Tuesday.* In 4683 (922/23)
New Year on Thursday, the year *regular* (354 days), Heshwān and Kislēw counting together 59 days (29+30), and
Passover on Sabbath.** In 4684 (923/24) New Year Monday (Postponement), the year *deficient* (353 days), Heshwān
and Kislēw counting together fifty-eight days (29+29), and
Passover on Tuesday.§

We may now return to Ben Meir, but for a full understanding of his position it is necessary to mention one more
point, namely that in the system of the Jewish calendar the
hour is divided not into 3600 seconds but into 1080 halākim
(parts).

As a learned man, the head of an academy, Ben Meir was
naturally well informed on the question of the Jewish calendar. The four principal rules of calendation had been known
for centuries,[154] and in the main he recognized them as
binding. All that he apparently asked, when he began the
controversy, was a modification of the rule which required
that to proclaim any day as *Rosh Hodesh* the new moon
must be discovered (or, in times of reckoning, be due
to appear) *before* noon.[155] Following either another computation or a definite Palestinian tradition,[156] he added 642
" parts " (about thirty-five minutes) to the time limit, so that
if, for instance, the new moon of *Tishri* was due to appear on
the Sabbath *at noon* or within the 642 halākim *after noon*,

---

*In Hebrew this order is marked by the letters ג"הש‎; ה, the fifth
letter of the alphabet, denoting Thursday, the fifth day of the week;
ש stands for שְׁלֵמָה‎, full, and ג, the third letter, for Tuesday
(Passover).

** In Hebrew ז"הכ‎, ה = Thursday, כ is an abbreviation of כסדרה‎,
which means regular, and ז, the seventh letter, = Sabbath.

§ Hebrew letters ג"בח‎, ב = Monday, ח stands for חסרה‎, meaning
deficient, and ג for Tuesday.

[154] See Bornstein, p. 25, n. 2; Epstein, *Ha-Goren*, V, 132, and above,
note 151.

[155] See Bornstein, p. 64, n. 4.

[156] See below, p. 80.

no postponement should take place. The Sabbath would thus
be declared *Rosh ha-Shanah*, while according to the accepted
calendar the festival had to be postponed until Monday
(Sabbath being ineligible on account of the belated appearance of the new moon, and Sunday on account of rule 1).

This being precisely what was due to happen in *Tishri*
of the year 4684 (September 923), Ben Meir, believing the
time favorable for the long-sought overthrow of the Babylonian authority, came out in the summer [157] of 4681 (921)
with the declaration that *Heshwān* and *Kislēw* of the ensuing
year (4682 = November and December 921) should both be
made *deficient*. Now the year 4682 could be declared deficient only when the year 4684 was to be declared full, that
is, if *Rosh ha-Shanah* of the last named year was not to be
postponed on account of a belated new moon, but was to
take place on the Sabbath of the new moon's appearance
In fact it was the anticipated postponement of the New
Year of 4684 which Ben Meir attacked. He contended
that inasmuch as in that year the new moon was due only 237
halāķim (about fourteen minutes) after midday and thus
much in advance of the allowed 642 parts, it was not to be
considered as late, and hence no postponement could be
admissible.*

Such, and apparently so technical if not trivial, was the
actual issue between Ben Meir and Babylon

The question forces itself upon us: What was Ben Meir's
reason for the addition of 642 parts to the given time limit?
It is hardly credible that a learned and pious man, as Ben
Meir undoubtedly was, should have undertaken to change
essentially one of the most sacred religious institutions of
the Jewish people, one upon which depended the celebration
of the festivals in their proper season, unless there were

---

[157] Epstein, *Ha-Goren*, V, 138, end of note 1

* Ben Meir's order for the three years was accordingly 682 הח"א,
i e., New Year Thursday (ה), deficient (ח), Passover Sunday (א) ,
683 גכ"ה, New Year Tuesday (ג), regular (כ) Passover Thursday
(ה) ; 684 וש"ג, New Year Saturday (ו), full (ש), Passover Tuesday (ג)

strong reasons to justify his action.[158] Moreover, it would
have been the most injudicious step for a leader to take, as
he could foresee that no conscientious Jew would follow
him, unless the religious expediency of his procedure was
proved. As a matter of fact, many Jewish communities in
Palestine and outside [159] accepted Ben Meir's view, and soon
after were ready to celebrate, or actually did celebrate, the
Passover of the year 4682 on Sunday instead of Tuesday.

Various views have been advanced in explanation of the
matter; among them that the accepted calendar being based
on the time in the city of Babylon, where noon is approximately 56 minutes earlier than in Jerusalem, Ben Meir,
claiming Jerusalem as the right basis, added 642 parts
(35 minutes) *partly* to offset the difference.[160] Against
this it has been properly pointed out [161] that the fixing of the
calendar was originally the prerogative of Palestine, and
it is therefore inconceivable that it should have been based
on Babylonian time.[162] Nor is there any proof that later
Babylonian authorities assumed to transfer the basis from
Jerusalem to Babylon. Besides, if this was the reason for the
addition, Ben Meir would certainly not have failed to mention it. Finally, the addition of precisely 642 parts (35
minutes instead of 56) would after all be an arbitrary and
futile act.

[158] Ben Meir guards himself against the reproach that his desire
to re-establish the authority of the Holy Land was the only reason
for his reforms, by pointing out to his opponents the correctness of
his calculation; comp. Bornstein, p. 51, n. 6, and above, note 148.

[159] As may be seen from a letter of Saadia to three Rabbis in Egypt,
published by Hirschfeld, *JQR.*, XVI, 290-297, the Egyptian communities too, or at least some of them, during the time of the quarrel
celebrated the festivals according to the computation of Ben Meir;
comp. also Bornstein, p. 12.

[160] Bornstein, pp. 20, 28, 34 ff.

[161] Epstein, *Ha-Goren*, V, 119 ff.

[162] This view is maintained by D. Sidersky in his recent work,
Étude sur l'origine astronomique de la chronologie juive, Paris,
1911; comp. his article in the periodical הצופה מארץ הגר, III (Budapest, 1913), 33, 37, top.

Another, more acceptable explanation is that Ben Meir's
real purpose was to reduce the number of postponements
provided for in the accepted calendar.[159] These postponements were, in his opinion, frequently the cause of celebrating the festivals at a time other than that prescribed in
the Torah. Most of them resulted from the rule concerning
the belated new moon, and when this operated in connection
with another rule, it might readily necessitate a postponement for two days. Finding that a slight extension of the
time set for the appearance of the moon around mid-day
would greatly reduce the number of such postponements, he
considered it a religious duty to issue a proclamation to this
effect. The claim that the rule opposed by him was based
on the authority of the Talmud did not appeal to Ben Meir,
as the passage in question is rather obscure and allows of
differing interpretations.[161]

Plausible as this explanation seems to be, it is still difficult
to see why he should have selected exactly the number of
642 for his addition, and the suggestion has therefore been
made that in this respect Ben Meir relied on a definite
Palestinian tradition.[162] Various passages in the controversial letters dealing with the subject seem to support this
view. It is quite possible that others before Ben Meir had
attempted to rectify the calendar by the same addition of
642 parts, but that the literary records, if there were such,
have not been preserved.

At this point the subject of the calendar may be dismissed,
and we may revert to the discussion of the course of events
connected therewith, which led to the defeat of Ben Meir
and ultimately to the rise of Saadia to the Gaonate.

Ben Meir's intention to make *Heshwān* and *Kislēw* of the
year 4682 deficient and to have the Passover of the same
year celebrated two days earlier than that fixed by the Babylonian authorities (Sunday instead of Tuesday) became

[159] Epstein, *Ha-Goren*, V, 125 ff.

[161] See above, note 153. A new interpretation of the passage is
offered by Sidersky, הצופה מארץ הגר, III, 41; comp. Ginzel, II, 514.

[162] See above, p. 77; Epstein, *Ha-Goren*, V, 133.

known in the summer of the year 4681 (921). In what
way he had manifested this intention, cannot be ascertained
from the available material. At that time it seems he had
not yet issued an official proclamation.[166] The rumor reached
Saadia in Aleppo. He at once addressed several letters to
Ben Meir, demonstrating to him the correctness of the established calendar and warning him against the change
advocated. This is reported by Saadia himself in the
two letters which he addressed during the subsequent winter
to his pupils in Egypt.[167] He further informs us, in the
same letters, that in Bagdad, whither he had gone from
Aleppo, he learned that his repeated warnings had had
no effect on Ben Meir, who had meantime issued his
official proclamation, much to the perturbation of the
Babylonian Geonim. The date of Ben Meir's proclamation[168] is not given by Saadia. In all probability it was
issued on *Hosha'na Rabbah* (the seventh day of the feast
of Tabernacles) in the year 4682 (autumn, 921), on which
day, as is known from other sources, it was customary
among the Palestinian Jews of that period to assemble
annually on the Mount of Olives (east of Jerusalem) for
prayer and solemn processions around the mount (Ḥaḳḳā-
fōt). The occasion was used for the discussion of the

---

[166] Epstein, *ibidem*, p. 138, end of n. 1.

[167] Bornstein, pp. 68, 70.

[168] The sources do not explicitly mention Ben Meir's proclamation.
In his first letter Ben Meir speaks of the proclamation of his son
(Bornstein, p. 51, line 10: הכריז חמודנו), which, as we know from
Saadia's *Sēfer ha-Mōʻadim* (Bornstein, p. 60), took place about three
months later, in *Tēbēt* (comp. Epstein, *Ha-Goren*, V, 138, n. 1, as
against Bornstein). In his second letter, however, he speaks of a
"proclamation of his pupils on the Mount of Olives" (הכרזת
תלמידינו בהר הזיתים; Bornstein, p. 91, bottom; 92, top), which
seems to refer to a previous proclamation on *Hosha'na Rabbah;* comp.
the text recently published by A. Guillaume, *JQR.*, N. S., vol. V. (1914-
1915), p. 555, l. 15. In the second letter of Saadia (Bornstein, p. 70)
we also read twice הכריזם with reference to Ben Meir. It is
possible, however, that the writers had in mind the proclamation of
Ben Meir's son; comp. below, *Appendix*, no. 9, pp. 415 ff.

6

various religious and communal needs of the people, and
decisions as to future actions were adopted.

As soon as the news of this proclamation reached Babylon
the Exilarch David ben Zakkai, in conjunction with the
Geonim of both academies and probably also Saadia,[168] addressed an official letter to Ben Meir setting forth in urgent
words the validity of the established calendar and warning
him against the contemplated change.[179] At the same time
the Geonim sent out circular letters to the various Jewish
communities, advising them to abide by the old order, and
not to heed the innovations proposed.

It was about this period that Saadia wrote to his Egyptian
pupils. The first half of his letter was given above (pp.
55 f.) : the second reads as follows :

" Know that when I was yet in Aleppo, some pupils came
from Baʿal Gad [171] and brought the news that Ben Meir intends
to proclaim *Ḥeshwān* and *Kislēw* deficient. I did not believe
it, but as a precaution I wrote to him in the summer [not to
do so]. The Exilarch, the heads of the academies, all the
'Allūfim,[172] teachers and scholars,[173] likewise agreed to proclaim *Ḥeshwān* and *Kislēw* full, and that Passover be celebrated on Thursday. In conjunction with their letters I

[168] This results from a passage in Ben Meir's letter (Bornstein,
p. 50, l. 8: והמתחבר אליהם סעיר בן יוסף אלדלאצי). It is possible, however, that Ben Meir refers here to letters he received directly
from Saadia, who, as stated, wrote to him from Aleppo.

[179] For the chronology of the various letters see below, pp. 410 ff.

[171] A town at the foot of the Lebanon Mountains (Joshua, 11, 17;
see Dillmann, *ad locum*). It is mentioned also by Judah Al-Ḥarizi,
Taḥkemōni, makāma 30, beginning, and in the *Itinerary* of Benjamin
of Tudela, ed. London, 1840, p. 27; comp. also *JQR.*, XVI (1904),
732, n. 3.

[172] For the meaning of this title see the references above, note 122.

[173] The phrase מבין עם תלמיד is taken from I Chronicles, 25, 8.
The word תלמיד in the usage of Arabic-speaking Jews has not
always the common meaning of *pupil*, but more often designates a
recognized *scholar;* comp. Ginzberg, *Geonica*, I, 32, n. 4; Davidson,
Sepher Shaashuim, New York, 1914, p. cx.

too wrote to most of the great cities,[174] in order to fulfill my
duty. Persist ye also in this matter and close up this breach,
and do not rebel against the command of God. None of the
people dare to profane the festivals of God wilfully, to eat
leavened bread on Passover, and eat, drink, and work on
the Day of Atonement. May it be the will [of the Lord]
that there be no stumbling-block and no pitfall in your place
or in any other place in Israel. Pray, answer this letter and
tell me all your affairs and your well-being. May your peace
grow and increase forever!"

Here we have Saadia's own testimony as to the part he
took in the struggle, and the rank to which he had attained
among the Babylonian authorities at this period. Not only
did they invite his co-operation in signing their official letters
in order to confer special weight upon their ordinances,
but Saadia issued such letters on his own account to the
largest congregations in and outside of Babylon—a proof of
the great fame and popularity he must have enjoyed in Jewry
in general.

Meanwhile Ben Meir, far from heeding the interdicts of
Babylonia, repeated his attack by sending his son[175] to
Jerusalem, to proclaim there, for the second time, the proposed changes of the calendar. To the charges of the
Geonim and of Saadia he replied in a disrespectful and
aggressive tone, denying their authority in matters of the
calendar, which, he claimed, should be left, as in former
times, in the hands of Palestinian scholars. In a lengthy
letter to his adherents in Babylonia, in which he sets forth

[174] Schechter, *Saadyana,* p. 25; Bornstein, p. 69: גם אנכי כתבתי עם
אגרותיהם אל רוב המדינות האדירות.

[175] Nothing definite is known about Ben Meir's sons to whom Ben
Meir refers as his "darlings" (המודיי), while Saadia calls them
עגלים! See below, note 188; Bornstein, p. 67, n. 2. According to
Poznański, *REJ.,* LXVI, 67, a son of Ben Meir by the name of Abra-
ham was the founder of the Palestinian Gaonate in the year 945.
He occupied the position several years, and was succeeded by his son
Aaron, who was named after his grandfather; see above, note 149.

with much detail the reasons for his reforms, he pours out his whole wrath on Saadia in particular, denouncing him and "his arrogant followers" in scathing terms. This is also significant of the rôle Saadia evidently played in the affair. In the meantime the feast of Passover was approaching. The congregations were bewildered by commands and countermands."[176] Some prepared to celebrate the festival on the date set by Ben Meir, others stood up for the accepted calendar A serious rupture was imminent in the ranks of Jewry, not dissimilar to that brought about previously by the Karaites. Saadia again addressed a letter to his pupils in Egypt,[177] and probably also to various communities elsewhere, imploring them to remain steadfast and to abide by the regulations of the Geonim. To his credit it must be remarked that in this letter there is not a single harsh word against Ben Meir, the originator of all the trouble

The repeated notes of warning did not bring about the desired result Most of the Palestinian and some of the Babylonian communities actually celebrated that Passover, and consequently the other festivals, two days earlier than the official date.[178] The schism must have assumed alarming proportions. Even a non-Jewish historian of the following century considered it important enough to include it in his account of historical events.[179] Twice more, so far as our

---

[176] So Ben Meir *apud* Bornstein, p. 92: והזכרתם כי רבו השימועות בגלל אחינו ישראל והאיגרות באות אליכם מכל צד

[177] The letter was published first by Neubauer, *JQR.,* IX (1897), 37; Harkavy *Ha-Goren,* II (1900), 98, Epstein (with French translation and notes), *RÉJ.,* XLII (1901), 200; Bornstein, p 69, comp. below, p 413, no 5.

[178] Comp. Bornstein, pp. 12, 90, n 1; Epstein, *RÉJ*, XLII, 179, n 1, on the testimony of the Karaite Sahl b. Mazliah *apud* Pinsker, *Likkūtē,* II, 36.

[179] Elijah of Nisibis (11th century) in Baethgen's *Fragmente syrischer und arabischer Historiker,* Leipzig, 1884, pp 84, 141. Cyrus Adler in an article "Jewish History in Arabian Historians," *JQR*, 11 (1890), 106, first called attention to the passage in the work of Elijah relating to the differences between the Babylonian and Palestinian Jews in the appointment of the festivals in the year 922. At

records give us information, the Babylonian representatives of Judaism expostulated with Ben Meir.[159] This happened in the ensuing summer. Again letters of warning and exhortation were sent to the " divided house of Israel," but to no effect. " The two parties indulged in mutual recriminations and excommunications, and even went so far as to charge one another with fraud and deception." [151] How long the quarrel lasted, and by what means it was brought to an end, cannot be learned from the scanty material that was discovered in the Genizah. From the report of the Syrian historian and from Ḳaraitic sources we know only that at the beginning of the year 4683 the quarrel was still in progress. *Rosh ha-Shanah* of that year was observed by the two opposing parties on different days in accordance with their divergent views.

We know, however, that Ben Meir and his supporters ultimately met with crushing defeat, and as may be plainly seen from Ben Meir's epistles, he attributed his downfall particularly to the activity of Saadia.[152] Ben Meir's judgment was doubtless right on this point. Neither the Geonim who presided over the two academies, nor any of the scholars among their followers had either the intellectual capacity

---

that time, however (1890), nothing was known about the controversy of Saadia and Ben Meir and the real importance of the passage could not even be guessed at. Several years later, when the various Genizah fragments were brought to light by Schechter and others, Poznański, referring to Adler's article, pointed out the full meaning of Elijah's report in its bearing on the subject under consideration; see his article in *JQR.*, X (1898), 152-161, and comp. Bornstein, pp. 7 f.

[150] That the Geonim wrote three times to Ben Meir is repeatedly stated by Saadia in the fragment of the *Sefer ha-Mō'adim*, Bornstein, p. 61, line 17; 63, line 3; comp. Epstein, *Ha-Goren*, V, 138.

[151] Poznański, *JQR.*, X, 154, based on the testimony of the Ḳaraite Sahl b. Maẓliaḥ; see the references given above, note 178, and Bornstein, pp. 7, 61, n. 5.

[152] Comp. Bornstein, p. 13, n. 3, particularly Ben Meir's letters *apud* Bornstein, pp. 56, 90.

or the complete command over the people to parry the determined onslaught of Ben Meir, whose influence reached far beyond the boundaries of his own country and whose contention was not without merit. In fact, it was partly because of the weakened standing of the Gaonate that Ben Meir could venture to assert his authority above that of Babylonia. But Saadia's fiery genius, his profound learning, and above all his superior literary skill proved more than a match for his opponent and finally brought about Ben Meir's overthrow.

It is characteristic of the situation, that, as Saadia himself tells us, the Babylonian authorities, having failed in all their efforts against the disturber, had thought of calling the government to their assistance.[153] For some reason not stated they gave up the plan and decided upon issuing a memorial-volume (*Sefer ha-Zikkaron*),[154] in which all the misdeeds of Ben Meir from the beginning of the controversy to its end, his errors in calculation, the proceedings of the Gaonate against him, and particularly the reasons for their continued upholding of the accepted calendar, were to be minutely recorded. The volume was to be spread broadcast among all the Jews of the Diaspora, with the

---

[153] This results from a passage in Saadia's *Sefer ha-Mō'adim*. Bornstein, p. 65: ולא התעשתו לקחת אגרות מאת המלך להסירו, which means that they did not make up their mind to invoke the government, at the same time suggesting that the appeal was considered. This does not contradict the passage in Bornstein, p. 92, bottom (better given in the *JQR.*, N. S., vol. V (1914-1915), p. 555, top), where Ben Meir reports that he was twice imprisoned and tortured (comp. Schechter, *Saadyana*, p. 22, n. 1), for there Ben Meir has reference to some previous entanglement with the Karaites, who denounced him to the government for some unknown reason and procured his punishment. Comp. Bornstein, p. 93, n. 2.

[154] This *Sefer Zikkarōn* is not identical with the *Sefer ha-Mō'adim*, as has been hitherto assumed, but is a separate work, which was written by Saadia at the request of the Exilarch and the Geonim for recitation in public. As I have shown elsewhere (see *Appendix*, No. 9) the lengthy fragment in Schechter's *Saadyana*, pp. 128-130 (Bornstein, pp. 99-102) is a remnant of this work.

special injunction, that it be read annually in public on the twentieth of *'Elūl,* before the approach of the high Holy Days, and thus serve as a warning against possible upheavals of a similar nature in all future generations. It was again Saadia who was charged with the composition of this important document. He wrote the book in the summer of 4682 (922), while the struggle was at its height. It was read publicly, as provided, in the month of *'Elūl* of the same year. Its effect on the communities was very great, apparently putting an end to the agitation, which had lasted for nearly two years. At all events, nothing more is heard of Ben Meir during the following years, though his main intention was to change the date of *Rosh ha-Shanah* of the year 4684 (923).[185]

How important a part Saadia had in the regulation of the present calendar can be seen also from the fact that eminent authorities of later centuries[186] describe him as the father and founder of the science of the calendar Most, if not all, of his work in this field was done in connection with the controversy with Ben Meir or his polemics with the Karaites. Its contemporary importance may be judged from the fact that it paved the way to Saadia's election to the Gaonate;[187] but the lasting moment of Saadia for the Jewish world and his influence on the development of mediæval Jewish literature have a better basis than his discomfiture of Ben Meir. Considering the acrimony—almost ferocity—with which the quarrel over the calendar was carried

---

[185] It must be borne in mind, however, that in all probability there were more documents relating to the quarrel, which have not yet come to light. Numerous fragments from the Genizah which are preserved in various public or private libraries, are still awaiting examination and publication. We may therefore expect that the continued search among the treasured documents will bring to light additional details bearing upon the various phases of the controversy and its final outcome.

[186] So the Tōsafist Jacob Tam (12th century); see for further details Bornstein, p. 25; below, note 625.

[187] See above, pp. 63-65.

on by both controversialists,[339] especially in the last stages
of the argument, one cannot but designate it as a deplorable
episode.

[339] Ben Meir's letters abound in personal denunciations and abuses
of Saadia, which reveal the extreme bitterness of the writer ; comp.
e. g. the passage Bornstein, p. 56: סעיד בן אלפיומי וחבריו הזידונים
המצרים והמינים, כרגע יאבדו ויזרו בארבע פינים. Not satisfied
with the attacks on the character of his opponent, Ben Meir tried to
defame also Saadia's family, asserting, as he says, " on good
authority " that the latter's father was a Muezzin in the service of the
Muhammedans, defiled himself by eating abominations, until he was
driven out of Egypt and died in Jaffa (בן פיומי הדלאצי אשר נתברר
לפנינו בערים ברורים וכשרים . . . . יהיה אביו מכה בפטייט בארץ
מצרים לעבודה זרה ואכל מרק פיגולים ונרחף מארץ מצרים ומת ביפו;
Bornstein, p. 90) ; comp. above, pp. 27, 63. Saadia retaliates by
adorning Ben Meir with the epithets המחשיך, " the obscurantist,"
and הממאיר, " the accursed one," both in satiric allusion to the
name מאיר; comp. Bornstein, pp. 58, n. 1; 62, n. 1. Ben Meir's sons
he terms " calves " (עגלים) ; see above, note 175.

Chapter V

SAADIA'S APPOINTMENT TO THE GAONATE
(4688=928)

In the course of the inquiry into Saadia's career, the Ben Meir controversy appears to the investigator like an islet emerging suddenly from a vast void, only to be swallowed up again almost as soon as he sets foot upon it. Even the information about Saadia's early departure from Egypt has come to us from one of the documents bearing on that controversy;[189] while for the period of the years between his emigration to the Holy Land and his appearance on the scene with Ben Meir (921), one searches in vain for data regarding the life and activity of the future Gaon. During the two years the quarrel appears to have lasted he is seen in the foreground of all affairs, but as soon as the controversy abates, he is lost to sight for another period of six years (922-28), at the expiration of which he is called to the Gaonate. The only trace of his existence during that period is a passage from one of his works, quoted by a later author,[190] in which Saadia refers to the year 926 as the time of his writing.

We must therefore abandon for the present all speculation as to events and happenings in the life of Saadia during the few years preceding his installation in the office of Gaon. Some of the unexplored and unidentified remnants of manuscripts from the Genizah which are treasured in various public and private libraries, possibly contain data to fill the gaps; but until such material turns up, we

---

[189] See note 88 [and *Postscript*].

[190] Abraham b. Ḥiyya, astronomer and mathematician of the 12th century, in his *Sefer ha-'Ibbūr,* London, 1851, p. 96; comp. Rapoport's *Biography* of *Saadia* in the Hebrew periodical בכורי העתים, 1828, p. 26, end of note 1; Poznański, *JQR.,* X, 245; Graetz, *Geschichte,* V, *Note* 20, no. 6; above, note 126.

are entitled to the assumption that nothing of importance
happened during these blank years to change the general
aspect of his personality. Saadia the scholar spent most of
his time in seclusion, studying and writing. Particularly in
the period before us, when he had been made a regular member of the official staff of the Sura academy, he doubtless
devoted his life entirely to the elaboration and completion
of his numerous works. Years of study and research
behind closed doors are not commonly fraught with personal
events of such general interest as to induce contemporary
chroniclers to record them for the benefit of future generations. As for the petty idiosyncrasies of a Jewish scholar
or the trivial incidents of his daily life, there was no Boswell
at hand to delight in watching and noting them. We may
pass over the interval between the Ben Meir episode and
Saadia's election to the Gaonate with the assurance that it
hides no phase of biographical importance.

The period now to be taken up is the only one in Saadia's
life, the details of which were known to the student of
Jewish literature before the discovery of the Genizah. Such
details may be derived partly from the works of Saadia
himself, partly from those of contemporaneous authors or
from well-authenticated later sources. Hence this period has
been more or less minutely treated in works on Jewish history in general or on Saadia in particular. It was practically
all that constituted the biography of the Gaon. But even
this part of Saadia's life has been inadequately described. In
the few existing monographs [19] on the Gaon, one regularly

[19] Separate biographies or occasional descriptions of Saadia's life
were written by the following authors (in chronological order):
Rapoport. תולדות רבנו סעדיה גאון וקורות ספריו. in בכורי העתים.
IX (1828), 20-37 (comp. *ib.*, X. 37 f., XI 83 f.), the classic source
of all subsequent writers on Saadia. The biographical sketch,
without the notes, was translated into German by Joseph Zedner
and published in Ludwig Stern's *Jüdische Geschichte in Lebens-
bildern*, Stuttgart, 1862, pp. 136-138.

S. Munk, *Notice sur R. Saadia Gaon*, Paris, 1838.

E. Carmoly, in his *Revue Orientale* (Brussels 1841-1846), II, 33-46.
L. Dukes, *Beiträge*, II (1844), 5 ff.

finds the few important events of his later life—his election
to the Gaonate, his subsequent quarrel with the Exilarch,
his deposition, and his final rehabilitation—put together in a
few lines; while the rest of the work is devoted to the pres-

A. Geiger, *Wissenschaftliche Zeitschrift*, V (1844), 281-316.
Steinschneider, *CB.*, *coll.* 2156 ff., and later in *Arab. Liter.* (Frankfurt a/M., 1902), pp. 49-69; comp. Kaufmann's *Gedenkbuch*, pp.
144-168.

Graetz, *Geschichte der Juden*, V, fourth edition by S. Eppenstein,
Leipzig, 1909, pp. 282-315; 523-533; Hebrew translation by S. P.
Rabinowitz, III (Warsaw, 1893), pp. 279-308; 465-473; English trans-
lation, III (Philadelphia, 1894), pp. 187-202.

M. Joel, in Wertheim's *Jahrbuch für Israeliten*, 1865, pp. 1-17.

S. J. Fünn ג"רס תולדות, in הכרמל, 1871, pp. 61-68.

G. Tal, *R. Saadjah Gaon*, in " *Lesingen gehouden in de Vereeniging
voor Joodsche Letterkunde en Geschiedenis*," Hague, 1887.

I. H. Weiss, ודורשיו דור דור, IV (1887), 4th edition, Wilna, 1904,
pp. 123-143.

A. Harkavy, *R. Saadia Gaon, istorico-literaturnoe chtenie, Voskhod*, 1887, pp. 82-104 (the same appeared also in Hebrew under the
title וחכים רב by H. Mirsky, in the periodical ישראל כנסת,
III, Warsaw, 1888, pp. 55-71); comp. also Harkavy, in *Zapisky . . . .
Ruskavo Arkheologicheskavo Obshchestwa*, V (1891), 179-210; VI,
340.

S. A. Taubeles, *Saadia Gaon*, Halle a/S., 1888 (a compilation
without value).

D. Kohn (Kahana), גאון ס"ר לתולדות ספר, Cracow, 1892 (reprint
from הספרות אוצר, IV, 292-328).

S. Bernfeld, גאון סעדיה רבנו, Cracow, 1892 (reprint from אוצר.
הספרות, IV, 329-346; 698-—, as a biography worthless).

M. Friedländer, *Life and Works of Saadia*, in *JQR.*, V (1893),
177-199.

G[regory] H[enkel], *R. Saadia Gaon, Opit Characteristiki evo
Proizvedenii, Voskhod*, 1893, IV, 12-25; V, 104-119; VIII, 121-138;
IX, 42-61; 1894, I, 118-143; II, 130-146; III, 136-146; VI, 119-132;
VIII, 112-126; XI, 7-32; XII, 131-138.

W. Engelkemper, *De Saadiae Gaonis vita* etc., Münster, 1897, a
learned dissertation.

S. Eppenstein, *Beiträge zur Geschichte und Literatur im geonäischen Zeitalter* (reprint from *MGWJ.*, 1908-1913), pp. 65-148; 215-218.

A brief account of Saadia's life and works is given by Bacher in the
JE., X, 579-586; and lately by H. Malter in Hastings' *Encyclopaedia
of Religion and Ethics, s. v. Se'adiah* (vol. XI); see also the present

entation of his teachings. No attempt is made to interpret these events in the light of contemporary history. We shall therefore not be bound by any of the existing presentations, but will dispose of the material from the old sources [192] in the way that seems best adapted to the plan and purpose of the present work. In accordance therewith it appears advisable to prepare the reader for a fuller understanding of the essential points in the development of the last and the most significant epoch of Saadia's life, by a brief account of the two important institutions of mediæval Babylonian Jewry—the Exilarchate and the Gaonate—and of their relations to one another.

The origin of the Exilarchate, which, according to the historical sources maintained its place in Babylon for over eight centuries, is not fully known. An old tradition claims

writer's article *Philosophy, ibidem,* vol. IX, pp. 873-877) ; comp. also A Kaminka in Winter and Wünsche's *Die judische Litteratur,* II, 28-31; ד״ר א. גינזבורגס אידישע דענקער און פאעטען אין מיטעלאלטער New York, 1918, pp. 21-33. Finally, biographical accounts of Saadia are to be found with more or less detail in the introductions to the numerous editions of Saadia's writings, mostly repeating the older authorities, as Rapoport, Munk, Geiger, Graetz, and Steinschneider. See the detailed *Bibliography* in the present work, especially sections I, V —An article on " The Time of Saadya " by S Koch (Hebrew Union College Journal, vol. VI, Cincinnati, 1902, pp 168-174) may here be recorded for bibliographers.

[192] These are in the main the *Report* of Nathan ha-Babli, a contemporary of Saadia, ed. Neubauer, *Mediæval Jewish Chronicles,* II, 77-88, the *Epistle of Sherira Gaon,* ed Neubauer, *ib.,* I, 39 f. Abraham b. David's account in his סדר הקבלה (Neubauer, *ib ,* I, 65 f.), which conflicts in many essential points with the reports of Nathan and Sherira, is disregarded as less reliable. Later authors, as Menahem Meiri (Neubauer, II, 224), Isaac Lattes (*ib.,* p 233) and Saadia Ibn Danan, חמדה גנוזה, ed Edelmann, Konigsberg, 1856, p 28, merely repeat the unfounded statements of Abraham b David, though for some points they may have had also other sources. For Nathan and the historicity of his Report see Ginzberg, *Geonica,* I, 22-36; comp Marx. *ZfhB ,* XIII, 169, and Poznański, *JQR., N S.,* vol. III (1912-1913), pp 400 f. In the following the *Report* will be referred to only by the word " Nathan," and the pages are those of Neubauer's edition The same edition is used also for the Letter of Sherira.

no less a personage than King Jehoiachin as the first
Babylonian Exilarch (597 b. c. e.). This tradition is based
on II Kings, 24-25, where it is told that Jehoiachin was
brought captive to Babylon and imprisoned, but later freed
by King Evil-merodach and given a place of honor. " The
craftsmen and the smiths," who were taken into captivity
together with the King (II Kings, 24. 16) are interpreted
homiletically to be the King's retinue of scholars and
prophets.[193] A chronicler of the eighth century,[194] the first
to mention the captive Judæan King as the founder of the
Exilarchate, in an effort to establish a continuous chain of
Exilarchs of Davidic descent,[195] makes up a list of such dig-

---

[193] *Sifre*, section האזינו, § 321, and *Seder 'Olam*, ch. 25, which are
the source of the Talmudim and Midrashim; see the references given
by Ratner in his edition of the *Seder 'Olam, ad locum*. These sources
do not designate King Jehoiachin as the first Exilarch. He receives
this title only in the works of a later period in which, however, the
authors gave expression to ideas only that were current among the
people long before; see the next note.

[194] I refer to the anonymous author of the סדר עולם זוטא. This
dry chronicle, covering only a few pages (in Neubauer's *MJC.*, II,
68-73), exists in various recensions and editions, also in Latin translations, and with commentaries. For the literature see Steinschneider,
Geschichtsliteratur der Juden, § 9, and additions on p. 173. The most
important and minute study on the subject is the one by Felix Lazarus,
Die Häupter der Vertriebenen, in Brüll's *Jahrbücher*, etc., X (the
entire volume), also separately, Frankfurt a/M., 1890. In the following I shall refer to this study by quoting only the name of the author;
comp. also Abr. Krochmal, פרושים והארות לתלמור בבלי, Lemberg,
1881, pp. 1-73 (Steinschneider, *H. B.*, XXI, p. 122). The chronicler
docs not state explicitly that Jehoiachin was Exilarch, though this
is obviously his view, but in a fragmentary version of the same
Chronicle, in Neubauer's *MJC.*, I, 195, it is said of the king: והוליכו
בגלות והמליכו על ישראל; comp. Lazarus, *ib.*, pp. 19, n. 4; 55, n. 1;
158, n. 1. Among other ancient authors who follow this tradition may
be mentioned the Gaon Ẓemaḥ b. Ḥayyim of Sura (882) in his Letter
concerning Eldad. (See Jellinek, *Bet ha-Midrasch*, II, 113); Sherira,
p. 26; comp. Ginzberg, *Geonica*, I, 5. Ebjatar in Schechter's
Saadyana, p. 87, line 27; p. 89, line 27, has reference to the same idea,
but in a derogatory sense, pointing to the wicked ancestors of the
Exilarchs, among them Jehoiachin.

[195] Zunz, *Gottesdienstliche Vorträge* (1892), p. 142; Steinschneider,
Geschichtsliteratur der Juden, § 9; comp. Lazarus, pp. 19, 29 f.

nitaries reaching down to the year 520 c e. The names of the earlier Exilarchs are all identical with those of the King's descendants enumerated in I Chron 3 17-24, all of whom according to the author lived and died in Babylon The names of the Exilarchs of later generations are taken partly from the Talmud and partly from unknown sources. The historicity of this list, so far as the Biblical part is concerned, is beyond control. The latter part, however, beginning about the middle of the second century c e., is authenticated by Talmudic and other evidence. Other lists of Exilarchs of still later periods, from 520 to 940. or even 1040, are preserved in various sources, more or less trustworthy [196] Leaving aside those whose names are recorded in the Bible, and whose Exilarchal dignity may be legendary,[197] there are still at least thirty-three Exilarchs [198] accounted for historically by recent investigation.

The history of the Exilarchate is thus divided into two distinct periods ; the first when Babylonia was under Persian rulers (the Arsacids and the Sassanids) and the second when it came under the Caliphate of the Arabs (651).

The exact circumstances under which the office came into existence are unknown. From the moment when the light of history falls upon the institution, it is evident that the Exilarch was the governor of Jewish Babylonia, appointed by the ruler of Persia and vested with full authority over his Jewish subjects [199] As such he was responsible only to the king His duties were to maintain order among the people under his jurisdiction and see to it that the taxes imposed upon the Jewish communities were collected and delivered into the imperial treasury. At certain festivities he had to

---

[196] See the various lists in Lazarus s work, pp 171-173, 180

[197] Comp Lazarus, pp. 62 f

[198] Beginning with a certain Nahum (about 140, c e.), who is supposed to be identical with one Ahiah, or Nehunyon, mentioned in the Talmud, and ending with David b Zakkai (died 940), the opponent of Saadia Comp Lazarus, pp. 65 ff, Bacher, *Jewish Encyclopedia*, V. 288.

[199] Lazarus, p 87, and in more detail, pp. 131 ff.

appear among the other dignitaries of the empire and participate in the court functions. In his dealings with the Jewish population he was entirely independent, often also overbearing and oppressive. In accordance with oriental custom, and being wealthy in his own right, he maintained his Exilarchal court with considerable pomp and circumstance, surrounding himself with a large retinue of servants and courtiers, who had to observe etiquette and official ceremonies similar to those practised at the Persian court. It was the prerogative of the Exilarch to appoint judges for the Jews from among the prominent scholars of the time, one of whom was the supreme judge. The latter had to reside at the Exilarch's court.[200]

Some of the Exilarchs, who were themselves learned in the religious law, are reported by the Talmud [201] to have acted as presidents of the judicial tribunal. On the whole, however, the Exilarch was not a representative of religious, that is to say, spiritual Judaism. His ambitions and aspirations were of a worldly and political nature. Such was the natural consequence of the fact that the office was hereditary in one family, which traced its pedigree to the house of David. Not only the Exilarchs themselves, but also the Jews in general looked upon their rule as a continuation of the old Judean kingdom.[202] Conscious of their dignity and power, the Exilarchs often placed themselves above the spiritual leaders of the people. Talmudic literature affords numerous

[200] Lazarus, pp. 143, n. 2; 148, n. 1; comp. Ginzberg, *Geonica*, I, p. 11, n. 4.
[201] Shabbat, 55a, Mo'ed Ḳaṭan, 16b, Ḳiddushin, 44b; comp. Lazarus, p. 96, n. 5.
[202] The verse, " The scepter shall not depart from Judah, nor a lawgiver from between his feet " (Gen. 49, 10), was accordingly interpreted as referring to the Exilarchs and Patriarchs of Babylonia and Palestine; see Synhedrin, 5a; comp. Ginzberg, *l. c.*, p. 1. Bacher, however, properly remarks (*JE.*, V, 289), that the Baraita intends to cast a reflection on the Exilarchs. Sherira, p. 27, puts upon the Baraita the interpretation of the Talmud, that Babylon is more important than Palestine; comp. *Tōsāfōt ad locum;* Lazarus, p. 142.

instances of the ill-treatment of eminent scholars by Exilarchs, and especially by their unscrupulous officials.[203]

This attitude gradually created a certain antagonism to
the ruling house among the people, notably among the learned
men, which has found expression in various passages of the
Talmud.[204] There is, however, no proof that the Exilarchs
ever made themselves so objectionable as to arouse a
general desire to see the office abolished. On the contrary,
whatever dissatisfaction may have been felt at times, it was
cheerfully suppressed in favor of this real or supposed Davidic dynasty, the only remnant of ancient glory. Thus, at a
later period, under the dominion of the Arabs, when the
privileges of the Exilarchs had been considerably curtailed,
and their former independence in dealing with the Jewish
population so reduced that the government would not recognize them unless they had been chosen by popular vote, the
people remained loyal to the traditional house of David and
regularly elected a member of the royal family.[205] Moreover,
a few of the Exilarchs of Talmudic times endeared themselves by great learning, noble conduct, and just administration. Many legendary stories were later woven about their
names, glorifying their memory.

Very little is known of the history of the individual Exilarchs under the Muhammedan rule, from 660, when a
prince by the name of Bostanai was elected to the office,
down to the time of Saadia. Several incidents that can be
adduced from the scanty sources indicate, however, that
the strained relations between the Exilarchs and the scholars
of the academies,[206] which marked the Talmudic epoch, continued also during the second period of the Exilarchate.

[203] Gittin, 14b, 67b; 'Abōdah Zarah, 38b; Shabbat, 58a, 121b;
Yerushalmi Baba Batra, end of ch. 5; comp. also 'Erubin, 26a;
Bacher, *JE.*, V, 291, bottom; Lazarus, p. 149.

[204] See Synhedrin, 38a; Shabbat, 54b, bottom; Lazarus, pp. 73, n. 6;
150, n. 1.

[205] Lazarus, pp. 131 ff.; 145.

[206] See the instances given below, p. 103.

When we reach the century of Saadia, the antagonism
between the two forces assumes a definite form, tending
toward mutual annihilation, until circumstances do practically put an end to the official existence of both.

If the Exilarchate may be looked upon as a shadowy
representative of the Jewish body-politic after the destruction of the Jewish state, the Gaonate, as a spiritual organiza-
tion, must be regarded as the informing and inspiring life-
principle of that body. In the history of the Jewish people,
perhaps more than in the history of other peoples, one may
observe, without special effort, the existence side by side of
two important factors, the political and the spiritual; but
with the spiritual always in the foreground. Even during
the time of Israel's political independence, the only period
when the two tendencies might have manifested themselves
equally, this aspect, one may unhesitatingly assert, was pre-
dominant.

The men in whose lives and activities the intellectual and
spiritual aspirations of the nation find clear expression, have
received from time to time different collective designations,
in accordance with the accepted usages and customs of the
respective ages. But whether they appear in history as Elders,
Prophets, Men of the Great Synod, Tannaim, Amoraim,
Saboraim, Geonim, or under the designations of intellectual
leadership in later ages—and while their activities naturally
differ in scope and compass with the varying conditions of
the times—their inspiration and their message are intrinsi-
cally the same throughout all the generations. Their endeavors serve the one great purpose of perpetuating the Torah
and making Israel the worthy people of God. In the
unbroken chain of great men who have worked successively
and successfully for the realization of this high purpose,
the Geonim are the links between the generations of the
Talmud and the Middle Ages. Through them, the heritage
of the Orient comes down to its successor, the Occident.

As is often the case with the great movements and institutions of a remote past, the beginnings of the Gaonate are
but imperfectly known. Nor is even the original meaning of

7

the title Gaon established beyond doubt. We are here not
concerned, however, with details; a few general points will
suffice.

The Geonim merely continued the educational work,
mutatis mutandis, of their predecessors, the Saboraim, who
in turn succeeded the Amoraim, the creators of the Talmud.[207] The two Babylonian academies, over which they
presided, were founded by two distinguished Amoraim, Rab
and Samuel, as early as the first part of the third century. Their work differed from that of their forerunners,
inasmuch as they did not feel themselves called upon to add
to the content of the Talmud or to change its form. They
confined themselves to its study, elucidation, and interpretation. Eventually they also issued legal and religious decisions in doubtful cases. Their function, thus, would hardly
in itself have justified the assumption of the new designation
(Gaon = Highness, Excellency). This title, then, whatever
the reason for its selection may have been, was not intended,
like the earlier class-names mentioned, to be descriptive of
the scholarly activity and significance of its bearers. It must
have attached itself to their names in their official capacity
as the religious representatives of Babylonian Jewry, recognized as such by the government. Its adoption as a symbol
of office must, therefore, coincide with the governmental
recognition and endorsement of that office.

There are no definite data enabling us to determine when
this recognition by the government took place. On general
grounds, supported by an incidental reference by the Gaon

[207] The differences between the Geonim and Amoraim pointed out
by Ginzberg, *Geonica*, I, 6, may readily be admitted, yet these differences are the natural result of changed times and conditions. The
general aspect of the development of Jewish tradition and its representatives is not altered thereby. In its basic idea this view coincides
with the doctrine of the uninterrupted continuity of Jewish tradition,
which is emphasized by all Jewish writers. That the scholars of
every generation are the successors of the prophets is often expressed
also by Saadia; see *'Emūnōt*, ed. Slucki, p. 40, bottom; Harkavy,
Zikron, V, 158, n. 5; Steinschneider, *Alfārābi*, 115, n. 49; comp.
Dieterici, *Weltseele*, pp. 139, 175.

Sherira, the historian *par excellence* of the Geonim, it may be assumed with a high degree of certainty that it happened under the fourth caliph, 'Ali, the son-in-law of Muhammed. In the year 658 he granted religious autonomy to the academy of Sura,[208] freeing it from the jurisdiction of the Exilarchs, who prior to that time had meddled in its affairs. It is true that the same Sherira designates as Geonim all the scholars that presided over the two academies long before the rise of the Caliphate, beginning with the year 589. This does not prove, however, that these scholars were actually invested with the title in their own time. Nor is there any evidence to prove that the title Gaon had come into use in the earlier period. It is known that the continuity of presidents of the two Babylonian academies, Sura and Pumbedita, had been interrupted for several decades previous to the year 589. Owing to persecutions by some of the Persian rulers, both institutions had to close their doors.[209] The period of the Saboraim had thus been brought to an abrupt end. But with the accession of the humane Chosru II (589) settled conditions returned, and the academy of Pumbedita resumed its work at once; the academy of Sura following, so far as is known, twenty years later (609).[210]

Sherira obviously considers the period during which the academies were closed as marking the end of the old line of presidents, known under the title Saboraim, and the inauguration of a new line. The later line, beginning with the year 589 and extending to 658, had no distinguishing title, except the one that has always been used as a general designation, *Reshe Metibata,* Heads of the Academies. Sherira, therefore, not caring to make a distinction between the presidents of the academies under Persian rule and those

---

[208] Graetz, V, *Note* 13; English edition, III, 90 f.; comp. Ginzberg, *l. c.,* p. 53. That the Caliph gave special privileges to the academy of Sura may be disputed, but the fact remains that the spiritual leaders of the people chose Sura as the institution representing Babylonian Jewry as an autonomous religious body.

[209] Graetz (English), III, 4 f.; comp. Brüll, *Jahrbücher,* II, 50-53.

[210] Graetz, *l. c.,* pp. 9 f.

under the Caliphate, applied the title Gaon, very general in
his days, to all the past presidents alike. For the same
reason he also designates as Geonim all the presidents of the
Pumbedita academy, although, as has been proved lately,
they probably received that title only under the Caliphate of
Al-Ma'mun (830).[211] He even applies the title, though not
so consistently, to Amoraim who happened to be presidents of the academies—for example to R. Ḥisda (died 309)
and R. 'Ashi (died 427).[212]

It is therefore unnecessary either to continue the period
of the Saboraim into the seventh century, or to reach back
for the origin of the title Gaon into the time of Persian rule.
The truth is that the Saboraic period ended in the middle of
the sixth century. Then followed a gap of about forty years
of total inactivity. When the work of the two schools was
finally resumed, their rectors had no specific titles differen-
tiating them as a class, until the second half of the seventh
century, when the Muhammedan rulers granted to the spiritual leaders of Judaism full religious authority with definite
rights and compensation. But even then only the heads of
the more renowned academy of Sura assumed the title " Excellency " (Gaon). Those of the sister academy in Pumbedita remained what they had been theretofore, rectors of
their institution, without special titles[213] or privileges. In
all official matters they had to submit to the jurisdiction of
the Exilarchs, whilst in religious questions they depended
upon the decisions of Sura. This state of affairs continued
until the year 830, when, under the new regulations of Al-
Ma'mun, they were put on an equal footing with the Geonim
in Sura, which meant, likewise, their liberation from the in-

[211] Graetz, V, *Note* 12, no. 6; English edition, III, 155, 177;
Ginzberg, *Geonica*, I, 54.

[212] Comp. Brull, Jahrbucher, II, 50, n. 72.

[213] Poznański (*JQR*, *N S*, vol III (1912-1913), p. 402), however,
thinks that the Pumbeditan rectors too may have assumed the title
Gaon, though they were not recognized as Geonim by the authorities
of Sura.

terference of the Exilarchs in their internal affairs.[214] Morally,[215] however, they did not gain the standing and recognition enjoyed by the chiefs of Sura, except perhaps for occasional short periods, when one or another among them happened to excel his rival in Sura through extraordinary learning or other personal qualities.

To this brief summary of the main points in the external history of the Geonim it remains but to add a few observations concerning the relations between the spiritual heads of Jewry and their political counterparts, the Exilarchs. It was noted before that a more or less outspoken antagonism between the Exilarchs and the leading scholars had existed as far back as Talmudic times. So long as the spiritual representatives of Talmudic Judaism were not organized into a regular religious body, with a well-defined religious policy, the antagonism of some of the worldly, often religiously lax, Princes of the Exile could express itself only sporadically and individually. With the growing importance of the academies, however, when their influence over all classes of the Jewish population, especially the humble pious masses, had become a factor to be reckoned with, the Princes, always jealously safeguarding their dignity and prestige, could not avoid misgivings that eventually led to open, inimical action.

The bad feeling between the two forces could only have been aggravated, when, under the leadership of a strong president, as, for example, R. Ashi, the academies suc-

[214] Nevertheless even after this time quarrels between the Exilarchs and the Pumbedita academy occurred quite often, due, as we shall see later, to the strained relations that existed between the two houses. The power of the Exilarchs, however, was gone, and at a later period we even find that the Geonim deposed unpleasant Exilarchs.

[215] Financially, too, there was a great distinction made between the two academies, Sura receiving two-thirds of certain revenues, while Pumbedita received one-third. This unequal distribution of the income was changed only by the Gaon Kohen Zedek in 926, when it was decided that both institutions should divide equally; see below, pp. 106 f.; Graetz (English), III, 93 f.

ceeded in lessening the authority of the Exilarchate and
abolishing some of its former rights and prerogatives.[216]
Of the relation existing between the two sides during the
short Saboraic period nothing is known. In the tur-
bulent times of the sixth century, when persecution followed persecution, there was hardly any spirit left in Babylonian Jewry for the adjustment of internal differences.
The academies had finally to suspend their work, and the
Exilarchate existed only nominally, if at all.[217] When under
the last Sassanid kings, at the beginning of the seventh
century, more favorable conditions for the Jews set in, and
the academies resumed their activity under the presidency
of the so-called earlier Geonim, the bickerings between them
and the Exilarchs must have assumed a grave character.[218]
There are no details relating to the inner history of the institutions under these Geonim. However, one statement of
Sherira, the only contemporary historian of the Geonic period,
regarding the conditions then prevailing, speaks volumes.
Having discussed the succession of the Pumbedita Geonim of
that early period, he declares : " The succession of the Geonim
at Sura in those earlier years (up to 689) is not quite clear
to me, owing to the disorders and revolutions caused by the
Exilarchs, who deposed Geonim and installed them again." [219]

It should not be thought, however, that the Geonim of
his own academy, at Pumbedita, fared any better, though
he appears to be better informed on their early history. A
glance at the report of Sherira proves, to the contrary, that
the Pumbedita institution was subject to the same ill-treat-

<hr/>

[216] Comp. Lazarus, pp. 104, 111-113.

[217] Lazarus, p. 128.

[218] Of the conditions prevailing during that period Sherira, p. 33,
has the following to say : " Under the Persian regime and at the
beginning of Muhammedan rule the Exilarchs wielded tyrannical
power and exercised great authority, for they bought the Exilarchate
with large sums of money. There were some among them who
harrassed the scholars and oppressed them greatly ; " comp. Lazarus,
p. 140.

[219] Neubauer, MJC., I, 136; comp. Ginzberg, Geonica, I, 15.

ment by the Exilarchs, and for a much longer period than
the one at Sura. As before noted, Sura had succeeded in
obtaining perfect religious autonomy as early as the year
658,[20] so that henceforth nothing is heard of any Exilarchal
interference with its management, while Pumbedita remained under the jurisdiction of the Exilarchs for nearly
two centuries longer. During that long period depositions
of Geonim, who for one reason or another had incurred the
displeasure of the Princes, and installations of others, who
proved subservient to their purposes, were of frequent
occurrence. In 719, to quote only one instance, the Gaon
Natronai I, a close relative of the Exilarch, wielded his
power so tyranically that the scholars of his institution fled to Sura, where they remained until after his
death.[21] To show the nature of Exilarchal interference
with the academy it is also interesting to note that in
828, when two Princes laid claim to the Exilarchate, each
of the pretenders appointed his Gaon, so that for a time
Pumbedita was blessed with two Geonim.[22] Friction of one
kind or another must have occurred even after the rescript
of Al-Ma'mun (830), when Pumbedita too became independent, though for a long interval no case is actually
recorded. About the year 920, shortly before the time of
Saadia's appointment at Sura, we hear again of a violent
feud of five years' standing between the Exilarch 'Ukba and
the Gaon Kohen Zedek,[23] or according to the account of
Sherira, between the Exilarch David b. Zakkai and the

---

[20] This date does not necessarily conflict with the statement of
Sherira, that there were troubles and disorders prior to 689. For
the words ואית בהון תפוכאתא וטריאתא need not be taken so
literally as to cover also the last three decades (658-689). The men
were not always at war, and there were also times of peace. Moreover, it may have taken some time before the Exilarchs got used to
the new order of things, and during that time friction may have
occurred, though no record thereof has come to us.

[21] Sherira, 35; comp. Ginzberg, *Geonica*, I, 16.

[22] Sherira, p. 38, top; comp. Ginzberg, *l. c.*, p. 21; Graetz (English),
III, 155 f.

[23] Nathan ha-Babli, p. 79.

Gaon Mubashshir of Pumbedita and his supporters.[24] There
are indications that even at Sura things were not always
very quiet, though the Exilarchs may not have dared to use
the same tactics as in Pumbedita. The fact that Sherira
does not record any instance of Exilarchal meddling with
the affairs of that academy, does not prove its total absence. Sherira, as is well known, was particularly interested in relating the history of his own academy (Pumbedita) and shows no intention of describing in detail the
events at Sura. It is hardly probable that the quarrel between the above-mentioned Exilarch David b. Zakkai and
Saadia, which we are now about to discuss, was the first in the
long history of the Sura academy since its emancipation in
the seventh century. Similar conflicts must have arisen at
previous times. They may not have been followed by such
grave consequences as in the case in question, and were
therefore passed by without special notice. Be that as it
may, the history of the Exilarchs and the Geonim shows
sufficiently that from the very beginning to the very end
of their dual existence conflicting ideas and interests were
at play, which filled both parties with mutual distrust and
suspicion and often moved them to acts of open warfare.
If we bear these facts in mind, the bitterness with which the
war was finally waged between those whom we may call

---

[24] Sherira, p. 40. Various attempts have been made at explaining
and reconciling the widely divergent reports on this dispute by the
two authors, Nathan and Sherira; see the discussion of the subject
in Graetz' *Geschichte*, V, *Note* 12, no. 7, and more recently Ginzberg,
Geonica, I, 55-66; comp. Marx, *ZfhB.*, XIII (1909), pp. 169 f.;
Poznański, *JQR.*, 1913, pp. 401 f. This much disputed problem
does not concern us here. To my mind a reconciliation between the
two contradicting sources is not possible, and credence should be
given to Nathan as against Sherira. Nathan writes like an historian
describing events with much detail. His account is thus supported
by internal evidence. Sherira, on the other hand, chronicles names
and dry facts, for which he is often the only source, thus escaping
our further control. Finally, Nathan is eye-witness of most of the
events he relates, Sherira relies on other chroniclers or tradition.
In the subsequent pages we therefore follow Nathan's account.

the last Exilarch on the one side and the last Gaon of Sura [225] on the other, will appear almost as the natural outcome of an age-old feud between two families struggling for supremacy. In this case particularly, however, personal differences seem to have given the first impetus to the opening of hostilities.

Before discussing this matter, however, we must consider the conditions that prevailed in the Sura academy shortly before the election of Saadia to the Gaonate and the immediate causes that led to that election.

In the life of an institution as in the life of an individual, there is a period of growth and development, a period of persistent strength and vigor, and naturally also the period of gradual falling off and final dissolution. The Geonic institution at Sura, not to speak of its sister at Pumbedita, which had a somewhat different career, manifested in a marked degree during the long stretch of its existence, all these signs of growth, vigor and decline. At the time with which we are here concerned, toward the end of the ninth century, it had long passed the culminating point of its vitality and was rapidly nearing its end. It had spent its vital energy and was about to die of exhaustion. It ceased to produce able men who could take charge of its affairs and keep it alive. The historian is wont to look for more immediate and definite causes to account for the decay of institutions, as a physician seeks for some special disease as the particular cause of death, although age and general decrepitude might be sufficient explanation. In the case of the Sura Gaonate it is not hard to find external causes to account for its decline. Sherira (p. 39) informs us that the Gaon R. Malka (about 887) died after an incumbency of only one month, and that during a period of three months at about the same time, an unusual mortality prevailed, carrying off

[225] About fifty years later, it is true, the Suran academy was reopened under the headship of Samuel b. Hophni (see below, note 281). His Gaonate however, is to be regarded as a detached relic of the past rather than a direct continuation thereof. The attempts to revive the Exilarchate were still less successful; see below, note 283.

most of the older scholars. No doubt their death was due to
some epidemic disease. In the years that followed things
went from bad to worse. The Geonim that succeeded one
another for the next three decades, to judge from the little
we know about them, were quite insignificant men. When
the Gaon Shalom b. Mishael died (911), Sherira says " Conditions at Sura became extremely bad, and there were no
scholars left." A certain R. Jacob b. Natronai was appointed
to succeed Shalom, and when he too passed away, after an incumbency of thirteen years, the Exilarch David b. Zakkai, in
order not to leave the chair vacant, saw himself compelled
to " ordain " a certain Yom Tob Kahana, " although he was a
weaver by trade." He occupied the chair for four
years (924-928). Upon his death it was first contemplated
to abolish the Gaonate of Sura altogether and to transplant
the resident members to Pumbedita. After some delibera-
tion, it was agreed to retain the Gaonate of Sura, at least
nominally, by the appointment of a titular Gaon, who was to
have his seat in Pumbedita. The choice fell upon an '_Allūf_
of the Pumbedita academy named Nathan, an uncle of the
Gaon Sherira. But the Gaon-elect died before he had a
chance to assume his dignity. His death seems to have been
taken as a sign of Providential disapproval of the intention
to abolish the old academy of Sura. The plan was given up,
although no acceptable candidate was at hand to fill the
vacancy.[226]

This was in brief the situation at Sura in the year 928.
It represents the nadir of a long downward movement, which
in the last few decades had been hastened considerably by
the newly strengthened position of the Pumbedita academy.
In the measure in which Sura lost in power and prestige,
the Pumbedita institution, by virtue of its more prominent
Geonim, gained in ascendency, attracting a larger number
of disciples. In 926 the able and energetic Gaon Kohen
Zedek even succeeded in diverting a part of the income of

the academy of Sura to the treasury of the college of Pumbedita, thus putting an end also to the financial supremacy
of Sura.[227]

These adverse conditions did not discourage the Exilarch
David b. Zakkai from trying to invest some scholar with the
honor of the Sura Gaonate. His first thought was to offer
the position either to Saadia, or to one Zemaḥ b. Shâhin, a
man of noble parentage and of some learning. It seems,
however, that neither of the two was entirely satisfactory
to him. Saadia, although for some years an active member
of the academy, was a foreigner by birth. Theretofore the
Geonic dignity had been hereditary in a few families, some
of whom even claimed Davidic descent.[228] To judge from
several instances recorded in the sources, they were all in-
terrelated, being in this respect, too, an exact parallel to the
Exilarchs, with whom they were also often linked by inter-
marriage.[229] Hence the appointment of Saadia involved the
breaking of all precedents. David b. Zakkai seems to have
entertained a natural reluctance to go to this extreme.[230]
But the other candidate, probably of Geonic origin, to which
the phrase " noble parentage " seems to allude, did not possess the necessary qualities for the presidency of the academy.

[227] Neubauer, *MJC.*, II, 78; Graetz, *l. c.*, pp. 183 f. There are some
doubts as to the authorship of the text preceding the report of
Nathan ha-Babli, for which see Ginzberg, *Geonica*, I, 34 ff.; comp.
Marx's review of Ginzberg's work in *ZfhB.*, XIII, 169, where this
point is also touched upon.

[228] Sherira, p. 33, points out with pride that he was a descendant of
an ancient Exilarchal family, which traced its pedigree to the house
of David; comp. Abraham b. David, סדר הקבלה (Neubauer, *MJC.*,
I, 66); Ginzberg, *l. c.*, pp. 9 f.; above, notes 18, 150.

[229] Sherira, p. 35, tells of the Gaon Naṭronai I (719), that he was
related to the Exilarchal house; comp. Ginzberg, *l. c.*, p. 16.

[230] As we have seen above (note 18) Saadia claimed noble ancestry,
tracing his origin to the Mishnaic teacher Ḥanina b. Dosa, or even as
far back as Shelah, the son of Judah. He voiced this claim, however,
at a much later period, when his enemies pointed with scorn to his
supposed lowly origin; see Harkavy, *Zikron*, V, 164, n. 10.

The Exilarch therefore decided to offer the position to R.
Nissi Nahrawâni, a blind man, who was generally respected
on account of his extreme piety. On a previous occasion he
had played an important part in bringing about a reconciliation between the same David and his opponent, the Gaon
Kohen Zedek of Pumbedita. Nahrawâni, however, declined
the honor on the ground of his blindness. Asked to make
some suggestion as to a possible candidate, he refused to
express himself. The Exilarch then solicited his opinion regarding Saadia and Zemah b. Shâhin. R. Nissi at once advised the choice of Zemah. He expressed the greatest admiration for Saadia's learning and character, but knowing
Saadia's independent spirit and the dictatorial disposition of
the Exilarch, he anticipated trouble between the two men.
" It is true," R. Nissi explained, " that Saadia is a great man,
of extraordinary learning; but he is absolutely fearless, and
by reason of his great learning and wisdom, eloquence and
piety, he does not consider anybody in the world." These
words of praise and caution produced the opposite effect
from that intended, for David now said: " I have decided
and will appoint Saadia." To this R. Nissi replied: " Do
as you have determined, I shall be the first one to sit at
his feet and hearken to his words." Thereupon [221] Saadia

[221] Nathan, on whose report the foregoing presentation is based,
has here: הנהיגהו אותה שעה בפני כהן צדק ובפני תלמידי ישיבת
פומברדיתא ומינוהו להיות ראש ישיבת סורא. Neubauer (p. 80)
reads הנהיגוהו, in the plural, probably because of the following
ומינוהו, but as the Exilarch is not mentioned separately, it seems pref-
erable to read הנהיגהו, the singular form thus referring to David,
who introduced Saadia to the assembly. However, this is not of
importance. More important are the words אותה שעה, which
certainly mean " at once," or " immediately." Unless the words were
overlooked, or Nathan disregarded as untrustworthy on this point,
it is hard to see why all modern biographers of Saadia, prior to the
discovery of the Genizah, should have assumed that he was living in
Egypt at the time of his appointment as Gaon. We need not contend
now against this erroneous view, which originated with Abraham b.
David. Nathan's report points to a meeting of the Exilarch, the
Gaon Kohen Zedek, and the leading members of both academies
either in the house of the Exilarch, or in the academy of Sura,

was invited to appear before the Gaon Kohen Zedek and
the other dignitaries of the Pumbedita academy, and was
solemnly installed as Gaon of Sura. This event took place
in the month of Iyyar, 928, Saadia being then thirty-six years
old.[232]

Only too soon did the blind man's apprehension prove true.
At first only slight friction occurred, without immediately
serious consequences.[233] But two years after Saadia's installation a fierce struggle broke out between the Gaon and
the Exilarch, which, in the bitterness manifested by both
parties, as well as in its far-reaching consequences for Babylonian Jewry, surpassed all similar quarrels known in the long
history of the Geonim.

The immediate cause of the rupture—a litigation by heirs
to a fortune, which the Exilarch decided so as to bring great
gain to himself—was important enough to explain Saadia's
opposition. Nevertheless, judging from what we know
about the administration of the Exilarchs in general and
that of David b. Zakkai in particular, we may take it for
granted that the incident in question was not the only one of
its kind to come to the notice of Saadia. It must have been
part of an established system of administrative abuses and
perversions of justice, which a man of Saadia's integrity and
love of right could not possibly countenance.

The special case which the Gaon probably regarded as a
capsheaf of iniquity, is characteristic of the conditions prevailing. The decision of the Exilarch in the lawsuit before
his court, would have put one tenth of the disputed amount
into his own coffers. To give legal authority to his decree
the Exilarch had to obtain the signatures of the two Geonim.

---

for which a Gaon was to be chosen. As soon as the choice fell
upon Saadia, he was called in and formally presented by the
Exilarch to the assembled board and the scholars of the Pumbedita
academy. To the scholars of Sura he needed no introduction, as
he had been a member of that academy for about six years prior
to his appointment.

[232] Sherira, p. 40, top [but see *Postscript*].
[233] Comp. Graetz (English), III, 194.

He sent the documents first to Saadia. The latter, upon
examining them, saw through the scheme and found it
impossible to affix his signature. Wishing to avoid un-
pleasantness, he advised the litigants to secure first the
signature of the Gaon Kohen Zedek of Pumbedita. He may
have hoped that his senior would recognize the unfairness of
the decree and would undertake to settle the matter in some
acceptable way. But Kohen Zedek was not so scrupulous
as Saadia. He signed the documents without raising any
objection, possibly without scrutiny. When the matter was
brought back to Saadia, he at first tried to escape the difficulty
by the statement that his signature was superfluous, since
those of the Exilarch and of the other Gaon had been affixed.
The litigants realized that this was only a pretext and repeatedly adjured him to tell them the real reason for his
refusal. The truth could be hidden no longer. Saadia had
to point out and to explain the points of illegality in the Exilarchal decision which made him withhold his assent. The
parties concerned returned to the Exilarch and informed him
of the situation. Aroused by the daring of the Gaon, the
Exilarch sent his son Judah to Saadia with the command:
" Go and tell him in my name that he shall at once endorse
the documents." Judah carried the message, and Saadia
received it with the words: " Tell your father that it is written in the Torah (Deuteronomy, 1, 17) ' Ye shall not respect
persons in judgment.' " The Prince of the Captivity, infuri-
ated by the answer, forgot all etiquette and through his
son reiterated categorically: " Sign and don't be a fool! "
The son, who was to deliver this order, thought it wiser
to suppress it, so as not to widen the breach. Instead he
implored the Gaon to yield, in order to avoid a rupture. But
Saadia was not the man to surrender in a question that involved a religious principle. David b. Zakkai, incensed beyond measure, sent his son again and again to Saadia with
abusive messages and threats, which were turned by the
princely messenger into friendly appeals and expostulations.
But all to no avail. Finally Judah, too, wearied of walking
to and fro with his father's fruitless orders. When his last

effort at persuasion had failed, in a moment of exasperation,
he raised his hand against the Gaon, threatening to strike him
if he did not sign immediately. Hardly had the prince finished
speaking, when he was seized by Saadia's attendants and
thrust from the room. The doors were locked to prevent
his re-entrance. Judah went home defeated, and, " with
tears running from his eyes," reported to his father what had
happened. Matters were now beyond repair. David b.
Zakkai excommunicated the obstinate scholar and declared
his office vacant. To the Gaonate he appointed a young and
insignificant Rabbi, one Joseph b. Jacob, called also Bar-
Satia.[234]   Saadia, not in the least discouraged, retaliated in
kind, excommunicating David b. Zakkai and declaring him
to be no longer Exilarch. To the vacant throne he appointed
Josiah Ḥasan, a brother, or, according to Sherira, a nephew
of David b. Zakkai.[235]

At once two opposing factions were formed, the one
siding with the Exilarch, the other with the Gaon. With
Saadia were the richest people of Babylonia, the scholars
of the academies,[236] and all the prominent men in the community of Bagdad, among them the wealthy and highly respected Naṭira family.[237]   David b. Zakkai, on the other hand,

[234] This Joseph seems to have been a member of a Gaonic family,
for he is described as גאון בן גאונים; see Harkavy, Zikron, V,
227, n. 6, 229, n. 9, and p. 233, line 10.
[235] The above presentation is a free reproduction of Nathan's
Report, p. 81.
[236] Nathan, p. 80, line 10 from below, says תלמידי הישיבות, in the
plural, which suggests that even some of the scholars of the
Pumbedita academy, whose Gaon sided with the Exilarch, sympa-
thized with Saadia. See, however, below, note 239.
[237] Nothing whatever was known about this family prior to 1903,
when a highly interesting manuscript from the Genizah, containing
a sort of a family history of the house Naṭira, was published in
Arabic, by Harkavy, in Berliner's Festschrift, pp. 34-43. The writer,
a contemporary of Saadia, tells of a plot by a high official of the
Caliph Al-Mu'taḍid (892-902) to exterminate the Jews, which was
frustrated by a dream of the Caliph that led to the elevation of
Naṭira. The latter, immensely wealthy and charitable, remained in
his high position at the court of the Caliphs until his death (916),

was supported by his courtiers, as also by the Gaon Kohen
Zedek, whose eagerness for the downfall of Saadia and the
Sura academy appears to have been prompted by the desire
that his own college might become the sole authority of Babylonian Jewry. He had, indeed, already disgraced his name
and office by signing, or perhaps even assisting in the composition of the Exilarchal "Letter of Excommunication"[238]
against Saadia. In the baseness of its tone and the vileness
of its accusations this document has its equal only in the
diatribe of Sarjâdah mentioned below.[238a] Prominent members of the Pumbedita academy[239] followed their chief's example, either because they had to do his bidding, or because
they shared his feeling.

---

when he was succeeded by his son Sahl, who, like another son,
Isaac, followed the example of his noble father, caring lavishly for
the poor and the needy, Jews and Muhammedans alike. It is these
two brothers to whom Nathan ha-Babli refers as the בני נטירא
(p. 80, line 6 from below). The father he had mentioned twice
before (pp. 78, line 4 from below; 79, line 11; comp. p. 83, line 8).
Harkavy, l. c., p. 34, remarks that no mention of Naṭira is made anywhere else in Jewish literature, but a few years later the "Sons of
Naṭira" appeared again in a fragmentary letter in Ginzberg's
Geonica, II, 87; comp. J. Friedlaender, *JQR.*, XVII, 753, who
suggests that the fragment on the Naṭira family published by
Harkavy and the Report of Nathan ha-Babli are portions of one and
the same book written by Nathan under the title אכבאר בגדאד,
" The History of Bagdad," which is not improbable; comp. p. 293.

[238] Published first by Geiger, *Jüdische Zeitschrift*, X, 172 ff., then
by Harkavy, *Zikron*, V, 231-234. This was not the only missile
David and Kohen Zedek directed against Saadia, as the Karaite
epitomizer mentions there (p. 231, lines 21-23) other, more extensive,
writings by the same authors.

[238a] See below, note 246a.

[239] Of these only one is known with some degree of certainty. In
his ספר הגלוי (Harkavy, *Zikron*, V, 167, line 15) Saadia mentions
among his enemies one Hananiah, whose name he changes disparagingly into 'Ananiah═the *lamentable* one. As Harkavy, l. c., p. 144,
properly remarks, Saadia has reference to Sherira's father, Hananiah
b. Judah, who later became Gaon of Pumbedita (938-43); comp.
above, note 236, and below, p. 126.

The most violent and most influential opponent of Saadia was one Aaron b. Joseph Ibn Sarjâdah [240] of Bagdad, a merchant of great wealth and at the same time a scholar and writer of no small accomplishments, who at a later period succeeded in usurping the Gaonate of Pumbedita. This man hardly deserves the respect and consideration usually accorded to him by modern authors. He may have been a great scholar, as is attested by contemporary sources,[241] and he may also have possessed other good qualities—liberality, devotion to communal interests, and the like. But from all that is related of him in the same sources, he was also a man of violent, quarrelsome, and vindictive temper, and of an absolutely tyrannical bent of mind. There is no doubt that he had himself aspired to the Gaonate of Sura [242] prior to the appointment of Saadia, but his candidacy, it

[240] His first name in Arabic was Ḫalaf (כֹלף), for which Nathan regularly substitutes the Biblical Kaleb (כלב), while Sherira, Abraham b. David, and others have Aaron. Saadia (Harkavy, *Zikron*, V, 167, line 14; *REJ.*, LXVIII, 9, top), playing on the name Kaleb, calls him כֶּלֶב. The meaning of the surname is unknown and even the writing uncertain. Steinschneider, *Arabische Literatur*, § 34, adopts סרגׄאדֹה, which I follow in the transliteration; comp. Steinschneider, *JQR.*, XI, 126, no. 282; Harkavy's note in the Hebrew translation of Graetz's *Geschichte der Juden*, vol. III, p. 291; Graetz, *Geschichte*, V, 4th edition, p. 293, n. 4.

[241] See Steinschneider, *Arab. Literatur*, § 34. In a marginal note of a MS. of Maimonides's *Guide* (see below, pp. 133 f.), probably written by Maimonides himself, Sarjâdah is mentioned among the learned men who wrote against the doctrine of the eternity of matter. A passage from his Arabic commentary on the Pentateuch, section וזאת הברכה, is quoted by Joseph b. Judah, probably the pupil of Maimonides, known as Ibn 'Aknin (comp. Poznański, *JQR.*, XVII, 168 f.), in a fragment of a work on calendar, published by Hirschfeld, *JQR.*, XVI, 690-694. Other passages from the same commentary were published (from a MS. work of Tanḥum Jerushalmi, 13th century) by Harkavy, in his חדשים גם ישנים, X (Warsaw, 1896, reprint from the Hebrew edition of Graetz's History, V), 23. Sarjâdah is also the author of a commentary on the tractate *Yebamōt*, quoted by Ginzberg, *Geonica*, II, 67.

[242] Comp. Geiger, *Jüdische Zeitschrift*, X, 172.

appears, was not even considered.[243] He is reported to have
been a good dialectician. On any question submitted to him
he was able to give more than one satisfactory answer.
Nevertheless Saadia's extraordinary learning and brilliancy
put him lamentably into the shade.[244] Morbidly vainglorious
and ambitious, he bore a grudge against the generally
admired scholar, which may have been enhanced by the latter's independent spirit and perhaps open disregard for his
person. Thus, when the quarrel broke out between Saadia
and David b. Zakkai he thought his opportunity had come
to get even with his stronger rival, and he at once joined
hands with the Exilarch.

The two parties arrayed themselves for the combat. Their
first weapons, as we have seen, were mutual excommunications and depositions, and the appointment of substitutes
to fill the two imaginary vacancies. That pens on both sides
were kept busy writing recriminatory proclamations and
circular letters goes without saying.[245] The battle of proclamations in the Ben Meir controversy was but an insignificant
skirmish compared with the present struggle. A Karaite
of the time, who, like all of his sect naturally rejoiced in the
trouble of their lifelong opponent, has done history the
service of preserving extracts from a scandalous diatribe by
Aaron Sarjâdah,[246] a sad example of the demoralized and
demoralizing spirit that invaded the ranks of Saadia's opponents. The document is full of the coarsest invectives,
and some of its accusations, repeated again and again, are
so vile and impudent that one shrinks from reproducing
them.[246a]

[243] As noted before, the Exilarch considered only Nahrawâni,
Zemah, and Saadia.

[244] Nathan, p. 80.

[245] See above, note 238.

[246] Published by Geiger, Jüdische Zeitschrift, X, 173-178; Harkavy,
Zikron, V, 225 ff.

[246a] " In virulence and obscenity it exceeds anything of the sort I
have ever seen—the manifesto of the Spaniards at the time of the
Armada scarcely comes near it" (D. S. Margoliouth, JQR., XII,
506).

We may take it for granted that in turn Saadia and his adherents did not spare their antagonists. They probably issued counterattacks no whit gentler, which subsequent generations have wisely allowed to fall into oblivion. But it is safe to assume that nothing similar to the defamatory libel of Sarjâdah ever issued from the pen of Saadia. We have one example of the manner in which Saadia defended himself during this quarrel, which fully bears out our assumption. In the Introduction to one of his works, called *Sefer ha-Galui* (*The Open Book* [247]) he replies to some of the charges brought against him by his enemies, such as David b. Zakkai, Aaron Sarjâdah, and others, whom he mentions by name. Aside from general derogatory epithets, like " wicked" and "ignorant," and rather childish plays [248] on the names of his opponents, which he tries to justify by citing similar literary diversions in the Bible, there is not one word of objectionable or abusive character. If we reflect that the work in question was written at a time when Saadia, having met with crushing defeat at the hands of his enemies, was compelled to live in retirement and seclusion, while the Exilarch's faction were rejoicing over his downfall, we can easily draw conclusions as to the difference in character and moral stamina between the two opposing parties. [249]

Violent and determined as the literary feud appears to have been, it did not produce the results desired by either side. Both Saadia and David b. Zakkai remained in their respective offices, supported and upheld by prominent and influential friends. In the course of time the situation became untenable, as the adherents of both sides often resorted

---

[247] This meaning of the title as well as the genuineness of the book and many other points relating thereto have been made the subject of long controversies; see for all details the *Bibliography*, below, section VI, pp. 387-394.

[248] See notes 239-240 and the references there given; Margoliouth, *JQR.*, XII, 527.

[249] For this point see the correct remarks of Harkavy (against Margoliouth), *JQR.*, XII, 533, 552 f.

to acts of violence.[250]   Appeals were made to the government of the Caliph. According to the Exilarch's "Letter of Excommunication " it was Saadia who first invoked the assistance of the government, and secured the imprisonment of some of his assailants [251] If this was the case, he is not to be blamed, for Aaron Sarjâdah, with characteristic brazenness, tells boastfully of severe blows and beatings administered to the Gaon by his opponents.[252] However that may have been, the reigning Caliph Al-Muktadir, a fair-minded and just ruler, did not show himself amenable to the wishes of the Exilarch and Sarjâdah, who tried to effect Saadia's forcible deposition and perhaps banishment. Sarjâdah offered ten thousand ducats [253] to the treasury of the Caliph for a decree favoring the Exilarch. The Caliph

---

[250] Riots, street-fighting, interference of the government, and imprisonment of the rioters are repeatedly mentioned in Sarjâda's *Chronique scandaleuse* and in the Exilarchal Letter of Excommunication; see Harkavy, *Zikron,* V, 227, lines 4-5; 230, lines 14-18; 232, bottom. The contemporary Arabic historian al-Mas'ûdi (quoted above, note 20) likewise reports riots.

[251] Harkavy, *l c.,* p 232, bottom This seemingly contradicts the Report of Nathan (above, p. 111); for according to that Report Saadia was excommunicated immediately after his refusal to sign the Exilarchal decree, and hence, prior to that excommunication, could have no time, and probably no cause, for appealing to the government and securing anybody's imprisonment However, Nathan does not mention any formal Letter of Excommunication (כתב חרם) issued on the spot by the Exilarch He merely states that the latter " excommunicated R. Saadia " (החרים), which no doubt refers to the Exilarch's general pronouncement against Saadia prior to the issuance of the official Letter of Excommunication During the intervening time both parties may have resorted to acts of violence. Moreover, the Karaite who reproduced the Letter of Excommunication, being inimical to Saadia, may have tampered with the text of the document, adding matter that would prejudice the reader against the Gaon; Harkavy, *l c.,* pp. 222 f.

[252] Harkavy, *l. c.,* p. 230, lines 14 ff. Saadia himself tells of " attempted assassinations " by his enemies (Harkavy, *l. c ,* p 155, line 11) and the same is related by Abraham b. David, Neubauer, I, 65; comp. Malter, *JQR , N S ,* III (1912-1913), p 498, line 5

[253] So Graetz (English), III, 196, top, Nathan, p 80, has ס׳ אלף זוז.

insisted that both sides be heard. He ordered a formal trial before the judges of his court under the presidency of the grand-vizir 'Alì b. 'Îsâ. For some reason the dispute was not settled one way or the other,[254] and Saadia maintained his authority as Gaon for about three years, in spite of all opposition and the rivalry of the counter-Gaon Joseph b. Jacob.

In October, 932, the Caliph Al-Muktadir was killed in a rebellion, and Al-Ḳâhir, an unprincipled and dissolute person, who besides was so poor that he had to borrow clothes for the ceremony of installation,[255] became his successor. The Exilarch and Sarjâdah saw the time opportune, and again resorted to bribery. This time they met with success. Al-Ḳâhir did not care a rap which of the two parties was right or wrong, only which gave the larger sum of money. Aside from the contributions of Sarjâdah and probably of other individuals, the large sums which David b. Zakkai, with the aid of the Caliph's officials, is reported to have extorted from various communities, were no doubt, to serve this noxious purpose.[256] The Exilarch and his followers thus came out victorious. Saadia was definitely deposed, probably not long after Al-Ḳâhir's succession to the throne.

[254] Mas'ûdi, *l. c.* (see above, notes 20, 250), only says that the parties were advised to settle their differences before the court, but does not state whether a settlement was reached or not. Instead he proceeds with the statement that Saadia maintained his authority over many of the Jews, and that they paid allegiance to him. It therefore appears that the decision of the court, if one was reached, was to the effect that each party should have the right to adhere to its respective chief without interference by the other. The passage in Mas'ûdi was misinterpreted by Graetz, *Geschichte,* V, *Note* 20, no. 9, and Engelkemper, *De Saadiae Gaonis Vita,* p. 12, n. 3.

[255] Weil, *Geschichte der Chalifen,* II, 644; comp. *ibidem,* pp. 649, 654.

[256] Nathan, p. 86. He adds that in the face of this injustice none of the heads of the two academies felt it his duty to object to the procedure. This censure of the Geonim certainly does not include Saadia, nor does it refer to Saadia's predecessor, but to Joseph b. Jacob and Kohen Ẓedeḳ; comp. Graetz (English), III, 194.

That his enemies tried to secure his banishment, may be assumed. It is certain that they succeeded only in driving
him from his office in Sura, and that for a time he lived as a
private scholar in Bagdad.[237] Josiah-Ḥasan, the brother of
David b. Zakkai, whom Saadia had appointed counter-
Exilarch, was exiled to Ḥorāsān,[258] where he remained until
his death. As late as the fourteenth century, several families
claiming Exilarchic descent trace their pedigree to this
Josiah.[259]

Al-Ḳâhir's reign lasted about a year and a half (November 1, 932-April 23, 934).[260] He was succeeded by the
Caliph Al-Râdi (934-940).[261] During the reign of the former and partly also under the administration of the latter,
who, although a pious and just ruler, need not have been
especially interested in the affairs of the Gaonate, Saadia was
compelled to live in retirement. He had fought corruption
within the ranks of his own people, but he could not fight
a vicious Caliph and corrupt vizirs. However, though out-
wardly defeated, he was not broken in spirit. Saadia was
not the man to stand or to fall with an office. He did not
derive his greatness and worth from the Gaonate. On the
contrary, it was the Gaonate that had received a further
grant of life by being vested in a Saadia. Despite all the
tribulations and anguish the prolonged struggle and its outcome must have caused him, he realized that his career as a
teacher and uplifter of his people was not over, and he resolved to carry on with even more vigor and energy the task

[237] See Graetz, Geschichte, V, Note 20, no. 10. To the proofs
adduced by Graetz may be added that from Nathan's description of
Saadia's reconciliation with the Exilarch it also becomes obvious
that prior to that reconciliation Saadia was living in Bagdad. Nathan
relates that while the Exilarch was waiting in Bishr's house the
latter betook himself to Saadia and brought him over to his house
to meet the Exilarch. This proves that Saadia was within reach.

[258] Sherira, p. 40; comp. Harkavy in Frankel-Graetz's Monatsschrift,
1882, p. 167.

[259] Comp. Lazarus, p. 179, no. xiv.

[260] Weil, Geschichte der Chalifen, pp. 644, 650.

[261] Ibidem, pp. 650, 677.

to which he had set himself. It was during these years of retirement and solitude, that he wrote his best and most original work, the " Book of Philosophic Doctrines and Religious Beliefs," which gave the world the first not alone, but a complete, philosophic system of the Jewish religion. Its contents and merits are discussed in a later chapter. But it may here be said in passing that even had Saadia written nothing else, this book would have been sufficient to entitle him to the first place among the great minds of mediæval Jewry. The freshness and originality with which it is written, prove that it was not the work of a recluse brooding in despair over a shattered career and seeking to drown his grief in literary occupation, but that of a great and highsouled thinker who, having gone through a trying experience, and having realized that from the very beginning it was a lost cause, dismisses the whole matter from his mind, and with serene superiority turns his attention to what was the real aim of his life, the elaboration of a system of Jewish thought. It is characteristic of Saadia's mental attitude while writing this work that he nowhere so much as alludes either to his former Gaonate or to any of its phases, although the long Introduction, in which he speaks of himself and his motives in the composition of the work, might have given him the opportunity to do so.[262]

In another work, it is true, in the so-called " Open Book,' written a little later,[263] he takes occasion to describe his experiences in the Gaonate and the trials he had passed through. But even there, at least so far as can be seen from the extant portion, he does not speak as one bewailing his lot and reproaching his enemies, but as a warrior who has fought a battle for God and religion and has come out victorious.

---

[262] Fürst in his German translation of the work (Leipzig, 1845), pp. 19 f., notes, suggests, however, that the words ומי שיש לו מהם אויב מזיק וכו' (*Emûnôt*, ed. Slucki, p. 6) allude to David b. Zakkai and other enemies of Saadia, which is not improbable; comp. below, note 496.

[263] See above, notes 247-249.

He states explicitly that his purpose in relating the circumstances and "how he had prayed unto God for deliverance," was merely that he might serve as an example to
others; that "if they had to endure similar insults and
injuries at the hands of the wicked, they might remain firm
and pray to God rather than lose heart and surrender." [204]
As that part of the work which contained Saadia's detailed
account of the events is lost, it is impossible to say what he
meant by his "deliverance." Even if it was merely a reference to his steadfastness and faith in God in times of trouble
and distress, it is obvious from the marvelous mental vigor
and activity manifested in the works he wrote during this
period, that his reverses did not dishearten him or weaken
his lifelong efforts to further the cause of Judaism and Jewish thought. Moreover, it is safe to assume that during the
time of Saadia's retirement he was supported morally and,
if need was, also materially, [205] by devoted adherents, thus
making it possible for him to give himself to his studies.
The intrigues of Aaron Sarjâdah and the extortion of money
from the communities by the Exilarch, whereby Saadia's
removal was effected, must have filled all right-thinking
people with horror and contempt for the victors and with
increased love and reverence for the victim. The numerous
admirers of the deposed Gaon in and outside of Bagdad no
doubt continued to recognize him as their teacher and spirit-

[204] See Malter, JQR., N. S., vol. III (1912-1913), p. 402.

[205] There is no sufficient ground for the assumption that Saadia
ever was in need of pecuniary support. We may assume, with more
probability, that he was a man of independent means. It is even
questionable whether he received a salary, while occupying the
Gaonate. Nathan ha-Babli only mentions that Joseph b. Jacob was
the recipient of a fixed salary. David b. Zakkai in his Letter of
Excommunication (Harkavy, p. 232), in speaking of the good he
had done for the supposedly ungrateful Gaon, does not allude to
a salary, but if the passage (ibidem, p. 233, lines 16 ff.) is correct,
accuses him of having appropriated to himself the donations of
the communities for the academy. However, the sources do not
allow of any categorical assertion in this matter; comp. Poznański,
JQR., N. S., vol. III (1912-1913), p. 400, top.

ual leader, and to befriend him in every way possible. Free from the cares and responsibilities of office, Saadia was assiduously devoting his time to literary work, when an unexpected incident brought a change in the situation, which led to his re-installation into office.

It was litigation between two parties that had brought about Saadia's deposition, and it was again litigation that opened the door to his rehabilitation as Gaon of Sura. Two litigants decided to have their dispute arbitrated by notables. The one chose Saadia, the other nominated the Exilarch. The latter, who considered it a personal insult that anyone should dare to recognize as judge a man whom he had deposed and excommunicated, at once sent for the offender, probably demanding of him to drop Saadia or prepare for punishment. The man had enough moral stamina to refuse the demand, whereupon he was seized and given a severe beating. Wounded and his clothes torn to shreds, he left the Exilarch's office crying aloud, and telling whomever he met on the street what had been done to him. The incident aroused great indignation in the community, especially as the man so maltreated was a stranger, or at any rate was not under the jurisdiction of the Exilarch, and therefore had a right to choose as his judge whomsoever he wished.

The people's patience had now reached its limit. Everybody in the community was tired of the long-standing feud, and public opinion demanded that the matter be settled. The last act of violence on the part of the Exilarch brought the Jews of Bagdad to their feet. Their representatives visited Bishr b. Aaron, one of the most prominent men in the community and the father-in-law of Sarjâdah, the apostle of hatred and feuds, and told him that the situation had become unbearable. Finally, they said to him: "Rise to action, for it is your duty, and we shall assist you in the effort to put an end to this strife, which is fomented only by your son-in-law Sarjâdah."[266] Bishr, probably himself not quite satisfied

---

[266] Nathan, p. 82. The words אלא תלויה שאינה המחלקת להסיר בחתנך do not mean that peace depended solely on Aaron Sarjâda, so as to warrant the conclusion that when peace was established, it was through the winning over of the latter, but declare that

with the policies of his son-in-law, realized the earnestness of
the plea. He agreed to take upon himself the task of restor-
ing peace. He called upon the influential men of the community, and arranged with them to meet in his house at an
appointed date. The Exilarch, too, was invited, and came.
Then, in the presence of the whole assembly, Bishr addressed
the Exilarch in the following way: "See what you have
done! How long will you keep up this quarrel without fear-
ing God's punishment? Fear your God and desist from
strife, for you know how grave are its consequences. It is
time now that you try to improve your conduct toward
Saadia, that you make peace with him, and abandon whatever grudge you have against him." Dabid b. Zakkai, instead
of resenting this unexpected admonition, showed himself
exceedingly conciliatory. Without argumentation, at least
as far as can be learned from the words of the narrator, he
at once declared himself ready for peace.

By this act of self-denial, as well as by the generosity
he displayed later on, David b. Zakkai fully redeemed himself.
It would seem that the wrongs he had committed toward
Saadia in the heat of conflict were not wholly due to faults
of character, but sprang rather from the ungoverned im-
pulses of a hot-headed aristocrat with a somewhat exag-
gerated opinion of his inherited dignity and place, who would
not brook interference on the part of one whom he had
himself appointed to office and naturally considered his sub-
ordinate. That he fully appreciated Saadia's high qualities,[207] he had manifested in the very beginning by the fact

his son-in-law was the only cause of the trouble, and that it was
therefore Bishr's duty to step in the breach and secure peace. That
Bishr actually "succeeded in overcoming the hostility of his son-in-
law" (Graetz (English), III, 200) is not warranted by the sources;
see below, p. 125.

[207] It is interesting to note that in his Letter of Excommunication
(Harkavy, p. 232, top, lines 18 ff.) the Exilarch enumerates the good
qualities of Saadia, as pleasant manner, modesty, meekness, etc., by
which he had won his heart and the hearts of the people, but
declares all these qualities to have been a sham, calculated to
deceive him and others.

that he had made the appoinment in spite of the caution of the pious Nahrawâni. But later, after the quarrel had broken out, even when passion and anger biased his judgment, he must often have deplored the turn affairs had taken. Unlike Kohen Ẓedek and the cunning Sarjâdah, he had the welfare of the Sura Gaonate at heart, and was desirous of maintaining it on a high level. What he had achieved through the long fight, however, was quite contrary to his purpose, for Sura must have lost appreciably in prestige and standing during the period of inner strife and dissension. Moreover, he had come to see that in spite of excommunication and deposition the best elements as well as the rank and file of the people remained loyal and friendly to the fallen Gaon.[268] Kohen Ẓedek, the Gaon of Pumbedita, who, in the interest of his own college, had joined the cause of the Exilarch, had in the meantime passed away (935), and his successor, a certain Ẓemaḥ b. Kafnai, was entirely insignificant. Altogether, David had come to the realization that he had been on the wrong side, which had turned out to be also the weak side.

In view of all this we need not be suprised at the radical change in the Exilarch's attitude, and his unqualified response to Bishr's appeal for peace. Bishr did not lose any time. As soon as he had the assurance of the Exilarch, he left the assembly room and betook himself to Saadia, whom he invited with all the people in attendance, to follow him to one of his houses, in the same enclosure, opposite the building in which the Exilarch and his party were waiting. Arrived there, Bishr addressed Saadia with a speech similar to that which he had made to David b. Zakkai, admonishing him to conclude peace. Saadia, of course, was only too glad to follow the suggestion, and without condition assured the mediator of his desire for harmony. Thereupon the leading personages present in both houses formed themselves in two divisions, the one conducting the Exilarch, the other Saadia, and each proceeded toward the other until they met. The

[268] So Nathan, p. 80, and Mas'ûdi, l. c. (above, note 250, end).

two men, who for the last six years had fought one another
so bitterly, now embraced and kissed, and their reconciliation,
as shown by later events,[209] was sincere and complete.

One of the happiest men in Bagdad was Bishr himself,
who felt that he had accomplished a great thing in bringing
about the longwished-for reconciliation. It happened that
the day on which this reconciliation took place was the Fast
of Esther.[210] Bishr in elation over his success, begged all
present not to leave his house, but to read there the Scroll of
Esther, and after breaking the fast to stay with him the whole
night for general rejoicing. The Exilarch and Saadia, however, declined the invitation, the former proposing instead
that either Saadia should dine in the evening with him, or
he should dine with Saadia in the latter's house. As each
party was anxious for the honor of having the other as guest,
it was agreed that the matter should be decided by lot. The
lot fell in favor of the Exilarch. Saadia accordingly went
to the house of David b. Zakkai, and stayed with him during
the two days of Purim. The two strong men had much to
discuss and many an incident for which to express mutual
regret, but the two days of happy conviviality wiped out the
old differences and banished unpleasant memories. When on
the third day, they were to part again, they keenly felt the
relief from the burden of enmity that had weighed so
heavily on their souls, and were resolved to atone for their
sins against one another by establishing and maintaining
a bond of genuine friendship and mutual respect.

Saadia was now about to be formally re-installed into his
former office. The Caliph Al-Râdi and his vizir 'Ali b. 'Isâ
were not unfavorably inclined toward him, so that no objection from that side was to be feared. Some embarrassment
seems to have been felt on both sides regarding the future
status of R. Joseph b. Jacob, whom David b. Zakkai had
appointed Gaon in place of Saadia, and whose services had
now become unnecessary. But R. Joseph, it appears, did

---

[209] See below, p. 127.
[210] The 27th of February, 936.

not raise any difficulty. He retired to private life with
the provision that his salary continue undiminished.
Saadia again became Head of the Sura academy,[271] and the
new order of things seems to have satisfied all parties concerned. The only man of importance who remained sore
and disappointed was Saadia's arch-enemy, Aaron Sarjâdah,
the troublesome son-in-law of the peace-maker Bishr. There
is not the least indication in our source that he had in any
way participated in the conciliatory proceedings instituted by
his father-in-law. It cannot be supposed that the narrator,
who appears to have been careful throughout in relating all
details, would carelessly have omitted so important a fact as
the winning over to Saadia's side of an opponent like Sarjâdah, who, next to the Exilarch, was the most conspicuous
figure in the opposition. Nor can the reconciliation of Sarjâdah be assumed as a matter of course on the ground that it
was his father-in-law who had brought about peace. On
the contrary, from the words of the several members of the
community who in first appealing to Bishr for mediation, said
that it was only his son-in-law who supported the conflict,[272]
it may be deduced that Bishr and Aaron were in disagreement
on the matter, and there is nothing to assure us that the latter
subsequently changed his mind. Sarjâdah was not of the same
spirit as the Exilarch. The latter was quite satisfied with his
Gaon. What he wanted was subordination, to which, he
thought, his position entitled him. Sarjâdah hated Saadia personally. As noted already, he had an eye to the Gaonate himself, and, besides, was always extremely jealous of the
haughty and independent foreigner in the chair. The out-

---

[271] Abraham b. David, p. 66, top, states explicitly that Saadia was not
reinstalled, but his statement seems to rest on a misunderstanding of
the words of Sherira, which are not quite clear on that point; comp.
Rapoport, תולדות ר"ס, n. 1; Weiss, דור דור ודורשיו (1904), IV, 141,
note (see on the other hand Brüll, *Jahrbücher*, IX, 120). Abraham b.
David is refuted also by the considerable number of Responsa written
by Saadia in his official capacity as Gaon. This matter, however,
cannot be discussed here and will be taken up at a later stage of the
present work; see below, note 276.

[272] See above, note 266.

come of the long feud, on which he had spent a fortune, could
only be most galling to him. Being a man of large means
and of imperious nature, he would not accept his defeat with
good grace. Various circumstances make it highly probable
that soon after the reconciliation he left Bagdad and settled
in Pumbedita, the seat of the rival Gaonate

Years before, Sarjâdah had been made the recipient of
great honors in that institution. The Gaon Mubashshir (918-
926) had assigned to him, on his visits during the Kallah
months, a seat in the "great row," a distinction usually
reserved for academic members of the rank next to that
of the *'Allufim*.[273] Some of the members of the academy, who, like the late Gaon Kohen Zedek, had opposed
Saadia, were naturally not satisfied with his coming into
power again. One of them, Hananiah, the father of the
famous Gaon Sherira, became Gaon of Pumbedita not
long after Saadia's re-installation (938-943) He is known
to have been at enmity with Saadia.[274] It is therefore quite
natural that after what had happened in Sura, Sarjâdah
should have affiliated himself with the rival academy from
which he had received honors, and where he found sympa-
thizers of note. He probably did all in his power to raise the
standard of that academy, supporting it with his means, and
strengthening it against the competition of Sura. At the
same time he was preparing the ground for the execution
of his long cherished plan of becoming Gaon himself, and
Pumbedita proved a much better field for his operations
than Sura. When the Gaon Hananiah died (943), he was
to be succeeded, according to the rules of the academy, by
a certain Rabbi Amram, but Sarjâdah exercised such power
over the authorities, and so intimidated the candidate, that
the latter did not dare voice his aspiration[275] Sarjâdah appointed himself Gaon and ruled with an iron hand until the
time of his death (961)

---

[273] Sherira, p. 41, top For the meaning of the "great row"
(דרא רבא) see Poznański, שוגנים 'עניינים שוגנים, Warsaw, 1909, p 47,
comp Ginzberg, *Geonica,* II, 315, n. 3

[274] See above, note 239

[275] Sherira, at the end of his Letter.

The description of Sarjâdah's career has carried us a little beyond our point. The digression needs no excuse, however. For the purposes of a biography it is essential to know of what calibre were the hero's friends and foes. Sarjâdah played too prominent a part in the dispute about the Sura Gaonate for us to have let him drop out of sight as soon as his part in the play was over. His subsequent career serves to bring out more clearly the character of the man against whom Saadia had to contend. But whatever the truth about Sarjâdah may be, whether he remained for a time in Bagdad or went at once to Pumbedita, it is certain that Saadia was not again disturbed in his Gaonate. His relations with the Exilarch remained peaceful and amicable to the end. From the large number of Hebrew and Arabic Responsa written by Saadia in his capacity as Gaon, to various communities in and outside of Babylon, many of which belong to this later period,[276] it appears that under his presidency Sura was again looked upon by all Jewry as the center of learning and authority. No doubt, he wrote and completed during this period some of his numerous scientific works, but they cannot be designated with certainty.

The period of renewed co-operation between Saadia and the Exilarch was rather short. About three to four years after their reconciliation David b. Zakkai passed away (940). He was succeeded by his son Judah, the same, who, ten years before, had raised his hand against the Gaon. Judah died at the end of seven months, leaving a son twelve years old. Saadia on this sad occasion again showed the nobility of his character. The orphaned boy was taken into his house and treated as his own son. The Gaon sent the lad to school and tried to give him a good education, fitting for his future position of Exilarch.[277] Providence, however, had decided otherwise: Both the Exilarchate and the Sura Gaonate were

---

[276] See above, note 271. The assumption that they were all composed in the last year of his Gaonate (Graetz (English), III, 201) is unfounded; comp. Harkavy, תשובות הגאונים, p. 389; Steinschneider, *Arabische Literatur*, p. 48.

[277] Nathan, p. 82.

soon to go out of existence. Within two years after the
death of David b. Zakkai, Saadia's earthly career was pre-
maturely ended, and the conditions that followed made the
continuation of either institution impossible.

Saadia was but fifty when he died, in September, 942, common era.[218] As he left no son fit to succeed him,[219] the ever
available R. Joseph b. Jacob, whom David b. Zakkai had
once appointed counter-Gaon, and who was retired after the
reconciliation of Saadia with the Exilarch, was again called
into office. This time he clearly demonstrated his incom-
petence. Lacking the support of a strong Exilarch, as David
b. Zakkai had been, and having as rival the learned and iron-
handed Aaron Sarjâdah, who about that time (943), seized
the Pumbedita Gaonate,[220] he was unable to keep the Sura
institution alive. Pumbedita received most of the revenues from the communities, and attracted large numbers
of pupils, while Sura declined more and more. Realizing

[218] This date is based on Mas'ûdi, _l. c._, p. 113 (Carra de Vaux,
p. 160; see above, note 20), who says that "Saadia's death occurred
after 330" of the Hegira. Other authors give the date 941/2, which
corresponds to the date 1253 of the Seleucidan era given by Sherira
(comp. Rapoport, בכורי העתים, 1828, p. 15, n. 1; Steinschneider, _CB._,
col. 2158) ; for the discrepancy between the dates see Engelkemper, _De
Saadiae Gaonis Vita_, p. 14, n. 3 [see in particular the _Postscript_].
Abraham b. David, p. 66, says that he died " of melancholia " (מִן הַמָּרָה,
הישחורה) which Steinschneider (_Arabische Literatur_, p. 47) cleverly
modifies by "_in_ (for _an_) _Melancholie_," adding that the great struggles and trials Saadia had gone through may indeed have hastened
his death. Some Kabbalistic authors volunteer the information that
Saadia was buried at the foot of Mount Sinai (Jehiel Heilprin,
סדר הדורות, Warsaw, 1801, p. 143) ; comp. Engelkemper, _l. c._,
p. 14, n. 4. The famous traveller Benjamin of Tudela in his _Itinerary_
(London, 1840), I, 60a, reports that Saadia was buried in Sura.

[219] See below, p. 132.

[220] That it was Sarjâda, who in his desire to do away once and for
all with the Suran Gaonate had gradually undermined the position
of the weak Rabbi Joseph and caused him to desert his place, is
significantly hinted at by Sherira, who with a fling at both men
remarks that R. Joseph's position had lost greatly in dignity, and he
could not hold his own even against R. Aaron (ולא הוה ליה פתחון
פה אפילו בהדי רב אהרן) !

the doom of his Gaonate, R. Joseph decided to abandon it to
its fate. He emigrated to Baṣra, where he remained until
his death. The academy was closed, after it had been in existence with but little interruption for over seven hundred
years. About half a century later it came to temporary life
again, under circumstances that have not been sufficiently
cleared up. It seems that great struggles had again broken
out in Babylonian Jewry, the famous Pumbeditan Gaon
Sherira and his staff having probably opposed the re-estab-
lishment of the Sura Gaonate, as the meagre revenues from
the communities did not suffice to support two institutions,
and perhaps also, for other reasons.[281] The fallen Gaonate

[281] The source of the information that Sherira fell into trouble
toward the end of his Gaonate is Abraham b. David, p. 67. He merely
states that malicious persons had arraigned Sherira and his son Hai
before the Caliph who ordered their imprisonment and the confisca-
tion of all their property, so that they were left without a livelihood.
Abraham does not even hint at the cause of this trouble, and modern
historians have suggested various theories. Graetz (English), III,
233 f., assumes that the people were dissatisfied with the rigor of
Sherira's administration. Weiss, דור דור ודורשיו (1904), IV, 154,
asserts that objection was made to Sherira's appointment of his son
Hai as successor. Neither of these explanations is satisfactory. To
my mind it was again contention between Sura and Pumbedita that
brought about the intervention of the government. Prominent
citizens of Bagdad probably endeavored to re-establish the Sura
Gaonate, perhaps under the headship of Dosa, the learned son of
Saadia (see p. 132). Sherira and Hai must have opposed the idea
bitterly, as at that time the revenues of the Gaonate had decreased
so much that Pumbedita, though alone in the field, could hardly keep
itself alive. As once before, in the time of Saadia, the contending
parties appealed to the Government, and the result was the Gaon's
imprisonment. Influential friends of Sherira and Hai secured their
liberation, whereupon a compromise was reached, to the effect that
the Suran Gaonate be restored under the presidency of a Pumbeditan
scholar, Samuel b. Hophni, as against Dosa. The two institutions
were then closely linked together by Hai's marrying the daughter of
Samuel, and henceforth both did their work in perfect harmony.
This course of events is strongly suggested also by a Genizah
fragment (*JQR.*, XIV, 308), in which Samuel b. Hophni appeals to a
community or communities for the support of Sura. He assures the
latter that by giving his daughter in marriage to Hai perfect peace

was, however, reorganized under the headship of R. Samuel
b. Hophni, a great scholar from the Pumbedita academy and
grandson of the Gaon Kohen Zedek, whilom opponent of
Saadia. Peace was finally established between the two
institutions. Sherira's famous son, the later Gaon Hai,
marrying the daughter of Samuel b. Hophni; and the two
academies got along financially as well as they could.

had been established between the two academies, and that Sura is
therefore entitled to its share. The words, כי נעשה שלום גמור
ועם גאון בנו, do not neces-
sarily mean that prior to this the issue was between him and Sherira
personally, as interpreted by Margoliouth, the editor of the fragment,
for what Samuel wished particularly to emphasize was that the two
academies made peace. But even if Margoliouth's interpretation were
correct it would not vitiate our argument, for Sherira and Hai must
have opposed the revival of Sura on principle, and would therefore
have objected also to a candidacy of Samuel. The arrangements for
peace, the fragment states, were made shortly before Sherira's death
(טרם אסיפתו ב' שנים; comp. Marx, in Neumark's *Journal of
Jewish Lore*, Cincinnati, 1919, p. 400). This tallies exactly with the
account of Abraham b. David, who makes the imprisonment of
Sherira occur towards the end of his life. The words of Abraham
b. David ונתלה רב שרירא בירו אחת והוא כבן מאה שנה ולא הוסר
מגאונות which so far have defied all attempts at interpretation (see
e. g. Graetz, *Geschichte* V, (4), 368, n. 2; Weiss, רד"ו (Wilna 1904),
IV, 154, note; Steinschneider, *AL.*, p. 98, n. 1; Selig Cassel, in
his famous article "Juden," in the Encycl. of Ersch and Gruber,
II, vol. 31. p. 192, n. 28, and later in his *Wissenschaftliche Berichte
. . . . der Erfurter Akademie* . . . . I, Erfurt, 1853, p. 161, who
quotes parallels from Oriental history of people being hanged by
one hand) will now receive the right sense. For בירו אחת, though
found with some variants in all MSS of the סדר הקבלה and in later
works (e. g. the זכר צדיק, Neubauer, *MJC.*, I, 92, 117), we should
read במלכות, meaning that after the imprisonment Sherira, through
the intervention of friends, "regained influence with the *government* and was not removed from the Gaonate." It is true that many
scholars of fame have offered other explanations for the corrupt
phrase (ונתלה רב שרירא בירו אחת) one proposing בידי אישה אחת,
another (Luzzatto, quoted by Graetz, *l.c.*) בידי אחותו, a third one
ונחלה כיד וימת, and so on (see Levy, *Neuhebr. Wörterb.*, s. v.
בירו): but all this is in the face of the fact that the same
Abraham b. David uses the phrase ונתלה במלכות in other passages of his work to express the same thought as that in the
passage before us. Thus, in his presentation of the quarrel

Samuel, who was one of the most learned Geonim, followed
entirely in the footsteps of his great predecessor Saadia, producing a considerable number of important works, among
them philosophical commentaries on the Bible.[282] He succeeded in keeping alive the Sura Gaonate for about forty
years, but it never regained the preëminence it had enjoyed
under Saadia. Samuel died in 1034, and the academy was
then closed for ever. Only four years later his son-in-law
Hai, the Gaon of Pumbedita, also passed away, and this
death ended the history of the Geonim.[283]

---

between Saadia and the Exilarch, when he reaches the point of the
latter's gaining the upper hand with the Caliph (Neubauer, *MJC.*,
I, 65, line 4 from below), he says ואח"כ נתחזק דוד ונתלה במלכות.
In the same sense he uses the phrase ונתלה במלך ("and we shall
gain influence with the king ") in the case of the brothers Ibn Ġau
(*ib.*, p. 70, line 6). In the latter passage also a number of nonsensical
variants are found in the MSS., proving that the copyists did not
know the meaning of the phrase. Later authors merely copied
Abraham b. David with the mistakes. It should be noted that the
verb תלה is used in a similar figurative sense in the Talmud *p.*
Berakot, 4, 1, near end: אשרי אדם שיש לו יתד להתלות בה. It
should be remarked that the phrase occurs in this sense also in
connection with ביד (comp. Mann, *JOR., N. S.,* vol. X, p. 123:
ויתלה עצמו ביד גוי), which would make it possible to accept the
emendation of Luzzatto. But it is improbable that a sister of Sherira,
of whom we hear nowhere else, should have been the one to exercise
such influence. See also B. Lewin, רב שרירא גאון, Jaffa, 1916, p. 29.
    Through the rectification of this error the whole sentence becomes
clear. The words והוא כבן מאה שנה do not intend to state Sherira's
age at the time he died, as interpreted by Weiss, *l. c.,* for this
the author had stated before (p. 66, line 8 from below). Besides,
the ensuing words ולא הוסר מגאונות would then be entirely out of
place *after* the announcement of Sherira's death. Abraham only
means to say that when Sherira regained his influence with the
government and was freed from prison he was nearly an hundred
years old, that is either 97 or 98 years, and after his liberation he was
allowed to resume the Gaonate. Owing to his old age, however, he
abdicated shortly after the occurrence (998) in favor of his son Hai.
    [282] See Steinschneider, *Arabische Literatur,* § 65.
    [283] " It is true " says Graetz (History, III, 253), " that the college
[of Pumbedita] immediately chose a successor [to Hai], who acted
at once as Gaon and as Exilarch, it seems only in order to have the

In conclusion a few words may be added about Saadia's family at the time of his death. As we have seen above,[234] Saadia was a father when he left Egypt In his letters to his former pupils he twice refers to his children.[235] If our assumption is correct, that the lengthy panegyric on a Gaon by his secretary has reference to Saadia, he had three or four sons and two married daughters at the time of his first occupancy of the Gaonate (928-932) The daughters, perhaps also one of the sons, must thus have been born in Egypt. A brother is mentioned often in the same panegyric.[236] He seems to have belonged to Saadia's household, as did the sons-in-law with their children We further learn from the eulogy that at the time it was written another child was about to be born to the Gaon.[237] This child was Dosa, who later attained fame. At Saadia's death (942), this Dosa was of tender age, and naturally could not be considered as his father's immediate successor. The older sons, as also the brother and the sons-in-law, if they all survived Saadia, probably lacked the scholarship and other qualities necessary for a Gaon. When Dosa grew up and was recognized as a great Talmudic authority, he may have laid claim to the position of his late father It is therefore probable that he had some part in the struggles that preceded the appointment of R. Samuel b Hophni to the Gaonate of Sura.[238]

But all this must remain a matter of mere conjecture so long as we have to rely on the sources now available. Some of

---

two offices buried together in the same grave with his person " In 1040 the successor, named Hiskiah, a descendant of David b. Zakkai, was slandered at court, imprisoned, tortured and then executed; see Graetz, *l c*, p. 254; comp Poznański, רב דוסא ברב סעריה גאון. Berditschew, 1906 (reprint from *Ha-Goren*, vol. 6), p. 7.

[234] See chapter 1

[235] See above, pp 55 f

[236] Schechter, *Saadyana*, p. 67, top, 69, top, 71, line 4 from bottom: Mann, *JQR, N S.*, vol IX (1918-1919), p 159, l. 15; comp in particular above, note 11.

[237] *Ibidem*, pp. 66, lines 25-26, 67, line 19; see above, notes 13, 14

[238] See above, note 281

the many unexplored Genizah fragments may, we hope,
shed new light on this dark period. Thus much, however,
is certain—this learned son of Saadia was looked upon as
one of the most eminent scholars of the time, not only by
the Jews of Babylonia, but also by those of foreign countries, especially Northern Africa and Spain. Various communities addressed religious and legal questions to him as
they had done to previous and contemporary Geonim.
Several of his authoritative Responsa are still extant, while
others are referred to in the sources. From a passage in
one of these Responsa [289] it appears that he was the head
of a college, whose location cannot be ascertained.[290] Later
authors often refer to him as Gaon. Aside from his Talmudic learning he occupied himself with philosophic studies,
following therein the example of his father. In a marginal
note to an Arabic manuscript of Maimonides' " Guide of
the Perplexed," the writer, in all probability Maimonides
himself, mentions Dosa among other authors who had refuted

[289] See Poznański's essay on Dosa (quoted above, note 283), p. 9,
whence all other details given in the text are taken.

[290] I am inclined to think that Dosa is the author of the fragmentary
letter in Ginzberg's *Geonica*, II, 87, in which the sons of Naṭira and
of Aaron Sarjâda are mentioned as the leading members of the
Bagdad community. Sarjâdah was already dead, as the writer adds
to the names זכר הנאספים לברכה, hence he must have been writing
after 960. As Ginzberg properly remarks, the whole trend of the
letter makes it appear clearly that the writer was a man of considerable influence and high position. That he was a Gaon is
precluded by the fact that he resided in Bagdad. But Dosa may have
continued the work of his father as the head of a college in the City
of Bagdad, which in the course of time gained great authority,
though it was not considered officially as a Gaonate. Later authors
were thus justified in referring to Dosa as Gaon; comp. Poznański,
l. c., pp. 9, 15, 21, bottom, 23 f., and especially the references in the
"Supplement," *ibidem*, p. 27. Dosa and his supporters, probably the
same sons of Naṭira and perhaps also the sons of Sarjâda, may have
tried later on to transplant the college to Sura and establish it there
as a regular Gaonate, with the result that not Dosa, but Samuel b.
Hophni got the position. Dosa reached an age of about 90 years; see
Poznański, *l. c.*, p. 8, and above, notes 13, 14.

the theory of the eternity of matter.[291] His fame reached also
Hisdai Ibn Shaprut (915-70), the renowned Jewish states-
man at the court of the Caliph 'Abdur-Rahmān at Cordova,
with whom he entered into correspondence. At Hisdai's request Dosa wrote the biography of his father, Saadia,
describing therein also all "the good he [Saadia] had done
for Israel."[292] This biography, which no doubt contained
all the material, the want of which has been so keenly felt
in the course of this presentation, is unfortunately lost

[291] Munk, *Notice sur Rabbi Saadia Gaon*, Paris, 1838, p 13, and in
Guide des Égarés, I, 462; Poznański, *l c.*, p. 25; comp. above, note 241.
    [292] Abraham b. David, p. 66; comp. Steinschneider, *Arabische
Literatur*, § 32, Poznański, *l c.*, pp. 9 f

PART II
THE WORKS OF SAADIA GAON

Chapter VI

SAADIA'S WORKS

Saadia's literary activity embraced nearly all the branches of knowledge known and cultivated among the Jews and Arabs of his day. His works, which have come down either complete or in a fragmentary form, or are known only from quotations in the writings of later authors, cover the following fields of learning with their respective subdivisions:

A) Hebrew *philology* (comprising *grammar, lexicography,* and *exegesis*) ;

B) *Liturgy* (including *poetics* in general) ;

C) *Halakah* in its manifold ramifications (covering the various branches of the Jewish religious and civil law) ;

D) *Calendar* and *chronology* (largely controversial) ;

E) *Philosophy* (especially the philosophy of religion and embracing the author's systems of *ethics* and *psychology*) ;

F) *Polemics* against the Ḳaraites and other opponents of traditional Judaism (of diversified content and written at various periods of the author's life).

There is no possibility of ascertaining the exact chronological order of the works of Saadia belonging to the various branches of learning enumerated.[203] So far as these branches

[203] In the various attempts that have been made at a chronological arrangement of Saadia's works, too much emphasis is laid on the references found in his writings, from one to another. Such references do not prove that the work referred to actually preceded in time that in which the reference is found. It is known that Saadia was constantly changing and improving upon his writings (comp. Harkavy, *Zikron,* V, 30) and of some, as the *'Agrōn* (see p. 139) the Sefer *Ha-Galui* (p. 269), parts of the *Kitâb al-Amânât* (p. 194), and several of his commentaries on Biblical books, he even prepared more than one edition. He may therefore have inserted in revising his works of an earlier period, references to others composed at a later date. Thus, in his Commentary on Proverbs (ed. Derenbourg, Paris,

themselves are concerned, it may however be assumed with
sufficient reason that they were taken up by Saadia for
literary presentation in the order here given, although some
works in the field of liturgy, or Halakah, etc., may have preceded in time some under the heading of philology. In the
following pages I shall attempt to give a general characterization of Saadia's writings without entering upon a detailed
account of the contents of each book or fragment   Such an
account would reach far beyond the limits set to the present
work.

PHILOLOGY

a) *Grammar and Lexicography*

Saadia was the father and founder of Hebrew philological
science.[20] He laid down for the first time, so far as is known,
scientific rules for a systematic treatment of the Hebrew
language. These were set forth principally in three books.

1) *'Agron* (אגרון), a Hebrew dictionary in two parts   In
the first part all the words (nouns, verbs, etc.) were arranged

---

1894) he refers twice (pp 94, bottom, 195, top) to that on Isaiah
(ed. Derenbourg, Paris, 1896), while in the latter (p 126) he refers
to the former; comp. Derenbourg's Introduction to his edition of the
Commentary on Proverbs, p vii, n. 2; Hirschfeld, *JQR.*, XVIII,
(1906), 318, Harkavy, *Zikron*, V, 30, n 7. Moreover, some of these
references may have been added on the margin by later readers and
then put into the text by copyists, comp. Harkavy, *Ha-Goren*, VI,
27. For a detailed discussion of the question of the chronology see
Graetz, *Geschichte* (4), V, *Note* 20, pp. 523 ff. Quite inconsistent in
this respect is S. Eppenstein in his *Beitrage zur Geschichte und
Literatur im geonaischen Zeitalter* (reprint from *MGWJ*, 1908-1913),
Berlin, 1913. The publication of the Genizah fragments has established the fact that Saadia had left Egypt not later than 915, when he
was in his twenty-third year. Eppenstein is well aware of this fact
(p. 90, n. 4)   Nevertheless he assigns (pp. 78, 89, 90, 119, 121) to
Egypt, aside from the *'Agrōn* and the *Kutub al-Lugah*, also several
commentaries on the books of the Bible, the *Kitâb al-Tamyiz* (written
in 926), the Commentary on the *Book Yezirah* (written in 931), and,
naturally, all the books mentioned therein, as the Commentaries on
Genesis and Isaiah (comp. Steinschneider, *AL*, p. 66, n. 23) and on
the Tractate Niddah (see Bibliography, III, no 10). It is neither
possible that Saadia wrote so many works before reaching the age
of 23, nor is there any proof that he ever returned to Egypt after his
sojourn in Asia (Eppenstein, pp. 103, 116). [See. however, *Postscript*, p. 420]

[20] See above, pp 34 f

in alphabetical order according to their initial letters, to help writers of poetry to make acrostics. In the second part, the final letters of the words were alphabetically arranged, to facilitate the making of rhymes. The whole was thus intended to be a guide in the art of Hebrew versification.

The definitions in this lexicon were Hebrew and there was a rhetorical Introduction in a pure Biblical vocabulary, provided with vowel points and accents, in which Saadia briefly summarizes the history of the Hebrew language, deplores its woful neglect by the Jews of his time, and urges them to devote themselves again to its study and cultivation. He then turns to the exposition of certain fundamental rules of Hebrew grammar.

Saadia wrote this work when he was about twenty. Several years later he issued an enlarged edition, in which each word of the dictionary was followed by its translation into Arabic. He furthermore inserted portions treating of the various subjects and forms of poetry. This addition induced him to change the title of the work and call it " The Book on Hebrew Poetics " (כתאב אלשער אלעבראני).[295] Finally he added an Arabic Introduction wherein he gives a brief account of the contents of the work, mentioning incidentally some of the early Payyeṭanim, such as Jose b. Jose, Yannai, Eleazar Ḳalir, and others. These references make this Introduction highly valuable.

Unfortunately only the two Introductions and a portion of the dictionary have been preserved.[296] Nor are the manuscripts of the Introductions in our possession quite complete, the Arabic being defective at the beginning and the Hebrew at the end.

2) *Kútub al-Luġah* (כתב אללגה), " Books on Language," a grammatical work in twelve parts, which the author sometimes designated as separate books, at other times collectively

[295] See, regarding this matter, Steinschneider, *AL.*, p. 61; Bacher, *RÉJ.*, XXXIX, 207; Eppenstein, *Beiträge*, p. 70, n. 5.

[296] See the *Bibliography*, *s. v. 'Agrōn*, p. 306.

as one book.[297] Of this work, the oldest grammar of the Hebrew language known, only a few fragments are extant.[298] Several passages from it are quoted by Saadia himself and in the works of later authors.[299]

3) *Tafsir al-sab'ina láfẓah al-fáridah* (תפסיר אלסבעין לפטֿה אלפרדה), "Explanation of the Seventy Isolated Words," a list of the so-called hapaxlegomena and other very rare Hebrew and Aramaic words of the Bible. Saadia interprets the words by way of analogy, quoting for each word a passage from post-Biblical literature (Mishnah, Babylonian and Palestinian Talmud, Targum, and Midrash) in which it occurs, thus leaving no doubt as to its meaning. The list actually contains *ninety* words. Probably a slip of the pen occurred in writing the Arabic word for ninety in the unique MS., which bears the title given above.[300] The

[297] Thus, in his Commentary on the *Sefer Yeẓirah*, p. 45, line 5, Saadia refers to the book as כתב אלרגׄיש ואלרפי, meaning those parts or chapters of the work that dealt with the question of *dagesh* and *raphe*, while on p. 75, last line but one, he refers to it under its general title *Kutub al-Luġa*, and quotes a lengthy passage from its first chapter (see the *Bibliography*, p. 307). In the *Sefer ha-Galui* (see below, p. 271) he again quotes it simply as "the Twelve Parts;" comp. Malter, *JQR.*, N. S., vol. III (1912-1913), p. 494, n. 25. Harkavy who maintained the erroneous theory that the work is identical with the *'Agrōn*, collected all the material relating thereto as remnants of the latter, and treated it as such (*Zikron*, V, 32-38, 60-132). This theory has been fully disproved by Bacher (*REJ.*, XXIV, 307 ff.) and others, and Harkavy himself subsequently modified his views (*Ha-Goren*, VI, 30).

[298] My statement (*JQR.*, N. S., vol. III (1912-1013), p. 494, n. 25) that "nothing" has been preserved of this work is to be corrected accordingly.

[299] Hebrew authors, as Dûnâsh b. Labrat, Abraham Ibn Ezra, and others quote it under the title ספר (כתב) צחות לישון הקריש, or ספר (כתב) צחות לישון העברי; comp. Harkavy, *Zikron*, V, 32, n. 3; Steinschneider, *AL.*, p. 60; Bacher, *Leben und Werke des Abulwalid*, p. 91, n. 3; *A. I. E. als Grammatiker*, p. 18; *Anfänge*, p. 39.

[300] This would indicate that the title and whatever Arabic there is in the book was written in Arabic characters (see note 305), as only in these *sab'ina* (70) can be read for *tis'ina* (90), the words being

booklet has been frequently published with learned notes.[301]

In addition to these works devoted almost entirely to grammar and lexicography, Saadia wrote occasionally on the same subjects in some of his other works. Especially in his Commentary on the *Sefer Yezirah* [302] are there numerous passages dealing with Hebrew grammar.[303]

b) *Biblical Exegesis*

Hebrew philology in its incipiency was not regarded as an independent discipline, but merely as an auxiliary science to Bible-exegesis. Saadia's work in the field of grammar and lexicography is therefore to be considered only as the scientific apparatus for the main object of his studies, the interpretation of the Scriptures. Indeed, exegesis was the chief occupation of Saadia's life. To it he devoted the . greater part of his literary activity. In all probability he began while he was still in Egypt, to make translations of Biblical books accompanied with commentaries and continued this work in the following periods of his vicissitudinous life, changing, correcting, and enlarging the exegetical portions as his knowledge increased. His translation of the entire Bible into Arabic, the first [304] to be made

---

distinguishable only through diacritical points, which may have been missing; see, however, Geiger, *Wiss. Zeitschrift*, V, 324; Peritz, *MGWJ.*, 1899, p. 51; see also as regards the real number of the words Steinschneider, *CB.*, 2196, no. 29.

[301] See the *Bibliography*, p. 307, no. 3.

[302] See below, p. 192.

[303] Most of the grammatical passages in the Commentary on the *Sefer Yezirah*, however, are repetitions from the *Kutub al-Luġah;* see above, note 297. A grammatical work of Saadia on punctuation, נקוד רב סעדיה, is quoted by Rashi on Psalms, 45, 10, but it is not certain that it was a separate work. It probably formed a part of the *Kutub al-Luġah;* comp. Bacher, *Anfänge*, p. 60, n. 2, and Steinschneider, *Vorlesungen über die Kunde hebräischer Handschriften*, Leipzig, 1897, p. 15.

[304] It is true that an Arabic translation of the Bible is said to have been prepared prior to Saadia by the Christian scholar Honein b. 'Isḥâk (809-873). This translation, however, was not made from the Hebrew text but either from the Greek or the Syriac; see

directly from the original (Masoretic) text, ushered in
a new epoch in the history of civilization in general and
of the Jews in particular. As the Septuagint in ancient
times was instrumental in blending Greek and Jewish
thought into what is known as Hellenism, subsequently
giving rise to the Christian religion; and as Mendelssohn's
German translation of the Bible in recent times introduced the new literary era of modern Jewry; so Saadia's
Arabic translation and his interpretation of the Scriptures, paved the way for the glorious Spanish-Arabic period
during which the Jews again became the mediators between
the Orient and the Occident, and themselves made original
contributions to all branches of mediæval science.

Saadia's translation has become the standard Arabic Bible
for all the Arabic-speaking Jews and for the Christian
scholarly world down to the present time. According to
Abraham Ibn Ezra,[305] Saadia wrote the translation in Arabic
characters, contrary to the general practice of Jewish authors, who wrote Arabic in Hebrew characters. His object
was in all probability to make the Bible intelligible to Muhammedans as well as to Jews who had not sufficient learning

---

Steinschneider, *JQR.*, XII, 498, n. 2, where further references are
given. For Saadia's acquaintance with some of Honein's works see
below, note 532. For a supposed translation of the Bible into Arabic
by Abû Kathir, the teacher of Saadia, see Steinschneider, *AL.*, § 23.
A recent attempt to disprove Saadia's priority as translator (*JQR.*,
N. S., vol. IV (1913-1914), pp. 537 f.) is based on too puerile arguments to require discussion.

[305] See Abraham Ibn Ezra's Commentary on *Genesis*, 2, 11. The
question was often disputed, but it is now generally assumed that
Saadia wrote all his Arabic works in Arabic characters, which were
subsequently changed by the copyists into Hebrew characters; see
for the literature on the subject Steinschneider, *JQR.*, XII, 613-616;
comp. Kaufmann, *Attributenlehre*, p. 89, n. 150; Ewald, *Beiträge*, p. 5;
Landauer's Introduction to the *Kitâb al-Amânât*, pp. xii ff. Among
the many Genizah fragments of Saadia's writings I know only one
in Arabic characters: Schechter, *Saadyana*, no. xlix, p. 132; comp.
the *Bibliography*, III, p. 347, no. 5.

to understand the original.[306] This is fully in keeping with
what is generally recognized as the characteristic features of
Saadia's exegesis. His chief thought was to make the
Bible a book accessible to all; to present the Scriptures in a
rational, intelligible form. Hence he does not always bind
himself to the rules of the Masorah, to grammar, or to common usage; but, aiming at the greatest possible clearness and
consistency, often disregards all difficulties arising from
rule and custom. He does not hesitate to insert words and
phrases, or to divide and connect verses and sentences in his
own way, when necessary to convey to the reader the intended
sense.[307] To this extent his translation is at the same
time an interpretation, and Saadia, being himself well
aware of the fact, called it *tafsîr*, which means both commentary and translation.[308] His work, however, is far from

[306] See Landauer's Introduction to the *Kitâb al-Amânât*, p. xii;
Eppenstein, *Beiträge*, p. 85, nn. 1, 2, where more references are given.
Of interest in this connection is an Arabic passage quoted by Merx,
Die Saadjanische Uebersetzung des Hohen Liedes, Heidelberg, 1882,
p. 5, n. 1. In his Introduction to the translation of the Pentateuch
(ed. Derenbourg, p. 4) Saadia states that he undertook the work at
the request of some [Israelites], who asked him to do so, "in order
that they might understand the meaning of the Torah," which likewise goes to show that in the time and country of Saadia Arabic was
better understood than Hebrew by the Jews in general; comp. *JQR.*,
X, 256, n. 2.

[307] Instances are altogether too numerous to be here adduced. They
were collected by various authors to some of whom reference may
here be made: Dukes, *Beiträge*, II, 85 ff.; Poznański, *MGWJ.*, 1902,
p. 370, and lately L. Bardowicz in his interesting work *Die Abfassungszeit der Baraita der 32 Normen*, Berlin, 1913, pp. 102-107. A
striking example of the liberty Saadia took in transposing the verses
in order to get the desired sense is found in his Commentary on
Proverbs (ed. Derenbourg, p. 51), where the verses 10-12 are taken
from the middle of chapter 9 and placed at the end thereof, so as to
get the proper contrast between the honest and dishonest, as described
there, vv. 1-9, 13-18.

[308] See Munk, *Notice sur Saadia*, p. 5, n. 1; Steinschneider, *CB.*,
2182; Bacher, *RÉJ.*, XXXIX 206, no. 8; *idem, JE.*, X, 583; Poznański, *Schechter's Saadyana*, p. 21, no. 2; Harkavy, *Zikron*, V, pp. 138,
n. 2; 180, n. 6; *JQR.*, XIII, 61, no. 77. See also *JE.*, III, 166, 189.

being a paraphrase. Saadia took liberties only when he found it necessary to clear away obscurities, otherwise he followed the Scriptural text word for word.[309]

Another characteristic of Saadia's translation is the anxious elimination of all anthropomorphisms.[310] In this matter Saadia was not an innovator; he followed the so-called " Targum Onkelos," [311] the ancient Aramaic translation of the Pentateuch, but he went far beyond his model. This often led him to quite arbitrary assumptions as to the possible meaning of certain Hebrew words

From the Targum he adopted also the method of translating the numerous proper names occurring in the Bible, particularly those designating tribes or nations and places.[312] Here, too, he " bettered the example." Abraham Ibn Ezra [313]

[309] Comp Hartwig Derenbourg's Introduction to the edition of Job, p xi.

[310] Here again no attempt can be made at gathering the many hundreds of instances that evidence Saadia's efforts to remove the anthropomorphic and anthropopathic conceptions of God as they appear in the Scriptures. I refer the reader to the numerous works quoted below in the Bibliography, I. pp 328 f, to which may be added Bacher, Die Bibelexegese der judischen Religionsphilosophen des Mittelalters vor Maimuni, Strassburg, 1892, pp 1-44. According to Guttmann (Die Religionsphilosophie des Abraham Ibn Daud, p. 31) the " Commentator " blamed by Ibn Daud (Emunah Ramah, p 89) for not having gone far enough in removing anthropomorphic ideas from the Scriptures through philosophic interpretations, is none other than Saadia; comp. below, note 607, end.

[311] Saadia's relation to the Targum has likewise been fully discussed in many of the works and articles referred to in the preceding note, especially by Munk, Geiger, Dukes (Beitrage, II, 81, n 4), and Bacher, comp. the latter's Abraham Ibn Esra's Einleitung zu seinem Pentateuch-Commentar, Vienna, 1876, p. 33; Schmiedl, MGWJ., 1902, pp 84-88, 358-361; S Galliner, Saadia Al-fajjumi's arabische Psalmenuber setzung, p 10, n 2

[312] For the literature on this point see in particular Dukes, Beitrage, II. 48-58; Bacher, Abraham Ibn Esra's Einleitung zu seinem Pentateuch-Commentar, pp. 33-36 The translation of proper names has also been observed in the fragments of Aquila (Reider, Prolegomena to a Greek-Hebrew and Hebrew-Greek Index to Aquila, 1916, p. 20)

[313] Commentary on Genesis, 2, 11, 4, 19; comp Dukes and Bacher, as quoted in the preceding note.

severely criticizes Saadia's procedure in this matter, but suggests as a possible excuse that the translation was intended also for Muhammedans, who, if they found a large number of words untranslated, might say that the Bible contains laws which the Jews themselves [314] do not understand.

Among other peculiarities of Saadia's translation may be mentioned the frequent rendition of Hebrew words by Arabic words of similar sound, even when the latter do not possess exactly the meaning required by the Hebrew text.[315]

It is characteristic of Saadia's zeal in his work on the Bible that he prepared a double translation of most, if not all, of the books. The first, associated with an extensive Commentary (in Arabic *sharḥ*) was intended for learned readers. The other, called *tafsîr*, rendered the text in a form intelligible to the general public, as described above.

The significance of Saadia as a Bible exegete, however, comes into light more through his Bible commentaries than through his translations. A detailed characterization of Saadia's exegesis, as it appears in these commentaries, is not within the scope of the present work. In general it should be pointed out however, that Saadia's special merit as an exegete lies in his philosophic handling of the material. He did not merely translate and comment upon the passages

---

[314] The passage is misunderstood by Merx, *l. c.* p. 5, who puts the words לא ידענום into the mouth of the Muhammedans.

[315] See the numerous instances collected by Munk, *Notice*, pp. 55-57; Geiger, *Wiss. Zeitschrift*, V, 290; Haneberg (as quoted in the Bibliography, I, 319), p. 369; comp. the Introductions to the editions of the Psalms by the various authors quoted in the *Bibliography*, I, pp. 318 ff., and Poznański, *MGWJ.*, 1902, pp. 370 f.; Merx, *Die Saadjanische Uebersetzung des Hohen Liedes*, p. 13 (comp. J. Loevy, *MWJ.*, X, 34). The tendency to render Hebrew words by like-sounding words of the foreign language has been observed also in the Greek translation of Aquila (Brüll, *Ben Chananja*, VI, 300, no. 8; Reider, *l. c.*, p. 26) and in the works of authors later than Saadia; comp. Bacher, *Abraham Ibn. Esra's Einleitung zu seinem Pentateuch-Commentar*, p. 36; J. Loevy, *Libri Kohelet versio arabica, quam composuit Ibn Ghijath*, Leyden, 1884, p. 24; Kaufmann in Judah b. Barzillai's פרוש ספר יצירה, p. 336, note *ad paginam* 66.

of the Bible in their order. In a general Introduction to each book the basic principles in the light of which that book was to be viewed as a whole, were laid down, its contents briefly summarized, and the inner connection between its various portions clearly shown.[316] The Introductions[317] to the Pentateuch, Job, Proverbs, and the Psalms are classic examples in this respect. To some books of the Bible he wrote double commentaries.[318] By far the greatest part of the translations and commentaries is unfortunately lost.

LITURGY

As in all other branches of Jewish learning, so in liturgy Saadia was the pioneer and pathfinder. This is acknowledged by the many eminent authors who subsequently worked in this field, among them Maimonides[319] Actuated by the desire to strengthen traditional Judaism against the onslaughts of its opponents, such as the Karaites and other schismatics, and realizing the necessity of enlightening the scattered members of the Synagogue on all essential questions of their religion, it would have been surprising if Saadia had not devoted attention to the field of liturgy, on which the different parties in Judaism had at all times fought their religious battles Moreover, liturgy is intimately connected with Halakah. It was, therefore of vital importance to fix the ritual in conformity with Halakic regulations[320]

---

[316] Comp. Eppenstein, *Beitrage*, pp. 80 f., and below, *Bibliography*, pp. 308, 311, 319 f In connection with Saadia's Commentaries it is interesting to observe that he was in the habit of designating each book by a special title.

[317] See the *Bibliography*, under the respective works, pp 308, 318-21.

[318] Comp. Eppenstein, *Beitrage*, p 81.

[319] Comp. Ginzberg, *Geonica*, I, 167.

[320] According to Ginzberg, *ZfhB*, IX, 104-7, *Geonica*, I, 121, 167, n. 1, Saadia wrote the *Siddūr* for the congregations of his native country, Egypt This may be accepted as a fact on the basis of the proofs adduced there by Ginzberg, as well as on general grounds (comp Elbogen, *Der jüdische Gottesdienst in seiner geschichtlichen Entwicklung*, Leipzig, 1913, p 361). It is not proved, however, that the work was undertaken at the request of these congregations

Saadia, therefore, set about the task of arranging a complete "Order of Prayers" for the whole year, embodying
therein, besides all of the ancient and generally accepted
standard prayers, many liturgical productions of famous
synagogue poets, as well as various pieces of his own composition. Some compilations of prayers had existed prior
to the time of Saadia,[321] notably the ritual of the Sura Gaon
Amram b. Sheshna (856), commonly known as the "Order
of R. Amram," with a history of its own, the influence of
which on the development of Jewish liturgy throughout the
Middle Ages has been by far greater than that of the ritual
composed by Saadia. But aside from its small intrinsic value
as a literary production, the work of Amram, on account of
its unusual popularity, underwent such radical changes at
the hands of later generations, that it is impossible to say
what its original form was, and how much or how little of
its present content can be attributed to the editor whose name
it bears. It is even questionable whether Amram had any
share in compiling the ritual, except for the Halakic rules
and regulations embodied therein, which themselves are not
free from later interpolations.[322] Compared with the work
of Saadia the Order of Amram, even in its present aug-
mented form, sinks into insignificance. Saadia may, therefore, properly be designated as the first scientific author in
the field of liturgy, though the compilation by his predecessor
may have been of some use to him. Saadia did not merely
collect the existing prayers and arrange them in a particular
order for private and synagogue use, as is commonly done
by editors of prayer-books, but, following his general method
in other branches of literature, he made the whole traditional

[321] As early as in the middle of the 9th century an order of the
"Hundred Benedictions" (סדר מאה ברכות), the number recommended in the Talmud (Menahot, 43*b*) for daily recital, was compiled by the Suran Gaon Natronai b. Hilai (853), which was recently
published by Ginzberg from a Genizah MS. (*Geonica*, II, 114-119) ;
comp. for further details Ginzberg, *Geonica*, I, 119-123; Elbogen,
l. c., pp. 358 f., 565, no. 4.

[322] Comp. Ginzberg, *Geonica*, I, 144; Elbogen, pp. 359 f.

liturgy the subject of scientific investigation. In an elaborate Introduction he showed the significance and necessity of prayer, its foundation in reason (שֵׂכֶל), and in the books of Holy Writ (כָּתוּב), and the historic development of the different prayers during past generations (מְקוּבָל). He also took into consideration the various practices of communities and individuals in including or omitting certain prayers, and in each case expressed his opinion as to the permissibility of such customs, stating the reasons for or against the reciting of a given prayer. To whatever section of the book one turns, he finds the masterful hand of the scientific, logical systematizer and classifier, whose chief concern is to bring the scattered material under some general head or heads, so that the student shall get a clear perspective of the whole subject under consideration. Thus, for instance, in taking up the numerous short benedictions (*berakot*) he would first, by way of introduction, divide them into several classes: such as benedictions that are occasioned by the *obligatory* performance of a Biblical or rabbinical law, benedictions prescribed before the *voluntary* partaking of the good things of this world, which afford either bodily or mental pleasure, and so forth.[323]

The ritual itself he divides into two main parts, the one comprising prayers for every day, the other those for Sabbath, New-moon, Feasts and Fast-days. Each of these principal divisions is again subdivided into two parts, the one dealing with the prayers of the individual, the other with those of the community in the synagogue. In connection with these prayers he discusses the Halakic points bearing on them, quoting, or tacitly basing his decisions on, passages in both the Palestinian and Babylonian Talmudim.[324]

---

[323] For all the details here given see Steinschneider, Neubauer, and Bondi, as quoted in the *Bibliography*, II, pp. 329 f.

[324] Saadia himself (quoted by Steinschneider, *CB.*, 2205) states explicitly that he will not quote all the passages in Mishnah and Talmud on which he bases his views. This tendency to avoid as far as possible quotations from rabbinical literature is observable in other

As already noted, Saadia incorporated in his Order
numerous liturgical productions of eminent synagogue
poets, for example, the famous *'Abodah* (hymn for the
Musaf-prayer of the Day of Atonement) of the Spanish
ritual (אתה כוננת) and another one by the Payyeṭān Jose b.
Jose (אוביר גבורות אלה), a selection of *Hōsha'nōt* (hymns
for the feast of Tabernacles), *Teḥinnōt,* and *Selīḥōt*
(penitential prayers), many of which are not preserved elsewhere.[325] Here again he introduces the various compositions by valuable remarks relative to their place in the synagogue service and their importance there.

Great as was Saadia in the field of liturgy as the first
scientific collector, systematizer, and expounder of the
ancient material, his efforts did not stop here. He had begun,
it seems, in early life to write religious poetry for private as
well as communal use. His first work, the *'Agrōn,* was intended, as we have seen, to facilitate versification. An enthusiastic devotee of the Synagogue, and prompted by deep
religious feeling, he endeavored to enhance the divine service by numerous liturgical compositions of his own. He
wrote synagogue poetry of nearly all the forms and descriptions in vogue in his time. He himself informs us that he
composed a large number of *'Abōdōt* for the Day of Atonement, but chose to embody only one in his Order because,
he says, it was the shortest.[326] He likewise wrote numerous
Hōsha'nōt, aside from those incorporated into his ritual.
These, however, have not all been preserved.[327]

---

writings of Saadia (see below, note 461; Müller, *Oeuvres,* IX, p. x;
Ginzberg, *Geonica,* I, 166), and the reason in each case is that the
works were intended also for the Ḳaraites, for whom that literature had no authority.

[325] See the enumeration in the *Bibliography,* II, pp. 330-335.

[326] See Bondi, *Der Siddur des Rabbi Saadia Gaon,* Frankfurt a. M.,
1904, p. 38.

[327] Comp. Halberstam, *MGWJ.,* 1895, pp. 111 f., and below, *Bibliography,* II, p. 333, no. 5.

Among the species of poetry cultivated by Saadia his *'Azhārōt* (exhortations)[228] deserve special mention. They contain 119 four-membered strophes, dealing in ten groups— according to the Ten Commandments—with the 613 precepts of the Bible. They were no doubt intended to be recited in the synagogue.[229] On the same subject he composed also a lengthy didactic poem,[230] in six sections of twenty-two double lines each, corresponding to the letters of the Hebrew alphabet. One section gives the alphabet acrostically in its usual order, and the next in its inverted order (ק″שר״ת), the last section containing, besides, the acrostic: " Sa'id (שעיד) ben Joseph 'Alluf,"[231] which proves that the poem was written between the years 922-928, when, as we saw in chapter three, Saadia occupied the position of an *'Allūf* in the Sura academy. We must likewise assume that the *'Azhārōt* were composed during that period, for it has been discovered that the first line has the same numerical value (469) as סעיד בן יוסף אלוף.[232] The last section of the *'Azhārōt*, however, has only the acrostic " Sa'id ben Joseph," without *'Allūf.*

Apart from these pieces, which, owing to their considerable proportions, may be regarded as separate works, though they were embodied in his *Siddur,* Saadia is known to have composed a large number of Penitential Prayers (*Tĕḥinnōt*

[228] *Bibliography,* II, p. 331, no. 3.

[229] See Müller, *Oeuvres,* IX, p. xviii, bottom.

[230] *Bibliography,* II, p. 330, no. 2.

[231] See Müller, *Oeuvres,* IX, 67, n. 11; in Zunz. *Literaturgeschichte,* p. 94, l. 4, read *sechste* for *erste.*

[232] Rapoport, in הצופה להמגיד, volume VI (1862), 325, see below, note 336, and for a similar signature of Saadia in another composition, below, p. 336, no. 4; comp. in particular Rapoport's Biography of Ḳalir, note 12, where numerous instances from the latter's *Piyyuṭim* are quoted, in which the author has signed his name by using words that have the same numerical value. Saadia took Ḳalir as a model in some other respects also; see above, p. 139 and below, p. 184. It should be noted in passing that the recently discovered portion of Saadia's Polemic against Ḥiwi, which was written about 927 likewise bears the acrostics סעיד אלוף and סעיד ראש כלה; see Davidson, *Saadia's Polemic against Hiwi,* New York. 1915, p. 34 f.

and *Selīḥōt*), some of which, in addition to those incorporated into the Siddur, have come to light only recently from the Genizah. From the same source came also an important *Tokēḥah* (Admonition) of eighty-eight lines, containing a fourfold alphabet in the acrostic.[333]

All these productions disclose Saadia's great imaginative power, and testify to his astounding mastery of the Hebrew language in writing verse. It is true that for our taste today, his verses are too artificial for poetic beauty. Moreover, his lines are often so obscure as to defy interpretation. This is not due to the inefficiency of the author in the use of the Hebrew language, but to the erroneous conception of style and rhetoric, prevalent among the Arabs and Jews of those times. It was thought that the more uncommon and obscure the words one was able to gather and weave into a composition, the more remarkable was his literary performance, and therefore the greater its merit. Authors would exhaust themselves in the search for the most out-of-the-way forms and phrases, and these would often be used in violation of all rules of grammar and syntax, thus making the verse or the rhymed prose largely unintelligible, or at least mystifying.[334] In his poetical productions Saadia followed this style to excess. He indulged in the most arbitrary formations of nouns and verbs, outdoing therein even some of the old Palestinian Payyeṭānim, by whom he was greatly influenced.

This general predilection for rare and abstruse words was accompanied by a fondness for all sorts of artificial rhymes, acrostics of names and alphabets, catch-words from Biblical passages, and the like. Such overloading of the verses produced obscurity. But these performances were admired,

---

[333] See the *Bibliography*, II, p. 334; 338, no. 8. For the origin of acrostics in general see Steinschneider, *Vorlesungen über die Kunde hebräischer Handschriften*, p. 3.

[334] Comp. Zunz, *Synagogale Poesie*, pp. 117, 119; M. Sachs, in קובץ מעשי ידי גאונים קדמונים (ed. Rosenberg), pp. 84 f.; especially the references in Harkavy, *Zikron*, V, 45, n. 7; comp. also Bardowicz, *Die Abfassungszeit der Baraita der 32 Normen*, p. 62, n. 2.

because it was considered that they demonstrated the extraordinary skill and resourcefulness of the author in the
handling of the language. To point out only one instance in
Saadia's productions, we may cite his Introduction (פתיחה)
to the '*Azhārōt*.[335] It contains fifteen four-membered
strophes following the order of the alphabet. Each line of
a strophe begins with a letter of the alphabet and rhymes
with the other three lines. In addition, the first line of each
strophe is preceded by a word from Ps. 68. 8 ff. (in consecutive order), which is more or less suggestive of the idea contained in the strophe, while the third line is led in the same
way by the first word of each consecutive verse from Canticles.[336] Besides all this, the author has managed to work
his name into the first line by an arithmetical device.[331] The
last six strophes go far beyond even this, the lines being
divided into hemistichs with the same rhyme and double
acrostics. In the '*Azhārōt* proper a similarly artificial system is adhered to throughout.

With such complexity of the technic, it is not surprising
that the author could not attain to beauty or even to any
degree of clearness. No writer who subjects himself to such
unreasonable restrictions can accomplish anything but a sort

---

[335] For other instances, see Elbogen, *Studien*, pp. 64, 82 f.; comp.
Landshuth, עמודי העבורה, pp. 288 f.

[336] By way of illustration I give here the first strophe:

אלהים   אצל יום הלזה מיכים ימימה
בל יתחרוהי רבי כל היום והאימיכה
יׄיׄר   גהית ענתה בו ותישר ימיכה
דוריׄתי לכין תורת ה' תמיכה
בא״י מין אברהם

The word אלהים (Ps. 68.8) is the leader of the strophe. The
first line, beginning אצל, has the numerical value of סעיד בן יוסף
אלוף = 469. The word יׄיׄר (Canticles, 1. 1) leads the third line and
can be read together therewith. The strophe is followed by the
eulogy of the first benediction of the daily prayer, to which the fourth
line contains an allusion in the word לכין. For the meaning of the
whole see the commentary *ad locum*.

[337] See above, note 332.

of literary hotchpotch. Even the *'Azhārōt* of Solomon Ibn Gabirol, the greatest poet of the Synagogue, fall short, for similar reasons, of the sublimity often attained by this author.[338] Where Saadia did not resort to such artificial means, as for instance, in the aforementioned poem on the 613 precepts or in the recently discovered *Tokēḥah* and in the Polemic against Ḥiwi,[339] his verses are on the whole clear and smooth, though they never rise to the heights of poetic beauty.

Taken all in all, Saadia's attainments as a synagogue poet cannot be rated very high. But he has written some prayers in plain Hebrew prose, which, in grace and purity of style and in the fervency of religious emotion, rank among the best the Synagogue has ever produced. Two of these, called *Bakkāshōt* (supplications), have been adopted, wholly or partly, into various rituals. They may be considered as classics.[340] The one, beginning "Thou art the Lord, Thou alone," was destined by the author for Sabbaths and Feasts; and the other, beginning "To-day, too, I know . . . . that the Lord is God," for Fast-days. An Arabic version of the latter was made by Saadia himself, and a later author, a certain Ẓemaḥ b. Joshua, translated the former into the same language.[341] Both translations are found in Saadia's Ritual along with the Hebrew originals. Maimonides,[342] who was not too well-disposed towards prayers proceeding from the schools of the Geonim, recommended these prayers of Saadia for recital on the Eve of New Year's Day; and Abraham Ibn Ezra in his famous criticism of Ḳalir[343] expresses

---

[338] Comp. Landshuth, עמודי העבודה, p. 292.

[339] See the *Bibliography*, II, p. 338, no. 8; VI, pp. 384 ff.

[340] For all details see the *Bibliography*, II, pp. 331 ff.

[341] See Steinschneider, *JQR.*, XII, 485; *AL.*, § 234; Landshuth, *l. c.*, p. 287.

[342] In a passage from an Arabic MS. Responsum, quoted by Steinschneider, *CB.*, 2214; comp. also קובץ תשובות הרמב"ם (Leipzig, 1859), I, no. 128; Zunz, *Literaturgeschichte*, p. 96, no. 6; Bondi, p. 18.

[343] In his Commentary on *Kohelet*, 5, 1; comp. Zunz *Synagogale Poesie*, p. 117, top; Landshuth, *l. c.*, p. 293.

himself with reference to them in the following words:
" The Gaon R. Saadia in his two *Bakkāshōt,* the like of which
no author ever composed, guarded himself against these
four blunders [of Ḳalir] His prayers are written in the
language of the Bible, with due regard to grammar, without
obscurities and metaphors, and without the use of Midrash."
Bahya Ibn Paḳūdah [344] likewise quotes approvingly a passage
from the first *Bakkāshāh,* although, according to the custom
of the Middle Ages, he does not mention the author by name
but refers to him as " one of the worthies." Owing to its
simplicity in style and to the deep religious fervor that
breathes through its lines, most of the second *Bakkāshāh,*
with some later, and even older, additions, has found its way
into the Penitential Prayers (*Seliḥōt*) for the Eve of New
Year, and in this form is referred to in mediæval literature as
the " *Widdui* (Confession) of R Saadia " There is, however, another short composition under this title, which is
likewise written in a beautiful Biblical style.[345] These and
other pieces assure to Saadia a place of honor among the
best liturgical writers of the Synagogue.

Here, perhaps, is the place to discuss another product of
Saadia's art of versification, though it does not strictly be-
long under the heading of liturgy It is his " Poem on the
Number of the Letters " (of the alphabet) occurring in the
Bible [346] It consists of twenty-eight [347] quatrains, twenty-

[344] *Duties of the Heart,* IV, 6, end. Luzzatto first identified the
passage (*Litteraturblatt des Orients,* XII, 170, comp Dukes, *Nahal
Kedūmim,* pp 2, 26, Landshuth, *l c,* p 293 Yahuda in his edition of
the Arabic original of Bahya's *Duties,* p 224, top, does not realize
that Saadia is here quoted; comp. Malter, *JQR, N S.* vol. VII (1916-
1917), p 384

[345] See the *Bibliography,* p 333

[346] For the Hebrew title and other details see the *Bibliography,*
pp. 339 ff According to Blau, *JQR,* VIII, 352, the poem gives only
the number of letters occurring in the Prophets and Hagiographa,
to the exclusion of the Pentateuch, see Marx, *Journal of Biblical
Literature,* XXXVIII (1919), 24, n 3.

[347] In Schechter's *Saadyana,* no xxvi, *verso,* line 3, the letters בכ are
probably to be corrected to כה

seven for the letters of the Hebrew alphabet, including the
five final letters, and one additional quatrain for the letter
taw, the last in the alphabet. The purpose of the whole is to
show how many times each of the letters is found in the
Scriptures, such counting having been commended in the
Talmud (Ḳiddushin, 30*a*). The manner in which Saadia
carries out this Masoretic task is extremely artificial, and
cannot be here described in all its details.[348] The first word

---

[348] As no description can give an adequate idea of the technicalities
of this poem, I subjoin, as an illustration, the first stanza of the
Hebrew text with a few explanatory remarks:

אֹהֶל מָכוֹן בְּנִינִי   שֵׁשֶׁם עָלוּ זְקֵנַי
הַקְהֵל עֵשׂ קָרְבָּנִי   וּלְזֶבַח תּוֹדָה בָּאוּ בְנִי

פרוש: מנין כל אלף שבמקרא ארבעים ושנים אלף שלש מאות
שבעים ושבעה סימן מ"ב אלף שע"ז והסימן להם>כל הקהל כאחד
ארבע רבוא אלפים שלש מאות וששים>ולזבח השלמים בקר שנים
אלים חמשה עתודים חמשה כבשים בני שנה חמשה.>

The Aleph of אהל indicates the first letter in the Hebrew alphabet,
to which letter the first quatrain is devoted; the letter מ of מכון,
numerically equalling 40, and the letter ב of בנני equalling 2, indicate the number 42,200, while the initial letters שעז of the second
hemistich equal numerically 377. We thus obtain 42,377, which is
the number of times the Aleph occurs in the Bible. The word הקהל
in the third hemistich alludes to the verse in Ezra, 2, 46, as quoted in
the "Commentary," which gives in words the number 42,360, while
the word ולזבח in the last hemistich recalls the verse in Numbers, 7,
17, which contains the numbers $2 + 5 + 5 + 5 = 17$; the two verses
thus make together $42,360 + 17 = 42,377$, which again indicates the
number of times the Aleph is found in the Scriptures; comp. J.
Derenbourg, *Manuel du lecteur*, in *Journal Asiatique*, 1870, p. 546
(separate edition, p. 238). As regards the custom of counting the
letters in the Bible and as to the correctness of Saadia's computation
see the exhaustive studies of Ludwig Blau, *JQR.*, VIII (1896),
343 ff.; IX, 122-144, 471-490; XVI (1904), 357-372; comp. also
Schapira, in the *Athenæum*, 1878, Feb. 23, no. 2626, p. 253.

In English the above quatrain would read as follows: "The Tent
(*i. e.* the Temple), the foundation of my structures, whither my
ancestors made pilgrimage, where the congregation offered my sacrifices, and whither my children came for the sacrifice of thanks-
giving." The word עש is the payyeṭanic form for עשה often used
by Saadia; comp. Derenbourg, *l. c.*, p. 447 (139), n. 6.

of each quatrain begins acrostically with a letter of the alphabet. The words that follow in the first two hemistichs begin with letters whose numerical value corresponds exactly to the number of times the letter in question is to be found in the Bible. The other two hemistichs contain each a word from a Biblical verse in which the number thus indicated happens to occur. The language of this mnemonic poem is very enigmatic and obscure, so that Saadia himself deemed it necessary to add to each quatrain a sort of " Commentary," to furnish a clue to its interpretation. I assent to the ascription of this *Perush* to Saadia for obvious reasons. It does not explain the stylistic difficulties and the real meaning of these peculiar verses. It merely states in plain words the number intended by the text and also quotes in full the Biblical verses mysteriously alluded to. I do not believe that anybody except the author himself could have found the key to this riddle. If any mediæval author had been so fortunate as to find the clue, he would certainly have furnished us with an extensive commentary.[349] It is needless to say that this composition is devoid of all poetic merit. Nor is it probable that the author ever intended to classify it as poetry. His object was to assist the memory by arranging the numbers of the letters in artificial rhymes. There is, however, aside from this didactic purpose, a general idea running through all the verses, and that is the expression of the hope that the Twelve Tribes of Israel will be freed from their captivity and return to the sanctuary at Jerusalem.[350] It is in keeping with this idea that most of the fifty-

---

[349] The anonymous author of the מחברת התיגאן actually ascribes the Commentary to Saadia; comp. Derenbourg, *Manuel du lecteur*, p. 547 (separate edition, p. 239) n. 1, who, however, does not sufficiently emphasize it, as the words וחזר ופרש clearly say that Saadia wrote the *Perush*. It should be noted that, as Derenbourg, *l. c.*, remarks, the editions as well as the MSS. contain only the second half of the commentary to each stanza, which gives merely the respective Biblical verses, while the first half, which indicates in each case the intended number, is to be found only in the מחברת התיגאן.

[350] Derenbourg, p. 548 (240). Some later writers, who saw no purpose in this poem, invented a curious story as the occasion of its composition, for which see below, note 661.

four Biblical verses which the author has chosen to indicate
the numbers contain either one of the names of the twelve
sons of Jacob, or a name of one of their descendants, or have
otherwise some bearing on the restoration of Israel and of its
ancient cult.[351]

HALAKAH

The study of the Talmud was at all times and in all
countries the most essential part of Jewish education. The
Talmud was the only subject in the entire range of Jewish
knowledge that, as we should say to-day, was considered
obligatory, although the Jews did not always have a com-
pulsory school system in the modern sense of the word.
It was a religious duty, incumbent upon every Jew, to study
the Torah, and Torah meant above all the Talmud, for even
the Bible was to be studied only through the spectacles of
the traditional law, its commentary. It is thus only in quite
recent times that a Jew, though he be a rabbi, may lay claim
to Jewish scholarship without having in the least familiarized himself with the Talmudic literature. All Jewish authors who attained to prominence in other fields of learning,
such as philology, philosophy, or even medicine and astronomy, were first equipped with a more or less thorough
knowledge of the Talmud. Only then did they indulge their
individual inclinations and choose their respective fields of
literary activity. Saadia, the future Gaon, was no exception
to this rule. The study of the Talmud and, as far as it
existed, of the Halakic literature in general, was one of his
earliest occupations. We are not in a position, however,
to designate any of his numerous Talmudic works as belonging to the earlier period of his life, and thus being the
immediate result of his first Talmudic studies. Nor is it possible to assign dates and periods to any of his various works
on Halakic subjects.[352] On general grounds it may be assumed that his literary activity in the field of Halakah began

---

[351] Comp. Derenbourg, p. 449 (141), n. 13.

[352] See above, note 293, and below, note 376; comp. also the *Bibliography*, III, p. 345, no. 3.

after he had settled in Babylonia as a member of the academy and reached its height during his occupancy of the Gaonate, though some of the Halakic treatises on single subjects, to be mentioned below, may date from an earlier time. It was hardly necessary for Saadia to prove his Talmudic learning by great Halakic works to justify his appointment on the academic staff. He was known to the authorities personally and, besides, his numerous writings on subjects other than Halakah as, for example, his polemics against the Karaites, Ben Meir, and others, showed incidentally his thorough familiarity with the literature of the Talmud.

It is highly regrettable that the number of lost Saadianic writings is largest in the department of the Halakah. It is in this department more than in any other that Saadia's importance in his capacity as *Gaon* should show itself. Of all his works in the domain of the Halakah only two [353] have been preserved *in toto*. Of some others [354] a few small fragments were recently brought to light from the Genizah, while the rest are known only by their titles, or from quotations in the works of later authors. In addition there are about fifty complete Responsa written by Saadia to various communities. While it is thus impossible to appreciate the full extent of Saadia's Halakic activity, we can see from what is left, that in this field as in all others Saadia was the most important author among the Geonim. Unlike his predecessors in the Gaonate, who confined themselves to issuing legal decisions or to writing explanatory notes on single Talmudic passages, he viewed the literature of the Talmud in its entirety. To it he applied the same scientific method of sifting, analyzing, and classifying which is identified with his name in every field of literary endeavor. He grouped

---

[353] Namely, the "Interpretation of the 13 Rules" (see below, pp. 159, 342) and the "Book on Inheritance" (below, pp. 163, 344). We might perhaps count also the so-called Commentaries on *Berakōt* and on the Order of *Tehārōt*, for which see below, pp. 161, 342 ff.

[354] *Bibliography*, III, pp. 345-347, nos. 2-5.

and arranged its contents under general heads, and brought system into what might have been considered an irremediable chaos.

Saadia's work in the field of Halakah may be divided into three main parts: (1) Methodology; (2) Interpretation; and (3) Codification.[335] Among his methodological works two should be mentioned:

1. *Kitâb al-Madḫal* [*ilâ al-Talmud*] (כתאב אלמדכל [אלי אלתלמוד]), "Introduction to the Talmud," which seems to have been much in use. It is referred to in several Genizah fragments and in the works of later authors. The book was extant in the Orient as late as the sixteenth century, but since then all trace of it has been lost. The short extracts preserved in the work of a sixteenth century author show clearly the methodological character of Saadia's Introduction.[336]

2. פרוש י״ג מדות " Interpretation of the Thirteen Rules," written originally in Arabic and translated into Hebrew by Nahum ha-Ma'arābī of the thirteenth century. It is a Commentary on the " Baraita of Rabbi Ishmael " which occurs at the beginning of the *Sifra,* an Halakic Midrash on Leviticus. The *Baraita,* which originated in the school of the Tanna R. Ishmael (first and second centuries), contains an enumeration of thirteen hermeneutic rules for the Halakic interpretation of Scriptures. This initial part is embodied in the daily prayers of the standard ritual. In its extended form, as it appears in the *Sifra,* it contains also ample illustrations, taken from the Mishnah and old Halakic Midrashim, for the proper application of each rule. Saadia, realizing the fundamental importance of these rules for the Halakah, undertook to explain them in his own methodical way. Unlike the old *Baraita,* which only quotes passages as examples for the application of the rules, Saadia first gives a clear definition of the meaning and significance of each rule, classifies the laws falling under it, and then proceeds to give copious examples showing

---

[335] Comp. Ginzberg, *Geonica,* I, 162.

[336] See the *Bibliography,* III, pp. 341 f.

its operation in given cases. He takes his material not only
from Halakic literature, but also from various portions of
the Scriptures, his avowed purpose being to extend the use
of these rules to questions of morality and good conduct
instead of confining it, as does the *Baraita*, to strictly Halakic
matters.[351]

A few instances may suffice in illustration. The first
rule deals with the "inference *a minori ad majus*," or
vice versa (וחמר קל). One of Saadia's illustrations is a
reference to Exodus, 21, 10, where a husband of two wives
is enjoined to fulfil his duty towards both, although no such
injunction is given regarding a man with but one wife.
Here, Saadia shows, the deduction by inference comes into
play. If a man is in duty bound to satisfy the needs of two
wives, although it may impose a great effort upon him, how
much more is it incumbent upon him to discharge his duty
as a husband if he has only one wife. Another illustration
is derived from the Biblical injunctions to bring back to one's
enemy his ox or ass that went astray and to release the
enemy's ass that had fallen under its burden (Exodus,
23, 4.5). The inference is that the same law naturally applies
to the ox and ass of a friend. Similarly, from the law that
forbids a man with two wives, the one beloved and the
other hated, to "make the son of the beloved the first born
(by leaving to him a double portion of his possessions) before the son of the hated who is the firstborn" (Deut., 21,
15-17), we must deduce by inference that if the son of the

---

[351] For all further details see Müller's elaborate Introduction and
notes, in *Oeuvres complètes de Saadia*, IX, pp. xxiii-xxxiii. Regarding the Baraita of the 13 Rules in general see Hoffmann, in
Berliner's *Festschrift*, pp. 55-71; comp. also *ibidem*, p. 56, n. 2, with
relation to Saadia. As to the supposed anti-Karaite tendency see
the references in Poznański's *The Karaite Literary Opponents of
Saadiah*, p. 68 (to p. 250). According to Weiss דו"ר (Wilna, 1904),
IV, 139, the פרוש י"ג מדות originally formed part of the דרבי
התלמיד, that is, the work mentioned here as no. 1. Steinschneider,
AL., p. 50, thinks that both may have formed one work together with
the סתו"א (see under *Chronology*, no. 2), which is not improbable;
comp. Bardowicz (quoted above, note 334), pp. 81-87, 100.

beloved happens to be the firstborn, the father cannot acknowledge as such the son of the hated, if for some reason
he might desire to do so. Saadia adds one more illustration
of this rule, and concludes by saying that in this way many
more laws and ideas should be derived from the Bible.[358]
With the same painstaking care the remaining twelve rules
are elucidated by numerous instances from the Scriptures.

Almost complete uncertainty prevails when we turn to
the second group of Saadia's Halakic writings, the interpretation of Mishnah and Talmud. Commentaries by Saadia on
the " Six Orders " are mentioned by an author of the twelfth
century.[359] It is not clear whether he means the Mishnah
only or also the Talmud. A so-called Commentary on the
whole tractate of *Berakot,* which, however, contains only a
few pages of lexicographical notes, was recently found among
the MSS. of the Genizah and published under the title פרוש
רב סעדיה על ברכות. Its authenticity is doubted by some;
others deny it altogether, but admit that it contains remnants of a larger Commentary on the Mishnah by the Gaon,
now lost.[360] Saadia's son Dosa speaks in one of his Responsa[361] of his father's Talmudic Commentaries (פרושי),
and references to such Commentaries by Saadia are found

---

[358] *Oeuvres,* IX, 74; comp. Ginzberg, *Geonica,* I, 162 f.

[359] I refer to the traveller Pethahiah of Ratisbon; comp. Graetz,
Geschichte, V, 4th ed., p. 531, no. 12; Bacher, *Abraham Ibn Esra's
Einleitung zu seinem Pentateuch-Commentar,* p. 20, n. 2; see also
Dukes, *Beiträge,* II, 69; Steinschneider, *CB.,* 2160, no. 1; Ginzberg,
Geonica, I, 164; below, note 642.

[360] See the *Bibliography,* III, pp. 342 ff. It should be noted that the
explanations of the words הימרות and איספרגום, quoted by mediæval
authors in the name of Saadia (see *Oeuvres,* IX, p. xxxv, n. 5), are
actually found in this booklet, pp. 9*b,* 17*a*; comp. also 13*b,* n. 101, and
the other passages noted by the editor, Wertheimer, p. 6, letter ג.
See, however, J. N. Epstein, *Der gaonäische Kommentar Zur Ordnung Tohoroth,* Berlin, 1915, p. 31, n. 1.

[361] See Schechter, *Saadyana,* p. 59, l. 2; Poznański, רב דוסא ברב
סעדיה גאון (reprint from *Ha-Goren,* VI), p. 11, n. 26; Eppenstein,
Beiträge, p. 118.

also in several Genizah fragments of Geonic origin.[342] None
of the passages makes it clear whether reference is had to
commentaries on entire tractates, or only to explanations
of single portions of the Talmud, such as are found in some
of Saadia's Responsa.[343] Moreover, the word פרושי may
refer to Saadia's commentaries on Biblical books, in which
explanations of single words occurred.[344] It is most probable, however, that the expression "commentaries" used
in these sources with reference to Saadia's writings is to be
taken literally. Saadia must at least have written such Commentaries on the tractates *Pesaḥim, Soṭah, Baba Mezï'a, Baba
Batra*, and on the whole Order of *Teḥārōt*.[345] He has, besides, commented upon special chapters of Talmudic tractates
in separate writings. One such Commentary, covering part
of the seventh chapter of the tractate *Shabbat*, is mentioned
in Genizah MSS. under the title "Interpretation (of the
Mishnah treating) of the Main Kinds of Work," which are
forbidden on the Sabbath (תפסיר אבות מלאכות).[346] However,
nothing definite can be said on the nature of Saadia's Talmud exegesis. With the exception of the short glosses contained in the later compilations on *Berakot* and on the Order
Teḥārōt, as well as a few quotations in other works, not
even a fragment has so far come to light.

[342] Schechter, *Saadyana*, no. xxxii, l. 2; xxxiii, l. 2; comp. Azulai,
שם הגדולים, ed. Benjacob, *s. v.* Saadia.

[343] See e. g. *Oeuvres*, IX, 87, n. 7; 103, n. 3; 125, n. 5.

[344] This is, indeed, the assumption of Poznański, *JQR., N. S.*, vol.
III (1912-1913), p. 410. See also J. N. Epstein (as quoted in n. 360),
n. 4.

[345] Ginzberg, *Geonica*, I, 164, n. 1; comp. Poznański, *JQR., N. S.*,
vol. III, p. 410; J. N. Epstein, *l. c.*, pp. 30 ff., who proves that the
Commentary on the Order of *Teḥārōt*, which has been ascribed to
the Gaon Hai, is essentially a work of Saadia, redacted by a later
author.

[346] It is mentioned in the book-list published from a Genizah MS by
Bacher, *REJ., XXXIX*, p. 200, no. 28; comp. *ib.* p. 203, and Schechter,
Saadyana, p. 128. Eppenstein, *Beiträge*, p. 110, suggests that it may
have been a commentary on the whole tractate Shabbat, which is not
very probable, as we would expect a more general title.

Our knowledge of the third group of Saadia's Halakic writings, those dealing with the codification of the rabbinical law, is not much fuller. A considerable number of treatises on various sections of rabbinic law is attributed to Saadia by mediæval authors and in old book-lists recently discovered in the Genizah. But of all these works only one [367] has been preserved completely. Of some,[368] scant remnants were brought to light lately, while others are known either by their original Arabic, or by (original ?) Hebrew titles. They may be enumerated as follows: 1. On *Inheritance;* 2. On *Pledges;* 3. On *Testimony and Contracts;* 4. On *Incest;* 5. On *Meat disqualified for Food (terefah)* ; 6. On *Usury;* 7. On *Defilement and Purity;* 8. On (legal) *Gifts;* 9. On the *Gifts due to the Priests;* 10. On the *Laws concerning Menstruation.*[369]

It is hardly probable that these treatises were the partial execution of a plan to codify the entire law by a succession of such monographs. There is no obvious reason why, if this were the intention of the author, he should have picked out from the bulk of the rabbinic law precisely the subjects enumerated. From a passage in one of the treatises[370] we learn that he had intended to write more monographs on questions of jurisprudence, but not that he had in mind to codify the entire Talmudic law in such fashion. In all likelihood most of the treatises were called forth by interpellations on their respective subjects[371] or by controversies between Rabbanites and Karaites.[372] Others the

[367] The *Book on Inheritance;* see the *Bibliography,* III, p. 344.

[368] Those mentioned below, nos. 2-6; see the *Bibliography* of the respective works, pp. 345 ff.

[369] From quotations in the *Tur* of Jacob b. Asher, הלכות צדקה, §§ 247, 251. it appears that Saadia wrote also a treatise on *Charity.* Nothing, however, is otherwise known about it. See also below, p. 397.

[370] The treatise on *Testimony and Contracts;* see the *Bibliography,* p. 345; comp. *Saadyana,* p. 66, ll. 10-13; Eppenstein, *Beiträge,* p. 120, n. 7.

[371] Thus the treatise on *Pledges,* see Harkavy, תשובות הגאונים, p. 393, top.

[372] Steinschneider, *AL.,* p. 50, top.

author may have been stimulated to write by similar monographs on legal questions in the literature of the Arabs.[313]
This seems to be particularly the case with the treatises on
Inheritance and on *Usury*. The former is the one that has
come down to us in its entirety. It may therefore serve
as an example of Saadia's method of treating Halakic problems. The Introduction to this work, its style as well as
its content—the very fact that there is an Introduction—is a
conspicuous example of Arabic influence. No Jewish
author before Saadia had written an Introduction to his
work. The Mishnah, the Talmud, the Midrashim, and,
so far as known, other works of the pre-Saadianic time
have nothing whatever in that form.[314] Moreover, a remarkable feature of this Introduction is its absolute lack of
bearing on the Halakic contents of the book itself. After
the fashion of similar prefaces in the works of Muhammedan writers, it contains enthusiastic praises of the Creator,
describing in a purely philosophic manner, His high
attributes, such as existence, eternity, and unity, empha-
sizing His infinite bounty toward all creatures, and showing the necessity of our belief in Him and our obedience
to His laws. The last idea is practically the only point
that may be construed as an Introduction to the book
itself, which is a classification of the laws of inheritance laid
down in Holy Writ and developed in the Talmud. More than
one hundred questions concerning the rights of relatives to
inherit movable or immovable property are systematically discussed and clarified on the basis of traditional literature.[315]
The influence of Muhammedan jurisprudence is obvious
throughout the work, a fact which leads to the assumption
that it was written after the author had sojourned for some
length of time in Babylonia, and had familiarized himself

---

[313] See the works referred to in the *Bibliography*, p. 344, no. 1.

[314] Not even the הלכות גדולות and others mentioned by Müller,
Oeuvres, IX, p. viii.

[315] Sometimes Saadia allowed himself to decide even against the
Talmud; comp. below, notes 462, 518.

thoroughly with the contents of kindred Arabic literature and the methods employed therein.[376]

In addition to these three groups of Saadia's Talmudic works, mention must be made of the Halakic *Responsa* issued by him from time to time in his capacity as Gaon. To publish legal and religious decisions in response to questions was the exclusive right of the heads of the Babylonian academies during the entire Geonic period.[377] About fifty of such Responsa issued by Saadia on various Halakic questions have been collected. Most of them seem to have been written originally in Arabic and translated later into Hebrew; others were written in Aramaic, the official language of the Geonim.[378] As an author of Responsa also, Saadia occupies a unique position among the Geonim. Here, as in all his writings, one can recognize at once a superior scientific method and the systematizing thought of the philosopher, who seeks a basis of broad principles for every subject he treats. Saadia's method is so distinctive that it is possible to discern his authorship of a Responsum though no other direct evidence be available. In the Responsa, as elsewhere, he numbers and classifies the points under consideration, bases his arguments on verses from Scripture and passages from Mishnah and Talmud, and then supports his deductions by the authority of reason. One instance out of many: Reuben advanced money to Simeon and Levi, partners, in consideration of a share in the profits of the partnership. Later Reuben withdrew his contribution. Subsequently the entire capital of Simeon and Levi was confiscated by the govern-

---

[376] The assumption of Müller (*Oeuvres*, IX, Hebrew Introduction, p. xvii, bottom, French, p. xiii), followed by Ginzberg (*Geonica*, I, 165, n. 3), that the book on *Inheritance* was the first production of Saadia in the field of the Halakah is therefore to be rejected; comp. Steinschneider, *AL.*, p. 48, no. 3; Eppenstein, *Beiträge*, pp. 121 f. Muhammedan influence is very evident also in the small fragment of the treatise on *Testimony and Contracts;* see the *Bibliography*, III, p. 345, no. 3.

[377] Ginzberg, *Geonica*, I, 8 ff.

[378] For all details relating to the *Responsa*, see the *Bibliography*, III, pp. 349 f.

ment. Judah, a creditor of the partners, tries to recover his debt from Reuben as partner of Simeon and Levi. Reuben defends on the ground that he was not a partner but a creditor; which plea was confirmed by Simeon and Levi. A court of arbitrators imposed an oath on Reuben to the effect that he was not a partner and that he had no money of the firm in his possession. Judah submitted. Later he changed his mind and renewed his claim on the ground that the defendant did not take the oath seriously, because it was informal. The matter was then brought before Saadia. The Gaon decided that Judah had no claim against Reuben, because the partners were Simeon and Levi, whereas the defendant was merely a creditor, like the plaintiff himself, and there was no privity of contract between them. The plaintiff had no more claim against the defendant on account of the defendant's contribution to the partnership than the defendant would have against the plaintiff for the plaintiff's contribution to the partnership. The arbitrators should, therefore, have dismissed the case outright. Moreover, the arbitrators had no right to administer to the defendant an informal oath, because where the necessity of a formal oath is in doubt, a compromise on an informal oath is not permitted. Now Judah's assigning as error the informality of the oath is without any ground. First: Judah was not entitled by law to any oath at all, but only to a declaration of a general ban against any one who was in partnership with Simeon and Levi and refused to acknowledge it. Second: The oath was not informal, because it was pronounced over a holy book; and third, which is most important, the plaintiff had no right to disqualify the oath of the defendant on the assumption that the latter did not attach sufficient significance to it. It makes no difference what a person thinks of the validity of an oath administered to him so long as it is recognized by the law. "The fire," Saadia adds, "burns alike those who believe in its burning effect and those who do not believe in it; the knife cuts into the flesh of him who recognizes its cutting capacity and of him who disputes it." This interesting comparison he finds indicated in the words of

Jeremiah, 23. 29: " Is not My word like as fire, saith the Lord, and like a hammer that breaketh the rock in pieces ? " [379] He then proceeds to prove that a deposition like the one in question, made by a party while holding a sacred object in his hand,[380] possesses all the sanctity and binding force of a regular Biblical oath. Several verses are quoted in support of this view.

Besides the collection of Responsa there is a large number of quotations from the Halakic writings of Saadia in the works of later authors. Altogether, over one hundred and fifty of such quotations, some of considerable length, have so far been collected. Two-thirds of them are of Halakic-liturgical content. They were mostly derived by the mediæval authors directly or indirectly from Saadia's Ritual-Order. The rest, with a few exceptions, were taken from the Halakic works of Saadia now lost.[381]

To complete the account of Saadia's activity in the field of Halakah, it should be noted that, not only are his liturgical writings based in the main on Halakic laws and regulations, but most of his works in other lines, especially those on the calendar, as well as his numerous polemic writings against the Ḳaraites, have as their object the defense of Talmudic Judaism and naturally discuss Halakic problems. Even in his main philosophic work, the *Kitâb al-'Amânât,* and in his commentaries on the Bible, he often resorts to Talmudic disquisitions.[382] Thus, wherever we turn, we are constantly reminded that the author was not merely a writer of philosophy or exegesis, but fundamentally a great Talmudist—a Gaon.

[379] *Oeuvres,* IX, p. 97, no. 10.

[380] Comp. Müller *ad locum,* p. 98, n. 5.

[381] For all details regarding the *Quotations* see the *Bibliography,* III, pp. 350 f.

[382] See below, note 462. In the *Sefer ha-Galui* too he devoted a chapter to the discussion of matters relating to the history of the Mishnah and the Talmud; see below, p. 270.

CALENDAR

In nearly all the writings of Saadia a tendency toward
polemics is observable. It cannot be admitted that his only,
or even his chief, purpose was to refute, directly or indirectly, the views of the Karaites and other dissenters, as
some scholars have recently asserted.[333] The most that can
be said is that Saadia was of a positive and aggressive disposition and often emphasized too vigorously his own views as
against those of others, even in noncontroversial works.
There are, however, among his productions, many writings
ostensibly purporting to solve the problems of one or another
branch of science, but which, as a matter of fact, were undertaken for the sole purpose of refuting opponents. To this
class belong particularly his disquisitions on the calendar.
These were not the natural result of Saadia's studies in a
specific field of learning, but were called forth by actual
happenings of a politico-religious character, which stirred
the communities of Oriental Jewry.

In an earlier chapter of the present work [334] the origin and
cause of this phase of Saadia's activity have been discussed
at length. I may therefore limit myself here to an enumeration of its literary product.[335] Some of these writings,
as will be seen below, were elicited by the authorities of the
Babylonian academies. Some of them have been preserved
only in a few fragments of the Genizah, or are known from
quotations only.

1. *Sefer Zikkārōn* (in full ספר זכרון ומגלה לדרות), "A
Record-book and Memorial-Scroll for (future) Generations," deals with the differences between the "Four Gates,"
—*i. e.*, the four principal rules of the Jewish calendar as accepted by the Babylonian authorities—and the rules advocated by their opponent, the Palestinian Ben Meir. The book
was written by Saadia during the summer of the year 922

[333] See below, notes 517, 548.

[334] See above, pp. 69-88

[335] For details regarding all the works enumerated below see the
Bibliography, under *Calendar*.

(common era) at the request, and under the name, of the Exilarch David b. Zakkai, and was designed to be read in public
on the twentieth of Elul. Copies were sent not only to the
communities in Eastern countries, but also to those in Egypt
and elsewhere.

2. *Four Gates* (ארבעה שערים), an exposition of the four
principles of the traditional calendar, mentioned as a work
by Saadia in ancient book-lists discovered in the Genizah.
It is quite improbable that the book is identical with the one
mentioned in the preceding paragraph. For although the
extant fragment of the *Sefer Zikkaron* likewise deals with
the " Four Gates," the object is not to explain their meaning,
but to refute the calculation of Ben Meir. Moreover, the
discussion of this matter is incidental, and not the main
burden of the book to justify the title ארבעה שערים.

3. *Sefer ha-Mo'adim* (ספר המועדים), on the appointment
of the Jewish festivals in accordance with the accepted calendar, written at the request of the Exilarch, probably soon
after the controversy with Ben Meir (about 922-923 c. e.).
Only a few, partly mutilated, fragments have so far come
to light from the Genizah.

4. Three *Letters,* two in Hebrew and one in Arabic, addressed to his pupils in Egypt, soliciting their assistance in
the suppression of Ben Meir's changes. The two Hebrew
letters were written in the winter 922, c. e., while the Arabic
letter is dated " Sixth day, the eleventh of Tebet," without the
year, which obviously is 923. In this letter, covering over
two printed pages, Saadia informs his pupils that he is
sending them two copies of his *Sefer Zikkārōn,* mentioned
above (No. 1), and he implores them to act, and make others
act, in accordance with its teachings.

5. *Seder (or Sōd?) ha-'Ibbūr* (סדר [סוד] העבור), " The
Order (or Mysteries) of the Calendar," referred to by several authors of the Middle Ages, as well as by a Muhammedan author of the tenth century. Nothing seems to have
been preserved of this work. The Arabic fragment published some years ago probably belongs to another work
by Saadia. If this be the case, it will also be open to

question whether the book under consideration was written
in Hebrew, as the title, if such it is, would seem[336] to indicate, or in Arabic, the language of nearly all of Saadia's
works.[347] It is possible, however, that the Hebrew authors
did not refer to any particular work of Saadia's bearing the
title given above. They may have used the expression
genetically to designate Saadia's theories on the calendar,[347a]
as laid down in his works on this subject, in his Bible Commentaries, and in his polemic writings against the Karaites,
all of which dealt with this perpetual subject of controversy
between Karaites and Rabbanites.

It has also been suggested that the work is identical with
the one to be mentioned below under the heading of Chronology (No. 1). This view does not commend itself, because
the Hebrew term 'ibbūr was used more particularly to designate the calculation of the calendar, concerning which
nothing is found in the chronological work referred to.

In conclusion it should be explicitly stated that Saadia
wrote about the calendar in many of his works in other

[336] The citation of a work by a Hebrew title is not sufficient proof
that the work was written in Hebrew. Later authors who wrote
Hebrew often quoted Arabic works by a Hebrew phrase, which
would properly indicate the contents (comp. for instance above, note
299), just as those who wrote in Arabic referred at times to Hebrew
works by an Arabic translation of the title.

[347] Among all the writings of Saadia only a few are known to have
been written in Hebrew. These are (aside from liturgical pieces and
two letters) the 'Agrōn (first recension, see above, pp. 138 f.), the
Sēfer ha-Galui, the Sēfer ha-Mō'adim, the Refutation of Hayawaihi
(Iliwi), the Poem on the Alphabet (pp. 154 ff.), and probably also
the ארבעה שערים. To these can now be added the Sēfer
Zikkarōn (see below, p. 414, no. 9) and perhaps also the Refutation
of Daniel al-Kumisi (see the Bibliography, p. 398, no. 10; comp.
Poznański, JQR., X, 261, n. 3. As regards the Responsa see the
Bibliography, p. 349; comp. Steinschneider, Die hebräischen Übersetzungen des Mittelalters, p. 909, n. 33. In view of these facts it
is not altogether improbable that the פרוש על סדר טהרות (see
below, p. 343) is not a translation but merely a recast of Saadia's
original work, by a later author, perhaps a pupil of Saadia; comp.
Eppenstein, Beiträge, p. 118, n. 3.

[347a] See, regarding this matter, the references given by Steinschneider, Bibliotheca Mathematica, 1895, p. 103, n. 11.

fields, including even liturgy, as, for instance, in his *Siddūr*.[388]
In the foregoing list, only those writings are included
which, so far as may be judged from the existing material,
dealt with the subject of calendar to the exclusion of all
else.

CHRONOLOGY

The chronological treatises that have come down to us
from the early centuries of the Middle Ages were not intended by their authors to serve as records of the history of
the Jewish people. Such historical consciousness did not
then exist among Jewish authors. The chronological lists
they drew up were modeled in form after similar productions by Muhammedan writers, but the purpose was mostly
religious. It was the continuity of Jewish tradition [389] that
they endeavored to establish by means of such data, culled
from the Scriptures and the subsequent traditional literature. This had become a necessity after the rise of
Karaism (eighth century) and other cults which disputed
the authority of the Mishnah and the Talmud as a foreign
element in Judaism, out of harmony with the genuine traditions of Israel.[390] Saadia, the most conspicuous champion of
Rabbinism, certainly could not afford to neglect this side
of the issue between him and his Karaite opponents. More
than once he took occasion to emphasize the uninterrupted
continuity of traditional Judaism.[391] For example, he contends that the system of the calendar, as observed in his
days, was of immemorial antiquity, and that even in Biblical times months and festivals had been determined by calculation; a view considered untenable even by the majority of
Rabbinical authors.[392]

[388] See Steinschneider, *CB.*, 2205.
[389] Comp. Steinschneider, *Geschichtsliteratur der Juden*, §§ 9, 18
(p. 24).
[390] As late as in the 12th century Abraham Ibn Daud wrote his
סדר הקבלה with the avowed purpose of refuting the Karaites; see
Steinschneider, *ibidem*, p. 46.
[391] *E. g. Kitâb al-Amânât*, pp. 23 (Hebrew, ed. Slucki, p. 12), 127
(66) ; see especially Guttmann, *Die Religionsphilosophie des Saadia*,
p. 147, n. 3.
[392] Comp. Poznański, *JQR.*, X, 159, 270 f.; *idem*, in Hastings's
Encycl. of Religion and Ethics, s. v. Calendar, p. 119.

Aside from casual discussions of the subject occurring
in his different writings, there are two separate works on
chronology attributable to Saadia. They are:

1. *Kitâb al-Ta'rih* (כתאב אלתאריך), "Book of Chronology." Saadia is quoted as the author of a work under this
title by Judah Ibn Bal'am, an eminent grammarian of the
eleventh century, who reproduces a passage therefrom and
points out an error. The same passage, with the error
referred to by Ibn Bal'am, is found literally in an anonymous work on chronology bearing the same title, *Kitâb
al-Ta'rih*. It was therefore suggested with great propriety,
that the latter is identical with the work quoted by Ibn
Bal'am. In support of this identification it has been pointed
out that the Arabic translations of the geographical names
of the Bible, which occur in large numbers in the anonymous *Kitâb al-Ta'rih*, agree with the renditions of the same
names by Saadia in his Arabic version of the Bible. All
doubts as to Saadia's authorship of the anonymous work have
been finally dispelled by the recent discovery of a short fragment of the initial part of the work, which agrees verbally
with the beginning of the anonymous text and contains
besides the definite ascription to Saadia.[203]

The work is divided into seven parts (*'aksâm*), covering
the history of the world from the Creation down to the
author's time. The Bible and the later traditional literature
serve as the main sources. The accounts reproduced from
the Scriptures are occasionally interpreted in the light of
Midrashic ideas. The last part, which is very short, shows
changes and additions by a later author or copyist, who

[203] For all details here touched upon see the *Bibliography*, under
Chronology, p. 353. With regard to the points of contact between the
Kitâb al-Ta'rih and other writings of Saadia (Bacher, *RÉJ.*, XXXII,
144) it should be noted that the reason for the longevity of the first
generations (from Adam to Abraham) advanced by Saadia in the
work before us (*MJC.*, II, 90, end of chapter 1) is found in greater
detail also in the recently published Introduction of Saadia to his
Commentary on the Psalms (Harkavy-*Festschrift*, Hebrew part,
p. 143, lines 5-15; comp. *MHJ.*, VIII, 16); comp. also H. Spiegel,
Saadia al-Fajjûmi's arabische Danielversion, Berlin, 1906, pp. 11 f.,
who adduces some parallels to passages in our work from Saadia's
translation of Daniel.

mentions the years 944 (two years after Saadia's death),
1125, and 1159. The data of this chapter (on account of
which Saadia's authorship was originally doubted) are
greatly confused, owing to numerous copyist's errors in the
text, especially in the numbers, which several scholars have
tried to rectify.[294]

2. *Sēder Tannāīm we-'Amōrāīm* (סדר תנאים ואמוראים),
"Chronology of the Teachers of the Mishnah and the Talmud." The discovery of fragments of such a work was
announced as early as 1886, but they were not published.
Possibly they are not part of a special work on chronology,
but of some other work, as the "Introduction to the Talmud," or the *Sēfer ha-Galui*, the second chapter of which
dealt with the redaction of the Mishnah and the Talmud.[295]

3. *Tōledōt Rabbēnū ha-Kādōsh* (תולדות רבנו הקדוש),
"The Genealogy of R. Judah the Patriarch," the redactor
of the Mishnah, which Saadia was asked to write while
sojourning in Mosul. Only a few lines have been preserved.[296]

4. מגלת בני חשמוני, *i. e.*, "The Scroll of the Ḥasmoneans," translated by Saadia from the original Aramaic into
Arabic. As is well known, the Scroll contains a detailed,
partly legendary, account of the Maccabæan victory over
Antiochus and his generals. Saadia, who in his *Sefer ha-
Galui* refers three times to the Aramaic Scroll, considered it
a work of the Ḥasmoneans themselves and hence important enough to warrant a translation into the vernacular. It
is also most likely that, as Arabic was then more commonly
understood by the Jews than Aramaic, the translation was
intended to counteract the Ḳaraites, who had rejected the
feast of Ḥanukkah as a Rabbanite invention.[296a]

[294] See Bacher, Steinschneider, and Marx, as referred to in the
Bibliography, pp. 353 f.

[295] See above, note 357, and below, p. 270; *Bibliography*, p. 354,
no. 2.

[296] Comp. above, note 107; Eppenstein, *Beiträge*, p. 91; *Bibliography*, p. 354, no. 3.

[296a] See Neubauer, *JQR.*, VI, 575. For further details see the
Bibliography, below, p. 355.

SAADIA GAON

A Greek thinker enunciated the idea that doubt is the first step toward knowledge;[207] it is through scepticism, and the refusal to accept things as they present themselves, that we arrive at a better understanding of their causes and a fuller comprehension of the universe. This doctrine, now the common property of all philosophers, is characteristic of the pagan conception of the origin of truth. For the heathen there is no ready-made truth, no pre-arranged system of thought to be relied upon in our conduct, or in our interpretation of nature. The Platonic ideas and a few mathematical axioms to the contrary notwithstanding, all knowledge is the product of our own mind, the fruit of our observation and experience. God himself is not a given entity, not an *a priori* truth, but merely an inference, something to be found by a logical process of demonstration.

In striking contrast thereto is the doctrine of Judaism. God, to begin with the point mentioned last, is not an object of reasoning and argumentation; His existence is a matter of course, an absolute fact neither to be doubted nor proved. He, the Creator of the world, is the source of all knowledge, the fountain of all truth. He revealed himself to His people, and gave them an eternal law, which was to make them live in accordance with His will, and He continued to guide them through His prophets and inspired teachers.

In a system based on such principles there is no room for doubt or scepticism. If scepticism is the generator of philosophic truth, Judaism, as a positive religion, could never become the bearer and promulgator of such truth. In fact, Judaism is not a system of philosophy, but a moral theology. It is not a scientific doctrine based on and developed by speculative thought. Leaving aside the legalistic elements, it is the immediate expression of religious feeling and emotion. Nor did Judaism ever produce philosophers on its own soil. It is only because of recent assertions to the contrary, that it becomes necessary to emphasize again the

---

[207] Ἐστι δὲ τοῖς εὐπορῆσαι βουλομένοις προύργου τὸ διαπορῆσαι καλῶς· ἡ γὰρ ὕστερον εὐπορία λύσις τῶν πρότερον ἀποροιμένων ἐστι (Aristotle, Metaphysics, B. ch. I, p. 995a, 27–29 of Berlin edition).

accepted fact, that the comparatively few Jewish authors who have become known as philosophers were all inspired by foreign thought. Some of the devotees of the Torah who had imbibed the foreign spirit were alive to the contrast between the Jewish and the heathen conception of God and the universe, and they held on to both in order to keep themselves from slipping between the two stools. The whole of Jewish philosophy was a product of the *Galūt,* and not indigenous Oriental Judaism. At the first collision between Jew and Greek on other than Palestinian soil, Philo the Alexandrian made a great effort to fuse the two opposing cultures into one. The artificial union was of comparatively short duration, and its effect on the subsequent development of the synagogue was of slight importance, except, perhaps, insofar as the Christian church may be considered an outgrowth thereof. For several centuries during the post-Alexandrian period, one looks in vain for a philosopher among Jewish scholars until, under the dominion of the Arabs in the Orient, Hebrew culture for the second time collided with Greek philosophy in the garb of Muhammedan literature. This encounter soon played sad havoc in the ranks of Oriental Jewry. The belief in the divine origin of the Torah was shaken, and the people took up with all sorts of religious vagaries then rampant in the Orient. Saadia was the first to enter into the breach. With his uncommon intellectual power and his vast knowledge of both Jewish and secular literature, he set up a comprehensive system of religious philosophy, culminating in the proof of the superiority of Judaism as compared not only with other religious systems, but also with the various doctrines of the philosophers, and of the compatibility of Jewish tenets with the dictates of reason. Saadia was, indeed, the first Jewish philosopher fully conscious of the basic difference between the Jewish and the philosophic conceptions of truth, and he gave especial emphasis to the fact that Judaism is primarily and essentially a religion based on historical experience; philosophic reflection being required only for the purpose of furnishing secondary evidence of the genuineness and worth of its manifold teachings.[398] And this constitutes his undying greatness.

As a linguist, a Talmudist, a liturgist, he has been greatly surpassed by many of those who followed in the paths he opened But as a systematizer and scientific expounder of the entire range of Jewish lore, as the builder of the most complete system of Jewish religious philosophy, he has been equalled by Maimonides alone Even Maimonides, superior though he is to Saadia in many respects, owed many of the basic ideas in his philosophic doctrines to the works of the Gaon,[399] though, following the literary methods of the Middle Ages, he never quotes them as his source.

The appreciation of Saadia as a master of philosophy should not be based merely on those of his writings that are specially devoted to the subject, but on the general trend of his works in all other branches of Jewish literature as well. Apart from the numerous philosophic ideas and expositions we meet with in most of his existing writings [400]— and doubtless there were many more in his lost works, especially in his elaborate commentaries on the Bible [401]— the philosophic spirit of the author manifests itself in the method and the

[398] This view is clearly stated by Saadia in his Introduction to the _Kitâb al-'Amânât_, pp 22-26, _Emûnôt_, ed. Slucki, Leipzig, 1864, pp 11-13

[399] This has been explicitly stated by Abarbanel, מפעלות אלהים, IX, ch. 1, beginning ... שכמה מדברי הגאון וטענותיו ימצאו בפרקי המורה עם היות שלא זכרם הרב בשמו. A full account of Saadia's influence on Maimonides in all fields of his literary activity, including Halakah, requires a monograph. Respecting Maimonides's indebtedness to Saadia in the field of philosophy see Guttmann, in the Israel Lewy-_Festschrift_, Breslau, 1911, pp. 308-326 (also in _Moses Ben Maimon_, II, 202) ; comp. below, notes 416, 446, 578

[400] E g his Introductions to the " Book on Inheritance " (_Oeuvres_, IX, 1-8), the translation of the Pentateuch (_Oeuvres, I_) the Commentaries on Job, Proverbs (_Oeuvres_, V, VI), and the Psalms (Harkavy-_Festschrift_, pp. 138-152), as well as numerous philosophic disquisitions embodied by the Gaon in the respective commentaries themselves; comp in particular the Commentary on _Proverbs_, pp. 183-203

[401] See the extracts from Saadia's lost Commentary on the Pentateuch in Judah b Barzillai's _Commentary_ on the _Sefer Yezirah_, ed. Halberstam, pp. 89-92, 197.

form of nearly everything he has written. This is what the
student recognizes as the peculiar Saadianic characteristic.
In the following exposition, however, we shall devote our
attention more particularly to those works of the Gaon which
come properly under the head of philosophy.

1. *Tafsîr Kitâb al-Mabâdi* (תפסיר כתאב אלמבאדי),
"Commentary on the Book of Creation"[402] written in
the year 931, soon after the struggle between Saadia
and the Exilarch David b. Zakkai broke out. Saadia is the
first known[403] commentator of this mysterious work, the
most puzzling literary production in existence. It might at
first seem surprising that a rationalist like Saadia, with his
pronounced aversion to all kinds of occult science, should
have taken the trouble of commenting upon such a mystical
document.[404] It becomes understandable when we reflect
that in the time of Saadia this work had not yet been divested

[402] Regarding the title see Steinschneider, *Hebräische Übersetzungen*, p. 443, n. 513. The date of composition is derived from a
passage in the Commentary (ed. Lambert, p. 52, bottom; French
text, p. 76, n. 1); comp. Harkavy, *JQR.*, XII, 539. The passage is
reproduced also in a Hebrew translation in Judah b. Barzillai's פרוש
ספר יצירה, p. 214, l. 13 (see the *Bibliography*, pp. 355 ff.), where the
date רמ״ז = 936 must be corrected to רמ״ב, as it is in the Arabic
original, not רמ״ו, as suggested by Halberstam in his note *ad locum*,
p. 325 (Steinschneider, *l. c.*, n. 517); comp. note 293 and below p. 185.
For all further details see the *Bibliography*, pp. 355-359.

[403] The book had been commented upon prior to Saadia, as he
quotes in his Commentary (pp. 81 f., see below, note 576) some other
interpreter, against whose interpretation he argues. No older
commentary, however, is known, as that of Isaac Israeli does not
exist in its original form, only some portions of it having been
embodied in the Commentary of his pupil Dûnâsh Ibn Tamîm
(London, 1902). It is possible that the interpreter quoted by Saadia
is indeed Israeli, for another passage, quoted on p. 42 (ll. 8 ff.), is
found in Dûnâsh's Commentary (p. 22) in the name of Israeli.
Regarding the complicated question of the authorship of that Commentary see Steinschneider, *AL.*, p. 44, no. 15; comp. above, p. 48.

[404] Against the explanation of Guttmann (*Saadia*, pp. 26, 49) see
the correct remarks of Lambert, p. viii, who, however, goes too far
in asserting that Saadia had acquired all his knowledge of philosophy
in Egypt. Lambert was not yet aware of the more recently ascertained fact that Saadia left Egypt when about 23 years old [see
Postscript].

12

of its original character as a philosophic attempt to explain
the process of the world's generation by the will of the
Creator. It still had a claim upon the earnest attention of
the scholar Moreover, Saadia seems to have had his misgivings as to the real value of the book and the acceptability
of its teachings. He expresses himself very cautiously
about the authorship of the work, saying that the general
belief which ascribes it to the patriarch Abraham can
only be sustained insofar as the ideas contained therein are
concerned, while in its literary form it is the product of
scholars who lived in Palestine. To support his view he
points to the Mishnah, which existed in oral tradition for
many centuries before it was put into writing. Even a part
of the Bible (Proverbs 25, 1 ff), he continues, went through
the same process [405] It is characteristic of Saadia's attitude
toward the book that he does not accept what he presents as
its basic theory of creation. He substitutes another theory,
which, he says, is that of the Torah,[406] a rather surprising
attitude in view of the circumstance that the theory of the
Sēfer Yezirāh is supposed to have been taught by the patriarch Abraham. He also realizes that the text had been
much tampered with, and cannot always be taken as a safe
guide He makes many emendations,[407] and " to prevent further alterations and misinterpretations " [408] gives the Hebrew
text in full, with a verbal Arabic translation (tafsir). This
is followed by a lengthy commentary (sharh). The Hebrew
text he divides into eight chapters, of which the first four are
subdivided into twenty-four paragraphs (halakōt), while
the latter four, which he considers merely as a more detailed
repetition and development of the former,[409] are given with-

---

[405] Tafsir, p 12, French translation, p. 28 (in the following notes
the references to the French translation will be indicated by figures
in parentheses); comp Jellinek, Beiträge zur Gesch der Kabbala,
I, 5 The same view as regards parts of the Bible he expresses in
his Commentary on Proverbs, 25, 1; comp Steinschneider,
Hebräische Übersetzungen, p 443, n. 515.

[406] Tafsir, pp. 11 (27), 91 (113), l 7; comp below, p. 182, top

[407] See Tafsir, pp 26, l. 9, 50, 3-9; 80, 14, 102, 8.

[408] Tafsir, p 13 (29), end of the Introduction.

[409] Tafsir, p. 89 (112), ll. 17 ff.

out further division and without the *tafsir*. The Commentary on this portion of the book, too, is comparatively brief, occupying about the tenth part of the whole (exclusive of the Introduction). In his introductory remarks to this part of the work, at the end of the fourth chapter (p. 98, bottom) he states that the Commentary on the following chapters will be limited to the explanation of rare words and the elucidation of new matter.

Whether or not Saadia succeeded in unravelling the mysteries of the *Sefer Yeṣirah*—let it be said distinctly that he did not—is not a matter of much concern. The Commentary, such as it is, is a valuable specimen of the early attempts to explain the book. It contains, however, a wealth of material of special importance for the appreciation of Saadia's achievements in various fields of knowledge, more particularly in those of Hebrew grammar and religious philosophy. A detailed account of Saadia's detached theories on these subjects, as they occur in this Commentary, is out of the question here. It would require the reproduction of a considerable portion of the book. Nor is this the place for a discussion of the doctrines of the *Sefer Yeṣirah* itself as presented by Saadia. A brief summary of the philosophic problems presented, and of some other literary and historical questions dealt with by the author in connection with his explanations of the text, will suffice to show the general character and literary significance of his Commentary.

We have seen that it was Saadia's scientific method to introduce his works, whether they were of an independent nature or in the form of commentaries, by a general outline of the subject under consideration, or by an analysis of the content, scope and purpose of the book to be commented upon.[410] The same method is adhered to in the Commentary on the *Sefer Yeṣirah*. A lengthy Introduction, occupying twelve pages of the Arabic text, begins with the brief statement, that the book is generally ascribed to Abraham the patriarch. After a short praise of God, cus-

---

[410] See in particular the Introductions to Job, Proverbs, and Psalms.

tomary in Arabic[431] works, he points out that the most
difficult problem that has troubled the mind of thinkers
among all nations is the origin of the universe. Even the
author of a Biblical book, King Solomon, had to admit that
his reasoning did not avail him to solve this problem
(Kohelet, 7, 24). Nevertheless it is not permissible to
abandon the study of this question, for " philosophy is one
of the noblest creations of God," and Scripture recognizes
in philosophy, so to speak, one of the occupations of the
Creator himself,[432] when it says (Job, 12, 22) : " He discov-
ereth deep things out of darkness and bringeth out to light
things obscure."

Having thus prepared the way for a philosophic investigation, he gives an historical account of the various
Greek theories of the origin of the world, and refutes them
one by one. It is Saadia's habit, observable in all his works,
not to mention the names of authors whose views he opposes,[432a] a custom departed from in but a few rare instances.
He follows here his common practice. The theories he discusses are, however, readily traceable to their respective
authors. The first, affirming the eternity of the world, is
that of the so-called *Dahriyya* (Eternalists), which differs
from that of Aristotle insofar as it eliminates the idea of a
prime mover [432b] ; the second, which he subdivides into three
somewhat similar branches, seems to be a combination

[431] The prayer is always followed by the formula אמא בעד, which
introduces the subject proper ; in Hebrew works under Arabic influence usually אחר היטבה לאל, or, as in the *Emunôt*, beginning :
ואחר כה יטפתחנו בו ; see the numerous instances collected by
Steinschneider, *HB.*, X, 98, n. 3 ; XII, 57, n. 1. The Arabs consider
the formula very important and credit David with its invention ;
see Steinschneider, *Vorlesungen über die Kunde hebräischer Handschriften*, p. 35.

[432] Comp. Guttmann, *Saadia*, p. 48, n. 3. Saadia's theory reminds
one of the dictum of K. F. Gauss, the great German mathematician :
ὁ θεὸς μαθηματίζει.

[432a] Saadia says this explicitly in his *'Agron*, Harkavy, *Zikron*,
V, 51.

[432b] Comp. Horovitz, Cohen's *Festschrift*, p. 243, n. 1 ; below, note
475.

of the doctrines of Plato and of the Greek atomists Leucippus (500 b. c. e.) and Democritus (460) ; the fourth, which postulates water as the prime matter, is the theory of the oldest known Greek philosopher, Thales of Miletus (640) ; while the fifth and the sixth theories, the one considering the element of air and the other that of fire as the prime matter, are those of Anaximenes (550) and Heraclitus (500) respectively. To these is added, as the seventh theory, the teaching of Pythagoras (586-506), that all existence originates through numbers.

It is obvious that Saadia did not follow chronology in thus disposing of the Greek thinkers. He seems to have arranged the theories in the order of his valuation of them, putting the least probable first, and proceeding by degrees to the most plausible. This will explain why he interrupted the order by inserting in the third place a theory which he evidently attributes to some unnamed Jewish authors, who maintain that the world was created, but, basing their inference upon an erroneous interpretation of a Mishnah (*Hagigah*, II, 1), forbid the study of how and by what means the creation was effected. Naturally, such restriction of the right to philosophize did not appeal to Saadia, and he put the theory where he thought it belonged.[413]

Having rejected, as to the origin of the universe, the seven views cited, Saadia turns to the theory of the *Sefer Yeṣirah*, which, according to him, differs from that of Pythagoras only insofar as, in addition to the ten numerals, it postulates also the twenty-two letters of the Hebrew alphabet as the creative mechanism and the essence of all creation. Saadia devotes much space here and elsewhere in his Commentary to the elucidation of this fantastic theory, which, together with that of Pythagoras, he endeavors to harmonize with the teachings of Judaism. The author of the *Sefer Yeṣirah*, he asserts,[414] did not mean to say that the numbers and letters pre-existed as separate entities, out of which the world was created, but only that they constituted an impor-

[413] For further discussion of the subject see below, pp. 202-204.
[414] *Tafsir*, p. 10 (26, top), ll. 15 f.

tant factor in the process of the world's formation as the underlying principles of order and symmetry in all nature.

But Saadia does not accept all the views of the *Sefer Yezirah*.[413] According to him there was no gradual process of formation such as described in that work, but, " as taught in the Book of Genesis, the four elements, fire, air, water, and earth, with all their compositions, combinations, and formations, were created by God (*ex nihilo*) at one stroke, just as the flesh, bones, veins, skin, and all that forms itself thereof originate all at once in the embryo ; the pulp, kernel, peel, stalk, and other components begin simultaneously in the fruit, and the elements of fire, redness, brilliancy, and ignition, appear all at the same time in the flame." [414]

Here the Introduction ends, but before taking up the text for interpretation the commentator discusses the question of Abraham's authorship. In this connection we receive historically important information about the differences between the Babylonian and Palestinian Jews in naming the letters of the Hebrew alphabet and in the pronunciation of the *resh*.[415] It is on the basis of these observations in the text of the *Sefer Yezirah* that Saadia assigns it to a Palestinian author.

Among the points of interest discussed in the Commentary proper the following may briefly be sketched.

[413] To minimize the importance of the theory of the *Sefer Yezirah*, as one advanced by Abraham, Saadia declares (*Tafsir*, p. 17 (35), bottom) that Abraham did not assert it as a positive truth, but merely suggested it as an idea that appealed to his imagination; comp. *Tafsir*, p. 12 (28), ll. 17 ff.

[414] *Tafsir*, p. 12 (27). It is interesting to note that Saadia quotes this passage from his Commentary on *Genesis*, now lost (comp. the *Bibliography*, p. 308). The question of the correctness of these illustrations from the viewpoint of modern science does not concern us. Saadia expresses the same view in the *Amānāt*, p. 88, ll. 17 ff. (*Em.*, p. 46). In both places he bases it on Is. 48. 13, as interpreted in the Talmud (*Hagigah*, 12a). Here again Maimonides (*Dalālat*, II, ch. 30; Munk, *Guide*, II, p. 234) follows Saadia, without referring to his source; comp. Guttmann, in Isr. Lewy's *Festschrift*, p. 322 (*Moses ben Maimon*, II, 212) ; above, note 399; below, notes 446, 515, 541a.

[415] Comp. Derenbourg, *Manuel du lecteur* (*Journal Asiatique*, 1870), p. 459, n. 1 ; 496; Brüll, *Jahrbücher*, II, 158 ff.; Bacher, *Anfänge*, pp. 22 f.

CHAPTER I (pp. 13-36). A lengthy discussion in which the distinction is drawn between things knowable and therefore to be studied with zeal, as, for instance, the content and meaning of the religious law, and things unknowable, as the laws of nature. " For if you ask the wisest among men why does fire tend upward and water downward, or why is the element of air in motion and that of the earth stable, he will not be able to say more than that they were so created and that this is their nature " [418]— as satisfactory a reply as the modern scientist makes when he refers a questioner dogmatically to the laws of " gravitation " or of " chemical affinity."

The author of the *Sefer Yezirah,* Saadia continues, who seems to have gone much farther in presenting his solutions of nature's mysteries, in reality did not pretend to know what is unknowable, but merely suggested that the numbers and letters may have been the instruments of creation, just as we believe in a *creatio ex nihilo,* though we have never witnessed anything coming out of nothing.[419]

Saadia's efforts to blend Judaism with Greek philosophy are characteristically illustrated in his interpretation of ten divine names used in the *Sefer Yezirah* and even of the Ten Commandments as indicative of the ten categories of Aristotle.[420] Needless to say, he turns many an exegetical somersault in order to accomplish his purpose. A little further on (p. 22) he attributes in the name of " scholars " a fourfold existence to all things : in reality, in speech, in writing, and

[418] *Tafsir,* p. 15 (32), ll. 15 ff. The same occurs, at still greater length, in Saadia's Commentary on *Proverbs,* 30, 3-4; comp. also Commentary on *Job,* 28, 28, and Bacher's note to that passage. The passage is quoted by Eliezer b. Nathan (see the references below, *note* 623) and Judah b. Barzillai, פס״י p. 155 (comp. also p. 275) from the Commentary on Proverbs, not from that on the *Sefer Yezirah,* as assumed by Kaufmann in his note *ad locum,* p. 339.

[419] *Tafsir,* p. 17 (35) ; comp. note 415.

[420] *Tafsir,* pp. 18-22 (36-42). Part of this exposition is quoted by Berechiah ha-Naḳdan, מצרף, pp. 118 f. (comp. the *Bibliography,* p. 358) ; comp. Judah b. Barzillai, pp. 276-278.

in thought. For this idea I do not know the source.[21]   In
connection with the alliterative passage *sēfer*, *scfār*, *sippūr*
(beginning of *Sefer Yeṣirah*), he points to similar alliterations in Bible (Isaiah, 24, 17), Talmud (Erubin, 65*b*, top:
בכיסו בכוסו בכעסו); Eleazar Ḳalir's liturgy (*Kerōbōt* to the
second day of Tabernacles: לסוככי למוסכי להסיכי בנסיכת
קדוש), and in the style of Hebrew letters prevalent in his own
time, of which he quotes several examples.[22]

Other points in this chapter worth mentioning are:
Saadia's correct explanation of the meaning of the dragon in
astronomy,[23] and his accurate description of the inequality
in length of days and nights in different parts of the world,
which ultimately results in some countries having continuous
day or night for a period of six months.[24]

CHAPTER 2 (pp. 36-55). The lengthy discussion of the
consonants and vowels of the Hebrew alphabet and their pronunciation by the Tiberians and Babylonians (pp. 42-46),
which is of great importance for the history of Hebrew
grammar, has been fully treated by competent scholars[25] and
may therefore be passed over. Among the points of interest
in this chapter we note Saadia's contention that the earth is
round, inclosed on all sides by the heavens, in opposition to
the author of the *Sefer Yeṣirah*, who considers it flat,
covered only on one side by the heavens " as the roof covers
the house." [26]   The endless diversity in the physical properties
of organic and inorganic bodies Saadia explains, like Aristotle, as the result of different combinations of the primary

---

[21] The idea is repeated in *Tafsir*, p. 44 (67), ll. 15 ff.; comp.
Judah b. Barzillai, pp. 230, l. 9 from below; 278, ll. 29 ff.

[22] *Tafsir*, p. 23; comp. Lambert's translation, p. 43. n. 7; Dukes,
נחל קדומים, p. 24; Steinschneider, *Kerem Chemed*, IX, 40; Harkavy, *Zikron, V*, 110; comp. J. N. Epstein (above, note 360), p. 45.

[23] *Tafsir*, p. 32 (52 f.), quoted also by Judah b. Barzillai, p. 209;
comp. Kaufmann, *ad locum*, p. 345.

[24] *Tafsir*, p. 33 (54); comp. Lambert's Introduction, p. x.

[25] Bacher, *Anfänge*, pp. 38-62.

[26] *Tafsir*, p. 48 (71), ll. 13 ff.; comp. Lambert, Introduction, p. x.

elements which constitute the bodies.[427] In illustration thereof
he points to the new meanings always arising from the permutation of letters in a word, or the transposition of words
within given sentences. Drifting into the field of astrology
(in which Saadia, in spite of his pronounced rationalism,
probably believed to some extent) he illustrates the same idea
by showing the varying influences of the stars on human
actions in accordance with their position in the zodiac.[428] For
the computation of the planetary motions he uses as a starting
point the day on which he was writing, so that we learn
incidentally the date of the work. It was Tuesday, the
twelfth of Sivan, 1242 *era contractuum* = May 31, 931, c. e.[429]

CHAPTER 3 (pp. 55-69). Numbers and letters occupying
so prominent a position in the "Book of Creation," Saadia
again and again takes occasion to discuss their qualities and
significance from various points of view. The number
"One" is extolled as the most important of all, being the
origin of all numbers with their infinite potentialities and preceded by none, resembling in this respect the Creator of the
universe.[430] The difficulties of the text often lead Saadia to
very curious conceits. The letter ש with its three arms ris-
ing from the base, symbolizes to him the upward striving
element of fire; the מ with its two sides dropping down,
represents the water; and the א with outspread wings the

---

[427] *Tafsir*, p. 51 (73 f.); Lambert, p. x. In a similar way he explains elsewhere in this work (p. 60, top) the causes of the differentiation between male and female; comp. Lambert, p. 82; Judah
b. Barzillai, p. 222, top.

[428] *Tafsir*, p. 53 (76 f.); Judah b. Barzillai, p. 214.

[429] See above, note 402. It may here be added that nearly all of
the second chapter is reproduced in a Hebrew translation in the
פס״י of Judah b. Barzillai (see the *Bibliography*, pp. 356 f.), but the
text is very corrupt.

[430] *Tafsir*, p. 56 (79), l. 4 from below; Judah b. Barzillai, pp. 260 f.
On p. 27 (48, top), ll. 11 ff., Saadia restricts this statement to the
effect that numbers, like time, are infinite only in comparison with
ourselves, but not when compared to God. Another paragraph is
devoted to the glorification of the number One; *Tafsir*, p. 68 (89 f.);
comp. Steinschneider, *Bibliotheca Mathematica*, 1895, pp. 23 f.

air.[431] A lengthy discussion on the permutations of letters[432] shows their endless progression with the increasing number of letters added to a word, so that the longest word occurring in the Bible and counting only eleven letters (והאחשדרפנים, Esther. 9, 3), permits of 39,916.800 combinations! He concludes this discussion with the following interesting remarks : " In similar proportions increases the gain of him who searches after knowledge. Each time he learns a point he derives therefrom another one, just as the profit of the merchant increases each time he adds something to the capital. Nay, even more ; the profit gained by study can always be added to the capital, while the profit of capital engaged in business in the beginning is spent so that it disappears, wherefore Scripture (Prov. 3, 14) says : The merchandise of it is better than the merchandise of silver, and the gain thereof than fine gold."

The Commentary on the " Book of Creation " is, so far as I know, the only extant work of Saadia in which he touches also upon the ancient idea of the parallelism existing between the universe as a macrocosm and man as a microcosm[433] ; an idea which, as I have shown elsewhere, has its origin in old Babylonian literature.[434] Following a Midrash,[435] Saadia interposes between these two worlds an intermediary world, which is represented by the Holy Tabernacle. He refers the reader to his "commentary on the construction of the Tabernacle," in which he draws eighteen parallelisms among the three worlds.[436] Here only two are given : to

---

[431] Tafsir, p. 59 (82) ; Judah b. Barzillai, pp. 221 f. ; comp. also Tafsir, p. 91 (113, bottom).

[432] Tafsir, pp. 62-64 (83-85) ; Judah b. Barzillai, pp. 244 ff. Judah (p. 243, bottom) quotes some other words of the Bible as the longest. Ibn Ganâh, Kitâb al-Luma'. p. 29 (רקמה, p. 7) uses Saadia, as usual, without name.

[433] Tafsir, pp. 67 f. (89) ; comp. also p. 91 (113 f.), end of chapter 4.

[434] Comp. Malter, Personifications of Soul and Body, JQR., N. S., vol. II (1911-1912), pp. 453 ff.

[435] See Jellinek, Bet ha-Midrasch, III, 175 f.

[436] Quoted by Abraham Ibn Ezra, on Exodus, 25, 40; see also his Short Commentary on Exodus, 25, 7 (Geiger, Wissenschaftliche

the two celestial lights (sun and moon) correspond the two
eyes in man and the lamps in the candlestick of the Tabernacle; the firmament which divided the water under it from
the water above it (Genesis, 1, 7) is paralleled by the veil
which divided between the holy and most holy place in the
Tabernacle (Exodus, 26, 33) and by the diaphragm,[437] which
separates the organs of nutrition from those of respiration in
man.

CHAPTER 4 (pp. 69-92). Most of this chapter is devoted
to the explanation of the theory of creation supposed to be
propounded by the *Sefer Yeẓirah*.[438] The believers, Saadia
begins, use various terms in trying to describe the process of
creation. They say, God created the world by his "breath,"
"spirit" (רוח), "word" (דבר), "power," "will," "desire,"
and the like. But all these terms have one and the same meaning. The author of our book uses "breath," which is used
also in Scripture (Job, 26, 13), "by his breath the heavens
are garnished." When the breath, or spirit, is conceived
as having assumed actual form, it is called "word." Thus
Scripture says (Psalms, 33, 6), "by the word of God were
the heavens made; and all the hosts of them by the breath
of His mouth." When the letters of a word are spoken into
the air, they shape themselves into substantial entities.
Through the vibration of the air they then reach the ear of
the listener. The word of God, being infinitely more effective, at once carried creation with it. He said and it was.

According to Saadia's interpretation of the *Sefer Yeẓirah*
the first thing God created was a certain intangible, rarefied,

---

Zeitschrift, V, 299); another author (see Steinschneider, *CB.*, 2207)
quotes 16 instead of 18, see the *Bibliography*, p. 312. For more particulars on this subject see A. Epstein, *RÉJ.*, XXI (1890), 92-97;
XXII, 1-4; Brüll, *Jahrbücher*, VII, 117; Malter, *JQR.*, N. S., vol. II
(1911-1912), p. 479, n. 99.

[437] Saadia uses here the Greek word (דייפרגמא = διάφραγμα),
hence also the translator Moses of Lucena; see Steinschneider,
Hebräische Übersetzungen, p. 448, and Epstein, *l. c.*, XXI, p. 93, n. 4.

[438] The first two paragraphs of this chapter (69-74) are given also
by Judah b. Barzillai, pp. 177-179, and partly by Moses Tachau, *Ozar
Nechmad*, II, 66 f. (see below, pp. 281 ff., 358).

pneumatic or ethereal substances,[439] which differs from the
tangible air that surrounds us by its greater tenuity and
sublimated quality. The next step was the creation of the
atmospheric air. At this stage the alphabet, or rather the
words of God formed therefrom, became the active instruments of creation, the air serving as the medium for the
transmission of God's will.

As pointed out before (pp. 178, 182), Saadia does not
accept this theory in full. According to him there were
no prior and posterior stages in the process of creation,
but all sprang into potential existence at once, and the
Biblical account of a six days' duration refers only to
the gradual development into reality. But he seems to
have admitted the differentiation between the ethereal substance and the atmospheric air, which he imputes to the
author of the *Sefer Yezirah*. He expatiates considerably upon the subject, and in connection therewith endeavors to prove also the omnipresence of God and to show
God's relation to the universe.[440] The pneumatic substance, or

---

[439] Saadia uses various terms to designate this substance, as *peculiar, simple, subtle, second, air*.

[440] Lambert, p. vii, contends that Saadia had given up this theory
when writing the *Kitāb al-'Amānāt*, or had never recognized it.
"Dans son traité de théologie, Saadya ne parle plus de cette théorie.
Là il cherche à prouver la création et son corollaire, l'existence de
Dieu, mais il ne tente plus d'exposer les relations de Dieu et du
monde." Probably following Lambert, S. Horovitz, *Über den
Einfluss der griechischen Philosophie auf die Entwicklung des
Kalam*, Breslau, 1909, p. 43, likewise asserts that there is no trace
of that theory in Saadia's main philosophic work. Both Lambert
and Horovitz, however, overlooked or misunderstood the parallel
passages, *'Amānāt*, pp. 88, 91 (*Emūnōt*, Leipzig, 1864, pp. 46, 48), especially p. 108, ll. 1-8(*Emūnōt*, p. 55, ll. 32 ff.; *Tafsir*, p. 71) which,
though not so explicit as in the *Tafsir*, are nevertheless based on the
same theory, and can only be understood in the light thereof; comp.
'Amānāt, p. 88, ll. 12 ff., and *Tafsir*, p. 70, top (Lambert's translation,
p. 91, is here incomplete); *'Amānāt*, p. 88, l. 3, and *Tafsir*, p. 72 (94),
l. 11, and especially *'Amānāt*, p. 91, ll. 17 ff., and *Tafsir*, p. 73 (95, bottom), ll. 9 f. (the text, l. 11, gives no sense, for עלי הם ואנבמא is probably to be read ואנבמא נעלי). Guttmann (Saadia, pp. 119, 127) correctly recognized the connection between the two works, but failed to
see that the passage, *Emūnōt*, p. 48, is likewise part of the theory that

ether, which he probably adopted from the Stoics,[441] pervades all existence, even the interior of the most solid bodies. It is through the medium of this sublimated air that God is omnipresent; it is, figuratively speaking, "the throne of God's majesty," [442] the agency of the divine spirit that animates and sustains all creation. Scripture therefore says (Psalms, 103, 19), " God hath established His throne in the heavens ; and His kingdom ruleth over all." In this sense Jerusalem,[443] the city from which God sent His messages to the world, is called " the throne of God " (Jeremiah, 3, 17). The same all-pervading ethereal substance is often designated in Scriptures by the name Kabod, " glory," as it is said (Isaiah, 6, 3), " the whole earth is full of His glory." It is by means of this " finer air " that the word of God was communicated to the prophets, and that all the miraculous phenomena became visible to their eyes. The Jewish nation later coined the special term Shekinah (שכינה), which also designates this imperceptible medium of power, the subtle air, charged, as it were, with divinity, in contradistinction to the perceptible atmospheric air, which serves as a vehicle for its manifestations. Even after the cessation of prophecy, the divine spirit continued to manifest itself, though in a lesser degree, to the sages of the nation. During this period the imperceptible substance, which thus establishes the relation between God and the pious ones, is called " the Holy Spirit " (רוח הקרש), or " Echo " (בת קול), that is, the resonance of God's voice.[444]

---

attributes to the air or ether a high degree of divinity. Hence Guttmann's efforts (pp. 113 f.) to explain the reason why Saadia discussed the matter in that place.

[441] Comp. Horovitz, Über den Einfluss, etc., p. 42; Goldziher, RÉJ., XLII, 184.

[442] Comp. 'Amânât, pp. 99 f., 102, 104, 106 (Emūnōt, pp. 51, 52, bottom, 53, 55).

[443] Arabic al-Ḳuds (Tafsir, p. 73, top), which is the name of Jerusalem, misunderstood by Lambert, p. 95, who translates sanctuaire; comp. 'Amânât, p. 143 (73).

[444] Tafsir, p. 73 (95).

The foregoing glorification of the imperceptible air as the
omnipresent divine spirit might easily lead to grave misunderstanding For in spite of Saadia's cautious remark that
the imperceptible air itself was created, and that his theory
is only to be taken as a metaphoric presentation of the idea
of God's omnipresence, the doctrine borders dangerously on
pantheism. Saadia is well aware of this danger, and therefore endeavors to save the personality of God as a distinct
entity, in no way immersed in the universe. In order to
reach some approximate idea of God's relation to the world,
he says,[415] we must, in the first place, compare His presence
in the universe with the presence of life in the animal or
human body Just as there is life in every particle of the
body, so God is in every atom of the universe. He is therefore described in the Bible (Daniel, 12, 7) as the *life of the
world* (חי העולם).[416] We then proceed a step farther and
conceive God as the life-governing principle, which in the
human body is the intellect. God thus becomes " the intellect of the world." The imperceptible air, of which we spoke,
is the vitality of the entire cosmos, permeating and vivifying
all its parts, just as life permeates the living organism. But
above this vitality stands a spiritual power which controls
its actions and gives it direction, as is obviously the case in
the life of the individual We may draw further compari-
sons and say, that just as the human intellect is not divided
by the division of the body and does not perish with it, so
God, the intellect of the world, is not affected by the divisi-
bility of the latter, and does not cease to exist, though it
should disappear. Moreover, as the intellect, though per-
vading every spark of life, its next substratum, is nevertheless
distinctly above it, so that life is actually guided by intellect,

[415] *Tafsir,* p 70 (91, bottom), ll 4 ff.
[416] This interpretation of the verse as well as the philosophic idea
underlying it, without making use, however, of the air as a medium,
were taken over by Maimonides, *Dalâlat,* I, chaps. 69, 72 (Munk,
Guide, I, 321, 371), who does not mention, however, his source; see
above, notes 399, 416, and below, notes 450, 472a, 473, 494, 515, 541a,
578

similarly God—though present in all parts of nature by means of the imperceptible air, His immediate agency—is nevertheless the extra-mundane guiding spirit of all. Finally, as the intellect is not defiled by the uncleanness and other imperfections of the body, so the Creator is untouched by the soilure and impurities of the world.[417]

It may be surprising, but it is nevertheless true, that if Saadia's presentation and solution of this most important problem be stripped of its Oriental floridity and ornateness, the doctrine here propounded will be found to be much the same as that of the German philosopher Schopenhauer. The imperceptible air is but an expression for the dynamic energy active in all organic and inorganic nature, constantly producing and reproducing life—in the phraseology of Schopenhauer, the *will to live*. The difference between Saadia and Schopenhauer is not in the definition and conception of the power in question, but only as regards its origin. According to Saadia the will—and it should here be added that Saadia uses this term (*mashi'ah, 'irâdah*) repeatedly [417a] to designate the imperceptible air—was implanted by God in nature for a special purpose, and its workings are everlastingly superintended and directed by Him. According to Schopenhauer the will is a blind, unconscious power, working to no purpose and gaining consciousness only in the higher stages of existence, where it becomes mind, as in man. The reason for this difference is obvious. The pious Gaon of Sura could not afford to lose his personal God. He fared better for it. For the Jewish sage could present his philosophy with a smile, while the German thinker was bound to plunge himself and his followers into a world of philosophic pessimism.

In keeping with the text of the *Sefer Yeẓirah* the philosophic exposition is here again interrupted to give place to a

---

[417] *Tafsir*, pp. 70-71 (92 f.) ; comp. Horovitz, *l. c.,* pp. 42 f., who adduces some parallels from Greek and other authors; Kaufmann, in his *Notes* on the פ״י of Judah b. Barzillai, pp. 340 f.

[417a] *Tafsir*, p. 69, ll. 16 f.; 70, ll. 2, 15.

lengthy paragraph (pp. 75-9) on Hebrew grammar and
phonetics, which is of importance for the history of that
science Saadia refers twice to his main work on Hebrew
grammar (*Kutub al-luġah*) and gives extracts therefrom,
the more valuable as the book in its entirety is lost.[448]

In a following paragraph (pp. 80-84) Saadia shows himself to have been familiar with the astronomical literature
of his time. He gives the various measurements of the
planets and other stars as compared with the size of the
earth The circumference of the latter is given as being
nearly 20,000 miles [449] As the Arabic mile is about 300 meters
longer than the English, the measure is about the same as that
given by modern scientists, namely, 25,000 English miles.
Saadia concludes that these measures were established by
ancient scholars with the help of instruments and by mathematical computations.[450]

The last four chapters of the *Sefer Yezirah* (pp 92-105),
are treated summarily, Saadia limiting himself for the most
part to the interpretation of difficult words and phrases.
Some of these interpretations are forced and can hardly
be accepted, although nothing better can be offered There
occur, however, numerous linguistic remarks of interest,[451]
as also some references of importance. Thus Saadia's reference to a book dealing with the decorative " crowns " of
certain letters in the Torah scrolls (ספר תגין), is the earliest

[448] This paragraph was published by Neubauer and later, with a
Hebrew translation, by Harkavy, for which see the *Bibliography*,
p 356

[449] *Tafsir*, p. 84 (107), l 12; comp Lambert, p. x

[450] It is interesting to note that in Saadia's opinion (*Tafsir*, p 83
(106), end of § 4) " the scholars properly choose mathematics and
geometry as the first subjects of instruction, because they are the
origin of all sciences." This view was also adopted by Maimonides
Dalâlat, I, 34 (Munk, *Guide*, I, 321) ; comp Malter, *JQR.*, N S , vol.
I (1910-1911), pp. 491, n 138, 402, n 143 The same view is
expressed in the *Commentary* on the *Sefer Yezirah* attributed to
Dûnâsh Ibn Tamim, London, 1902, p 16

[451] So on p 94 (115) (discussed by Derenbourg, *Manuel*, p 130,
n. 6) , 97 (116), 102 (119).

known.[452] He speaks also of people who believe in the
efficacy of amulets (קמיע), and suggests the origin of the
belief.[453] In the sixth chapter he discusses in detail the
functions of various internal organs of the human body,
showing his acquaintance with Arabic works on the subject, to which he refers in another passage as "books of
anatomy" (kutub al-tashrîh).[454]

2. Kitâb al-'Amânât wa'l-I'tikâdât (כתאב אלאמאנאת
ואלאעתקאדאת, in Hebrew: ספר האמונות והדעות, "Book
of Philosophic Doctrines and Religious Beliefs,"[455] Saadia's
most important philosophic work, written in Bagdad during the time of his seclusion, in 933.[455a] The printed Arabic

[452] *Tafsir*, p. 94 (114). The book was published with a Latin
Introduction by J. J. L. Bargès, Paris, 1866 (in an entirely different
recension also in the מחזור ויטרי, pp. 674-685; comp. p. 800), preceded by a lengthy essay on the origin of the book by Senior Sachs;
comp. Bargès, Introduction, pp. X f.; Schechter, *Abot di R. Nathan*,
p. xi; Dukes, נחל קדומים, p. 24; Steinschneider, *Hebräische Übersetzungen*, p. 443, n. 514; *Vorlesungen über die Kunde hebräischer
Handschriften*, pp. 4 f. The book is also mentioned in an ancient
list, *JQR.*, XIII, 55, no. 90; Wertheimer, לקט מדרשים, p. 13. None
of the editors knew that the book was quoted by Saadia; see above,
note 52.

[453] *Tafsir*, pp. 89 (111), 94 (114).

[454] *Tafsir*, p. 91 (114), l. 14; also in *'Amânât*, p. 201 (*Emūnōt*, pp.
100 f.); comp. below, *Bibliography*, VII, p. 398.

[455] The Hebrew title has been variously translated by recent authors
and mostly mistranslated. The word אמונה usually means belief,
faith, or creed. Ibn Tibbon, however, imitating the Arabic *'amânât*,
used it in the sense of a philosophic doctrine, or *system* of belief; see
Saadia's own definition, p. 11, ll. 4 f., *Emūnōt*, p. 6, l. 7, where, however, אמונה stands for i'tikâd, not *'amânah*, showing that Ibn Tibbon
used the Hebrew term indiscriminately for both. See Steinschneider,
H. B., XI, p. 141, n. 3, end; XXI, 19; *Hebräische Uebersetzungen*,
p. 439, n. 482.

[455a] The date of composition is derived from a passage in the work
itself, p. 72, Hebrew, p. 37 (here and in the following quotations of
the Hebrew text the edition of Slucki, Leipzig, 1864, is referred to).
For the literature regarding the date see Landauer, p. v, and the
numerous references given by Steinschneider, *l. c.*, p. 439, n. 483.

13

text covers 320 pages of the usual octavo size. The book
seems to have originally been written and issued in separate monographs, later combined by the author into an
organic whole preceded by a general Introduction. Traces
of this development are still found in various parts of the
book.[456] In its present form the work consists, apart from
the long Introduction (pp. 1-30), of ten distinct *treatises*
(*maḳâlât*), each bearing a special title, indicating the subject
treated thereunder. The seventh treatise is still extant in two
different recensions, the one probably forming the original
monograph and the other being a recast thereof to suit the
plan of the bigger work.[457] In the following analysis I
shall refer to the individual treatises by the more general
term of chapters.[458]

GENERAL CHARACTERISTICS

One of the main features of this great work of Saadia
is its fundamental theory, that philosophy and religion not
only do not contradict one another, but from the very start

[456] Thus several of the chapters are quoted in the work itself
under their respective special titles, although this is not carried
through with consistency; see *'Amânât*, pp. 55, top, 116, 1. 13
(*Emûnôt*, pp. 29, 60) : שׁער הצדק=באב אלעדל, *i. e.* chapter 4;
Am., p. 77, 1. 10 (*Em.*, p. 41) : שׁער החדוׁישׁ=באב חדת אלעאלם (so
read for the corrupt שׁער הֹמדע), *i. e.* chapter 1; *Am.*, pp. 159, l. 9;
254, bottom (*Em.*, pp. 81, 129) : מאמר=מקאלה (באב) אלתוחיר
(שׁער) היחוד *i. e.* chapter 2; comp. Kaufmann, *Attributenlehre*, pp. 87,
146, and p. 504 *ad locum*, and below, *Bibliography*, section VI. p. 384,
no. 4. The third chapter seems to have been known as a separate
book under the title *Kitâb al-Sharâi'* (Book of Laws), see the
Bibliography, section VII, pp. 400 f., while the tenth chapter is designated (*Am.*, p. 286, bottom, *Em.*, p. 147), as *Kitâb Zûhd*, כתאב זהר=
ספר פריישׁות, *i. e.* Book of Abstinence, Ethics, see below, note 530.
In Hebrew too several of the chapters circulated as separate
treatises (see below, p. 247, bottom, 267, and the *Bibliography*,
pp. 362 f., nos. 1-2; 367, no. 4; 395, 401).

[457] See the *Bibliography*, p. 360.

[458] In the older Hebrew translation, the so-called *Paraphrase*, the
individual treatises are called מגלה (see Zunz, *Gesammelte
Schriften*, III, 232), while Ibn Tibbon uses מאמר.

were destined to help and supplement each other in the finding
and propagation of truth. For both reason and religion
sprang from the same divine source; hence neither one, if
properly used or interpreted, can teach anything that is
incompatible with the teachings of the other. By religion
Saadia naturally understands the faith revealed to Moses
on Mount Sinai and later amplified and developed by the
divinely inspired prophets of Israel.

With this theory as a basis Saadia sets out to examine the
various philosophic doctrines which seem to be at variance
with the teachings of the Mosaic religion, and endeavors
to prove that the supposed antagonism between the two is
due either to fallacious reasoning or to a misinterpretation
of religious sources. It is therefore a matter of prime importance to find out the criteria by which we are to recognize the ways of sound reasoning, as well as to establish
certain rules for the proper interpretation of the Biblical
documents.

All our knowledge is commonly derived from three
sources: 1. sense-perception; 2. direct cognition or apprehension of the mind (intuitive, or immediate knowledge);
3. syllogistic reasoning (inferential, or mediate knowledge).[458a] In addition to these three general sources of knowledge " we, the followers of monotheism," recognize also a
fourth one, *i. e.*, the Bible. If, as often happens, the word of
Scriptures appears to contradict what we had assumed as true
on the basis of one or the other of the three general sources
of truth, or even of all of them, it becomes our duty first
to submit the assumed truth to a careful examination. For
it may be found that it is based either on an imaginary
experience or on false reasoning. If, upon conscientious
revision, we still feel convinced that the Biblical word is
in conflict with experience or reason, then we are not only
entitled, but in duty bound, to interpret the Scriptural pas-

[458a] Regarding this important matter see Horovitz, *Die Psychologie,*
etc., pp. 48 f., and in Hermann Cohen's *Festschrift (Judaica),* p. 251.

sage in question allegorically, so as to bring it into harmony
with the accepted truth.[459]

The "Book of Doctrines and Beliefs," which is devoted
entirely to this work of harmonization between reason and
religion, thus assumes the character of philosophic her-
meneutics. There is hardly a single thought in the whole
book that is not viewed in the light of some Scriptural verse,
which either confirms or refutes it. Even for our recognition of the senses and of reason as bearers of truth we
get the authorization, as it were, from certain passages of the
Bible.[460] The teachings of the Bible, though named by
Saadia in the fourth place, are actually recognized by him
as the first and most reliable source of truth. Thus, at the
beginning of every paragraph in which some new point is
to be discussed, he quotes a verse or verses in which, according to his opinion, the teaching of the Bible in the matter
is clearly stated. Then the contrary opinions of various
thinkers are taken up and considered from all sides, and
finally it is proved that reason or experience or both come
to the support of the Biblical view. At the end of the paragraph additional verses are quoted and interpreted in a
way that makes them corroborate the original statement.
It is astounding with what ingenuity hundreds of verses
taken from all parts of Scripture, are made to bear on the
remotest ideas and most subtle philosophic questions.
Nearly thirteen hundred verses, approximately the number
of verses in the Book of Isaiah, are thus interpreted. It is

---

[459] See *Am.*, p. 83, bottom, *Em.*, pp. 44: ‏ובכלל אמר כל מה שימצא‎
‏בספרים ובדברינו אנחנו המיחדים מלישון בספור בוראנו או מעשיו‎
‏חולק על מה שמחיבו העיון האמתי בלי ספק שהוא דרך העברה מהלישון‎
"In general I say: any description of God or of His actions occurring in the Scriptures or in the words of others among us, the mono-
theists, which is found to contradict what is demanded by sound
reasoning, is undoubtedly a figure of speech." The same idea is
expressed with more detail, p. 212 (109); (comp. Guttmann, *Saadia*,
p. 221, n. 1), so also *Em.*, p. 133: ‏וכל פרוש מסכים למה שייש‎
‏בישכל הוא האמת וכל מה שכביא אל מה שהוא חולק בישכל הוא הבטל‎.
[460] *Am.*, p. 14, ll. 6 ff.; *Em.*, pp. 7 f.

obvious that this work is of great importance also for the history of philosophic exegesis.

While Saadia is so profuse in the use of the Bible, he refrains conspicuously from bringing into play the vast treasures of traditional literature. In the whole book there are only twenty-nine direct quotations from the Mishnah and both Talmudim. Nearly all of them occur in the eschatological chapters, which deal with specifically Jewish problems.[461] The reason for this procedure is in all probability to be looked for in the fact that the book was intended to carry conviction not only to the adherents of traditional Judaism, but even more to those who antagonized it, as the Karaites and other sectaries, whom the author so forcibly describes in the Introduction to the work. It should be noted, however, that many of Saadia's views, particularly in the eschatological chapters, are based entirely on passages in Talmud and Midrash, although he neither quotes nor refers to them.[462] For completeness' sake it may here be

[461] The same attitude toward the Talmud is observable in Saadia's Bible Commentaries, see Derenbourg, *MWJ.*, VII, 133. They too, like the *'Amânât*, were probably calculated to impress also those who did not believe in Jewish traditions; comp. notes 305, 470. In our work Saadia occasionally, as it were, excuses himself for not making more use of traditional literature, saying that the passages are so many that it would be impossible for him to discuss them; see *'Amânât*, chapter VII, in the edition of Bacher, Steinschneider-*Festschrift*, p. 109, top; *Emûnôt*, p. 114, further *'Am.*, p. 223, l. 5; *Em.*, p. 133. Aside from the 29 direct citations there are some instances in which Saadia merely states that the Rabbis expressed a certain view, without quoting a passage; see p. 175 (88), l. 14; 204 (102), ll. 15 f. (allusion to *b. 'Abôdah Zârâh, 20b*); see also the references above, note 324.

[462] The instances are too numerous to quote. For the sake of illustration I refer to *Am.*, p. 181, ll. 2-7, *Em.*, p. 91, ll. 2-5 (*Baba Kamma, 94b*) ; *Am.*, p. 214, ll. 7 ff., *Em.*, p. 114, ll. 4 ff. (*Synhedrin, 91b*) ; *Am.*, p. 278, *Em.*, p. 141 (*'Erûbin, 19a; Shabbat, 153a*) ; see also below, note 485. On the other hand Saadia at times tacitly opposes the Talmud, see *Am.*, p. 182 (91) the interpretation of *Exodus, 20, 12, Deuter., 22, 7*, as against *Kiddûshin, 39 b;* comp. below, notes 482, 518, 603.

added that he quotes once the Book of Sirach,[463] several
times the Targum Onkelos,[464] and once refers to three old
liturgical pieces [465] that are still recited on the Day of Atonement. Of his own works he mentions his commentaries on
Genesis, Exodus, Job, and on the *Sefer Yezirah*, and a
" Refutation of Hiwi of Balkh." [466] No names are mentioned
in the book, with the exception of those of Anan, the founder of Karaism (once), and of the Karaite Benjamin
Nahâwandi (twice).[467]

The foregoing characterization of Saadia's method in
the work under consideration brings out the fact that his
original purpose in composing it was not to create a new and
independent system of cosmic philosophy on the basis of
the many Greek and Muhammedan doctrines he consulted,
but to define the position of Judaism in the light of these
doctrines and to demonstrate that it rests on much firmer
ground than all other proposed solutions of the great world-
problems. In pursuing this aim Saadia could not afford to
bind himself to any of the existing philosophic systems in
its entirety, but had to adopt from each one those elements
which in his opinion were essential to Judaism and compatible
with his understanding thereof. Whether an idea originated
with Plato or Aristotle or in the mind of some Muhammedan
thinker was immaterial, so long as it could stand the test
of reason and experience, and was *ipso facto* consonant
with the teachings of the Bible. Saadia's method in this
work was thus that of an eclectic. This is not to be taken,
however, in the technical sense of the term. For he did not

---

[463] *Am.*, p. 301 (153) ; comp. Guttman, *Saadia*, p. 274, n. 3 ; below,
p. 252, no. 6, end.

[464] *Am.*, pp. 95, 178, 264 (50, 89, 134) ; comp. above, note 311.

[465] *Am.*, p. 179 (90) ; comp. Guttmann, *Saadia*, p. 187, n. 1, where
further references are given.

[466] Commentary on *Genesis: Am.*, pp. 20 (10), 37 (20), 84 (44) ;
on *Exodus:* p. 105 (54) ; on *Job:* p. 15 (8) ; on *Sefer Yezirah:*
p. 37 (20) ; *Polemic* against Hiwi: p. 37 (20).

[467] *Anan:* p. 190 (96) see below, p. 223; Benjamin: p. 201 (100)
see below, p. 227. On the same page he refers also to " Books (or
Book) of Anatomy," see above, note 454.

aim at eclecticism as such, but was concerned only in the interpretation and systematization of the Jewish religion. Any idea that lent itself to that purpose and helped to establish the religious truth was welcome material. However, the question whether or not Saadia should be designated as an eclectic is mere quibbling over words, since it is generally admitted that in his philosophic works he drew upon a variety of systems, which on the points in question, do not agree with one another. Saadia's merit in the field of philosophy is not to be sought in any originality of his as an inventor and propagator of new philosophic doctrines, but in the extraordinary skill with which he was able to bring a vast amount of foreign thought into subservience to the great religious *Weltanschauung*, which he was about to build up for the benefit of his people. For it is not always the original content of a thought that lends it particular value in the realm of human knowledge. As often, it is the new aspect under which an idea is conceived and the individual interpretation put upon it, that give it a special character and make it stimulative of fresh thought and new complexes of ideas. From this point of view Saadia is justly recognized as the creator of a new epoch in the history of the philosophy of religion. It was his " Book of Doctrines and Beliefs " that gave the impetus to the subsequent development of the whole of Jewish philosophic literature.

CONTENTS OF THE *Kitâb al-'Amânât*.[468]

A detailed presentation of the full content of this work, tempting as it is, cannot here be entered upon. Such an attempt would require a volume equal in size to Saadia's. Not even the full development of the main problems of the

---

[468] As the presentation of the content of the *'Amânât* generally follows the order of the original text, no references to the passages will be given, except in the case of direct quotations or in a few instances in which it seems advisable to point out a particular context. Parallel passages in the works of later Hebrew authors will also be referred to in exceptional instances only.

work, as the unity of God, free-will, immortality, and the
like, can be undertaken in the limits set to the present volume.
A brief summary of the more important topics treated of by
the author must suffice to convey to the reader an idea of the
substance and profundity of this work and its significance for
the history of the mediæval philosophy of the Jews and
partly for that of the whole scholastic world.

In the Introduction, beginning with the usual laudation
of God,[469] the author first states the causes which in his
opinion are responsible for all the error and confusion prevalent among the people. They are mainly ignorance and
superficiality. He then describes the sad conditions among
the people at large and especially among those of his own
race who, constantly wavering in their philosophic opinions
and religious beliefs, were unable to determine upon a definite
course. These circumstances led him to the composition of
this work which, he hoped, will prove a guide for the perplexed. " My heart grieved for mankind," [470] he writes,
" and my soul was moved on account of our own people
Israel, as I saw in our times many of those who adhere to
their faith entertain impure beliefs and unclear ideas, while
those who deny the faith boast of their unbelief and tri-
umphantly deride the men of truth, albeit they are themselves
in error. I saw men sunk, as it were, in a sea of doubt and
overwhelmed by the waves of confusion, and there was no
diver to bring them up from the depths and no swimmer to
come to their rescue. But as God has granted unto me some
knowledge by which I can be useful to them, and endowed
me with some ability which I might employ for their benefit,
I felt that to help them was my duty and guiding them aright
a moral obligation upon me." [471]

[469] See above, note 411.

[470] This declaration makes it probable that the book was intended
not only for Jews but also for Muhammedans; see above, note 461.

[471] *'Amânât*, pp. 4 f. (*Emunot*, p. 3) ; comp. Graetz, *History* (English), III, 197 f., and especially Horovitz, in Hermann Cohen's
Festschrift (*Judaica*), pp. 238 ff.

Saadia then takes up the question of why men are made subject to doubts and mistakes in their search after truth instead of being given immediate truth. The answer is, that immediate truth is only in the power of God, and for man to ask for it is tantamount to asking that he be made the equal of his Creator. Man being part of nature, his thinking must run through the whole scale of causes and effects, which requires time and patience.

The author is now prepared for the discussion of the four sources of knowledge, as described above. Much space is devoted to the demonstration of the manner in which the three natural sources of knowledge should be used in order to be assured of the correct results. Here, however, the question arises: If a man is capable of arriving at the truth by his own reasoning, what purpose was there in teaching him the same truth by religion? To this Saadia replies that the majority of men have not sufficient reasoning power to be relied upon, and even those who do possess it would have to go a long way before they could reach the truth through their unaided efforts.[472] In the meantime they would be without trustworthy guidance. Revealed religion was, therefore, an absolute necessity. It gave to the people, so to say, a ready-made truth, coming from God Himself, and provided them with a complete system of rules and regulations by which to govern their lives. This system has the advantage of affording a safe-conduct also to the uneducated, to women, and to those who by reason of youth or incapacity cannot avail themselves of philosophy. Adherence to religion does

[472] In the third chapter of the work Saadia takes up the same question in connection with prophecy and gives additional reasons for the necessity of religion. Everybody, Saadia argues, may recognize the idea of justice, and it would seem that no special messenger is needed to recommend it to our reason. However, it is not a question of the idea as such, but of the proper ways and modes in which it is to be carried into practice. For these you must have rules and regulations based on divine authority, so as to command the respect and the obedience of the people; comp. Guttmann, *Saadia*, 140 f. Judah Halevi adopted this view from Saadia, see *Kuzari*, I, 79; II, 56; III, 7; see also the following two notes.

not, however, free us from the duty of thinking for ourselves. On the contrary, only when we examine its teachings by the light of reason, can we grasp their true meaning and fulfill their demands."[72a]

Saadia has a peculiar fondness for numbers. In this book he often carries it to an extreme. Like a conscientious book-keeper he puts upon record the number of all the arguments and counter-arguments for and against a theory, keeps careful account of the points he has scored against his opponents, lays special emphasis on the number of theories about certain subjects and of the causes that produce such and such effects. Here, too, he winds up the Introduction by enumerating eight causes that lead to infidelity."[73]

(I) The first chapter, the longest in the book, deals with *creation*. After a brief characterization of the great difficulties this problem offers to the philosophic investigator, the author gives a full presentation of thirteen different theories concerning it. His own theory, which according to him is that of the Bible, he puts first—that the world was created by God *ex nihilo*. To support the Biblical doctrine he adduces four philosophic proofs, the principal elements of which are derived partly from the writings of Aristotle and partly from those of the Muhammedan philosophers known in literature under the collective designation of Mu'tazilites. The remaining twelve theories, which he refutes one after the other, are given anonymously, but they can all be traced with more or less certainty to their respective Greek, Arabic, and Persian authors.

[72a] All this reasoning was tacitly adopted by Maimonides (*Dalâlat*, I, 34) ; comp. Guttmann, in *Moses ben Maimon*, II, 208 ff.

[73] The same causes are enumerated by Maimonides, *l. c.*, who no doubt followed Saadia; see Guttmann, *l. c.*, p. 210, n. 2; above, notes 416, 446.—Guttmann, *Saadia*, p. 53, n. 1, has pointed out numerous passages of the work in which the same playing with numbers occurs. This mystic love for numbers seems to have made Saadia go to the trouble of figuring out that no less than 19,169 forms can be derived from every Hebrew verb! Comp. Geiger, *Jüdische Zeitschrift*, IV, 202; Bacher, *Anfänge*, p. 54; below, pp. 218, 312, and note 531.

In the arrangement of these theories Saadia reversed the order he had adopted for the enumeration of the nine theories of the world's creation in his Commentary on the *Sefer Yezirah*. There, as we have seen, he begins with the theory that he considers the most objectionable of the nine, namely, the doctrine of the Eternalists (*Dahriyya*), who, asserting that the world is eternal, deny creation altogether. He then proceeds according to the respective degrees of unacceptability from the least to the most probable, rejecting all theories until he reaches the last, which is his own.

In the *Kitâb al-'Amânât*, on the contrary, he states first his own view, which he bases on the Bible, and then arranges the following twelve theories on the principle of the least objectionable first, followed in turn by the others in the order of their probability."[*] The result is that the theory (a combination of atomism and Platonism) which in the Commentary on the *Sefer Yezirah* was rated as being next to the most unreasonable, appears here as next to the most reasonable. In both books it is put in the second place! The explanation lies in the fact that aside from the Biblical theory (*creatio ex nihilo*),which, as is to be expected, occupies first place in the one arrangement and last in the other, only two of the other eight theories discussed in the *Sefer Yezirah* are taken up also in the *Kitâb al-'Amânât*. For the six theories in the former work, ten entirely different ones are given in the latter. According to the standard set up by the author for the valuation of the various theories, it is proper that one which in comparison to the others treated in the same book should be considered as coming near the worst, is recognized as being close to the best of those treated in the other book. The same standard

---

[*] This is not a mere conjecture, but is indicated clearly enough by Saadia himself, who at the beginning of each refuted theory repeats the stereotyped phrase, "and the adherents of this theory are still more ignorant than those of the preceding theory" (*e. g. Am.*, p. 49, l. 4: והאולאי אגֹהל מן אלאולין). This remark is missing only at the beginning of the eighth theory, probably by oversight.

required that the theory of the theory of the Eternalists, the first in the Commentary, be put tenth in the present work.

The principles upon which Saadia built up his standard for the valuation of the theories cannot be set forth here. It would involve a detailed presentation of all his arguments against the theories themselves, which space forbids.[475] But it has been necessary to present the facts, since they have been heretofore overlooked. It should also be pointed out in particular that the doctrine of the author of the *Sefer Yeẓirah*, for the elucidation of which Saadia had composed his Commentary on that work, is entirely disregarded in his present enumeration of the theories on creation. This is not to be interpreted, however, with a recent writer, as a proof that Saadia " did not take that doctrine seriously enough to include it among the theories historically authenticated." [476] Though he did not identify himself with the doctrine of the *Sefer Yeẓirah*, he certainly considered it more acceptable than any of those here rejected. Its omission is due to the fact that in this work he deals with the one theory which in his opinion was positively true and with those which were positively wrong. The theory of the *Sefer Yeẓirah*, on the other hand, was recognized as tolerable, by way of a special exegesis which brought it essentially into harmony with the true Biblical theory. Thus, it was covered in the exposition of the Biblical theory, making further discussion of it superfluous. Moreover, the Commentary is referred to by Saadia in another passage in this first chapter of the *Kitâb al-'Amânât*.[477]

(II) The discussions contained in the first chapter led to the conclusion that the world was created. Hence there must

[475] On the whole see Guttmann, *Saadia*, pp. 33-75, which is so far the clearest presentation of the subject. Various points in Guttmann's presentation were severely criticized by D. Neumark, *Geschichte der jüdischen Philosophie des Mittelalters*, Berlin, 1907, pp. 460-469. As to his identification of the tenth theory with that of Aristotle (p. 468), see Horovitz as quoted above, note 412a.

[476] Guttmann, *Saadia*, p. 26.

[477] See above, note 466.

be a Creator. The next task was to define the essence and
nature of the Creator, thus logically demonstrated. This is
the object of the second chapter, which bears the heading
" Chapter of Unity." At the outset Saadia tries to meet the
objection of those who deny the existence of God because He
is not perceptible by the senses, the most reliable source of
our knowledge. It is true, he says, that human knowledge
originates in mere sense impressions, but we all know that it
never stops there. From the most ordinary sense experiences
which we have in common with the animals we proceed by
degrees to higher and more abstract thoughts, and the
farther we advance in our upward course, the more subtle
become our ideas and concepts. This onward movement of
our mind does not mean that we are losing ground in our
search after truth. On the contrary, with every step forward the original truth derived from experience becomes
more general and comprehensive, embracing a multitude of
realities. In spite of incidental deviations from the straight
course in our intellectual pilgrimage to the source of ultimate truth, we are constantly approaching nearer to the desired goal. There is, however, a natural limit to such intellectual progress. Man being finite, his thinking capacity must
be limited. A point is reached at which the ideas become so
subtle and abstract that they are beyond man's grasp. The
God-idea is of the utmost subtlety, and hence past human
comprehension. But, as we have seen, the finer and subtler
an idea is, the more truth and reality it is bound to contain.
The transcending subtlety of the God-idea is therefore in itself an irrefutable proof of its verity. God is the necessary
postulate of our reason, the ultimate truth, *the sum total
of all reality.* To demand that He be perceptible by the
senses is a retrogression from the higher stages of comprehension to the lower stages of animal sense-perception.
Indeed, a perceivable, corporeal God is a contradiction in
itself. What we are looking for is an extra-mundane cause
of all existence, which necessarily transcends the category
of bodies.

After these preliminary remarks, Saadia refutes some
other erroneous ideas about God that had come to his knowledge, and then turns to the discussion of the main subject, the
unity and uniqueness of God, involving the very important
question of the Divine attributes.[475] The author adduces
numerous verses from the Scriptures which describe God
as *One,* excluding all plurality or diversity from His
nature; as *Unique,* excluding the existence of any other
God besides Him; and as *living, omnipotent,* and *omniscient.*
The Scriptural testimony to the oneness of God is substantiated by three positive proofs based upon reason. These
are followed by a controversy against the doctrine of dual-
ism. The arguments against this doctrine serve indirectly as
further proofs for the doctrine of unity. In the ensuing
paragraph the other three essential attributes of God are
taken up for detailed discussion. Special emphasis is laid on
the demonstration that life, omnipotence, and omniscience
do not constitute a plurality in God's essence. They merely
designate this essence in accordance with the aspect under
which it is viewed. The idea of a Creator necessarily implies
life, power, and knowledge. In explicating these attributes
we add nothing to His essence. They are enumerated
separately by reason of a shortcoming of language, which
possesses no single term to convey all of them at once.
At this point Saadia enters upon a lengthy controversy
against the Christian doctrine of the Trinity, showing that
it originated from a misinterpretation of the same three
essential attributes of God. In connection therewith he
discusses and refutes the various theories regarding the
person of Jesus, evidencing his thorough acquaintance with
Christian polemics on this point.

Having established the idea of God's absolute unity,
Saadia devotes several pages to another important matter

[475] For a detailed discussion of this subject see Kaufmann, *Geschichte der Attributenlehre in der judischen Religionsphilosophie des
Mittelalters,* Gotha, 1877, pp 1-77, Neumark, *Geschichte,* II, Berlin,
1910, an exhaustive study, to which the entire volume is devoted,
comp Guttmann, *Saadia,* pp. 90 ff.

with direct bearing on the problem under consideration. Numerous passages in the Bible speak of God in terms clearly implying corporeity. Strictly taken, they contradict the idea of a spiritual unity. They depict God as equipped with human organs—as hands, eyes, ears—and possessed of the qualities, affections, and emotions characteristic of human beings. Saadia classifies these anthropomorphic terms under the ten Aristotelian categories, and shows that, as none of these categories is applicable to God, so none of the terms falling under them can be literally applied to Him. By numerous quotations from the Bible he proves that in the ordinary use of the Hebrew language all such terms have, besides their literal meaning, a figurative sense. Whenever they are used of God, therefore, they must be taken in the latter significance; that is, as figures of speech.

In a concluding paragraph Saadia describes, in a highly poetical manner and with deep religious emotion, the state of happiness and peace of mind that falls to the lot of him who has attained to a true conception of God, and is permeated by the firm belief in His love and benevolence toward mankind. There is a rhythm in the evenly-balanced sentences of this paragraph, and a religious fervor that cannot fail to impress even the modern reader, despite his widely divergent mode of thought.

(III) The investigation, so far, has brought to light the facts that the world was created and that its Creator is *indivisible, unique, incorporeal.* The question which now forces itself upon our mind is the purpose of the Creator in forming His world. To the solution of this question Saadia accordingly devotes the third chapter of his work, bearing the title "Command and Prohibition." Unhesitatingly he declares at the very beginning of the discussion that creation was an act of grace on the part of the Creator, who desired to make His creatures happy. To assure their happiness He gave them a code of laws, injunctions and prohibitions, by obedience to which they would realize His purpose, that is, to be happy. Here we are confronted with the difficulty, that God could have granted happiness without impos-

ing the burden of the law upon mankind. To this objection
Saadia replies that nothing whatsoever will give man perfect
happiness unless he feels that he has a right to what he possesses, that somehow or other he has personally merited it.
Wherever this consciousness is lacking, he will not enjoy
happiness completely. To enable us to be perfectly happy
with the material and spiritual blessings God intended for
us, He enjoined upon us numerous laws and ordinances, the
observance of which requires great sacrifice and much self-
restraint on our part, thus giving us a chance to acquire,
through our own efforts, the ultimate state of perfect happiness in store for us.

These introductory remarks on the purpose of the divine
law lead the author to a general characterization of the latter
and its educational value for humanity. He divides the Biblical laws into two main classes, those dictated by human
reason ('akliyyât = שכליות), and those which have their
origin in divine revelation (sam'iyyât = שמעיות)—a distinction adopted by Saadia from Muhammedan literature and
later accepted by Jewish mediæval philosophers.[49] Saadia
endeavors to prove that even the laws based on revelation,
though we cannot always recognize their *raison d'être*, are
by no means irrational, and have, besides, a moral discip-
linary value, inasmuch as they train us in submission to a
higher will.

In connection with the idea of revelation Saadia discusses
the subject of prophecy, its credibility, and its necessity for
the people; divides the essential content of Scriptures into
three branches, the narrative, the legal, and the prophetic;
and tries to prove their historical trustworthiness from the

---

[49] Maimonides (*Eight Chapters*, ch. 6), however, strongly opposed
this classification of the law, which is to be found also in Saadia's
Introduction to the Commentary on Proverbs; comp. Steinschneider,
CB., 2165; see for the literature on the subject the references given
by Joseph I. Gorfinkle, in his scholarly study *The Eight Chapters of
Maimonides on Ethics*, New York, 1912, p. 77, n. 3; comp. also
Steinschneider, *HB.*, X, 173; Goldziher, *Kitâb ma'âni al-nafs*, Berlin,
1907. pp. 22 ff.; Guttmann, *Saadia*, p. 135, n. 2; *Festschrift* of Isr.
Lewy, p. 315, n. 6 (*Moses ben Maimon*, II, 206, n. 3).

viewpoint of reason. The object of the lengthy discussion
was in all probability the refutation of the doctrine of a
Hindu sect, who denied the need of prophecy, and whom
Saadia mentions further on in the same chapter under the
name of Barâhima (Brahmans)—by the way, the only sect
mentioned by name in his work.

The defense of the Bible as a reliable historical record suggested another important problem for immediate treatment,
the question whether the Biblical dispensation was given for
all time, or was to be abrogated at some subsequent period
and replaced by another dispensation. The matter was much
in dispute among Jews, Christians, and Muhammedans
alike.[480] The adherents of Christianity and Islam maintained,
on the basis of numerous passages in the Bible as well as
general reasons, that the original law was, from the very
first, intended only for a limited time, and was to be replaced
by their respective systems of religion. Saadia refutes their
arguments. He shows that they have misinterpreted the
Biblical passages adduced by them. One of these refuted
arguments may here be briefly reproduced. There is no
cogent reason, the opponents say, why we should be bound
to believe in Moses because of the miracles he performed
more than in other prophets (Jesus and Muhammed,
respectively) who performed similar miracles. Saadia declares that when he first heard this argument, he was greatly
surprised, for our belief in the prophecy of Moses is not due
merely to his performance of miracles. It is based on the
intrinsic ethical value of the message he carried.[481] For
that matter we believe in any prophet who brings us a similarly acceptable message. The miracles are but a secondary matter. If a miracle-worker, claiming prophetic inspiration, asks us to accept what our reason considers posi-

[480] For the literature see Steinschneider, *Polemische und apologetische Literatur*, pp. 322 f.

[481] This view is actually taken up again by the most recent Jewish
scholars on the subject; see for instance Max Wiener, *Zur Geschichte
des Offenbarungsbegriffs*, in the Hermann Cohen-*Festschrift* (*Judaica*), pp. 12, 16, 18.

14

tively wrong (such as the Christian dogmas of the Trinity, Incarnation, etc.), we refuse to heed his miracles. No miracle can evidence the truth of that which is inherently untrue. Saadia illustrates the point by the example of two different sorts of claims laid before a court by a litigant. If one should sue a man for the sum of thousands of denarii, the court will hear the witnesses summoned to testify to the rightness of his claim, but if his contention be that the defendant owes him the Tigris, the court will at once dismiss the case as nonsensical, without the hearing of any testimony

In the last portion of this chapter Saadia defends the authority of the Bible against the attacks made upon it by the Jewish heretic Ḥiwi of Balkh, who, however, is not mentioned by name in this connection. Of the many objections of Ḥiwi to the Bible, said to have numbered two hundred, Saadia selects twelve for refutation.[482] In all proba-

---

[482] One of the twelve points refuted by Saadia (the fourth, *Am*, p. 141, *Em*, p. 72) deserves special notice here. The opponent is quoted as objecting to the Biblical institution of sacrifices on the ground that sacrifices are the cause of great cruelty to animals. Saadia replies: " God has decreed death upon all living beings. In the case of man death comes naturally at the expiration of the time-limit God sets to his existence. But in the case of animals any moment when they are taken to be killed is the time-limit set to their existence With them the killing takes the place of natural death. Should it be true that killing causes more suffering to the animal than a natural death, then God certainly knows it. Justice would require that He reward the animal after death in proportion to the additional suffering inflicted upon it. We accept this view— provided the additional suffering is made plausible—because reason demands it, not because it is prescribed by the revealed law." This strange theory of a reward to animals in the hereafter, adopted by Saadia from the Mu'tazilites, is not in keeping with rabbinical teachings (comp מסכת כלה, ed. Coronel, ch. 2, p 4 בהמה לשחיטה עומדת ואין לה חלק לעוה"ב, and *Kohelet rabba*, 3, 18: מה הבהמה נדונת בחריגה ואין לה חלק לעוה"ב כך הרשעים וכו', comp. Jellinek, בהמ''ד, I, 151, bottom) and is another instance of Saadia's disagreement with some Talmudic traditions (see above, note 462, and especially below, note 518). The theory was accepted also by some other Geonim (comp תשובות הגאונים,

bility the whole paragraph is reproduced by Saadia from his polemical work against this heretic (quoted above, p. 198) under the title "Refutation of Ḥiwi of Balkh," which will be considered under *Polemics*.

(IV) Human happiness—so Saadia had sought to prove— was the ultimate purpose of God in creating the world, and the law was shown to have been handed down as a means to that happiness.[433] This doctrine can be accepted only on the supposition that man is perfectly free in his actions, so that whatever he does, good or evil, may be set to the account of his own deliberate choice. Otherwise, *i. e.*, if man's actions are predetermined by his physical nature, or—what is meant by our author—by the higher will of God, they would count for nothing, and he should receive neither reward nor punishment for his obedience or disobedience of the divine law. We thus encounter the perplexing problem of free will, that has troubled the philosophers of all nations in bygone ages, and fills the pages of many a philosophic work of our own day. To its solution Saadia devotes the main part of his fourth chapter, which bears the title "Obedience and Disobedience."

As is to be expected, his theory, for which numerous verses of the Bible are quoted, is that men are free agents and therefore fully responsible for their actions. But before entering

---

ed. Harkavy, p. 190, no. 375; see also *ib.*, p. 373), who were, without naming, opposed by Maimonides, *Moreh*, III, 17; comp. also his Commentary on the Mishnah, *Baba Ḳamma*, 4, 3, and Ibn Ṣaddiḳ, עולם קטן, ed Horovitz, pp. 60, 72. In particular the Ḳaraites, who generally followed the theology of the Mu'tazilites, favored this view; see Munk, *Guide*, III, 128, n. 4, whose assertion "dans les écrits de Saadia, nous n'en trouvons aucune trace" is due to oversight of the passage in Saadia's *'Amânât* quoted above; comp. Kaufmann, *Attributenlehre*, p. 503; Steinschneider, *Polemische und apologetische Literatur*, pp. 337, 356, top; *Hebräische Uebersetzungen*, p. 438. n. 481; Gutmann in Isr. Lewy's *Festschrift*, pp. 313 ff. (*Mos. b. Maim.*, II, 204); Malter, *JQR.*, *N. S.*, vol. IX (1918-1919), p. 239. For details regarding the other objections of Ḥiwi see Guttmann, *MGWJ.*, 1879, pp. 260-270, 289-300; Graetz, *Geschichte* (4), V, 533-535 (end of *Note* 20; *JE.*, VI, 429 f., X, 582, no. 6; comp. also below, *Bibliography*, section VI. pp. 384 ff.

[433] Comp. Maimonides, *Guide*, III, 27.

upon the subject proper, he raises the question as to what constitutes the most important part and the real object of creation. An examination of nature reveals that the most essential
part of any organic body is placed in its center. The kernel,
which is indispensable for the generation of the plant, is in
the middle of the fruit ; the yelk, in which the chick develops
to life, is the center of the egg ; the heart, as the seat of vitality, is likewise in the center of the body. If, then, we
find that the earth, too, is in the center of the universe, sur-
rounded by the celestial spheres, we may safely conclude
by analogy that it [484] is the most important part of all creation.
Now, if we turn to the inhabitants of the earth, we shall
certainly recognize human beings as the superiors of
all. Hence it is man that is the ultimate aim of the whole
cosmic plan. This view is fully in keeping with the fact that
God created man last, " just as the architect, who erects a
palace, furnishes it, puts everything in order, and then invites the owner to its occupation " [485]

[484] Landauer, who usually follows the Oxford recension of the
Arabic text, here (*'Amânât*, p 146, l. 11) made an exception, choos-
ing instead the reading of the St. Petersburg recension, followed also
by Ibn Tibbon (p 75: הַמָּכוֹן בבריאה הוא בָּאָרֶץ), according to
which Saadia intended to say that "the purpose of creation is *on*
earth" (Arabic הי פי אלארץ). This reading, however, is wrong,
as is evident from the following text, and the Arabic preposition פִּי,
though attested also by Ibn Tibbon, is probably a corrupt repetition
of the immediately preceding הִי.

[485] *Am.*, p 146, l. 16 (*Em* p 75), based on a passage in *b. Synhedrin*,
38a. The view here proposed by Saadia, that man is the final purpose
of creation, hence superior to all celestial hosts, the angels and stars,
which are created for man's service only, found many opponents in
the ranks of mediæval Jewish authors. The subject is too large to
be treated in a note A few references will lead to the literature in
question Among the distinguished authors who disagreed with the
Gaon in this matter are Hananel of Kairwân (1050) (see Rapoport,
Bikkûrē ha-'Ittim, XII, 24, end of note 15); Abraham Ibn Ezra
(*Commentary* on *Genesis*, 1, 2; *Short Commentary* on *Exodus*,
23, 20), who is extremely severe against the Gaon on this point
(comp Reggio and Luzzatto, *Kerem Chemed*, IV, 104-108, 136 f.;
Mortara, *Ozar Nechmad*, II, 209, M Friedlaender, *Essays on the
Writings of Abraham Ibn Ezra*, p. 115, n. 1), Maimonides (*Guide*,

Here we must ask ourselves: Wherein consists man's particular importance, that he should be thus distinguished and
recognized as the crown of all creation? In nothing else, we
reply, than in his being endowed with reason, with that
divine soul which, in the words of the Psalmist, makes him
but "a little less than God himself." At this point Saadia
waxes enthusiastic in depicting the excellence of human
reason and the great things man is able to accomplish
through his reason. "With his reason man embraces the
past and the future; by it he subdues the animals, that they
till the ground and carry in its produce; by it he is able to
draw the water out of the depth of the earth to its surface,
nay, by it he even invents hydraulic implements that pump
the water automatically; by it he builds lofty palaces, makes
magnificent garments, and prepares dainty dishes; by it

III, 13; Munk, pp. 95 f.), and his numerous followers down to the
end of the fifteenth century, e. g. Jedaiah Bedersi (בחינת עולם)
chapter 12; comp. Schorr, *Kerem Chemed*, VIII, 204), and his
commentator Moses Ibn Ḥabib (about 1500), who in his commentary
on the latter work (Ferrara, 1552), 61a, speaks with little respect of
the Gaon and expresses his great satisfaction with Ibn Ezra's
thorough refutation of his theory (ויותר מגונה מזה הוא דעת מי)
שחושב כי האדם יותר נכבד מן המלאכים כאשר חשב רבנו סעדיה
בספר האמונות והדעות בתחלת המאמר הר' וחשב שהביא ראיות
על זה להורות כי המכוון בכל הנבראים הוא האדם וכבר סתר דעתו
הראב"ע בפרוש התורה והפיל כל ראיותיו ארצה בפרשת ואלה
המשפטים).
Ibn Ḥabib, it may be noted in passing, shows very little
appreciation of the whole book *Emūnōt;* see his remark at the end
of the commentary, 122b: לא הגיע אלינו ספר מחובר באמונה מן
הגאונים זולת ספר האמונות לרבנו סעדיה ואיננו מספיק אחת מני
אלה למה שכלל בו הרב המזרה. While Maimonides's *Guide*, as a
philosophic work, is, no doubt, superior to Saadia's *Emūnōt,* Ḥabib's
statement nevertheless contains a gross exaggeration; comp. also
below, note 607. Saadia's view is in keeping with that prevailing in
traditional literature (see e. g. b. *Berakōt, 32b; Ḥullin, 91b,* bottom),
hence it was upheld by the more orthodox mediæval Jewish authors.
among them Baḥya b. Asher (comp. Bernstein, *MWJ.,* XVIII, 172,
n. 32). For further material see Geiger החלוץ, II, 20; Luzzatto, כוכבי
יצחק, V, 33; D. Kohn (Kahana), תולדות הראב"ע, pp. 51, 86;
Halberstam, in his notes on פס"י of Judah b. Barzillai, p. 307;
Schmiedl, *Studien,* pp. 83-85; comp. also below, note 508.

he leads armies, equips military camps, and manages the affairs of state, so that men become civilized and orderly; by it he learns the nature of the celestial spheres, the course of the planets, the size of their bodies, their distances from one another, as well as other astronomical matters."

"In view of all this it is only natural that man should have been commissioned with carrying out God's law, be rewarded for its keeping and punished for its transgression, for he is the axis of the world and its foundation (*kuṭb al-ʿālami wa-ḳâʿida-tuhu*, Ibn Tibbon: קטב העולם ומכנתו)."

"This belief of ours in man's superiority is not merely an imagination, or the result of our desire to exaggerate our importance, nor is it out of boastfulness or arrogance that we make such claims, but it is positively true and perfectly legitimate. Why, then, should God have equipped man with that supreme power of reason that makes him the master of all creation? For no other purpose than to make him the beneficiary of the law (through which, as explained in the preceding chapter, he is to attain to happiness), as it is said in Scripture (Job, 28, 28): And He said unto man, Behold, that thou mayest fear the Lord, was wisdom bestowed upon thee, and understanding, that thou mayest depart from evil." [456]

Following these introductory remarks Saadia tries to meet eight [457] objections that might be raised against his views. One might ask, for instance, how is it possible, considering his physical smallness and insignificance, to assume that man is the purpose of creation? The answer is, that "though his body be small, his soul is larger than heaven and earth, for through it he reaches even what is above them and the cause of them, the Creator Himself." The short duration of man's life on earth is contrasted with his eternal

---

[456] *'Amânât*, p. 147 (76). All this is ridiculed by Abraham Ibn Ezra, in the passages referred to in the preceding note. For Saadia's interpretation of the verse here quoted comp. above, note 418.

[457] Saadia says *seven* (*Am.*, p. 150, l. 14; *Em.*, p. 77), but actually counts *eight*. Similar mistakes in counting happen to him several times in this book; comp. notes 526, 528.

life hereafter, the latter being a compensation for the former. The frailty of the human body, its composition of the four humors and consequent impurity, are declared to be the necessary result of man's being part of this earthly world of the four elements. To demand that man be otherwise, that is, simple and eternal, is tantamount to asking that he be made a star or an angel, or that, for example, the earth should be fire, which contradicts all logic. Man, such as he is and should be, is the finest organism possible on earth. As to his being subject to diseases and accident, the author finds that they are for man's good, since they make him pray to God for relief and teach him to fear punishment. It is also true that man's life is often imperiled by his passions. These, too, are necessary for his own preservation. Without desire for food, sexual intercourse, and the like, he could not exist. His task is to control these passions and to use them in a proper, permissible way. That a human being should at times be put to death for the commission of crimes is likewise fully justified. Reason demands that a degenerate individual, who endangers the life of others, be destroyed for the safety of the rest of mankind, just as it is sometimes necessary to cut off a diseased limb in order to save the rest of the body.

Having thus demonstrated God's justice and benevolence toward man, the author feels prepared for the discussion of the main subject, the freedom of the will. It was one of God's benevolent acts toward men, he declares, that He granted them freedom of will, by which they can determine for themselves the course they are to follow, thus working out their own salvation. That we actually possess free will the author proves by Scriptural verses and lengthy philosophic arguments, which cannot here be reproduced. The main difficulty in the way of this assumption is its apparent incompatibility with the idea of God's omniscience. If God knows in advance how man is going to act in a certain instance, as the idea of prescience requires, man is evidently bound to act in accordance therewith, else God's prescience would be nullified. We are thus compelled to

sacrifice either God's foreknowledge or man's independence
of decision—a dilemma which baffled the minds of all the
philosophers of the Middle Ages. Saadia tries to do away
with the difficulty by declaring that God's knowledge of
what will occur does not necessitate its actual coming into
existence. Man is therefore free to do as he pleases. Moreover, God's knowledge always extends to man's ultimate
decision, whatever this may be, so that there can be no contradiction between the two. This is about as satisfactory
a disposition of the question as the hitching of two horses to a
wagon, each one pulling in a different direction, and thus
neither one bringing the load forward. Later philosophers,[43] indeed, refused to accept this solution, but Saadia
himself does not seem to have suspected the inadequacy of
his arguments.

The idea of God's prescience causes a number of other
difficulties. They are taken up by Saadia, one by one, and
if we accept the author's premises, they are successfully explained. A closing paragraph is devoted to the interpretation of numerous Biblical passages which appear to emphasize the fact of God's interference with man's will, depriv-
ing him of the power of self-determination. Saadia classifies the respective passages, to which, he says, many more
can be added from the Bible, under eight general headings,
and tries to show that in each case the difficulty arises only
through a misunderstanding of the true meaning.

(V) Man is a free agent, the law was given to him for
his benefit, and it is for him to follow it. This is the net
result of the investigation so far. But what if we are over-
come by doubts and misgivings as to the value and useful-
ness of the law for us? What if a given law contains
nothing that appeals to our reason and recommends it for
acceptance? What if, as experience often shows, those
who conscientiously obey the law live in poverty and distress, while those who disregard it are prosperous and
happy? These and similar questions the author proposes to

[43] See Guttmann, Saadia, p. 170, n. 1.

treat in the fifth chapter, called " Merits and Demerits."
As usual he opens the discussion by quoting verses from the
Bible, which, in his opinion, enlighten us on the subject.
" Repeated acts of obedience to the law are designated in
the Bible as merits, while acts of disobedience are called
demerits, and both, we are told, are put to man's credit or
discredit. We are further informed that the deeds of a man
leave an impress on his soul, either ennobling or debasing
it, and although this escapes the knowledge of men it is
patent to God." [489] These sentences, based on Scriptural
verses, are the key to the solution of all the questions raised.

In a lengthy paragraph the author proceeds to show the
correctness of the Biblical ideas from the point of view of
reason. We should not always be ready to deny the importance of a thing merely because we are ignorant of its use-
fulness. There are hundreds of things even in the material
world the value of which is not known to the majority of
us, but only to a few experts. It is only the numismatist who
can distinguish between valuable and worthless coins, the
physician who understands how to diagnosticate the nature
of a disease, and the jeweller who can tell the difference
between the various kinds of precious stones. The same
applies to every art and science. Inaccessible to the multitude, they are known to the few initiated in the secrets.
If this be the case with things material, how much truer
must it be when we deal with things spiritual. The soul
is admittedly the most spiritual entity under human observation. What wonder that we have no knowledge as to the
effect certain practices and customs of ours may have on it.
We cannot tell the influence on our soul or character that
is exercised by the observance of ceremonies, the dietary
laws, and the like. We must assume that God, the Creator
of our soul, knows the benefits that accrue to it from law-
ful acts and the harm that it suffers if we go counter to
His ordinances. It is therefore best for us to carry out God's
commands to the letter. The reward is certain to follow.

[489] *'Amânât*, p. 165 (84), beginning of the chapter.

The general ideas of merit and demerit having thus been
made clear, the author divides all men into ten classes, according to the degree in which these two aspects of human
life manifest themselves in their religious conduct   The
division seems to be, in part, rather arbitrary and due to the
author's fondness for numbers, though he founds it on
Talmudic passages. The first two classes are pious and impious men. In order to be recognized as pious, it is not necessary that man should have only merits to his account. It is
sufficient that his meritorious deeds or good qualities should
preponderate over his bad ones   Such a man is designated
in Scripture as pious, as we call a man healthy if he is in a
generally good physical condition, though his health may not
be absolutely perfect. The same holds good also with
regard to the impious person   He may possess a number of
commendable qualities, but he is to be judged according to
the evil traits dominant in his character. The status of men
in the world to come depends upon the major number of their
actions. For the minority, good or bad, men are rewarded or
punished in this world.[489a]

With these statements, derived from the Talmud, Saadia
prepares for the answer to the important question, formu-
lated above, why the righteous are so often subject to suffering and affliction, while the wicked enjoy well-being and
happiness—a question repeated again and again in the
Bible[490] and the puzzle of the theologians of all creeds.
Men being judged according to the nature of the majority
of their deeds, Saadia says, the pious are destined to eternal
bliss in the hereafter, while the impious are doomed to lasting infelicity. Each of the two classes, however, has to be
rewarded or punished also for those deeds, good or evil,
which are in the minority, and as this is to take place in this
world, it results therefrom that the righteous suffer and the
wicked prosper   It may happen, however, that the righteous
or the wicked change their respective courses, or by a certain action invalidate their past records. In this case their

---

[489a] This is the teaching of R 'Akiba. *Bereshit rabba,* ch 33, 1
[490] Thus Jeremiah, 12, 1, comp *b Berakot,* 7a

status in this world has to be reversed. As most of the actions of our fellow-men and their inner motives are beyond our control, we can never account for their standing in life, and are therefore often inclined to doubt the justice of the distribution of worldly blessings. It also happens that the righteous are afflicted merely because God knows that they will stand the test and remain faithful and submissive, as was exemplified by Job. This is of great educational value for others. The firmness and steadfastness of the righteous man serve them as a model in similar situations; while he who has thus been tried is compensated in the future world for his undeserved sufferings. The sufferings of innocent children, too, can only be explained by assuming that they are to be rewarded therefor in the world to come.[490a]

For the prosperity of the wicked there are additional reasons, of which Saadia suggests six: among them, that transgressors are sometimes spared because they are to be used as instruments for the punishment of others, or because they are sure to repent and reform at some future time, as in the instances of king Manasseh and others.

Saadia now turns to the other eight classes of men, which he briefly characterizes in accordance with Talmudic passages. To these he adds a special class, consisting of men whose good and evil deeds balance each other. In connection with the tenth class, that of penitents, he gives a definition of true repentance, points out seven instances in which prayer for forgiveness is not accepted,[491] three kinds of sins which

---

[490a] This question of the suffering of children has been touched upon also by Plato (*Republic*, X, 615). Saadia reverts to it twice in the following; see below, notes 511a, 525a.

[491] The source of this enumeration is probably a Baraita in the tractate דרך ארץ in the recension of the מהזור ויטרי, p. 725, where, however, not seven, but *ten*, mostly different instances are enumerated. Saadia must have had a different recension of the Baraita. He in turn was the source of Judah he-Ḥasid, ספר חסידים, § 612 (ed. Berlin, § 36) and of Eleazar of Worms (רקח, § 28, repeated in § 216; comp. also § 29), who added two points to the seven of Saadia; comp. Friedmann, נספחים לסדר אליהו זוטא, Vienna, 1904, p. 9, who overlooked Saadia as the source of Judah and Eleazar. Both Judah and Eleazar follow the text of the Paraphrase as against that of

cannot be forgiven although the sinner has repented (seduc-
ing others to iniquity, calumniating, and robbing without
readiness to restore the goods),[402] four sins for which punishment is meted out in this world (false oath, murder, adultery,
and bearing false witness), and finally three virtues, which
are recompensed in this life. These are: honoring father and
mother, compassion with animals, and perfect honesty in
one's dealings. All these statements are supported by verses
from the Bible.[403]

A paragraph is devoted to the description of the relative
value of the moral or immoral conduct of an individual
under given circumstances. For instance, the virtue of
temperance is to be more appreciated in a young person
than in the old, while licentiousness is more contemptible
when found among the latter; giving aid to an enemy is
one of the higher virtues, and injuring a friend reveals
special viciousness; modesty on the part of a great man is
particularly praiseworthy, while the pride of the plebeian is
particularly detestable; cheating the poor, or the learned or
other public benefactors is objectionable to a high degree;
robbing a multitude of people is an aggravated crime (exacting a thousand denarii from a thousand men is worse than
exacting the same sum from half the number), while on the
other hand charitableness and uprightness on the part of the
poor are of special credit to them. Here again each statement is proved by a Biblical verse.

The last portion of this chapter speaks of sins in thought
and sins committed out of ignorance, thoughtlessness, or
under the stress of circumstances. Evil thoughts are not

Ibn Tibbon; comp. Bibliography, p. 362, no. 1. The passage
was made use of also by the moralist Judah Ḥaláz of Tlemçen,
Algeria (1490), in his ספר המוסר (Mantua, 1560), fol. 30a, without
mentioning the source; see note 403; Bibliography, p. 368, top.

[402] Comp. Baba Ḳamma, 94b; the passage was made use of by
Abraham b. Ḥiyya, הגיון הנפש, Leipzig, 1960, pp. 28, 32.

[403] Saadia adds here a description of five classes of penitents, one
higher than the other. This is again given anonymously by Judah
Ḥaláz (see note 401) fol. 19b, who adds a sixth class.

punishable, except those denying the existence of God; for belief and unbelief depend entirely upon one's thoughts.[494] Among evil thoughts Saadia counts the misinterpretation of Scriptures that leads to false conceptions of God, and the like.[495] A judge who misconstrues the law and punishes the people to serve his own purposes [496] " is destroying his own life." Ignorance of the law is no excuse for unlawful actions, nor is drunkenness. The sufferings of those who are afflicted with illness, or of Israelites who are oppressed by their enemies, do not justify them in uttering complaints against God; they ought to endure and hope for God's mercy. All this is borne out by verses from Scripture and partly also by passages from the Talmud. Saadia concludes with the remark that it would lead him too far to gather all the material pertaining to the subject, but that he has selected the most obvious points, which, he hopes, will prove beneficial in stirring up the people to their religious duties.

(VI) The entire system of Saadia's philosophy, as presented in the preceding chapters, has the immortality of the soul as its necessary postulate. The misery and wretchedness prevailing in the world, the brevity and uncertainty of our lives, the injustice and iniquity so overwhelmingly present in all human affairs—all this is out of harmony with the proposed view that man is the culminating point of creation and points unmistakably to the existence of another world, where all evil is turned into good, and all wrong made right. The inhabitants of that world are the departed immortal souls. It thus becomes a matter of prime importance to probe into the nature of the human soul and define its essence. Incidentally the phenomenon of death is to be discussed, and a few suggestions made regarding the mysteries of the future

[494] Comp. Maimonides, *Eight Chapters*, II ; הלכות עכו"ם, II, 3, 6; Malter, *JQR., N. S.*, vol. I (1910-1911), p. 485, n. 90, where additional references will be found.

[495] This is probably an allusion to the biblical critic Ḥiwi al-Balḥi, see below, pp. 267 f.

[496] Here no doubt the Exilarch David b. Zakkai is alluded to ; comp. above, note 262.

life. The sixth chapter is accordingly entitled "On the
Essence of the Soul, on Death, and What follows it."[401]

At the outset Saadia briefly announces his theory: God
creates the soul, which takes its seat in the heart at the
moment the body is completed. He sets a time-limit to the
combined existence of body and soul, at the expiration of
which they have to part, and when the number of souls God
has seen fit to create is completed, body and soul will be
resurrected to renewed and combined life. This is testified to
by Scripture, proved by the prophets, and accepted by all
Israel. It remains now to prove the truth of the Biblical
doctrine by way of speculation. The first thing to be investi-
gated is the essence of the soul. Saadia remarks that the
subject is much disputed and that he refrains from quoting
all the theories, but will select seven, the last of which is
his own. What is adduced by Saadia as the first theory is
a combination of five different Greek doctrines on the soul.
Saadia takes them as one because, as he says, they have all
the one view in common, that the soul is not a substantial
entity, but merely an accident of the body, having no
separate existence. It is natural that Saadia should
oppose this theory with all its ramifications, as it denies the
existence of a soul altogether. The second and the third
theories, the one asserting that the soul consists of air and
the other that it is fire, are both opposed by Saadia on the
ground, that they deprive the soul of its spirituality, air and
fire being two elementary substances. The fourth theory is
more complicated. It assumes that the soul consists of two
parts, the one rational and imperishable, with the heart as
its seat, and the other irrational, present in the entire body
and perishing with it (vitality). This theory is likewise
rejected, because it destroys the unity of the soul. The fifth
theory holds that the soul consists of two kinds of air, the
one dwelling permanently in the body, the other coming

[401] For details on the contents of this chapter see the monograph of
Horovitz, Die Psychologie Saadias, Breslau, 1898; comp. also
Neumark Geschichte der jüdischen Philosophie, I, 536-551; Guttmann,
Saadia, pp. 194 ff.

from without through breathing, mixing with the former
and sustaining it. This theory denies both the spirituality
and the unity of the soul, and is therefore to be rejected.
The sixth theory identifies the soul with the blood. While,
as usual, no authority is mentioned for any of the preceding
theories, an exception is made by our author in favor of the
sixth. He ascribes it to Anan, the founder of Ḳaraism,
who, Saadia says, was misled by a too literal interpretation
of a scriptural verse, "the blood is the soul" (Deuteronomy, 12, 23).[498] Saadia is wrong, however, in stating that
Anan is the only advocate of this theory. It was common
among various ancient peoples and is mentioned by Aristotle[499] and also in the Midrash.[500] All the Greek theories
mentioned by Saadia anonymously have been variously assigned to their respective authors; and the subject has been
fully treated elsewhere.[501]

Having refuted the foregoing doctrines on the essence of
the soul, Saadia turns to the presentation of his own view.
By way of introduction he observes that the investigation
of this subject is extremely difficult, and compares in this
regard with the question of *creatio ex nihilo* and of the
nature of the Creator, which accounts for the fact that so
many conflicting theories have been advanced on the subject.

---

[498] Landauer (p. 191) and some of the Hebrew editions give here
the wrong verse, Leviticus, 17, 11*b*. They were misled by Saadia's
referring a little further to Leviticus, 17, 11*a* as "preceding" the
verse quoted before. But the word in question (קודם) does not
mean preceding *immediately*. Speaking of a verse in Deuteronomy
he refers to a verse in Leviticus as preceding it.

[499] Aristotle, *De Anima*, I, 1; comp. Horovitz, *Psychologie Saadias*,
p. 21, n. 36; Dukes, *Philosophisches aus dem zehnten Jahrhundert*, p. 58; Harkavy, *Jahrbuch für jüdische Geschichte und Literatur*,
1899, p. 119. The theory is mentioned also by Seneca, *Questiones
Naturales*, VII, 24; comp. Adolfo Bonilla, *Hist. de la filosofia Española*, Madrid, 1908, I, 130.

[500] *Bereshit* rabbah, c. 14, § 9; comp. Theodor *ad locum*, p. 133;
Ginzberg, *Die Sage bei den Kirchenvätern*, p. 22.

[501] See Malter, in the Hebrew monthly השלח, XXVI (1912), pp.
128-137.

This remark serves him as a basis for the interpretation of the verse (Eccles. 3, 21), "Who knoweth the spirit of men, whether it goeth upward, and the spirit of the beast, whether it goeth downward to the earth"? which seems to doubt the immortality of the soul. The problem being so difficult, the verse referred to means only to express admiration for him who succeeds in solving it. Saadia is very anxious to remove the difficulty, and offers two more explanations of the verse.[502]

Saadia's theory, based on Bible verses and on speculative arguments, is that the soul like every other being, is a creation of God. Its creation takes place at the moment the body, its seat, is complete and about to come into the world.[503] This statement is intended to express Saadia's opposition to the belief in the pre-existence of the soul, which makes it co-eternal with God. While the soul has thus a beginning in time past, it is nevertheless immortal, that is, it has no end in time to come. This point, however, is not discussed here,

---

[502] This verse, which apparently doubts the immortality of the soul, greatly disturbed the Jewish interpreters; see Luzzatto, בית האוצר (ed. Lemberg), I, 35; Epstein, מי מנרבונה הדרשן ר׳משה. Vienna, 1891, p. 46 (see below, note 618) ; Zohar, on Genesis, 4, 1. One of Saadia's interpretations of this verse was adopted by Abr. Ibn Ezra and by Rashi ad locum, who supports it by the same verse from Joel, 2, 14, which is here quoted by Saadia. Joseph Ibn Saddik, עולם קטן, ed. Horovitz, p. 35, ll. 30 ff., likewise makes literal use of Saadia's interpretation. The Karaite Salmon b. Jeroham (see Isr. Günzig, Der Commentar des Karäers Jephet ben Ali Halevi zu den Proverbien, Cracow, 1898, p. 34, n. 15) may also have used Saadia (comp. JQR., XIII, 340). Comp. also Goldziher, Kitâb ma'âni al-nafs, Berlin, 1907, pp. 46 f.

[503] See on this point Guttmann, Saadia, p. 199, n. 2 (where read ברנע for בהגע, as in Berechiah's המצרף, p. 148, bottom), followed by Horovitz, Psychologie, p. 24, n. 40, and Neumark, I, 544. The same view was taught also by some of the Church Fathers. Thus, Isidore of Seville (d. 636): Animam non esse partem divinae substantiae vel naturae; nec esse eam priusquam corpori misceatur, constat; sed tunc eam creari quando et corpus creatur, cui admisceri videtur (Sententiarum, liber I, c. XII) ; comp. Bonilla, Hist. de la filos. Española, I, 243. Comp. also Goldziher, l. c., German part, pp. 17 f.

but in the ninth chapter of the work."¹ The substance of the soul is as fine and brilliant as that of the celestial spheres, nay, it must be even finer than the latter, for, unlike the spheres, it is endowed with reason. As the substance of the spheres is illuminated by the stars, so is the substance of the soul made bright and luminous by the light of wisdom. By wisdom, Saadia understands that which is acquired through the study of the divine law and through a moral and religious life in harmony therewith. This is fully in keeping with his view regarding the influence of human actions on the condition of the soul, as propounded in the preceding chapter. Good deeds ennoble the soul and add brightness and splendor to its substance; immorality, on the contrary, degrades and darkens it. The power of reasoning is an essential attribute of the soul and in this regard it is independent of the body. For the manifestation of this power the soul is necessarily bound up with the body, as its physical instrument, without which it cannot act. In its combination with the body the soul appears under three different aspects, viz. as a cognitive, a spirited, and an appetitive power.⁵⁰⁵ These three powers are

---

⁵⁰⁴ *'Amânât*, 273 (138 f.). Speaking of the soul, Saadia draws there the line between existence without beginning, which is inadmissible, as it excludes creation, and existence without end, which is admissible, because, once the soul is created, it can be coëternal with its Creator. This view is based ultimately on a scholastic distinction between *perpetuity* and *eternity*, which is clearly expressed by Isidore of Seville (*l. c.*) in the following words: *Sicut angeli, ita et animae; habent enim initium, finem vero nullum. Nam quaedam in rebus temporalia sunt, quaedam perpetua, quaedam vero sempiterna. Temporalia sunt quibus inest ortus et obitus; perpetua quibus ortus, non terminus; sempiterna, quibus nec ortus, nec terminus.* There is, in my opinion, no reason for doubting, with Horovitz (*Psychologie*, p. 23, n. 38; comp. p. 65, n. 128), Saadia's positive denial of the preexistence of the soul, the assertion of Abraham Ibn Ezra (Commentary on Is. 48, 16) to the contrary notwithstanding.

⁵⁰⁵ This is the well-known Platonic division of the soul, which was accepted by several Jewish philosophers. I have prepared a special essay on the subject and refrain from discussing it here; comp. Guttmann, p. 201; Horovitz, pp. 30 f.; Malter, *JQR.*, *N. S.*, vol. I (1910-1911), p. 460. Saadia discusses the three faculties of the soul also at the beginning of the tenth chapter.

15

not to be taken as three separate souls, but as different
manifestations of one and the same psychic entity. The seat
of the soul, the author states again, is in the heart, the central
organ of the nervous system and thus the power-house of all
sensation and motion. It is true that some large arteries
ramify from the brain, but these have no psychic, only
physical functions[506] It is because of the heart's being the
physical organ of the soul that Scripture always uses heart
and soul (לב ונפש) as synonyms.

It might be objected, the author continues, that if the soul is
such a sublime being, even finer than the celestial spheres, why
should God have sent it down into an ignoble physical frame?
This objection, Saadia says, implies that God, the Creator,
acted unfairly toward one of His own creations, which is
absurd, as it contradicts the very concept of God, the just
and benevolent Moreover, the question in itself has no
sense, for soul means nothing else than a spiritual being
acting in and through a body An active soul without a body
is as imaginable as a fire burning without combustible material. Body and soul are two correlatives, absolutely depending upon one another. In combination they constitute
man In a previous chapter, this combination, representing
man, was set forth as God's purpose in creating the world,
the ultimate purpose in creating man being that he should
attain to happiness through his own merits. This is only
possible when, in the constant struggle between the two
partners, between the noble aspirations of the soul and the low
desires of the body, man follows the counsel of his better
half, the soul; that is, obeys the Law.[507] To demand that the

---

[506] This is in contradiction to what he says in his Commentary on
the Sêfer Yezirah, p 27 (French, 47), ll. 4-5, where he places the
cognitive faculty in the brain (Plato). It is possible, however,
that in the Commentary he does not give his own view, but that of
the author of the Sefer Yezirah, as he understands him. The question
here discussed is treated also in the Commentary, pp. 33 f (55):
comp Kaufmann, Die Sinne, p 63. Horovitz, Psychologie, p 30,
n. 50
[507] Comp Malter, "Personifications of Soul and Body," in JQR,
N. S., vol II (1911-1912), p. 473.

soul should have been left alone, therefore, reveals a failure
to understand God's purpose, and is tantamount to declaring
all creation as meaningless. One might just as well ask that
the soul should be a star in heaven or an angel. It might be
one or the other, but then it would not be a soul.[503]

The investigation into the substance of the soul is here
closed, and the author turns to the discussion of the other
two points announced in the description of the chapter,
namely, " death and what follows." Body and soul together,
he declares, are only one agent, as indicated in the Bible
(Genesis, 2, 7), hence reward and punishment can only be
meted out to both together as a unit. This statement was
necessary, he says, because many people have confused ideas
in this matter, some asserting that the soul alone is the subject of reward or punishment, while others affirm the same
of the body alone. The Karaite Benjamin Nahâwandi,
basing the assertion on certain verses (Ezekiel, 32, 27, and
Psalms, 35, 10), singled out the bones as the part of the
body that is punished or rewarded. All this confusion is
due to ignorance of the proper usage of Hebrew. The
Bible often ascribes sins and virtues either to the soul (*e. g.*
Leviticus, 4, 2) or to the flesh, "bāsār" (*e. g.* Psalms,
145, 21). These verses are taken literally, and various
theories built upon them. What is overlooked is that in each
instance the words are to be understood in the sense of
person, including both soul and body. The same applies
to the theory of Benjamin. Saadia quotes numerous verses
from the Bible corroborating his view, and winds up with the
citation of the famous Talmudic parable (*b.* Sanhedrin, 91*a*)
of two men, one blind and the other lame, who, when called
to account for the despoliation of the king's garden which
they were appointed to watch, denied the deed on the ground
of their physical disabilities. The king placed the lame man
on the shoulders of his blind companion and demonstrated
how they had committed the crime. So body and soul dis-

---

[503] This argumentation is in keeping with Saadia's view, that man
is superior to the angels, regarding which see above, note 485.

own responsibility for their deeds in this world, as neither
of them can act without the other. God then reunites them
and metes out punishment to both together.[509]

Death is merely a dissolution of the partnership of soul
and body. At the very entrance upon life every human being
is equipped by God with a certain amount of physical power,
which suffices for a corresponding period of earthly existence. Sometimes God sees fit to shorten or lengthen this
natural term of a given individual ; then He adds to or takes
away from the original measure of vitality. Various instances are quoted from the Bible.

Saadia describes also some circumstances attending death.
Here, however, he does not speak as a philosopher, but as
a believer in certain common views and traditions prevalent
among the Jews and, in a modified form, among the Muhammedans. At the moment a person is to die—so the
Talmud (b. 'Abôdāh Zārāh, 20b) says—the Angel of Death,
all of yellowish fire and covered with eye-like spots of bluish
fire, appears with a drawn sword aimed at the sick person.
Beholding this sight, the victim is greatly shocked. At this
moment the soul departs from the body. Saadia adduces
several Bible verses to sustain the Talmudic tradition. The
passage in the Talmud does not contain all the particulars
given by Saadia.[509a] The fire and its different colors were
added from some other source. Nor does the spontaneous
departure of the soul accord with the Talmud. There it is
a bitter drop falling from the sword into the open mouth of
the terrified person that brings about death. That the soul
is not seen when departing from the body is explained by
the fact of its extreme fineness and transparency, as, for the
same reason, we cannot see the substance of the heavenly
spheres. " If one should take ten lamps of fine, transparent

---

[509] See Malter, JQR.. N. S., vol. II (1911-1912), pp. 454 f.

[509a] Moses Tachau, the severest critic of Saadia among the mediaeval Rabbis (see below, notes 597-616), does not fail to make use of
this point against Saadia (see Ozar Nechmad, II, 93). For parallels
from Greek and Christian mythology see Wünsche, Lewy's Festschrift, p. 97; Bender, JQR., VI, 333 ff., 669 ff.; comp. below, notes
518, 603.

glass, put one into the other, and place a light in the middle, no one at a distance would think that the light is inside of ten lamps. Due to the transparency of the glass, his vision passes straight through it and strikes the light therein." [510] This illustration is to explain why the celestial lights alone are visible to the human eye, while the spheres in which they are set, and which, in ancient astronomy, were supposed to be ten in number, cannot be discerned. Indirectly it serves also as an explanation for the invisibility of the soul, which is of transparent material like the spheres.

Upon its departure from the body, the soul of the righteous soars up to heaven, while the soul of the wicked roams about restlessly. For this view the author quotes the authority of the Talmud (*b*. Shabbat, 152*b*) and supports it by verses from the Bible. During the process of the body's decomposition the departed souls are greatly disturbed on account of what happens to their former abode, just as one is overwhelmed by grief when he sees the house in which he lived for a long time laid in ruins. This suffering is greater in the homeless souls of the wicked. The separation between the souls and their former bodies lasts until the end of days, when, as was stated at the beginning, the number of souls, which God in His inscrutable wisdom has decided to create, is complete and the time for resurrection has arrived. All souls are then reunited with their bodies forever.

The ideas here touched upon belong to the large subject of Jewish eschatology. The author is not prepared to discuss such matters at this point, and refers the reader to the ninth chapter, which is devoted entirely to questions of eschatology. The closing portion of the present chapter is taken up with the refutation of the very ancient belief in the migration of the soul after death, which has found adherents in many sections of Jewry, especially the Kabbalists.[511] According to this theory the souls of the dead

[510] *'Amânât,* 205 (102), bottom.

[511] The doctrine of the transmigration of the soul, which in Greek antiquity was represented by Empedocles and Pythagoras, found

migrate into other bodies, with which they start upon another
earthly career. This may be repeated several times. Some
aver that human souls often migrate into animal bodies and
vice versa. The adherents of the theory adduce various
arguments, among them that children often undergo great
suffering, which can be explained only by assuming that they
are expiating sins which their souls committed previously,
while residing in other bodies."[511a] The Jewish followers of the
doctrine try to prove it by numerous verses from Scripture.
Saadia is strongly opposed to this idea in all its phases.
He refutes the arguments adduced by the advocates of
metempsychosis and shows that all the verses quoted in support of the belief have been misunderstood and misinterpreted. He concludes with the remark that he would have
considered it beneath his dignity to polemicize against such
crude and superstitious notions, were it not that he feared
the evil influence they may have on the credulous.

(VII) Saadia distinguishes three periods in the life of
the soul after its departure from the body. The first period
is that of separation, during which, as was shown in the
preceding chapter, the souls of the righteous abide in heaven
"under the throne of God," while those of the wicked
wander about, homeless. This period lasts until all souls to
be created have passed through their earthly career. When
this time arrives, creation is naturally discontinued. This
does not mean that the world comes to an end, for then the
second, more auspicious, period sets in, that of resurrection, when most of the departed souls will be reunited with
their former bodies and begin life anew. As we shall see

many adherents among the various peoples of the Orient. Anan,
the founder of Karaism, who borrowed the theory from the Muhammedans and spread it among the Jews, is said to have written a
special work thereon; see Harkavy, JE., I, 555, and in the place
quoted above, note 499; The Karaite Kirkisâni (Semitic Studies in
Memory of Kohut, pp. 449 f.) combats the belief in transmigration
with weapons borrowed from Saadia; comp. also ibidem, p. 438, the
references given by Poznański.

[511a] See above, note 490a, and below, note 525a.

later, Saadia identifies this period with the Messianic time.
At the expiration of the second period the present material
world will dissolve, and a new spiritual world will be created,
into which *all* souls, including those of the wicked, will be
transferred, the place in which they will remain forever—
those of the righteous enjoying eternal bliss and those of the
wicked doomed to everlasting suffering. This is the world
called *'Olam ha-bâ'*, " the world to come," in which final
judgment is held, and reward and punishment are meted out.

As the status of the soul during the first period has been
treated of in the foregoing chapter, Saadia proceeds to consider the second period, to which he devotes the seventh
chapter of his book, with the special title, "On the Resurrection of the Dead in this World." The addition " in this
world [512] " is significant, as it expresses the principal contention of Saadia, who, in opposition to others, maintained that
resurrection will take place in this world of ours as a natural phenomenon. He informs us at the beginning of
the chapter that this is the view of the majority of the Jewish
people, who take the predictions of our prophets in their
plain, literal sense. Some, however, are of the opinion that
the numerous verses in the Prophets promising resurrection
simultaneously with the arrival of the Messiah, are to be
taken figuratively, and that resurrection is to be one of the
events of the " world to come," where the present order of
things will be overthrown.

The demonstration of the correctness of his view, as
against that of the minority mentioned, was to Saadia a
matter of great importance, for it involved God's justice
toward the people of Israel. According to Saadia the world
to come is not intended for Israel alone. The pious of all
nations will have a share in it, a view expressed in the
Talmud [513] What is Israel going to receive as a reward for

[512] In the presentation of this chapter I have combined the contents
of both the Oxford and the St Petersburg recensions, for all the
details regarding these two texts see the *Bibliography*, below, p 360.

[513] *Tosefta* (ed. Zuckermandel), *Synhedrin*, 13, 2, see Zunz, *Zur
Geschichte*, pp. 371 ff.; Guttmann, p 216.

all the indescribable sufferings and unparalled martyr-
dom experienced at the hands of its oppressors during the
long period of its dispersion? Is it conceivable that a just
and merciful God should select a particular people to be the
guardian and disseminator of His Law and then abandon it to
the cruelty and persecution of other nations, without any
prospect of a reward for its unflinching loyalty? To be
sure, our prophets assure us that Israel's redemption will
come, that God will send His messenger, the Messiah, to
vindicate the name of His people and restore it to its
pristine glory. But what of all the innumerable martyrs
who suffered torture and death for their faith and for
the sanctification of God's name? What of all the pious
men and women in Israel, who in ages gone by lived a life
of misery and affliction because of their faithful adherence
to the God-given religion? Have they lived and suffered in
vain, and are they never to witness the vindication of their
cause and the restoration of Israel? To say that the administration of justice is reserved entirely for the unknown
world to come, as was partly assumed in the case of individuals, would be a very unsatisfactory solution of this
problem. Our minds are not set at rest thereby, and they
humbly demand that justice be done in this world.

It is by such reflections that we are strengthened in the
belief that the Biblical promises of the revival of the dead
are not mere metaphors, but are meant literally; that simultaneously with the advent of Israel's redeemer, the promised
Messiah, the dead of the faithful and penitent of the nation,
to the exclusion of those who led a wicked life and died unrepentant, will revive to see with their bodily eyes the redemption of their people and its rehabilitation on " the Mount
of God."

Saadia, as a rationalist, naturally cannot stop here. The
questions that crowd upon his mind and try to overthrow
his belief are many. Is bodily resurrection a possibility? Is
it at all conceivable that human bodies, after having been
decomposed and dissolved into atoms for thousands of years,
should unite again and reassume their original form?

Saadia admits that for those who believe in the eternity of the material world and the immutability of the laws of nature, resurrection is an impossibility. For us, however, the believers in monotheism, who recognize in God the Almighty Power that created all nature and keeps it under His control, the belief in resurrection does not involve more difficulties, nay involves even less, than the belief in a *creatio ex nihilo*, in which we all agree. Nature, as we know, does not destroy anything; it merely resolves the constituents of a given body into its original elements, which are indestructible. Now if we are all ready to believe that God has created even the elements out of nothing, why should we deny the possibility of His rebuilding bodies out of their original and undestroyed elements? We do not claim that the dispersed atoms will spontaneously join together and by a natural process, come to life again,[514] for we have never witnessed such a phenomenon in the realm of nature. What we say is that resurrection is one of the miracles which God, through His prophets, has promised to perform for His people at the time of their redemption. There is no obvious reason why we should deny the possibility of this miracle more than of all other miracles reported in the Bible, none of which appears more natural and more acceptable. The Bible even relates definite instances of the revival of the dead through the prophets Elijah (I Kings, 17, 22) and Elisha (II Kings, 4, 35), which belongs to the same category of miracles as resurrection.

Having thus disposed of the question from the point of view of reason, the author turns to the examination of the numerous Scriptural verses that have some bearing on the subject. A large number of these verses, as the whole famous vision of Ezekiel, chapter 37, the prophecies of Isaiah (26, 19), Daniel (12, 1-3), and others, positively express the promise of a bodily resurrection in this world.

---

[514] This is found only in Landauer's text, p. 213, ll. 12-13; comp. the parallel passage in the other recension, Steinschneider-*Festschrift*, p. 100 (*Emūnōt*, p. 107), ll. 5-10.

The opponents of this belief maintain that all these verses must be taken in a metaphorical sense, and they adduce various instances of similar verses which are commonly taken as metaphors. Saadia, although in many other relations he himself resorts to metaphorical interpretations, denies the admissibility of the method in the present case. In this connection he establishes a famous exegetical canon which has proved of great importance in the development of Bible study, through its acceptance by eminent commentators of subsequent ages.[213] According to this canon we are entitled, or even in duty bound, to interpret the Scriptural word in a figurative sense under four conditions only: first, when the literal meaning contradicts a truth based on sense-perception; second, when it is absolutely incompatible with the dictates of reason; third, when it is in positive conflict with another passage of the Bible; and, fourth, when it denies a well-established ancient tradition. For each of these cases he adduces examples from the Bible. In the case of the verses bearing on resurrection none of these rules applies, and we are therefore constrained to take them in their literal sense. If we were at liberty to construe Scriptural passages indiscriminately as metaphors, there would eventually be nothing left to construe in a plain natural sense. We could easily take all the narratives of the Bible and all its laws and

[613] The question of the permissibility of allegorical interpretations (ta'wîl, in the language of Ibn Tibbon סברא) was hotly disputed among the various schools of the Muhammedan theologians, especially the 'Ash'arites and Mu'tazilites; see Goldziher, in Die Kultur der Gegenwart, I, 5 (1913), p. 305, and in the periodical Der Islam, III (1912), pp. 226-230. From the Muhammedans the problem was taken over first by the Karaites, Anan (Harkavy, Jahrbuch für jüdische Geschichte und Literatur, Berlin, 1899, p. 113) and some of his followers. A discussion of the subject as viewed by the mediæval Jewish philosophers requires a monograph. As to Saadia, whom Maimonides follows, see Bacher, Die Bibelexegese der jüdischen Religionsphilosophen, etc., pp. 8 ff.; Guttmann, Saadia, pp. 21, 221, n. 1, and (with reference to Maimonides) in Isr. Lewy's Festschrift, pp. 319 f. (Moses ben Maimon, II, 210 f.); above, note 446; comp. כתאב אלרסאיל, edited by J. Brill, Paris, 1871, p. 57.

precepts as mere figures of speech. For instance, the law, " ye shall kindle no fire on the Sabbath day " might be interpreted to mean ye shall not go to war on the Sabbath day, for in Numbers, 21, 28 war is designated as fire. The law that forbids taking from a nest the " mother-bird with the young " (Deuteronomy, 22, 6) might mean that in conquering an enemy we should not kill the women with their children, for the same phrase is used in the latter sense (Hosea, 10, 14).⁵¹⁶ Saadia cites numerous other passages for further illustration, showing the absurdity of such interpretations.

The opponents of the idea of bodily resurrection point, however, to several verses in Scripture that seem to bear out their view, e. g. (Psalms, 78, 39) : " And he remembered that they were but flesh, a wind that passeth away and cometh not again "; or (ib., 103, 15-16) : " As for man, his days are as grass, as a flower of the field, so he flourishes, for the wind passeth over it, and it is gone, and the place thereof shall know it no more "; further (Job, 7, 9-10) : " As the cloud is consumed and vanisheth away, so he that goes down to the grave shall come up no more; he shall return no more to his house, neither shall his place know him any more "; and (ib., 14, 12) : " Man lieth down and riseth not, till the heavens be no more they shall not awake, nor be roused out of their sleep." In answer thereto Saadia contends that these and similar verses have no reference to the question of resurrection; they merely emphasize the weakness and transitoriness of human life, the inability of man to fight death or to rise after death.⁵¹⁷ It should be remarked that Saadia here disagrees with the Talmud (Baba Batra, 16a), where the verse from Job, 7, 9 is quoted as a proof that Job denied resurrection.⁵¹⁸

⁵¹⁶ The same arguments, applied to verses of the Korân, are used by the Muhammedan theologian Faḫr al-Din Râzi (13th century), see Goldziher, in *Der Islam*, III, 228 f.

⁵¹⁷ The same interpretation he gives in his Commentary on Job in the verses here cited.

⁵¹⁸ For other instances of Saadia's deviation from the Talmud and the Midrash see above, notes 462, 482, 509a and below, note 603;

In addition to the proofs from the Bible, Saadia then quotes several passages from the Talmud corroborative of his view. The latter, he remarks, are too many for all to be quoted. The closing portion of the chapter is devoted to the answer of ten questions that either were asked or might be asked, in connection with the idea of resurrection. Some of these are: Who will be excluded from resurrection? Answer: Only the heretics and atheists among the Israelites who do not repent before death. Will the revived dead die again? Answer: They will not die, but live through the whole second—that is, the Messianic—period, until the beginning of the third period, when they will be transferred to the eternal world to come. Will the earth hold so many people? In answer to this question Saadia enters upon a detailed computation, which results in the assurance that a hundred and fiftieth part of the surface of the earth would be sufficient to supply the needs of all. It should be remarked in passing that Saadia's computation is based on his belief that the time of the Messianic redemption was not very distant.[518a] The other questions refer mostly to the mode of life which will obtain among the people during those blessed times. (See below, pp. 244 ff.)

In one of the two different recensions [519] of this chapter the author concludes with the expression of the hope that the belief in resurrection as here explained may prove a source of comfort to his oppressed people and strengthen their faith in God. Finally he utters the prayer that in

Müller, Oeuvres, IX, p. xxxvi, n. 11; Davidson, Saadia's Polemic against Hiwi Al-Balkhi, New York, 1915, p. 42, n. 96; p. 48, n. 126; p. 54. n. 157; p. 58, n. 177; comp. also J. N. Epstein, Der gaonäische Kommentar zur Ordnung Tohoroth, Berlin, 1915, pp. 38, 41, bottom. The Kommentar in question is essentially a work of Saadia; see below, p. 342, no. 1.

[518a] There is much speculation as to the year of redemption according to Saadia's Computations; see the references given below, notes 521, 522.

[519] The so-called St. Petersburg recension (edited by Bacher in the Steinschneider-Festschrift), which was followed by Ibn Tibbon.

reward thereof he, too, may be found worthy of beholding that glorious time.

(VIII) In the foregoing chapter Saadia endeavored to prove that the resurrection will be a special feature of the Messianic redemption of Israel. In so far, resurrection presupposes the coming of the Messiah. As a matter of reasoning, the belief in the final redemption of Israel is based on the supposition that it would be wholly incompatible with God's justice to abandon His people to its fate forever, after having chosen it as the bearer and promulgator of His truth, for which it was to endure the greatest sufferings. The same argument, as we have seen, served the author also as a proof for resurrection. This is quite natural, as resurrection is, in his view, an incident of the Messianic time. On the whole the matter might have rested here; but owing to the magnitude of the Messianic idea and its national importance for the Jewish people, the author devotes a special chapter to it, entitled " On the (final) Redemption," in which he proposes to discuss the subject in its manifold phases.

In an opening paragraph, the author, as is his wont, refers to the explicit statements of the prophets, containing definite promises of Israel's deliverance; mentions briefly the argument of reason given before; and depicts, in a highly poetic style, the power of Almighty God, as it manifests itself in nature and in the history of mankind—all of which tends to show that for Him the liberation of a people can involve no difficulty. The nations around us, who see our misfortune, mock and deride us and consider our hope as foolish; but this is because they have never gone through our experience and have never believed as strongly as we do. " A person that has never seen seed sown, when for the first time he sees the husbandman throwing grain into the fissures of the soil to sprout there, is apt to consider the sower a fool, and will realize his own ignorance only in the time of harvesting, when he sees that a measure cast forth produces twenty or thirty measures. Scripture says: ' They that sow in tears shall reap in joy.' (Psalms 126, 5.) Furthermore a person

that has never witnessed the bringing up of a child, when he
observes a father undergoing all sorts of hardships in order
to give his son a good education, may ridicule him, saying,
What is the use of all this? But after the child has grown
up, has become a scholar or a philosopher, a governor or a
general, then the taunter realizes that it was he that made
himself ridiculous." [520] The great sufferings of Israel have
likewise only a preparatory character and an educational
purpose. Out of her present decline will spring new life and
fresh vigor, to the amazement of those who had held her
in contempt; for, says Scripture: " The Lord thy God is a
merciful God, He will not fail thee nor destroy thee."
(Deuter., 4, 31.)

Proceeding from the prophecies of Daniel, chapters 10-12,
Saadia makes an attempt to fix the time for the coming of
the expected Messiah. His computation is too complicated
to be reproduced. Various theories have been advanced by
recent scholars [521] as to the year of redemption resulting from
these computations, but none of them is satisfactory. The
matter has been treated elsewhere [522] in full. Saadia adopts
the opinion of the Talmud (p. Ta'anit, I, 1; b. Synhedrin.
97b), that the appointed time for the redemption of Israel
will be adhered to only in case the Israelites do not prove
themselves worthy of a speedier deliverance from the
exile. If they repent of their sins and better their conduct, they will not have to wait for the extreme time-limit.
If, however, the appointed time is reached, and the conduct of the Jewish people does not warrant their deliverance, God will bring upon them the persecutions of base
kings, who will expel them from their countries, and by
all sorts of oppressive laws will drive them to despair,
so that many of them will leave their faith. Those who,
after this purifying process, remain steadfast and loyal

[520] Amânât, p. 232 (Em., p. 119) ; comp. Munk, Notice, etc., p. 27 ;
Michel A. Weill, L'Univers Israélite, 1870, pp. 271 ff.

[521] See Poznański, MGWJ., XLIV (1900), 400 ff.

[522] See Malter, " Saadia's Messianic Computation," in Neumark's
Journal of Jewish Lore and Philosophy, Cincinnati, 1919, pp. 45-59.

to their religion will then be redeemed. Using traditions
supposed to have originated in the earlier Geonic period,
Saadia mentions a king by the name of Armilus,[523] who is to
bring terrible suffering upon the house of Israel. This
king is in all probability identical with Romulus, the founder
of Rome, which stands for the Church. According to
the Talmud (Sukkah, 52a, b) a scion of the tribe of
Joseph will appear as the Messianic precursor of the real
Messiah of the house of David and conquer Jerusalem for
the Jewish people; but king Armilus will wrest it from him,
kill him and many of his followers, and usher in the period
of the great persecutions. Finally the real Messiah will arrive and wreak vengeance on the persecutor. Saadia finds
all the details of these great struggles and of the ultimate
victory of Israel predicted in numerous verses quoted from
the prophets, on the basis of which he draws a glorious
picture of Israel's ultimate salvation.

Having thus established his view that the Messianic predictions of the prophets refer without exception to a future
time in which they are sure to be fulfilled, the author, in a
lengthy, controversial paragraph, feels constrained to turn
against those who maintain a totally different opinion.
There are some so-called Jews,[524] he says sarcastically, who

[523] See Ginzberg, *JE.*, *s. v. Armilus*, also in אוצר ישראל, II, 201.

[524] Various views have been advanced as to the persons here alluded
to. In particular, see for the literature Kaufmann, *Attributenlehre*,
p. 84; Guttmann, *Saadia*, p. 214, n. 1; Poznański, *MGWJ.*, 1895,
pp. 441 ff., and later in *Semitic Studies in Memory of Kohut*,
Berlin, 1897, p. 438 (comp. also his *Karaite Literary Opponents of
Saadiah*, p. 98, and *ZfhB.*, III, 176); see also David Joel, *Der
Aberglaube*, etc., Breslau, 1883, II, 3; Horovitz, *Psychologie*, p.
69. Saadia uses the same phrase in his argument against the believers in the transmigration of the soul, *Am.*, p. 207, bottom, *Em.*,
p. 103 (see above, note 511) and in the *Sefer ha-Galui* (see Malter,
JQR., N. S., vol. III (1912-1913), p. 497, l. 9). To my mind neither
here nor there was any particular sect meant by Saadia. Adherents
of such theories were found among the Rabbanites as well as among
the Karaites and other sectaries (see below, note 577). This, however, is not the place to prove it; I have dealt with the question in
detail in my forthcoming edition of the *Emūnōt*.

claim that most of the Messianic promises of the Bible were
actually fulfilled during the time of the Second Temple,
while the others, which were not fulfilled, were definitely
withdrawn, because they were originally made on the condition that the religious conduct of the Israelites would
prove them deserving of the benefits intended for them,
which was not the case Saadia strongly opposes this theory,
and proves that it is based on false premises and on a misunderstanding of the Biblical passages. He points in particular to fifteen characteristic features of the Messianic
time as described in the Bible, and shows that none applies
to the condition of the Jews during the period of the Second
Temple and the times following it. For instance, we are told
that in the Messianic time all humanity will believe in one
God (Zechariah, 14, 9), that all nations will be free, none of
them being forced to serve the interests of the other (Isaiah,
62, 8), that all wars between the nations will be abolished,
and perfect peace will reign all over the world (*ib.*, 2, 4),
and so forth. But what we actually see to this day is the
very opposite of such conditions.

These arguments, Saadia continues, hold good also against
the adherents of Christianity, for they too claim that the
Messianic promises have been fulfilled in the past, with the
only difference that according to them the Messianic time
did not begin with the period of the Second Temple, but 135
years before its destruction—that is, with the birth of Jesus.
There are several other objections to be raised against the
Christian theory in particular Saadia therefore devotes the
closing portion of the eighth chapter to the refutation of the
Messianic doctrine of the Christian religion, showing especially the mistakes made by the followers of the Church
in interpreting certain passages of the Bible as referring to
Jesus of Nazareth

(IX) The ninth chapter, "On Reward and Punishment
in the World to Come," concludes Saadia's eschatological
studies In accordance with the method adopted by
him, he opens the chapter with the statement that the Bible
tells us of the existence of a future world in which all differ-

ences will be adjusted (Malachi, 3, 17-18). The proofs
thereof from reason, Scripture and tradition, he says,
have been adduced in previous chapters. There are, however, additional proofs requiring special attention in this
place. From the point of view of reason, to start with, it
appears impossible that "the amount of happiness God
intends for humanity should consist exclusively in the pleasures and enjoyments attainable in this world, for every
material good is counterbalanced by an evil that lurks
behind it, all happiness is neutralized by hardship, all pleasure by pain, and all enjoyment by grief; nay, the evil usually
outweighs the good. As this is obvious, it is absurd that a
wise God should have appointed these delusive worldly
pleasures as the final goal of our strivings. Another abode
must be in store for us, in which perfect life and unalloyed
happiness will be ours. Moreover, among the people I have
met I have never found any that were fully satisfied and
content with this world, even if they had attained the greatest power and the highest degree of dignity." [825] This inevitable dissatisfaction, Saadia asserts, is an inner voice
which tells us that this world with all its restlessness and
vicissitudes is not the final stage of our life, that there must
be something that surpasses it in grandeur and sublimity.
Hence the constant longing of our souls for a good unknown,
the instinctive yearning for a world undefinable. He adduces,
in further elaboration of the argument, the conflict that arises
between conscience and inclination in the presence of temptation—as to commit adultery or theft, or to take vengeance
on an enemy, and the like. On such occasions it would be
quite natural for us to yield to temptation and indulge in
pleasure. But God has implanted in us a certain instinct
which invariably makes us realize what is morally wrong and
sinful and bids us refrain from the evil. We often follow
that better instinct and practice renunciation, though it causes
great pain and suffering. Is it proper to assume that God

[825] *'Amânât*, p. 255, bottom, *Em.*, p. 130.

16

created men with consciences, the immediate causes of such
suffering, without providing also some reward for the suffering? God has likewise equipped us with a sense of duty and
the faculty of realizing that, for example, justice, honesty,
and uprightness are good and commendable. In most cases,
however, if we abide by our moral duty and carry out the
demands of justice, we expose ourselves to the enmity of
men; we must suffer persecution and even death. It appears
impossible that God, who created in us love for justice,
should let us perish for it without rewarding us therefor.
Other instances are mentioned in addition, which make it
clear that happiness and misfortune are not properly dis-
tributed in this world, and some sort of adjustment is our
due. In some cases we are not in a position to administer
justice even if we so desired. If a person commits one murder and another one commits ten, we can do no more than
execute them both. How are the nine additional murders
punished?

These arguments, obviously based on general reasoning,
are followed by thirteen proofs taken from Scriptures. The
first six are merely inferences from what happened to greater
or lesser personages, as related in the Bible. Thus (1),
Isaac was ready to be burned on the altar, because God had
so ordered; Hananiah, Mishael, and Azariah allowed themselves to be thrown into the fire, rather than worship an
idol; and Daniel was thrown into the lions' den, because he
prayed to God; (2) Moses endured the greatest hardships
while ministering to the needs of his people, yet he was
denied the privilege of entering the Holy Land and enjoying
the fruit of his labors; (3) Elijah procured food for others
(i Kings, 17), while he himself had to starve (ib., c. 19),
and Elisha revived the dead, but died himself; (4) the
Sodomites were utterly destroyed because of their sins,
while other peoples, just and wicked alike, prosper; (5) the
Israelites were exiled because of idolatry, other nations
worship idols and remain undisturbed; (6) innocent children perished in the flood of Noah, and likewise in the battle
against the Midianites it was ordained that children be

killed (Numbers, 31, 17).[525a] All this makes God appear as a decidedly arbitrary and unjust ruler of the world, unless we assume that a proper reward is meted out after death.

The remaining seven proofs are based on numerous Bible verses, which, according to the author's interpretation, contain unmistakable allusions to the future world. All these verses are arranged according to their contents under seven general headings—*e. g.*, verses describing life and death, or containing promises and threats, or referring to records kept in heaven of the deeds of men, and so forth. Each group is construed as a proof that the belief in the world to come has found expression in the Bible. There is the great difficulty that in the most important passages of the Bible in which the Israelites are admonished to obedience or warned against sin, as, for instance, in the famous Exhortations (Tōkāḥōt), Leviticus, 33 and Deuteronomy, 28, only promises of material happiness are held out, or misfortunes of a physical nature announced. The reason therefor, Saadia explains, is twofold. We find, in the first place, that the Torah never expatiates upon things that are self-evident. The belief in reward and punishment after death is, as we have seen, demanded by reason. If men sin, it is mostly not because they deny the existence of a future world, or because they do not care for its rewards, or are not afraid of punishment therein, but merely because of weakness of character. In order to restrain them from sin, it will not suffice to remind them of the hereafter. That is something of which they are fully conscious. It is only the promise of prosperity or the threat of severe punishment in this world that will prove effective. Secondly, it was the purpose of the Bible, as a book intended for the education of the people, to give ample directions in matters that concern the immediate present or the near future. The Biblical passages referred to have relation to the time when the Israelites were about to conquer the Holy Land. It was necessary to describe in full detail the happy conditions

[525a] See above, notes 490[n], 511[a].

which would obtain in the promised land if they were faithful to the laws and ordinances of God, and on the other hand,
to warn them of the sure failure awaiting them, if they disregarded these. There was thus no need at that time to refer
in any way to what was going to happen in the world to come.
Such things are briefly alluded to in various passages of the
Bible, as shown before.

As to the proofs from traditional literature, Saadia continues, the passages are too many to quote all of them. Only
five passages from the Talmud and two from the Targum
on the Pentateuch are adduced. The passages occurring
in the Targum on the Prophets are likewise too numerous
for quotation. The existence of a future world is thus established from every point of view.

Over two-thirds of the entire chapter are now devoted to
the discussion of ten (actually eleven) [526] eschatological
questions, nearly all of which had been briefly considered by
the author at the end of the seventh chapter. Here each
point is taken up in a different arrangement and treated at
great length. Owing to the latter fact Saadia's presentation
cannot be reproduced here. The questions at issue are:
the nature of reward and punishment in the hereafter
(counted as two) ; are the categories time and space applicable to the future world? (also counted as two) ; are reward
and punishment eternal, or only for a certain period, according to the gravity of the case? (two) ; (7) if reward and

---

[526] The Hebrew text (p. 134) is here quite corrupt, and the order of
the questions much confused by uninformed commentators, especially
Dines in the edition used here by us (see the *Bibliography*, p. 371.
no. 5), who, however, puts the responsibility on the "printers and
copyists, who did not understand the text" as well as he. Saadia,
with his particular habit of playing with numbers, announces the
discussion of *ten* questions, but *de facto* enumerates *thirteen*, of which
he actually discusses *eleven*, and yet by an uncommon twist of logic
insists at the end of the paragraph (*Am.*, p. 279, l. 13, *Em.*, p. 142,
l. 21) that he had dealt with "ten only." The reason for this insist-
ence on ten is that the questions here treated are to be equal in
number, as they are also in content, to those treated in the last
portion of the seventh chapter (above, p. 236) ; comp. notes 487, 528.

punishment are eternal (Saadia's actual assumption), how about the reward and punishment for a single act? (8) If, as is again assumed by the author, the rewards and punishments, even for single meritorious acts or single reprehensible acts are to last eternally, the difference then being one of degree only, what about the great variety in classes that would result therefrom? Are all the righteous and all the wicked ranked in accordance with the number of merits or demerits they have to their account? (9) Which class of the wicked has to expect the severest punishment? (10) Will the righteous and the wicked be able to behold one another in the hereafter? In addition [527] to these ten points the author discusses the question whether the righteous will continue to be under obligation to worship God and to obey certain laws. Answering in the affirmative, he refers the reader to the seventh [528] chapter, where he stated that for such worship and obedience they will be additionally rewarded, and that the righteous of the world to come will never sin. As to the wicked, being in a state of suffering and affliction, they, Saadia says, will not be put under any obligation.

With a few exceptions the answers to the foregoing eschatological questions are all based on very numerous passages from Scripture, to which a Talmudic passage is occasionally added for corroboration. At the end Saadia admits that to attempt a detailed description of the real nature of reward and punishment would be presumptuous. The world to come must needs be totally different from ours, so that we have no proper standard of appreciation. Nor is it desirable that we should know exactly the reward and punishment of a certain deed or misdeed. This would

[527] See the preceding note.
[528] *'Amânât,* p. 228, l. 9, Steinschneider-*Festschrift,* p. 111, *Em.,* p. 116 (eighth question). Both the Arabic (p. 279, l. 10) and the Hebrew text (p. 142, l. 18) refer to the " end of the *eighth* chapter," which is a mistake, perhaps of Saadia himself. In the eighth chapter (*Am.,* p. 246, l. 8; *Em.,* p. 125, l. 9 from below) the matter is mentioned incidentally only, and it is not at the *end* of the chapter; comp. above, note 487.

interfere with freedom of action. We may hope, however, that in the Messianic time, intermediary between this world and the world to come, we shall be enlightened also about the latter.

So far as he felt justified by the indications contained in certain Scriptural verses, the author had previously attempted to describe the nature of the future world. According to these verses, as interpreted by Saadia, God, at the proper time, will create a sublime essence which will fill the world with magnificent light and splendor. On the souls of the righteous this light will have the most beneficent effect. It will imbue them with the knowledge of things divine, bringing them nearer to the presence of God and the heavenly hosts, and making them participate in a life of continuous joy and happiness. On the wicked it will have the opposite effect, dazzling and burning them eternally.[528a] These two effects are symbolically designated in traditional literature as *Gan Eden* (paradise) and *Ge-Hinnom* (Gehenna, hell), because the former was known from the story of Adam and Eve as a place of pleasantness, and the latter is mentioned as a place of abomination (near Jerusalem; Jeremiah, 7, 32, 19, 13) There will be neither time (that is, division into days and nights) nor space (that is, heaven and earth) nor atmospheric air in the world to come, as the people, though consisting of body as well as of soul, will not have to subsist on material food and will not need to breathe God will keep them alive by that fine light-shedding essence which he is to create We find the same exemplied in the life of Moses, who was with God for forty days and nights without food, sustained solely by the divine light (Exodus, 34. 28-29).

Saadia's answers to most of the other eschatological questions have been indicated above. The eighth question is answered in the affirmative, but only seven different degrees among the righteous and correspondingly seven among the

---

[528a] This entire exposition, for which Saadia gives no source, is based on the passage (Nedarim, 8*b*) אין גיהנם לעוה"ב אלא הקב"ה מוציא חמה מנרתיקה צדיקים מתרפאין בה ורשעים נדונין בה; comp. Theodor, *Bereschit Rabba*, Berlin, 1912, p. 46, n. 5.

wicked, are described by the author, as he finds them suggested in Bible verses. By way of answering the ninth question, he points to the atheists and polytheists and the per-
petrators of grave religious sins unrepentant at death. The
righteous and the wicked will see one another (tenth question) from a distance; the former, among themselves, however, will meet only when they happen to be of equal or not
greatly different rank, while among the latter, occupied as
they will be with expiation for their sins, no association, the
author conjectures, will be possible.

Saadia's philosophic system is here brought to a close.
As a summary of his eschatological views a few of the
leading thoughts may be restated. Soul and body are a unit.
The soul is created at the moment the body is completed and
takes its seat in the heart. Death separates the two. They
remain in separation until the Messianic time. At that time
the bodies will be resurrected and will reunite with their souls.
Resurrection is restricted to the pious ones in Israel as a
special reward for their sufferings; the wicked of Israel, as
well as the dead of other nations will not rise from the graves.
Their souls and bodies will remain separated until the Messianic period, lasting many generations, is over. At the
close of the Messianic period the present world will be
destroyed and a new eternal world created. This will be
the world of final judgment. In it the wicked of Israel, who
did not see the Messianic time, as well as the dead of all
nations will come to life again, though under a different, as
yet not fully intelligible system. The righteous of Israel,
who lived through the Messianic period will be transferred
bodily to that world. The righteous of all other nations will
also have their share in the reward of the eternal world to
come.

(X) The last chapter of the *'Amânât,* "About That which
is the Best for Man to do in this World," is not a continuation
of the thoughts developed in the chapters preceding it; nor
does it in any other way fit into the general plan of the work
before us. It has been suggested that the work was written
originally in separate essays under special titles, with a view

of later combining and arranging them so as to form a systematic whole.[529] The present essay, dealing with ethics, is
related in content to chapters 4 and 5 which deal with the
principal ethical problems as part of the system of the Jewish religion. The great latitude indulged in by the author
in treating the subject of this essay made its inclusion in the
body of the book appear inexpedient. It was therefore
appended here with the avowed intention of giving to the
reader some practical advice as to the course he should
choose in order to be able to live in conformity with the
religious doctrines laid down in the work.[530]

As is the author's wont, he opens the chapter with a few
general remarks leading to the subject under consideration,
in which he first points out that plurality and variety are
the very nature of all created beings, just as absolute unity
is an essential attribute of the Creator. All the units we see
in nature are only apparently such. Upon closer examination we realize that what appears to our eyes as a unit is
merely an aggregate of a multitude of smaller composites,
constituting a body, an organism. So it is in the whole of

---

[529] See above, note 456.

[530] Landauer's contention (Introduction, p. xx), that this chapter
was not considered at all in the original plan of Saadia, and did not
belong to the book, is disputed by Schreiner (*REJ.*, XXII, 70) on
the basis of a passage which is quoted by Moses Ibn Ezra (*Kitâb al-
Muhâdarah*) as occurring in chapter *nine* of the *'Amânât*, but is
found in the present chapter *ten*. Schreiner therefore suggests that
it was the *seventh* chapter (on resurrection) that was originally
excluded from the plan of the book. This is not at all conclusive,
as in the time of Moses Ibn Ezra (12th century) there may have
existed copies of the *'Amânât* in which the seventh chapter (in the
so-called *second* recension) formed a separate part, or was not included at all; comp. Bacher in the Steinschneider-*Festschrift*, (German part), pp. 219-226. We must also reckon with the possibility of a
mistake in the text of Ibn Ezra. Be that as it may, it is safe to assume
that both the seventh and the tenth chapters belonged to the original
plan of the author, as is evidenced also by the table of contents at
the end of the Introduction, and by a passage in chapter V of the
work (p. 179, top, *Em.*, p. 89); comp. Guttmann, p. 258, n. 1.

organic and inorganic nature and even in the superlunary world, for the heavenly bodies, too, are composed of various parts.

Precisely the same is true as regards our moral and intellectual world. Our entire thinking apparatus and our physical instinct are not units tending and working in one direction only. Each is a combination of multifarious thoughts, or tendencies, or inclinations, making up our diversified psychic world. As a tree would not be a tree by reason of its leaves alone, man would not be what he is, if he consisted only of one or the other of his components, and as the heavens do not shed their light through one star only, so a single instinct would not afford us the full variety of human life. Even in the sphere of human activities we must, for all purposes, make use of a combination of things. In building, manufacturing, and preparation of food for our sustenance, we must select our material from various quarters, in order to assure success.

By overlooking this truth most people go morally wrong. Contrary to the lessons of nature they bind themselves to one theory of life or follow a particular inclination to the neglect or exclusion of all others, with the result that they defeat their own purpose and go to wrack and ruin even physically. From among the many methods of living adhered to by the majority of people, the author selects thirteen for careful consideration, in order to exemplify to the reader the moral and material dangers that lurk behind each one, if pursued exclusively. A cursory perusal of these thirteen doctrines of life as presented by the author, makes it at once doubtful whether they had all come to his knowledge from personal observation. Some of them, as we shall see, are of such a nature that while they may at all times find here and there an individual advocate, they would hardly ever or anywhere become the common view of a larger, organized section of a people, and thus deserve to be raised to the dignity of a doctrine, as is here proposed by the author. Doubtless, Saadia has here again fallen under the spell of his peculiar

fondness for numbers.[531]   A brief reproduction of these doctrines under their respective headings will suffice to make this
clear.

(1) The doctrine of the *hermits,* who teach that the best
course for a man to pursue is to turn his back on the world,
isolate himself in the mountains, and weep and mourn over
the misery of human life   They repudiate marriage and all
pleasures of life, and subsist on whatever they happen to find
near them, until they are relieved by death of their wretched
existence

(2) The doctrine of *sots* and *gluttons,* who hold that good
eating and drinking is the highest purpose in life.   With the
greatest enthusiasm they picture the wonderful feeling after
a rich meal and the cheerful effect produced by wine   All
human enterprise, they say, has as its sole purpose the
gratification of the stomach, all friendships and social enjoyments are based on conviviality.   Saadia is equally extravagant in depicting the opposite effects of this epicurism.

(3) The doctrine of the *voluptuaries,* who aver that the
gratification of sexual desire is the highest aim one should
strive after   " Sexual intercourse," they assert, " is the consummation of human happiness, it cheers the soul, drives
away all worry and melancholy, and, what is more, it main-
tains all existence '   Saadia opposes this doctrine most emphatically, showing the sad results of excessive sexuality.

(4) The doctrine of *lovers*[532]   Love is the most exalted
feeling a human being is capable of.   To experience love

----

[531] See above, notes 473, 526, Guttmann, p. 263, n 2   For some of the
theories various parallels were adduced by Guttmann from Greek
and other sources.

[532] For this doctrine see in particular Guttmann, 269-273, who quotes
the parallels from Plato   So far as I know, it has never been noticed
that what is here reported by Saadia is found in the *Apophthegms*
of the famous translator of Greek works, Honein b 'Ishâk (died 873),
which were translated from Arabic into Hebrew by Judah al-Harizi
(comp Steinschneider, *Hebraische Uebersetzungen,* pp 348 ff)   The
Hebrew translation was edited by A. Loewenthal, under the title
מוסרי הפילוסופים, Frankfurt a/M , 1896 Thus, on p 25, no 43, the
theory that love is due to the influence of the stars is presented with

should therefore be one's highest pursuit in life. "Love
ennobles the mind, purifies the character, and transports the
soul with joy." The followers of this view further theorize
that "love is an extremely delicate substance produced by
nature and infused into the human heart, originally through
an incidental *coup d'oeil* and, once there, it assumes the
aspect of a feeling of hope and desire. Through this feeling
the substance becomes firmly rooted in the heart, then other
elements (sexual passion) are added to the original substance, which make it endure. They even declare that love
is due to the influences of the stars: If two people were born
in the ascendant of two stars facing each other in full or in
part and both standing under the influence of one zodiacal
sign, the two persons will attract one another on sight.
They go still further and assert that love is a divine institution. The souls, so runs their theory, were created in the
form of globes, each globe consisting of two souls. Then
the globes were divided into two equal halves and each half
placed in some human being. When a person possessing the
one half of a certain globe happens to meet the person who
possess the other half of that globe, the two feel irresistibly
drawn toward one another by love. Finally they venture
to ascribe to love a religious significance, contending that
God affected men with this powerful passion in order to
make them suffer humiliations and thus learn to be humble
and to submit to His will."

Saadia argues against this panegyric of love with exceptional vehemence, and even excuses himself for discussing

---

full detail in the name of Plato, while on p. 38, no. 64, the theory of
the "globes" is given in the name of Ptolemy (בטלמיום, which is
a mistake for אפלטון, see Steinschneider, *l. c.*, p. 353, n. 687) ; comp.
also p. 36, no. 9, another theory in the name of Galen. Ḥonein is
probably the source of Saadia. This is strongly supported by the fact
that the description of the origin of love (a substance sunk into the
heart) and of its bad effects (melancholia and coma), especially
the latter, are found in the *Apophthegms* of Ḥonein (p. 35, no. 10)
almost verbally, under the heading איפוקראט [י]מוסרן, "moral
sentences of Hippocrates." Ḥonein was the source also of Joḥanan
Alemano, שער החשק, *ed.* Halberstadt, 1862, *fol.* 29a.

so base a conception of life. The reason for his particular
objection to the love-doctrine is that, as becomes apparent
from some of his arguments, its eulogizers, as he knew them
from Greek sources through the medium of Arabic, did not
confine their praise to love between different sexes, but
included the abomination of sodomy.[533]

(5) The doctrine of *materialists,* who advocate the accu-
mulation of wealth. " They insist that the only proper course
for man to take is the pursuit of money. They base their erroneous [534] view on the fact that all the pleasures and neces-
sities of life can be obtained only with money, that all business
transactions, government affairs, social relations, matrimony,
and so forth center around it." In opposition thereto,
Saadia describes the great evils resulting from the hunt after
money: The nervous strain and restlessness, the deterioration
of the moral character through the oppression of the weaker,
the utter disregard of truth and honesty,[535] and the like. Nor
should the dangers attending the possession of wealth
be overlooked. Wealth arouses the envy of the poor and
invites maltreatment and extortion by the mighty. Finally,
its possession is never assured; often it happens that a degenerate son throws to the wind the ill-gotten fortune of his
father.

(6) The doctrine of those who see the greatest human
happiness in the possession of *children.* " Children are the
joy and the delight of their parents, the only object of one's
sincere love and affection, a treasure and comfort in old

---

[533] See Guttmann, p. 269. This is also evident from Saadia's argument, that " if love had the origin they claim for it, we should never
find that Zaid would love 'Amr without 'Amr's reciprocating his
love " ('*Am.* p. 269, l. 3; in *Em.,* p. 150, the names Reuben and Simeon
are substituted, as usual, for Zaid and 'Amr).

[534] For והישלמת, in the Hebrew text (p. 151) read וְהִשְׁלוֹם (hif'il of
שלה), to delude, mislead, not והטעו, as proposed by Guttmann,
p. 273, n. 3.

[535] The Hebrew text (p. 152, l. 6) has here העברת הכוערים, which
means " breaking of promises." Guttmann read the latter word as
plural of כּוֹעֵר, festival, and translated accordingly (*Übertretung
der religiösen . . . . Gebote*).

age, the only ones who remember us in love when we are dead." Saadia shows the other side of the medal. He points to the great difficulties in supplying children's needs and in giving them proper education, without which, he says, they are no blessing; recalls the dangers of disease and death, and of the disgrace that depraved sons or wayward daughters may bring upon their parents; and concludes with the citation of a passage from the Book of Sirach,[536] which relates to the latter point.

(7) The doctrine of those who maintain that one's sole occupation in life should be making the *earth* habitable (ישוב העולם), especially the cultivation of the soil, because all life depends upon the produce of mother earth. Besides, occupation with building and agriculture invigorates mind and body, induces thrift and procures prosperity. Saadia admits in general the importance of agriculture, but ridicules the idea that occupation therewith should be considered the sole source of human happiness.

(8) The doctrine of *longevity*. " The adherents of this doctrine claim that man's greatest care in this world should be the prolongation of his life, for through it he can accomplish all he desires in religious as well as in worldly matters. In order to attain long life, they advise, one should indulge in the pleasures of life with great moderation, always endeavor to keep up good spirits, and under all circumstances avoid dangerous situations." Saadia, in the first place, denies that longevity can be assured by following out the advice given. "We find that many people who live according to this prescription, die a premature death, while others who disregard it, reach a high age. Often people of strong physique die suddenly, while others of a delicate constitution live long." Moreover, it is not true that life, as such, is the highest good. He points to the innumerable and unavoidable troubles of life in its various stages, particularly to the infirmities of old age, and contends that this life should only be regarded as a preparation for life in the world eternal.

[536] See above, note 463.

(9) The doctrine of those who consider the acquisition of *power* and *dominion* as the foremost object in life. " They say that the ambition for the possession of greatness is a natural instinct, that the human mind resents humiliation and submission to others, that the consciousness of power cheers [537] the soul, raises the spirits, encourages enterprise, and widens the sphere of activity, and that without power and authority there would be no civilization." Saadia very pointedly remarks that these advocates of power knowingly suppress the real truth in the matter. Order and civilization are not effected by power and authority as such, but by the wisdom and foresight with which these are exercised. Authority based on power alone is a misfortune to the world and in the end also to the one who possesses it. A powerful but unwise individual will interfere with all human activities, and will arrogate to himself final authority on art and science, politics and religion. Should he succeed in usurping the government, he will turn everybody into an enemy, so that he will have to take even his meals under guard, " live as under the edge of a sword, as if his entire existence hung upon a hair."

(10) The doctrine of *vengeance*. " Its adherents praise the practice of vengeance as the most desirable occupation in life, because it frees the soul from worry, relieves mental strain, disposes of the necessity of constant scheming and plotting against the adversary, fills the avenger with satisfaction, and serves as a warning to other enemies." It is only natural that Saadia should strongly object to so unholy a view. For religious reasons and on general grounds, he denies that taking revenge ever gives lasting satisfaction. We may at times experience such feeling when our enemy falls through his own wrongdoings, but not when we have caused him to fall.

<hr />

[537] Thus the Arabic text (p. 305, l. 12: תסרׄהא) ; Ibn Tibbon (p. 154, line 6 from below) has מחזקת, strengthens. He must therefore have read תישׄדהא, or תישׄדרהא. The text of the second Arabic recension, followed by Ibn Tibbon, is here missing.

(11) The doctrine of *scholars*. "Some scholars believe
that man's only occupation in this world should be study and
research, for through it he will arrive at the knowledge of
everything on earth, as the elements of nature and their compositions, and of much [538] that is in heaven, as the stars and the
spheres. Besides, knowledge has its special charms, gladden-
ing the soul and, like medicine, curing it of ignorance.
Knowledge is the spiritual food of the soul and an ornament [539]
to man, as jewels are to kings, and he who does not strive
after it nor appreciate it, is not to be accounted fully a human
being." Our author recognizes the elements of truth contained in this view, but opposes its exclusiveness and onesidedness. Exclusive devotion to learning brings poverty and
destitution, and thus makes the scholar dependent upon the
good will of others. A poor scholar is despised, his opinion
is neither sought nor relied upon, his learning, consequently,
worthless. Should he try to maintain his independence
and subsist on dry bread and the like, he will find that his
learning deteriorates, for poor living is harmful to the mind.
Moreover, the world cannot exist by the study of the sciences
alone, without any practical occupation. The devotees of
the scholarly view defeat their own purpose. Nor is it
proper to advocate the study of the sciences [540] to the exclusion of the study of law and religion, for the knowledge

[538] The Hebrew text has in all editions הבורא, for which must be
read הרבה.

[539] Here again all Hebrew editions have either ואינו, or ועינו,
which makes no sense. Read: וזינו, which in the sense of *ornament*
is used only in Arabic. Saadia quotes here Proverbs, 1. 9. In his
Commentary on Proverbs *ad locum* (p. 16, top) he indeed says:
אלעלם ואלדין גמיעא המא זין אלאנסאן, "learning and piety combined are the ornament of man."

[540] This is the meaning of Ibn Tibbon's חכמת היצירה, *i. e.*,
"science of nature," or natural science, not as Guttmann, p. 280
(comp. p. 281, n. 1), translates: *speculative Wissenschaft*. Saadia
speaks here of physics, not of metaphysics; for details see Malter,
"Mediæval Hebrew Terms for Nature," in the Hermann Cohen-
Festschrift (Judaica), pp. 253 ff.

of the sciences [341] is intended only as a means towards a better understanding of religious duties.

(12) The doctrine of *penance*. "There are many who proclaim that the best thing for a man to do is to devote himself solely to the worship of God. He should fast during the day and spend the nights in prayer and praise of God. He should relinquish all worldly occupations and leave it to God to provide him with all the necessaries of life. The worship of God affords us the greatest pleasure, thrills us with joy and rapture, and, besides, assures us of the reward of the world to come." Saadia here has the Christian monks in mind, and refutes their theory of life on the ground that a life of penance counteracts the purpose of God in creating the world. Mankind needs but to indulge in such practices for a single generation, and there would be no other generation to take its place, as we should all die of inanity, childless, and thus penance itself would exist no more. The laws and ordinances of any religion have a meaning only in connection with human activities. If we renounce life altogether for the sake of doing penance, we have no chance whatever to obey or disobey any of the religious precepts. What, then, is the object of doing penance? Its advocates might say that they would encourage others to attend to the practical needs of the world, while they would cling to their method of living; but then it is the others who are the real servants of God in carrying out His will, not they who persist in doing nothing. As to their reliance on God, that He will supply them with a livelihood, they might better rely on Him to provide them with the desired reward in the world to come without their incessant prayers for it.

(13) The doctrine of *idleness*, "Some teach that rest and inactivity is the best conduct in life, for it gives composure and serenity to the soul, furthers digestion, promotes the growth of the body, and strengthens the senses.

[341] The editions have העולם (אהבת). According to the Arabic text we should expect זאת (אהבת), the latter word referring back to חכמת היצידה.

In all his toil and labor man looks forward with eagerness
to the pleasure of rest which is to follow." " I find," says
Saadia, " that these people are the most ignorant of all, and
misunderstand their own words. The very idea of rest
presupposes work and activity. Rest that is not preceded
by work is a mere word. In reality such rest means sluggish-
ness and indolence, and these lead to poverty and physical
misery." Saadia enumerates ten special diseases caused by
laziness, which might be interesting for the history of medicine, among them hernia, tumors, podagra, nephritis, and
elephantiasis. Even those, he adds, whose needs are provided by others should not sit idle, but should work for the
sake of work.

As said before, not all the theories here described were
actually in vogue among the people of Saadia's acquaintance.
In his desire to carry his point against all bias and narrow-
mindedness in the conception of life, he selected for criticism
a number of ideas found in the works of individual Greek
and Muhammedan authors, who expressed themselves in
favor of the one or the other, either incidentally or in ex-
pounding their systems of life. He labored the point that
whether a particular course in life be vicious or virtuous,
dogmatic and onesided adherence to it is bound to lead to
failure; for in all walks of life it is prejudiced onesidedness
that works moral and material injury. Saadia advises that
man live in accordance with the requirements of his natural
inclinations and propensities, but keep them under strict
control. One must beware of exaggerations and excesses,
carrying out all functions of life at the proper time and in
the proper place, refraining therefrom when reason or
religion so demands.[541a] Among the thirteen tendencies dis-

[541a] The underlying idea of Saadia's disquisition is the famous
Aristotelian doctrine of the *Golden Mean*. Saadia is thus the first
mediaeval Jewish thinker who utilized this doctrine for Jewish Ethics. He was followed by a host of others, particularly
Maimonides, who has treated the subject in all its aspects. For further details see Malter, *Shem Tob Palquera*, *JQR.*, *N. S.*, vol. I (1910-
1911), pp. 160, n. 15; 484, n. 88; Gorfinkle, *the Eight Chapters of*

cussed, he designates those to despotism, vengeance, and indolence as absolutely immoral, and therefore entirely to be
avoided. He compares his method with that of the physician
who prescribes medicine composed of various ingredients in
unequal parts according to the needs of the case, but excludes therefrom whatever he thinks to be positively
injurious to the patient.

We might expect the foregoing remarks to be the end of
the disquisition on the subject. The matter would seem to
have been viewed from all sides, leaving nothing essential
to be added. The author realizes this, but, he says, he deems
it fit at the close of the chapter "to add gratuitously" a
special paragraph in which he purposes to show that in the
realm of nature, also, it is mixture and composition that
produces the highest and most pleasing effects. This, he continues, will serve as an illustration of what was said above
regarding our moral world and the necessity of employing
jointly all our natural instincts and intellectual endowments
in order to make life complete. He selects for this illustration
the impressions made by the objects of nature on the senses of
sight, hearing, and smell, leaving out the sense of taste,
because too obvious, and that of touch, because, according
to some ancient theory of physiology, it responds with
pleasure only to a single quality, that of softness.[440] As to
the sense of sight, we know that any elementary, unmixed
color, as white, red, yellow, or black, is hard on the eyes, if
they are persistently fixed upon it for some time. Besides,
these colors do not produce any cheering effect on the soul.
Only when they are mixed with others, the composition may

Maimonides, New York, 1912, pp. 54 ff.; Guttmann, in Isr. Lewy's
Festschrift, pp. 323 f. (*Moses ben Maimon*, II, 213) ; comp. above,
note 399. As to the popularity of the doctrine among Muhammedan
writers see Goldziher, *Muhammedanische Studien*, II, 398.

[440] A contrary view regarding the sense of touch is held by Abra-
ham Ibn Daûd; comp. Guttmann, *Die Religionsphilosophie des
Abraham Ibn Daud*, p. 82. For details see Kaufmann, *Die Sinne*,
Leipzig, 1884, pp. 172 ff.

in various ways be soothing to the eye and stimulate the
different faculties of the soul to action.[542a]

Saadia proceeds to describe the different effects certain
combinations of colors have on the soul, the one producing
vigor and strength, the other sadness and melancholy, and
the like. The same holds true with regard to the sense of
hearing. A single sound or tone has only one effect, and
this one often unpleasant. Only the concord of different
notes is capable of producing harmony and sweetness. Here
again Saadia enters upon a detailed description of the eight
fundamental musical tones and their intervals, or semitones,
and defines the effect of certain musical compositions on
soul and character. Finally, the sense of smell is taken up,
and treated in a similar way, and he shows that in odors, too,
the best results are achieved by combinations.[543]

If, as we have seen—so Saadia concludes—even in the
physical world it is only through a proper distribution and
co-ordination of forces that we arrive at the highest possible good, how much more is it desirable that we should
follow the same method in our moral and religious conduct,
for it is only through achievement of inner harmony and
equilibrium that we can attain to a perfectly sound and
godly life.

[542a] " Red combined with yellow," Saadia says, " stimulates the
choleric humor and its properties; the soul then manifests energy
and vigor. Yellow mixed with black makes the *phlegmatic* humor
predominate, producing in the soul a state of dejection. A combination of black, red, yellow, and white sets into action the *sanguine*
humor; the soul then manifests a will to power and dominion.
Finally, a combination of green and yellow stirs up the *black* humor
(melancholia), producing in the soul timidity and sadness. In
like manner the increase or diminution of each of the ingredients
in the mixture of colors brings about a corresponding change in
psychic qualities."

[543] The text of this entire paragraph, particularly the portion dealing
with music, offers great difficulties, which I have endeavored to
explain in my forthcoming edition of the *Emūnōt;* comp. Guttmann,
pp. 285-289; Ackermann, in Winter and Wünche's *Die jüdische
Litteratur,* III, 500; below, *Bibliography,* p. 369.

In accordance with his usual method Saadia quotes
numerous verses from the Bible, particularly from the Book
of Ecclesiastes, and interprets them to make them bear out
his ethical theories. Several of these verses serve him as
a basis for the commendation of certain good habits and
qualities which one should try to acquire, among them the
effort to leave a good name to posterity, mindfulness of
human frailty, zeal for the honor of God, patience and endurance, association with scholars and pious men, and consciousness of one's failings and shortcomings.

Saadia now closes his work with the following lines:
" Nothing in this book will be of benefit, save to him who has
purified [64] his heart and is intent on his moral elevation, as it is
said (Job, 11, 13 ff) : If thou set thy heart aright and stretch
out thy hands toward Him, surely then shalt thou lift up thy
face without spot." A few other verses are quoted to the
same effect.

POLEMICAL WORKS

Polemics is a natural result of intellectual life and activity
Wherever there is a great display of mental energy and
devotion to some cause on the part of an individual or a
multitude of men imbued by the same spirit, it is bound to
arouse the opposition and antagonism of others whose interests and opinions go in a different direction. This is, as
everybody knows, the origin of all sects and schisms known
to history. In the history of the Jewish people schismatic
tendencies and actual defections from the general cause were
not of infrequent occurrence. But at no time has there been
so much dissension among the Jews and so much proneness
to the formation of new sects as was the case in Oriental
Jewry during the last two centuries before Saadia. The air
was filled with religious unrest. Rationalists and mystics,
demagogues and dreamers of all sorts succeeded one another
and found adherents among the people, each one con-

---

[64] The Hebrew text is here corrupt, hence Guttmann's incorrect
translation, " die Herzen zu reinigen " For כי אם לזכות הלב
read כי אם עם זכות הלב, as in Arabic: מע אבלאין אלקלוב

tributing his share to the general confusion. None of the numerous sects, it is true, that arose in eastern Jewry during the period in question, survived for any length of time; but the repeated uprisings of these schismatics against the authority of traditional Judaism brought about a state of religious and intellectual commotion that continued its destructive effects long after the original causes had disappeared. Saadia himself, in his preface to the *Kitâb al-'Amânât,* gives a forceful description of these conditions, part of which was quoted above.[545]

More than all other sects it was the sect of the Karaites, founded by the energetic Anan b. David, in 760, that threatened to overthrow the authority of official rabbinic Judaism. To what extent the Geonim, the representatives of that Judaism, tried to counteract the spread and influence of the new sect, cannot be ascertained from the existing sources. In all probability they did nothing in this direction; either because they were too busy with the interpretation of the traditional law and the adjustment of the constant quarrels between them and the Exilarchs, as well as between the two rival academies which they represented, or—what is more likely—none of them possessed enough general education and literary skill to take up the fight against the very active and energetic propagators of the new doctrine. It required a man with the comprehensive learning, the sharp, tireless pen, and, above all, the fighting disposition of Saadia, to set himself against the manifold heresies that had invaded the minds of the Jewish people, and especially against the alarming spread of Karaism, which threatened the very existence of traditional Judaism. Indeed, Saadia was the first and the last great scholar in eastern Jewry who, single-handed, waged a fierce literary war on all Jewish sectarians, particularly on the Karaites. As early as his Egyptian period, when he was only in his twenty-third year, he struck at the very root of Karaism, in a book against Anan, the founder of the sect.

---

[545] Conditions like those described by Saadia prevailed at that time also among the Muhammedans. An interesting parallel will be found in August Müller, *Der Islam,* I, 591.

It is easily possible that it was this book which aroused the great enmity and persecution on the part of the Egyptian Karaites that made it necessary for him to leave his native country.[546] Saadia persisted in fighting Karaism with literary weapons; and throughout his checkered life he continued to combat its apostles with unrelenting vigor, so that he became the most dreaded and most hated opponent of the sect down to our own times. We need not go so far as to assume with one recent investigator that everything Saadia has written in the numerous branches of Jewish literature had as its sole purpose the refutation of Karaite doctrines.[547] There are several works by Saadia in which anti-Karaite tendencies can be discovered only by a considerable stretch of the imagination.[548] It must be admitted, however, that polemic against heresies in general and Karaism in particular, direct and indirect, is a very conspicuous feature in most of Saadia's writings. His commentaries on the Bible, the *Kitâb al-'Amânât*,[549] and many other works contain numerous controversial passages directed against Jewish schismatics, especially the Karaites, although he does not always mention them by name. Our present discussion naturally excludes incidental controversies occurring in the works treated under the different branches to which they

[546] See above, p. 58 [and especially the *Postscript*].

[547] Hirschfeld, *JQR.*, XVII, 714 f., and recently in the Cohen *Festschrift*, pp. 265 f., and with still more emphasis in his latest article, *JQR., N. S.*, vol. VIII (1917-1918), p. 166. He is followed by Davidson, *Saadia's Polemic against Hiwi Al-Balkhi*, p. 36.

[548] Thus one will hardly discover any trace of opposition to Karaism in Saadia's Commentary on the *Sêfer Yeẓirah*, nor is there reason to believe that his grammatical works ('*Agrōn*, etc.) and poetical compositions (as the שיר על האותיות) were intended against the Karaites. For the תרי"ג מצות see Müller, *Oeuvres*, IX, p. xix; for the פרוש י"ג מדות see above, note 357; below, *Bibliography*, III, p. 342.

[549] Comp. Poznański, *JQR.*, X, 257 f. As to the passages about the "so-called" Jews referred to by Poznański, *l. c.*, see above, note 524. For anti-Karaite passages in the various writings of Saadia see Poznański, *ibidem*, and additions thereto in his *Karaite Literary Opponents of Saadiah*, pp. 97-99.

belong, and limits itself to the works devoted exclusively to polemics. It should be here observed that none of Saadia's polemical writings has been preserved. Of some a few fragments have been brought to light lately from the Genizah. Others are known only by quotations in Saadia's own works or in those of other authors, Ḳaraite as well as Rabbanite. Though all the controversial writings turned about points of the Law, later ages, when the Ḳaraite movement had lost its original significance, did not attach enough importance to these works to preserve them for posterity. They were allowed to fall into oblivion.[550] The following are the works thus far ascertained:

1. *Kitâb al-Radd 'alâ 'Anân* (כתאב אלרד עלי ענן), "Refutation of Anan."[551] Saadia's first polemical work, written in 915[551a] in Egypt. Nothing definite can be said as to the extent and content of this book. A Ḳaraite author, in quoting two passages from Saadia's lost commentaries on Genesis and Leviticus, refers to his "Refutation of Anan." From this it appears that he took Anan to task on questions of the calendar, which, according to the innovations of Anan, was to be fixed by observation instead of the rabbinic method of calculation. Besides questions of law and Biblical interpretation the book seems to have contained personal attacks against the founder of the sect, accusing him of low motives and selfish interests. It was in existence at the end of the twelfth century, but since then no reference to it has become known.

2. *Kitâb al-Tamyîz* (כתאב אלתמייז), "Book of Distinction." Probably Saadia's most important and most voluminous polemical work, written in 926-7, by which time, as I have demonstrated (pp. 63 f.), the author had been officially connected with the Suran academy. Unlike Saadia's other polemical writings, this work was not directed against any

---

[550] It is also very probable that all the polemical works of Saadia were systematically destroyed by the Ḳaraites, against whom they were directed; comp. Pinsker, *Likḳūtē*, I, 112; Hirschfeld, *JQR.*, *N. S.*, vol. VIII (1917-1918), p. 177.

[551] For the literature see the *Bibliography*, p. 380.

[551a See *Postscript*].

particular author, but against the Karaites in general. Several extensive fragments have come to light from the Genizah. Besides, a Karaite author of the tenth century has preserved considerable portions of the book in his Bible commentary. He reproduced them verbally in order to give the reader a clear notion of the work. Saadia himself quotes it together with his " Refutation of Anan " in the passage from his commentary on Genesis referred to above (p. 263), which was preserved by the same Karaite author. He quotes it also in his " Refutation of Ibn Sâkawaihi," to be discussed below. Moreover, several Rabbanite authors, as for instance, Moses and Abraham Ibn Ezra, refer to it under the hebraized title ספר ההכרה or ספר המבחן, and give some indications of its contents. These fragments and quotations show that nearly all points of divergence between Rabbanites and Karaites were discussed in the work. The question of the calendar must have formed the greatest portion of the controversial matter.[562] Other questions are about the lighting of lights on Sabbath, the date of the Feast of Weeks, and the validity of the Oral Law. One of the fragments,[563] which forms the concluding chapter of the book, mentions a " Judah al-Iskandarâni," who, as has been assumed by recent scholars on sufficient grounds, is none other than Philo of Alexandria.[564] The closing lines of the work are : " I adjure by God those who study this book that they do it with a pure heart and strive after the truth, whether it be far or near, that they devote themselves to the Scripture and the Mishnah and to correct reasoning. Then they will arrive at [the truth] laid down in this book, and will thus re-

[562] This is apparent from the lengthy fragment in Schechter's *Saadyana*, no. ix ; see also Poznański, *JQR.*, X, 252 ; *Karaite Literary Opponents*, p. 96.

[563] The one edited by Hirschfeld, *JQR.*, XVI, 102-105 ; see the *Bibliography*, p. 381, letter *b*.

[564] See Poznański, *REJ.*, L, 10-31 ; *Karaite Literary Opponents*, p. 95 ; comp. *JQR.*, XVII, 65 ; B. Revel, *The Karaite Halakah*, Philadelphia, 1913, pp. 86 f.

move from their hearts all doubts and errors—with the help of the Merciful."[555]

3. *Kitâb al-Radd 'alâ Ibn Sâkawaihi* (כתאב אלרד עלי אבן סאקויה), "Refutation of Ibn Sâkawaihi" (or Sâkûya) written after the "Tamyiz." Various hypotheses have been advanced as to the identity of this Karaite, but none of them is sufficiently assured. So far as can be gathered from the scant sources, Ibn Sâkawaihi, provoked by Saadia's anti-Karaite writings, wrote a book under the title "Kitâb al-Fadâih" (Book of Shameful Things), in which he attacked the most essential parts of the rabbinic law. The title "Shameful Things" is meant as a derogative designation of the rabbinic law. Saadia's work was a rejoinder to that of the Karaite. Several extensive fragments, covering about twelve pages in close print, have of late been discovered.[556] From these we learn not only the scope and content of Saadia's Refutation, but get sufficient information also about the nature of the work of Ibn Sâkawaihi. The latter was divided into ten sections, each dealing with a special subject of rabbinic law in an antagonistic spirit, accusing the Rabbis of attributing to God bodily qualities, of misinterpreting the Bible, and of falsifying the calendar. Saadia takes up all the points of his opponent, to whom he often refers as "that ignoramus," or "that tyro," and refutes them one by one. The title "Shameful Things," he says, is appropriate to Ibn Sâkawaihi's work, for it reveals the author's own shame and impudence (כויה). It may be mentioned that in one of the fragments[557] the author makes allusion to the year when the Messiah may be expected. The computation is on lines different from those given in the eighth chapter of his *Kitâb al-'Amânât.*

[555] The ending is almost in the same words as that of the *'Amânât,* above, p. 260. Hirschfeld's translation of these lines (*JQR.,* XVI, 99) is altogether incorrect.

[556] See the *Bibliography,* pp. 382 ff.

[557] *JQR.,* XVI, 101; comp. Malter, in Neumark's *Journal of Jewish Lore and Philosophy,* Cincinnati, 1919, pp. 45-59.

4 *Kitâb al-Radd 'alâ al-Mutaḥâmil* (כתאב אלרד עלי
אלמתחאמל), "Refutation of an Overbearing Antagonist,"
whose name the author does not mention. It is not impossible that this is another rejoinder to the same Karaite, Ibn
Sâḳawaihi.[558] Of this polemical writing only one fragment
has been discovered, and that, recently. It deals with the question of the proper appointment of the Festival of Passover.
According to the rabbinic rules of the calendar, Passover
could never fall on Monday, Wednesday, or Friday.[559] The
Karaites opposed this rule, and Saadia shows that their opposition is based on a wrong interpretation of the Scriptural
verses relating to the question Another point of controversy in this fragment is the day on which the showbread
was set on the table in the Tabernacle. The Karaite author argued against the plain meaning of the verse (Leviticus,
24.8), that it was on Friday, and this opinion Saadia refutes.
From the points of controversy it is obvious that Saadia's
antagonist was a Karaite and not a rabbinical dissenter.
That we have here again a part of the preceding work
(No. 3) and not a separate treatise is quite improbable,
because several sources refer to a separate work under the
title "Refutation of the Overbearing Antagonist,"[560] and
the fragment in question, too, addresses itself to such
(הרֹא אלמתחאמל). As to the time when this controversy was written, nothing definite can be said. An author of the earlier part of the twelfth century[561] quotes a
passage from a controversial work by Saadia against a
heretic, probably a Karaite, in which reference is made by
Saadia to the "Book of Unity," and the same passage occurs in the second chapter of Saadia's *Kitâb al-'Amânât*,
which bears this title. The controversial work in question
might, accordingly, have to be assigned to a time subsequent

[558] Comp. Hirschfeld, *JQR.*, XVIII, 113 f.; Eppenstein, *Beitrage*,
p 109, n 4

[559] *JQR.*, X, 271.

[560] See the *Bibliography*, p. 384

[561] Judah b Barzillai, פס״י, pp 20 ff , see the *Bibliography*, p 383,
letter *d*.

to the composition of the *Kitâb al-'Amânât* (933). It is doubtful, however, whether the passage quoted by the twelfth century author was taken from the work under consideration, or, what is more probable, from the Refutation directed against Ibn Sâkawaihi. Moreover, as previously stated,[562] various chapters, if not all, of the *Kitâb al-'Amânât* were issued by Saadia as separate essays, prior to the appearance of the book as a whole. The controversial work, whichever of the two it might be, might therefore have reference to the single treatise and, like the latter, precede the *Kitâb al-'Amânât*. Finally, it should be borne in mind that aside from the polemics here enumerated Saadia wrote works of the same kind against other heretics and Karaites, the titles of which have not been preserved. He also engaged in frequent oral disputations with various opponents of Rabbinism, and subsequently embodied their arguments as well as his counter-arguments into his numerous works, especially into those on the calendar and into some of his commentaries on the Bible, which are likewise lost.[563] A quotation in the works of later authors, such as the one referred to above, may therefore have been taken from one or the other of these lost works of Saadia. No definite inference as to its particular source should be made, unless supported by other evidence.

5. *Kitâb al-Radd 'alâ Hayawaihi* (*vulgo* Ḥiwi) *al-Balḥi* (כתאב אלרד עלי חִיוִיה אלבלכִי), "Refutation of Ḥiwi al-Balḥi," *i. e.* of Balkh, Persia. Written in Hebrew rhymed prose and referred to by Saadia himself in his *Kitâb al-'Amânât* and in his later work, the *Sēfer ha-Gālui*. Ḥiwi was not a Karaite nor a follower of any particular sect, but a Jewish radical, who denied not only the validity of the Talmud, but also that of the Bible, either in its entirety or in part. Guided by certain heretical works of Muhammedan and Persian authors, severe critics of the Korân, he applied their criti-

---

[562] See above, note 456.

[563] Thus Abraham Ibn Ezra's quotations of Saadia's refutation of the Karaite Ben Zuṭa (on Exodus 21, 24, Leviticus, 23, 15) in all probability refer to a verbal dispute between the Gaon and the Karaite; see below, *Bibliography*, section VII, p. 398, nos. 9, 10.

cism to the Bible, trying to prove that its statements often
contradict one another, and that many of its teachings are
against reason. He is reported to have written a book in
which he raised two hundred objections to the Scriptures.
Of these none has been preserved directly, but their nature
and purpose are known from the recently published fragment of Saadia's " Refutations," which were partly embodied also into his *Kitâb al-'Amânât*, and from quotations
of later authors, especially Abraham Ibn Ezra. From these
we see that Ḥiwi believed in the eternity of the world, and
denied free will and the possibility of miracles. He also
attacked the Biblical passages that required the Israelites
to build a tabernacle and to offer sacrifices, and he doubted
the veracity of various Scriptural narratives, thus endeavoring to destroy the very foundation of the Jewish religion.
He is said to have prepared an abridged Bible, from which
he eliminated all objectionable portions, and to have introduced it as a text-book into Jewish schools. Owing to the
religious unrest that prevailed among the eastern Jews of that
time, as depicted also by Saadia, his ideas found many followers and his text-book seems to have had a wide circulation.[564]

We can imagine with what fervor and determination
Saadia took up the fight against these dangerous heresies.
Aside from the special work in refutation of them, a considerable portion of which has only been recovered recently,[565]
he carried on actual war against the writings of Ḥiwi and, as
we are told by the twelfth century chronicler Abraham Ibn
Daud, he succeeded in having the expurgated Bible banished
from the schools. In his *Sêfer ha-Gâlui* (p. 177) Saadia
points to his Refutation of Ḥiwi as a specially meritorious
deed of his.

[564] For all the details here mentioned see the references in the
Bibliography, pp. 384 ff.

[565] This very interesting portion, covering about one sixth of the
whole work, was found and published by Dr. Israel Davidson. A
full account of it is given in the *Bibliography*, p. 386.

6. *Sēfer ha-Gālui* (ספר הנלוי), " The Open Book," a title borrowed from Jeremiah, 32. 14. Saadia wrote this work during the years of his seclusion, after having been removed from the Gaonate by the Exilarch David b. Zakkai (931-934). It was composed in Hebrew in a highly rhetorical style, divided into verses, vocalized and accentuated after the manner of the Bible. The author's main intention was to justify his position in the struggle with the Exilarch and to defend himself against the attacks of his numerous adversaries. Incidentally it was to serve as a model of elegant Hebrew style. His enemies were not convinced by his expositions, and his imitation of the Bible, which they considered an act of arrogance and irreverence, only gave them additional ground for renewed opposition. Saadia then issued a second work (935-6), this time in Arabic, to which the original Hebrew text, perhaps in a revised and enlarged edition, may have been added. In this work, which he describes as *Al-Kitâb al-Târid* (אלכתאב אלטארד), " The Book that Refutes," he translated and commented upon the difficult Hebrew text, defended various points of grammar and style, which had been made the object of criticism by his opponents, and inserted some other material of a literary and controversial nature. The whole was preceded by a lengthy Arabic Introduction, in which the author summarized the contents of the book and related the causes that had led him to its composition.[566] Several extensive fragments[567] of both the Hebrew and Arabic texts, one of which covers nearly the whole Arabic Introduction, have been recovered, altogether about forty printed pages. In the Introduction[568] we receive most valuable information regarding the history and

[566] The proofs for all these statements, which in many points are at variance with the generally accepted view, will be found in the discussion given in connection with the *Bibliography* on this book.

[567] See the description in the *Bibliography*, pp. 387-394.

[568] The portion of the Introduction which is sketched in what follows was published by Malter in the *JQR., N. S.*, vol. III (1912-1913), pp. 487-499, where further details concerning the text and contents are given.

content of the work. In a few preliminary remarks, the beginning of which is missing, the author defends himself against the accusation of having assumed the rôle of a prophet by giving his book the appearance of a Biblical text. He avows that the division into verses and the addition of vowel-points and accents are merely means of facilitating the reading and understanding of a Hebrew book. He points to several post-Biblical authors before him, among them Sirach and the five sons of Mattathiah, the Hasmonean, who did the same without being censured. He then gives an outline of the whole work, from which we learn that it is divided into seven sections. The first contains a description of the value of learning and of the proper methods for its attainment, and the second deals with historical questions, *e. g.,* the duration of prophecy in Israel and the time of the redaction of the Mishnah and the Talmud. The reason for this historical investigation, he says, is that those who are called or call themselves Rabbis in his time, are quite ignorant in these matters. In the third section he describes the misfortune bound to befall a people that is ruled by a despot (as David b. Zakkai), and in the fourth he endeavors to prove from the history of Israel that God provides every generation with a sage or teacher who counteracts injustice and leads the people in the right path. With the self-confidence characteristic of Saadia, he points to his own Providential position as a leader in Israel and defender of the Law. The fifth chapter contains an exposition of the principles of the Torah and some computation as to the time of the Messianic Redemption. The sixth gives an account of the author's sufferings at the hands of his unjust enemies. The final section presents the ideas expressed in the Bible regarding the wicked who oppress the innocent and how they are punished. The purpose of this presentation, he says, is that the wicked of his own days may discover themselves in the picture and be induced to give up their evil conduct. Aside from the seven special subjects enumerated, the book as a whole, he continues, has three general purposes, the gist of which is that it is to serve the people as a model for

their Hebrew compositions;[569] for through the spread of
Arabic and Aramaic[570] they have of late forgotten the
proper usages of the Hebrew language. In this connection
he refers to his earliest known work, the *'Agrōn,* and to the
" Book on Language," both composed for a similar purpose.[571]

Aside from this general outline, the Introduction, as well
as the fragments of the work itself, contains numerous
remarks of exegetical and historical interest. If we may
judge from the material at hand, the loss of this work is
from many a point of view highly regrettable [572]

[569] See the article quoted in the preceding note, pp. 492 f., nn. 20, 22;
p. 494, n. 26.

[570] The text has נבטיה, *i. e*, Nabatean, by which Aramaic is here
meant; comp. Bacher, *JQR.,* XII, 705; Margoliouth, JQR, XIII, 157,
n. 1.

[571] See above, p 40

[572] See above, pp. 119 f., Steinschneider, *AL*, p 62, lines 9 f., from
below.

CHAPTER VII

SAADIA'S INFLUENCE ON LATER GENERATIONS

After all that has been said in the preceding chapters about
the life and activity of Saadia Gaon, there is no need to emphasize the importance of both his life and his work, not
only for the Jewry of his time but also for that of all later
generations. It is almost gratuitous to speak of the influence
of one whom we know to have been the actual originator of
a given development. Saadia did not merely influence the
Judaism of the Middle Ages, but, to a very large extent
at least, he created it. It is true that Saadia was neither
the first nor the only Jewish scholar of the Geonic period
who produced literary work either on strictly Jewish or
on general lines. In the field of the Halakah he was preceded by several eminent authors, such as 'Aḥa of Shab-
ḥeha (750), the Geonim Yehudai (760), Amram (856-
874),[573] Nahshon (874-882), who wrote on the calendar,[574]
and Zemaḥ b. Palṭoi (872-890), who composed a lexicon to
the Talmud.[575] Besides these and the earlier Masorites and
synagogue poets, like Ḳalir and others, whose productions
were of basic importance for the later development of
the respective branches, there were also grammarians,

[573] Aḥa is the author of the "Sheëltôt" (*Quaestiones*), a considerable work containing Halakic disquisitions interspersed with Haggadic elements. The book appeared twice with commentaries. To
Yehudai Gaon is attributed the "Halākôt Gedōlōt," while Amram
is credited with the compilation of the first Order of Prayers; see
above, p. 147, and the *Bibliography*, p. 335; for details regarding
these works see Ginzberg, *Geonica*, I, 73 ff.

[574] The treatise is known as the '*Iggūl* (Cycle) of R. Nahshon
and was often printed; comp. Steinschneider, *Bibliotheca Mathematica*, 1894, p. 101, no. 14; Ginzberg, *Geonica*, I, 154-158.

[575] The work existed as late as the sixteenth century, but since then
all trace of it has been lost; comp. Ginzberg, *l. c.*, pp. 159 f.

exegetes, and philosophers prior to and contemporaneous with Saadia,[576] whose works had some influence upon mediæval Jewish literature.[577] However, while many of Saadia's predecessors and contemporaries may have had a share in moulding the ideas of their time or of subsequent generations, the general development of our literature along all lines of knowledge and research actually began with Saadia. It was his comprehensive literary activity that welded numerous and diverse subjects of study and research into a rounded system of religion; that opened new perspectives to the thinking minds of the generations after him, and gave them a fresh and forceful impetus to continue to deepen the work he had begun.

It is further true that many great men of the first few centuries after Saadia, as the grammarian Jonah Ibn Ganàḥ, the exegete Abraham Ibn Ezra, the Talmudist and philosopher Maimonides, and numerous others, likewise exercised

[576] This is obvious from very numerous passages of Saadia's writings, especially from passages in his Commentary on the *Sefer Yeẓirah* and in the *Kitâb al-'Amânât*, in which he refers to or argues against predecessors; comp. *e. g.* Commentary on the *Sefer Yeẓirah*, ed. Lambert, p. 81, last line; p. 82, l. 13, where another commentator of the same work (בעיץ אלמפסרין, see Steinschneider, *Bibliotheca Mathematica*, 1895, p. 24) is mentioned; *Kitâb al-'Amânât*, p. 207, last line (*Em.*, p. 103); 247, l. 3 (*Em.*, p. 126, l. 4; comp. *ZfhB.*, III, p. 176, n. 22, where the passages are unnecessarily referred to Karaites); Introduction to his Commentary on Psalms (edited by Eppenstein in the Harkavy *Festschrift*), p. 149, bottom; comp. Rapoport, *Bikkūrē ha-'Ittim*, IX, p. 27, n. 6; J. Cohn, *MWJ.*, VIII, p. 73, n. 1; for Saadia's contemporaries see above, pp. 45, 66 f.

[577] Thus, the view that all the prophetic promises had reference to the time of the Second Temple, when they were fulfilled, a view against which Saadia, in one of the passages referred to above (*Kitâb al-'Amânât*, pp. 247 f.; *Emūnōt*, pp. 126 ff.; see above pp. 239 f.) argues with so much vehemence, is maintained also by Moses Ibn Giḳaṭillah of the eleventh century (comp. Poznański, *Moses Ibn Chiquitilla*, Leipzig, 1895, p. 27), who was strongly opposed by Naḥmanides (ספר הגאולה, London, 1909, pp. 16 ff.) and others. The matter is referred to also in an Arabic fragment of a Karaite polemic against Saadia published by Hirschfeld, *JQR., N. S.*, vol. VIII (1917-1918); see *ib.*, p. 174.

18

tremendous influence in their respective fields of work. But
they all built on the foundations laid by the Gaon; their
works are full of direct and indirect quotations from his
writings; and in some instances they could not have been
conceived without Saadia's epoch-making utterances.

It would be an interesting task, and of real value for the
history of the development of Jewish thought, to follow up
the traces of Saadia's ideas in the works of mediæval authors and to show in detail how much they were, directly
or indirectly, consciously or unconsciously, indebted to the
works of the great Gaon.

It should be borne in mind that in measuring Saadia's
influence it is not merely the direct citations found in the
works of various authors that are to be taken as a criterion.
Mediæval writers were not much concerned about stating the
exact origin of the views they expressed. Any idea in the
works of contemporaries or predecessors that appealed to
them they appropriated readily, and gave it further publicity
in their own works without the least consciousness of
plagiarism.[578] If, on the other hand, a certain view did not
meet with the approval of an author, he would argue against
it or simply deny its validity, without mentioning the one
responsible for it. The question was of the value of an
idea; its author was immaterial. The result, especially in
Jewish philosophy, was that theories were repeated by
various authors as if new and original, and subsequent
writers, when they happened to cite the source, would credit

[578] Even the Gaon Hai, so near the time of Saadia, used much of
the eighth chapter of the 'Amânât almost verbally (see below, note
614) without mentioning his source; and the same practice is observable also in the works of others. Authors of great scientific accuracy,
such as Ibn Ganâḥ (see MGWJ., 1902, p. 367, top) and Maimonides,
are no exceptions. For the latter see Guttmann, in Isr. Lewy's Festschrift, pp. 308-326 (Moses b. Maimon, II, 216); idem, Die Religionsphilosophie des Abraham Ibn Daud, Göttingen, 1879, p. 9, and above,
notes 399, 416, 446; see also above, p. 154, regarding Baḥya Ibn
Bakûdah. For some cases of conscious plagiarism see the references
in Steinschneider's Hebräische Uebersetzungen, p. 16, n. 110; Bibliotheca Mathematica, 1895, p. 103, n. 14.

the one from whom they quoted, without troubling themselves much about the accuracy of the attribution.[578a]

The literary practice here described naturally found many
exceptions. Particularly in the field of the Halakah, in
accordance with a Talmudic dictum,[579] there existed a great
anxiety to ascertain in each case the authority for a given
statement. Unlike questions of philosophy, exegesis, etc.,
it was not a matter of general reasoning, in most instances
of no immediate consequence for the religious life of the
people. The problems of the Halakah concern matters of
law and the decision is based essentially on authority and
tradition. Here, naming of the sources is of special importance. The personal element in Halakic works, excepting, of course, their method and form which were often
tacitly borrowed, becomes conspicuous, revealing the extent
of an author's dependence upon his predecessors. In all
other branches of Jewish literature anonymity and mixing of
sources are pervasive factors. To determine the influence
exerted directly or indirectly by the works of a given author
upon those of later ages, it would be necessary to go over
the entire field, comparing the related writings both in form
and content, with a view of establishing the parallels. The
immensity of such a task in the case of Saadia is obvious. If,
in addition, we consider the mixture of languages in the literature of the Jewish Middle Ages, the fact that translations
from one language into another contribute in no little measure

---

[578a] Thus, to quote a few instances only, Abraham Bédersi (13th c.),
in his חותם תכנית, Amsterdam, 1865, p. 149, quotes in the name of
Saadia what is found verbally in the translation by Ḥarizi of Maimonides's *Guide*, I, 15, while on the other hand Joseph Ibn Yaḥya
(1494-1539), תורה אור, Bologna, 1538, ch. 8, cites Maimonides for
what is originally Saadia's. Similarly, Saadia's discussion of the
permutation of letters (see above, p. 186, with reference to Esther,
9. 3) is quoted twice in the name of Eleazar of Worms (12th c.) by
Judah Moscato in his קול יהודה, a commentary on the *Kuzari* (Wilna
1905) ; see *ib.*, p. 25 *ad Kuzari*, I, 1, and p. 121, *ad* IV, 25.

[579] כל האומר דבר בשם אומרו מביא גאולה לעולם, "Whosoever
reports an idea in the name of its originator brings redemption to
the world" (*b.* Meg., 15a).

to the obliteration of identity and, finally, that the texts of
most of Saadia's works are lost, we shall realize the difficulty, if not the hopelessness, of any present-day attempt
at systematically tracing the Saadianic elements in the Judæo-
Arabic and Hebrew mediæval literature.

Be that as it may, no such investigation, useful as it might
be for our knowledge of Jewish literary history, can be
undertaken here. It would require a special volume, of considerable proportions. For our purpose it will suffice to
quote a few passages from the works of some of the most
famous mediæval authors in the different fields of Jewish learning. These will demonstrate the high respect and
almost unlimited recognition accorded to Saadia by the great
minds of subsequent ages, and thus serve as an indication—
but not a measure—of his undying influence. To begin
with, Sherira Gaon (about 900-998), who may have known
Saadia personally, in deciding a certain Talmudic question
against a decision attributed to Saadia, declares it to be
spurious, " because," he says, " Saadia was so great a scholar
that no important law could have escaped him." [580] About
the same time the philologist Menahem b. Sarūk, finding
himself at variance with Saadia on certain grammatical
points surrenders his own position in the following words:
" As to R. Saadia, who has arranged these nouns under
the letter He, I do not know what prompted him to do so,
and what was his opinion thereon. But the accuracy of his
interpretations and the comprehensiveness of his linguistic work testify to his understanding; it is therefore a
matter of propriety and loyalty not to criticise the way
he arranged his material." [581] Half a century later one
of the most eminent scholars of the time, the Talmudist
and mathematician Isaac b. Baruk Ibn al-Bâliya (1035-
1094), excuses himself for contradicting Saadia on

[580] Responsa שערי צדק, 18a, no. 11; comp. Steinschneider, AL., p.
64, n. 6.

[581] מחברת מנחם, ed. Filipofski, London, 1854, p. 69; comp. Luzzatto,
בית האוצר, I (Lemberg, 1881), 37.

a question of the calendar, as follows: "No one should reproach me, saying 'How dare you contradict a man great and distinguished far beyond your own greatness and distinction?' For, I answer, it is true that he [Saadia] was greater in every science than I am, but Moses our teacher was also a Gaon, and the greatest man in all Israel, and yet this did not prevent Eleazar the priest from doing what Moses had failed to do (Numbers, 31. 21). How much more should one be permitted to say that a view of Saadia does not appeal to him?"[582]

The renowned grammarian Jonah Ibn Ganâh, rebuking the Talmudists of his time for their neglect of Hebrew philological studies, points to Saadia as an example of a broadminded Talmudist, in the words: "Not as such are known to us the great Talmudic masters of former times, for R. Saadia, of blessed memory, displayed great efforts in this direction attaining the highest end he was capable of. He strove toward the aim which with his comprehensiveness he had set himself in explaining the language, laying bare its roots and clearing up its branches in many of his compositions, both in those written especially for the purpose, as the work entitled 'Book of the Language,' and those which were not written especially for this purpose."[583] Judah Ibn Bal'am, a great grammarian and exegete of the eleventh century, would not decide a question on which Saadia and Hai Gaon disagreed, saying that it is too difficult to decide between two such great authorities, whom he calls " everlasting (or the world's) foundations " (Proverbs, 10. 25). To justify this attitude he points to another author, who, for the

[582] Quoted by Abraham b. Ḥiyya in his ספר העבור, edited by Filipofski, London, 1851, p. 59; comp. Steinschneider, *Bibliotheca Mathematica*, 1895, p. 100.

[583] Introduction to his *Kitâb al-Luma'* (edited by Joseph Derenbourg under the title *Le livre des parterres fleuris*, Paris, 1886), p. 3, ll. 18-23; Hebrew translation of Judah Ibn Tibbon under the title ספר הרקמה (edited by Goldberg and Kirchheim, Frankfurt a/M., 1856), p. v. For the "Book of the Language" mentioned in this passage, see above, p. 139.

same reason, would not pass an opinion in a matter on which
Aristotle and Galen differed."[84] The poet Moses Ibn Ezra
(about 1070-1140) likewise mentions Saadia and Hai together as " the two princes in the knowledge of the Law
(Halakah) and the mightiest among the theologians."[85]
The famous moralist Bahya Ibn Bakûdah closes the Introduction to his " Duties of the Heart" with the following
words: " Understand of the Torah of thy God that to which
I called thy attention. In order to accomplish this, avail
thyself of the works of Rabbi Saadia, may God make shine
his countenance and sanctify his spirit; for they illumine
the intellect and sharpen the mind, they guide aright the
negligent and stir up the indolent."[86] Abraham Ibn Ezra,
though he often criticized Saadia's views,[87] styles him " the
chief spokesman everywhere,"[88] and " the pillar of the
Torah,"[89] and usually quotes him as " the Gaon," without
adding his name. Abraham Ibn Ezra's pupil, the lexicographer Solomon Ibn Parhon, takes occasion to character-
ize Saadia as " the chief preceptor and pioneer exegete, who
interpreted Scripture in the proper way and placed it on a

<hr />

[84] See Steinschneider in Geiger's *Jüdische Zeitschrift*, II, 308;
idem, *Polemische und apologetische Literatur*, p. 273, n. 73, and *AL.*,
p. 64, n. 6; comp. Dukes, *Beiträge*, II, pp. 186, 196. It should be
stated, however, that the same Ibn Bal'am in opposing Saadia's translation of Is. 1, 8 (*REJ.*, XVII, 183) refers to him as " one who has
no knowledge about the roots of the Hebrew language."

[85] Steinschneider, *AL.*, p. 64, n. 6.

[86] Arabic text edited by Yahuda, Leyden, 1912, p. 33; comp. Munk,
Notice sur R. Saadia Gaon, p. 6, n. 1; see also above, p. 154.

[87] For a general characterization of Abraham Ibn Ezra's relation
to Saadia see Bacher, *Abraham Ibn Ezra's Einleitung zu seinem
Pentateuch-Commentar*, Vienna, 1876, pp. 29ff; see also below, note
607.

[88] See above, pp. 52, 154.

[89] This title (עמוד התורה) he makes Saadia share with Onkelos,
thus placing both on the same level: comp. Bacher, *ibidem*, p. 31, nn.
2, 3. The designation of Saadia as " the Gaon " without further
specification is very common also in the works of other authors, but
sometimes applies also to the Gaon Hai; comp. Steinschneider,
Polemische und apologetische Literatur, p. 249, n. 13.

firm basis, so that all exegetes profited by his wisdom. He knew the holy language thoroughly, as also the language of the Arabs and other languages."[590] Maimonides, who disagreed with Saadia on many a point, nevertheless says that " were it not for Saadia, the Torah would almost have disappeared from the midst of Israel; for it was he who made manifest what was obscure therein, made strong what had been weakened, and made it known far and wide by word of mouth and in writing."[591] Maimonides's celebrated pupil, Joseph Ibn 'Aknin, in mentioning his predecessors who had served him as models in the composition of his Commentary on Canticles, gives the first place to Saadia, " whose light we have used in order to illumine our way, and in whose path we have walked."[592] The Provençal Shem Ṭob Palquera (1225-1290), a man of great literary insight, says " R. Saadia, of blessed memory, commented upon the Torah and the books of the Prophets; his expositions are laudable, they contain true ideas of a scientific nature, but also views of the earlier Mutakallimûn, which

[590] מחברת הערוך, s. v. פרח. Ibn Parḥon's statement regarding Saadia's knowledge of "other languages" is borne out by the פרוש על סדר טהרות (see below, p. 342, no. 1) which shows Saadia's acquaintance with Greek and Persian and his intimate knowledge of various Oriental dialects; comp. J. N. Epstein, *Der gaonäische Kommentar zur Ordnung Tohoroth*, Berlin, 1915, pp. 32, 51-74.

[591] אגרת תימן (in קובץ תשובות הרמב"ם, part II, Leipzig, 1859), p. 5, col. b; comp. Rapoport, *Bikkūrē ha-Ittim*, XI, 83 f. For Abraham Ibn Daud see below, note 607.

[592] As the Commentary is in MS. only, I adduce here the passage from a copy made by Steinschneider, which is in my possession: וקד ראינא תפסיר אלמקדמין להדא אלכתאב מנהא תפסיר מעלّם הדה אלטריקה֗ וריסהא ועטימהא אלגאון אלמעלّם רבנו סעדיה גאון ז"ל אלדّי בנורה אסתצّינא ועלי מנהגה משינא comp. Steinschneider, *AL.*, p. 64, n. 6; 231, no. 6 (line 4 from below read 105 for 100). Similar praise is bestowed upon Saadia by Judah Ḥasid (12th c.) quoted by Marx *JQR., N. S.*, II, 263. The famous mystic Abraham Abulafia (13th c.) likewise prides himself on the knowledge he derived from his study of Saadia's *Sefer ha-Emūnōt* (Jellinek, גנזי חכמת הקבלה, Hebrew part, p. 18; comp. below, note 622).

were refuted by later Mutakallımûn." [592a] Towards the end
of the thirteenth century we hear the opinion of an author of
high repute, the philosopher and poet Jedaiah ha-Penini of
Beziers, who in his *Letter of Defence* of the study of philosophy, addressed to Solomon b. Adret, points to Saadia with
the following words · " The most distinguished advocate of
secular learning among all the Geonim and other ancient
sages under Arabic rule, whose fame has reached us, is the
great Gaon R. Saadia al-Faȳûmi, who has enlightened the
eyes of the generations by his precious works; we possess
his scientific Commentary on the *Sefer Yezirah* and his
Emūnōt, in which he elucidates various doctrines and produces many arguments and interpretations of verses from
the Torah and the Prophets, which he brings as near to the
understanding as possible." [593]

Somewhat reserved is the praise of another Provençal,
the Talmudist Menahem Meiri of Perpignan (died 1306).
After having discussed the Geonim prior to Saadia, he says,
". . . . until the time came for R. Saadia, who was brought
from Egypt to Babylonia, who composed numberless books
on the oral and written Law, on grammar, and on some secular sciences, most of which are trustworthy. In his *Sēfer
ha-'Emūnōt*, however, he wrote certain things which are not
acceptable, and a pious man should not follow them." [594]
Meiri, unfortunately, did not point out the objectionable passages he had in mind. Finally, we should mention one more
author who expressed his admiration for the Gaon. It is

[592a] מבקש (ed. Hague), 24a. For Palquera see Malter, *JQR., N.S.*,
vol. I (1910-1911), pp. 151-185, 451-501. For Palquera's designation
of the Mutakallimûn as חכמי המחקר see Steinschneider, *Jewish
Literature*, pp. 296, 310, comp. Delitzsch, חיים עץ, pp. 311, f.

[593] כתב ההתנצלות, "Letter of Defence," printed in Solomon b.
Adret's *Responsa*, I (Bologna, 1539), no 418; also separately, under
the title אגרת התנצלות, with notes by Samson Bloch, Lemberg, 1809,
comp. Renan, *Les écrivains juifs français du XIVe siècle* (volume
XXXI of the *Histoire littéraire de la France*), Paris, 1893, pp 377-
382.

[594] בית הבחירה, or Commentary on *Pirkē .1bōt*, edited by Stern,
Vienna, 1854. Introduction, p. 16b, comp. Dukes, נחל קדומים, p. 25.

the Italian Jewish bard Moses b. Isaac of Rieti (died 1457), the so-called "Dante Ebreo," who in his Hebrew imitation of the "Divina Comedia" assigns to Saadia a place of honor in the fancied paradise. As a merit of Saadia he points out "his books and polemics against dissenters, which brought light into darkness." [595]

A search through mediæval Jewish literature would no doubt reveal a large number of similar appreciations of Saadia Gaon and his writings on the part of later authors. There is no need, however, of multiplying such testimony; the few examples quoted show sufficiently the high place accorded to Saadia by the greatest thinkers of subsequent centuries. [596]

Among the numerous rabbinical authors of the Middle Ages only one is known, who saw in Saadia an innovator and promulgator of heterodox ideas and therefore spoke of him disparagingly. This one is the learned zealot Moses b. Ḥisdai תקו, *i. e.* of Tachau, Bohemia, or, as recently asserted, [597] of Tackau, near Erfurt, Germany (about 1170-1230). Moses Tachau, who was a recognized Talmudic authority and also a liturgist of some standing, [598] wrote a book under the name of כתב תמים, of which only a part has been preserved. [599] The work is directed both against the

[595] מקדש מעט, ed. Goldenthal, Vienna, 1851, p. 95a; comp. Dukes, *ibidem*, p. 4.

[596] See also Saadia Ibn Danan (about 1470), in the collection חמדה גנוזה, edited by Edelmann, Königsberg, 1856, p. 28 (mostly taken from Abraham Ibn Daud's סדר הקבלה; comp. Steinschneider, *Geschichtsliteratur der Juden*, § 81).

[597] Tycocinsky, in *MGWJ.*, 1910, pp. 70 ff. The author raises some doubts as to the identity of Moses b. Ḥisdai and Moses תקו. We deal here with the כתב תמים, whoever its author. Comp. J. N. Epstein, *REJ.* LXI, 60 ff.

[598] Zunz, *Literaturgeschichte der synagogalen Poesie*, pp. 315-317; Landshuth עמודי העבודה, p. 223. The *JE., s. v.* "Moses Taku," has a cross reference to "Taku Moses," but there is no such article.

[599] Published by R. Kirchheim in the periodical אוצר נחמד, II (1860), 54-99, comp. Steinschneider, *HB.*, III, 62; *Hebräische Uebersetzungen*, pp. 442.

philosophers and the mystics,[600] who interpret Haggadic
passages of the Talmud relating to God, angels, resurrection,
and the like as figures of speech or symbols. The author
accepts even the most extravagant anthropomorphisms in
their literal sense. He pours out his wrath on Saadia, whom
he declares responsible for all the mischief done by the Jewish philosophers in falsifying the words of the Torah and
the Rabbis. " I deplore," he says " the damage done by the
Sēfer ha-'Emūnōt. It brought us the secular sciences and
increased the evils, weaning away the multitude from sincere piety ; casting doubts on everything, so that the people
do not know where they stand ; strengthening the hands of
the scientists, who have a grudge against the teachings of
our Rabbis, which are perfect, and setting in the place of
the latter the empty talk of the former."[601] Referring to
philosophic authors as a class, he says mockingly : " They
all feed on the wisdom of the *Sēfer ha-'Emūnōt*,[602] leaving
out things and adding others and writing books and dis-
courses on many topics and on the reasons of prophecy.
Indeed, prior to Saadia nobody dared give new interpretations, which deviate from the plain sense of the Scriptures
and from the trustworthy and well-established words of
our Rabbis.[603] It is the physicians and astronomers[604] that
despise our learning and those that adhere to it." In another

[601] See below, note 615.

[601] *Ozar Nechmad*, II, 64, top ; see also below, note 604

[602] *Ibidem*, p. 68, top ; comp. p. 65, l. 11.

[603] Further on (p. 75, l. 11) he accuses Saadia, on rather trivial
grounds, of having tyrannized over the people and forced on them
" a new Torah, unheard of since the days of Adam." Tachau feels
particularly provoked by the Gaon's opposition to the Talmud, in
proof of which he points out numerous passages in Saadia's Commentary on the *Sēfer Yezirah* and his *Emūnōt*, see pp. 74, where
אמונות (l. 13) is a mistake for פס״י, and 93 f. ; above, notes 462,
509a, 518

[604] By " physicians and astronomers " he derogatorily designates all
those who follow scientific methods in their studies, though they had
nothing to do with these disciplines. Thus, in the passage referred to
above (note 601) the Hebrew expression for " scientists " is הוברי
שמים (Isaiah, 47, 13), which is commonly translated by *astrologers*.

connection [605] he quotes a " Commentary on Chronicles," [606] according to which Saadia was imprisoned for thirteen years. In the prison, Moses assumes, he must have come in contact with non-Jewish scholars with whom he had religious disputes, so that certain ideas became fixed in his mind and were maintained by him later on. " There he got also into the habit of grandiloquence, trying to force the multitude into his ways of thinking by high metaphors and " fourfold " repetitions of one and the same thought—yes, he might have written in five tracts (קונטרסין) what he wrote in fifteen." [607] To refute Saadia's theories the author quotes

[605] *Ozar Nechmad,* II, 69, ll. 8 ff.

[606] The Commentary here referred to was published by Kirchheim, Frankfurt a/M., 1874, and the passage quoted by Tachau is on p. 36. For further details on the Commentary, which is ascribed to a pupil of Saadia, see the *Bibliography,* p. 327. Regarding the story of Saadia's imprisonment for thirteen years, quoted by Tachau from that Commentary, see the references in L. Bardowicz, *Die Abfassungszeit der Baraita der 32 Normen,* Berlin, 1913, p. 80, n. 29 ; comp. Steinschneider, *H. B.,* III, 62.

[607] It may be noted that charges of diffuseness and verbosity were brought against Saadia also by authors who were no antagonists of his. Thus Abraham Ibn Ezra, in his fondness for puns, plays on the words שערים and שעור, saying that the *Sēfer ha-Emūnōt* contains chapters of limitless length : והגאון רבנו סעדיה חבר ספר באמונות יסוד מורא) ויש בו שערים שאין שעור לדבריו, chapter I, end) ; comp. also his censure of Saadia's longwinded methods in Bible exegesis at the beginning of his Introduction to his Commentary on Genesis. Still harsher is his criticism of the Gaon in his *Short Commentary on Exodus* (23. 20) ; see Reggio and Luzzatto in *Kerem Chemed,* IV, 104 ff., 136 f. The famous Hebrew satirist Immanuel of Rome (1270-1330), poking fun at a very tall man, says, " Mr. Soandso is as tall as Saadia's works are long." (מחברות, V, ed. Lemberg, 1870, p. 42), which hardly refers to the " large number " of the Gaon's works, as suggested by Steinschneider, *HB.,* XIII, p. 62, n. 7 ; comp. Dukes, *Beiträge,* II, 78. Berechiah ha-Naḳdan, the epitomizer of Saadia's *Emūnōt* (see the *Bibliography,* p. 361), in his מצרף (edited by Gollancz, London, 1902), p. 141, l. 6, likewise alludes to Saadia's diffuseness (אריכות מלין) ; see, however, Bacher (*Abraham Ibn Ezra's Einleitung zu seinem Pentateuch-Commentar,* Vienna, 1876, p. 19), who, with Dukes, repudiates these charges as unfounded.

numerous passages from his Commentary on the *Sefer
Yezirah*,⁶⁰⁸ especially from the *Emūnōt*, each time adding
some slighting comment. Tachau's method of criticism is
best illustrated by the passage in which he attacks Saadia
for having declared the statement of the Talmud, that besides
this world God created eighteen thousand other worlds, to
be the opinion of an individual teacher, which was not
generally accepted.⁶⁰⁹ "What an ignoramus," he exclaims,
"Of the words of an '*Amōra* revealed by holy inspiration
and derived from tradition we are to say that they were not
agreed to by all Israel? But who has agreed to his worthless talk?"⁶¹⁰ In this strain he argues against many other
points, and on one occasion even expresses his doubt as to
the authenticity of the *Sēfer ha-'Emūnōt*,⁶¹¹ because the copy
which he happened to use did not bear Saadia's name. It is
interesting to note that Judah b. Barzillai, who quotes the

___

As to the exceptions taken to the *Emūnōt* in particular, they are
due, I believe, in most part to the fact that the critics (Berechiah,
Moses Tachau, probably also Abraham Ibn Ezra, in whose time the
Arabic original was already very rare) read the work in the so-called
Hebrew *Paraphrase*, which indeed has no parallel as regards turgidity
and windy phraseology. The stricture of Meiri (above, note 594)
is based on purely religious grounds. On the other hand Abraham
Ibn Daud (1161), while recognizing the great merits of the work in
general, declares that upon investigation he found it to be inadequate for his purposes: אמנם כאשר הקרנוהו לא מיצאנוהו מספיק
אמונה רמה) למה שצריך לנו, p. 2); comp. above, note 310. Ibn Daud,
however, borrowed many essential points of his own system from
the work of Saadia; comp. for details Guttmann, *Die Religionsphilosophie des Abraham Ibn Daud*, Göttingen, 1879, p. 12. A much
later author, Moses Ibn Ḥabib (about 1500), likewise attributed little
value to the *Emūnōt*; see above, note 485. For the attitude of
Dûnâsh Ibn Tamim to Saadia see above, note 75. For Ibn Bal'am
see note 584.

⁶⁰⁸ See the *Bibliography*, p. 358.

⁶⁰⁹ The passage here referred to by Tachau is in Saadia's Com-
mentary on the *Sefer Yezirah*, p. 5, bottom (Lambert, pp. 19 f.).

⁶¹⁰ *Ozar Nechmad*, II, 70, top; comp. also above, note 509a.

⁶¹¹ *Ozar Nechmad*, II, 70; comp. p. 96, l. 6; Steinschneider, *Hebrä-
ische Uebersetzungen*, p. 442.

same passage about the eighteen thousand worlds,[612] finds nothing wrong therein except that Saadia, relying on his memory, happened to misquote part of the Talmudic passage, a stricture without bearing on the question at issue. It should finally be remarked that while our author directs his arrows mainly against Saadia, "the first to speculate about the creations of God,"[613] he is no less opposed to all whom he considers followers and admirers of the Gaon. Even Hai Gaon[614] and men like the pious mystic Judah Hasid,[615] he finds, were under the influence of the Sēfer ha-'Emūnōt; but he naturally shows more animosity against Maimonides and especially against Abraham Ibn Ezra, who "was always accompanied by demons."[616] All this goes to show that even in the strictly orthodox circles of twelfth century Jewry, Saadia was known as the founder and originator of that critical, scientific epoch in Jewish literature which so disturbed the mentality of men like Moses Tachau.

Of special significance for a correct appreciation of the authority and importance attached by his contemporaries and successors to Saadia's works, is the fact that some of them

[612] פרוש ספר יצירה, ed. Halberstam, Berlin, 1885, p. 174.

[613] Ozar Nechmad, II, 77.

[614] Ibidem, p. 92; Tachau has in mind a Responsum of Hai which was published by Eliezer Ashkenazi in טעם זקנים, Frankfurt a/M. 1854, pp. 59 ff. The whole Responsum, with the exception of the "Questions" discussed below (Bibliography, pp. 365 f.), is indeed, as suggested by Tachau, taken without acknowledgment from Saadia's Emūnōt; see above, note 578; Bacher, in Steinschneider's Festschrift, p. 225.

[615] Ibidem, pp. 73, 95, and passim; comp. the Bibliography, p. 362, no. 1.

[616] Ibidem, p. 97: Ibn Ezra, Tachau reports, denied the existence of demons, but the latter proved to him that they do exist; for once Ibn Ezra was riding through a forest in England, when a pack of black dogs, which in reality were demons, suddenly appeared before him and their fierce eyes frightened him so that he died soon after; comp. Steinschneider, HB., III, 62; idem, Abraham Ibn Esra (in Supplement zur historisch-literarischen Abtheilung der Zeitschrift für Mathematik und Physik, 1880), pp. 81 f.

became known in European countries, even among the
Franco-German Jews, at a very early period. Numerous
scholars of the eleventh century in France, Germany,
and other non-Arabic countries, quote Saadia directly or
indirectly, or show familiarity with his views. Among them
may be instanced Rashi,[617] perhaps also his precursor Moses
Darshan of Narbonne,[618] Nathan b Jehiel of Rome, author
of the '*Arūk*,[619] and Tobiah b Eliezer of Castoria in Bulgaria,
author of the Midrash " Lekah Tōb." [620] During the twelfth
century Saadia's influence becomes general in all branches of
Jewish literature, even in the works of authors who show a
decided tendency toward asceticism and mysticism, as Judah
Ḥasid [621] and his disciple Eleazar of Worms [622] The leading

[617] For quotations of Saadia in the commentaries of Rashi see
Reifmann's note, in קובץ מעשׂי ידי גאונים קדמונים, edited by
Rosenberg, Berlin, 1856, p. 53, comp. Rapoport, בכורי העתים, 1828,
p 35, bottom; p. 36, n 43, Dukes, *Beitrage*, II, p. 98, n. 9, Geiger,
פרישׂנדתא, p 7 (of Hebrew part), Harkavy, *Ha-Goren*, I, 89.

[618] See Epstein, ר' מישׂה הדרשׂן מנרבונה, Vienna, 1891 (comp.
Neubauer, *JQR.*, IV, 157), p 46, where the interpretation of Eccl,
3 21, appears to be based on that of Saadia, *Kitâb al-'Amânât* pp. 192,
194 (*Emûnōt*, Leipzig, 1864, pp. 96, 98, top), comp. above, note 502.

[619] '*Aruk*, s vv הכיר and ענה; comp *Oeuvres complètes de Saadia*,
IX, 167, nos 110, 111 From a remark in the latter passage (רו"ג
פריׂש כרס"נ) it would seem that Rabbenu Gershom, too, (died in
Mayence, 1040) was acquainted with some of the writings of Saadia

[620] See Buber's Introduction to his edition of this Midrash (Wilna,
1884), pp 11, 22, no 29; comp J. Nacht, *Tobia ben Eliescr's Commentar zu Threni*, Berlin, 1895, pp. 6 f ; 30, n. 123.

[621] See the *Bibliography*, p. 362, no. 1, comp also note 615.

[622] Comp Steinschneider, *HB.*, III, 62; idem, *Abraham Ibn Esra*
(as quoted above, note 616), p. 82, n 84; Dukes,נחל קדומים, p. 24,
note; Geiger, *Parschandatha*, p 50; above, note 491 Mystics of
later ages were particularly attracted by Saadia's Commentary on
the *Sefer Yezirah* Eleazar's Commentary on that book is based on
that of Saadia, comp Jellinek, גנזי הכמת הקבלה, German part,
p 21, above, note 491 Even Kabbalists like Abraham Abulafia
(13th c) availed themselves of Saadia's philosophic teachings Thus
the latter's doctrine as to the sources of human understanding (see
above, p. 195,) is tacitly adopted by Abulafia; comp Jellinek ib.,
p 29, above, note 502 By virtue of a false attribution to Saadia

Halakists of the time, like Eliezer b. Nathan of Mayence,[623] Jacob Tam of Ramerupt, grandson of Rashi, and some of the Tosafists,[624] refer to him as to one of the most authoritative Geonic sources. A thirteenth century author,[625] in the name of the aforementioned R. Jacob Tam, quotes the sentence, " R. Saadia, on the words of whose mouth we live and who handed the secret of the calendar down to us."

Through what channels the various Jewish authors of European countries outside of Spain became acquainted with the writings of Saadia, or with his teachings, cannot always be ascertained. Some of these authors, like Rashi, his contemporary Joseph Kara, Joseph Bekōr Shōr (12th century) and others, certainly knew no Arabic, and all the quotations of Saadia found in their writings, as they often state explicitly, are based on hearsay, or are taken from the Hebrew works of authors who understood the Arabic language and drew upon the original sources.[626] Others, like

---

of another, mystic, commentary on the *Sefer Yezirah* (see the *Bibliography*, VIII, p. 404) some of the later admirers of the Kabbalah even acclaimed the Gaon as their own, crediting him with a device for the creation of a *homunculus* by means of certain manipulations with the alphabet. So Judah Moscato in his commentary to the *Kuzari* (קול יהודה), IV, § 25 (ed. Wilna, 1905, p. 94, bottom) and Joseph Solomon Delmedigo, מצרף לחכמה, Basle, 1629, *fols.* 9b, 20 a. The passage quoted by them as proof is found in the spurious Commentary on the *Sefer Yezirah* (II, § 4) marching under Saadia's name; comp. below, note, 660.

[623] ראב"ן, no. 119; comp. Halberstam, in his edition of Judah b. Barzillai's Commentary on the *Sefer Yezirah*, Berlin, 1885, p. 309, l. 13; *JE.*, V, 118; S. Hurwitz, Introduction to מחזור ויטרי, p. 46; see above, note 418.

[624] See *e. g.* Müller, *Oeuvres* IX, 157, no. 73, also the Tōsafists mentioned below, notes 636, 639. For Aaron b. Meshullam of Lunel (1200) see the *Bibliography*, p. 368.

[625] Zedekiah b. Abraham 'Anaw, in his ritualistic work שבלי הלקט, ed. Buber, Wilna, 1886, no. 28; comp. Rapoport בכורי העתים, IX, 29, n. 23; Bornstein, מחלקת רס"ג, p. 25, n. 1.

[626] Geiger, *Parschandatha* (Hebrew), pp. 6-16. For Joseph Bekor Shor see *ibidem*, p. 50; Poznański, *Kommentar zu Ezechiel—von Eliezer aus Beaugency, Warsaw*, 1914, Introduction, p. lxvi, n. 1; p. 227, note on pp. lxiv; p. 228, note on p. lxxxviii.

Moses Darshan,[627] Nathan b Jechiel,[628] and perhaps also
Tobiah b. Eliezer,[629] knew the language of the Arabs and
may have used or quoted Saadia directly. But whatever
the case may have been as regards individual authors, we cannot explain the general deference paid to his authority except
by assuming—and this is what I wish to bring out here—that
some of Saadia's works were translated into Hebrew, either
in part or in whole, long before the period of the Tibbonides,
though most of those translations are lost. Thus Judah
b. Barzillai, at the close of the eleventh century, made use
in his Commentary on the *Sefer Yezirah* of two or three
different Hebrew translations of Saadia's Arabic Commentary on the same book [630] These translations differ from
that of one Moses b. Joseph of Lucena, whose date is uncertain, but probably prior to 1148.[631] The famous fabulist Berechiah ha-Nakdan,[632] whose date has likewise not been defi-

---

[627] See Rapoport's *Biography of Nathan b. Jechiel* (בכה"ע, X),
note 47; Epstein, *Moses ha-Darschan*, Vienna, 1891, p 8.

[628] Rapoport, *Biography*, note 14

[629] Comp מדרש לקח טוב, on Exodus, ed. Buber, p 188, n 4;
Buber's Introduction, p. 36, line 3, Rapoport, *Biography of Hai Gaon*
(בכה"ע, X), note 16, refers to a passage in Tobiah's Midrash which
is taken from an Arabic Responsum of Hai

[630] See the *Bibliography*, p. 357.

[631] Steinschneider, *Hebraische Uebersetzungen*, p. 444, his doubts as
to the priorty of the translator Moses to the year 1148, when the
Jewish community was expelled from the city, are not sufficiently
founded   The style and strange terminology of the translation
(MS copy of the late Halberstam, now in the Jewish Theological
Seminary of America in New York) may rather be looked upon as
a proof that the author lived prior to the period of translators
inaugurated by the Tibbonides, in 1167.

[632] מצרף (ed. Gollancz, London, 1902), p 118, l 5 from below to
p 119, l 21, which, with some deviations, corresponds to Saadia's
text, ed Lambert, p. 18, l 16 to p 20, l. 3   So far as I know this
passage escaped the notice of scholars For the question of the time
and country of Berechiah and his knowledge of Arabic, which are
still disputed, the origin of the Hebrew translation of this passage
is of great importance, and its identification would eventually solve
the problems. A comparison of Berechiah with Moses of Lucena
shows convincingly that the authors are independent of each other;
see the *Bibliography*, p 358

nitely established, some placing him in the twelfth, others in the thirteenth century,[633] and the Talmudist Moses Tachau (around 1200),[634] quote lengthy passages from Hebrew translations of that Commentary of Saadia's, each one of which differs from those mentioned before.

As in the case of the Commentary here discussed, so also in that of Saadia's great philosophic work, the Kitâb al-'Amânât, we possess more than one Hebrew translation. Aside from the one prepared in 1186 by Judah Ibn Tibbon of Lunel, generally known under the title 'Emūnōt we-Dēōt, there is also an anonymous Hebrew version written in a very peculiar style, which resembles closely that of the liturgical compositions of Eleazar Ḳalir and others. Much thought has been spent in the attempt to find out something definite about the author, the time and the country of this as yet unprinted version, or rather paraphrase, of Saadia's work.[635] A colophon in one of the MSS. shows the date 1095, but it is doubtful whether this is the date of the translator or of the copyist. At any rate we have here the work of an author, who lived in the eleventh century, if not earlier. In spite of the obscurity of its payyeṭānic phraseology, or perhaps because of it, precisely this version of the Arabic original and not that of Ibn Tibbon, became widely known among the Jews of France, Germany, and other European countries. This is evident from the fact that the aforementioned Berechiah ha-Naḳdan issued the whole work in an abridged form, and otherwise[636] made extensive use of its contents; that Moses Tachau, the Spaniard Jacob b. Reuben, the mystic Judah he-Ḥasid of Ratisbon, and the Tosafist Samson b. Abraham of Sens, all authors of the twelfth century, quote

[633] See Gollancz, The Ethical Treatise of Berachya, Introduction; Jacobs, JE., II, 54.

[634] See the Bibliography, p. 358, and above, pp. 281 ff.

[635] For further details see the Bibliography, p. 360.

[636] Berechiah's work in the publication of Gollancz consists of two treatises, the one of which is the epitome of Saadia's Emūnōt, and the other, under the name of מצרף, is a compilation from the works of various authors, among them Saadia.

lengthy passages therefrom,[636a] and that throughout the
Middle Ages entire chapters [637] of the work were current in
Germany, France, and Italy as separate books.

That the Commentary on the *Sēfer Yeṣirah* and the *Kitâb
al-'Amânât*, both belonging under the category of religious
philosophy, were not the only ones of Saadia's works that
reached the Franco-German Jews of the eleventh and twelfth
centuries in Hebrew translation, hardly requires proof.
Saadia's Halakic and liturgical writings, for instance, were
known very early to Talmudic authors in Christian countries,
as is evident from the numerous quotations collected from
their works several years ago.[638] It may be admitted that
some of these authors understood Arabic, and were thus in
a position to use the originals, while others may have derived
their knowledge of the contents from Jewish-Arabic scholars
with whom they came in contact.[639] It is hazardous, however, to be satisfied with so narrow a basis for the comparatively wide diffusion of Saadia's Halakic views among
scholars who were not acquainted with Arabic. Much more
probable is it that some of Saadia's treatises on Talmudic
literature as well as his Halakic disquisitions on questions of
liturgy, which he had embodied in his Ritual-Order (Siddūr), were current in Hebrew translations. Their non-
existence at the present time proves nothing against this
assumption. Nearly all of the Arabic originals are also
lost, whereas quite a number of Saadia's Arabic *Responsa*
exist only in Hebrew versions, of whose makers but one is

[636a] See for these authors the *Bibliography*, pp. 368, 362, no. 1, 365,
respectively. According to Steinschneider (*HB.*, XVIII, 66) the
Introduction of the Tosafist Samuel of Falaise to his ספר המיצות
(Vatican MS. no. 429) is that of Saadia to the *Emūnōt*, but he does
not state which translation was used.

[637] See the *Bibliography*, pp. 362 ff.

[638] Müller, *Oeuvres*, IX, 145-173; *Israelsohn, REJ.*, XXII, 295.

[639] Comp. for instance Samson b. Abraham of Sens in כתאב
אלרסאיל (ed. Brill, Paris, 1871), p. 136. The אחד מיהחברים to whom
Samson refers is probably the same Abraham b. Nathan (see next
note) mentioned there, p. 107, as the carrier of Samson's letter;
comp. *Bibliography*, p. 365.

known by name.[640] All this merely corroborates what is partly known through other evidence, that in the centuries following close upon that of Saadia there was a lively exchange of ideas between the Jews living under Muhammedan rule and those living in Christian countries, and that the latter were anxiously endeavoring to acquaint themselves with the literary products of the former. For this purpose they sought scholars with a sufficient knowledge of Arabic to be able to interpret to them orally the contents of works written in that language or to prepare for them written translations. We may therefore take it for granted that Saadia's grammatical and exegetical works, or at least some of his numerous Biblical commentaries, soon became known among European Jews. This was brought about not only by Hebrew translations of whole works, or, what is more probable, of special parts and chapters in which certain scholars happened to be particularly interested, but also by occasional long excerpts embodied in the works of Hebrew authors, such as we find in Judah b. Barzillai's Commentary on the *Sēfer Yeẓirah* and in the Hebrew works of some Karaite authors.[641]

That the works of Saadia in all branches of learning were eagerly studied by the Oriental, North African, and Spanish Jews soon after their appearance and in subsequent centuries, need not be proved in detail.[642] The Geonim Hai and Samuel b. Hophni, especially the latter, modelled their entire literary activity after that of Saadia; the scholars of Northern Africa, such as Jacob b. Nissim and his son Nissim, Hananel b. Ḥushiel, Dûnâsh Ibn Tamîm, and Isaac Alfâsi,

---

[640] Abraham b. Nathan of Lunel (1204) who translated one Responsum; comp. Steinschneider, *Hebräische Uebersetzungen*, pp. 909, 935, n. 217; Cassel, in Zunz's *Jubelschrift*, pp. 125, 131.

[641] See the *Bibliography*, pp. 320, 346, no. 4, 356 ff.

[642] The traveller Petahiah of Ratisbon (1180) relates that in passing through Babylonia he found the Jews studying the Bible and the six orders of the Mishnah with the commentaries of Saadia; comp. Graetz, *Geschichte*, V (4th ed.), 531; above, note 359, where further references are given.

undoubtedly were familiar with the writings of the Gaon, and made use of them, each one in his chosen field, whether we find direct quotations in their works or not.[642] As to Jewish-Spanish authors no names need be mentioned. There is hardly an author of an original work who did not draw upon the rich treasures in the writings of Saadia. Many advanced far beyond his theories in various fields of research, and, as frequently happened, even criticised them very severely; but despite opposition and criticism he was always recognized as the first expounder of Jewish thought, the master whose keys had opened the gates of scientific research.

It goes without saying that Saadia had also a large number of personal pupils, who spread his teachings by word of mouth and in writing. We have seen that even as a very young man, while still in Egypt, he had gathered around him a circle of friends and disciples, who recognized him as their authority, and remained faithful to him many years after his departure from his native country.[644] Later, when he was made the head of the Suran Academy, he became *ipso facto* the spiritual guide and teacher of all the scholars of the institution. Unfortunately, only a very few of Saadia's immediate disciples have become known by name. Among them is the famous grammarian and poet Dûnâsh b. Labraṭ, who is designated by the pupils of his opponent, Menahem b. Sarûḳ, as "the least important of the pupils of Saadia,"[645] no doubt an exaggeration born of the desire to belittle an antagonist. Other pupils of prominence mentioned by name are Jacob b. Samuel, whose family name is thought to have been Ibn Ephraim, under which name he is quoted by Abraham Ibn Ezra, and who is assumed

[642] For the relation of Nissim and Hananel to Saadia see Rapoport's *Biographies* in בכה"ע, XII, 27, n. 21; 28, n. 29; 81, n. 40, end; for Nissim in particular see Goldziher, *REJ.*, XLII, 179, 184 ff.; Schreiner, *Der Kalâm*, p. 12; comp. Graetz, *History* (English), III, 249. For Dûnâsh Ibn Tamim see above, p. 48.

[644] See above, pp. 55 f.; below, p. 413, nos. 4-5; p. 418, no. 11.

[645] See Bacher, *JE.*, V, 11.

also to be identical with Jacob b. Ephraim, referred to by the Karaite Jephet b. 'Ali (10th century) as the author of a commentary on the Palestinian Talmud;[646] Sahl b. Naṭira, a member of the prominent Naṭira family, which played so important a rôle in the reconciliation of Saadia and the Exilarch David b. Zakkai;[647] Abraham al-Ṣairafi,[649] author of a work of uncertain content referred to in a recent Genizah fragment; a certain R. Menahem who addressed some scientific questions to the Gaon. At the end of his letter of inquiry he eulogizes Saadia in a poem showing the acrostics סעריה and מנחם and also applies to him the words addressed by Huram to Solomon: " Because the Lord loveth His people, He hath made thee king over them " (II Chr. 2, 10).[648a]

Finally, we should mention in this connection the tremendous influence of Saadia on the Karaites and their literature. Their entire activity in the fields of philology, exegesis, and Jewish law received its impetus from the works of the Gaon and his followers. A very considerable portion, perhaps the larger part of the existing Karaite literature, down to our present time, while antagonizing Rabbinism in general, actually aims at the refutation of the theories of Saadia, who, in the opinion of the Karaites, was not alone their most determined adversary but also the strongest exponent of Rabbinic Judaism. For nearly a thousand years after the disappearance of the Gaon from the arena, the Karaite authors unrelentingly attacked their dead opponent and

[646] This very plausible identification was suggested by Poznański in the Kaufmann *Gedenkbuch*, pp. 169 ff., where all the details are clearly set forth; comp. also Poznański, *The Karaite Literary Opponents of Saadiah Gaon*, London, 1908, p. 27.

[647] See Harkavy's article on the Naṭira family in Berliner's *Festschrift*, pp. 34-43; comp. above, note 237.

[649] See the *Bibliography*, p. 402, nos. 15, 16. The Commentary on Chronicles edited by Kirchheim (above note 606; *Bibliography*, p. 327) is very probably the work of a pupil of Saadia, whose name, however, cannot be ascertained; comp. also Vogelstein-Rieger, *Gesch. der Juden in Rom*, I, 184.

[648a] See Harkavy, *Ha-Goren*, I, 91.

denounced his views. Notwithstanding this bitter enmity to
Saadia they often appropriated his ideas or claimed that
these had originated with some of their ancient teachers,
with whom Saadia had studied or from whom he had
plagiarized. This is not the place for a detailed discussion
of this matter [649] I wish merely to point out the fact that
while Saadia has contributed, as no other Rabbanite in the
history of Jewry, to the disintegration of the Karaite sect as
such, he is, on the other hand, chiefly responsible for the
development of what is known as Karaite literature

In the foregoing sketch of Saadia's influence on later ages
I have merely outlined the ground upon which a future,
more detailed work may be undertaken. I have tried to
show only the channels through which Saadia's scientific
labors reached, within a comparatively short time, the entire
Jewry of the Diaspora Of what benefit they have been
to the Jewish people and of what interest Saadia's life
and literary bequests should be to us to-day, the reader, who
has patiently gone through this volume, may decide for himself. Perhaps some of the traits in the Gaon's character
may seem unadmirable and much of his reasoning may be
found obsolete and unproductive But a great man is entitled
to minor faults of character , they make him the more human
and the more interesting. If, furthermore, certain of his
ideas and contentions impress us as being somewhat behind
our age—this is what we should expect, since their author
preceded us by a thousand years They are, besides, greatly
outweighed by a wealth of genuine observation and sound
learning, which will retain its value throughout all ages.
Taken all in all, Saadia must be considered a remarkable
phenomenon in the history of the Jewish nation, a milestone
on the long road of Israel's development as a " people of the
Book." We may, indeed, with himself. recognize in him

---

[649] For the literature on the subject see Harkavy's article "Karaites "
in the JE. and particularly Poznański, The Anti-Karaite Writings of
Saadiah Gaon, JQR . X, 238-276 , idem, The Karaite Literary Opponents of Saadiah Gaon, London, 1908 (reprint from JQR. XVIII-
XX)

the man sent by Providence, whom—if with some not un-
pardonable egoism, yet in all sincerity—he describes in the
following words: "God does not leave His nation at any
period without a scholar whom He inspires and enlightens,
so that this one in turn may so instruct and teach her, that
thereby her condition shall be bettered." [650]

[650] ספר הגלוי, ed. Harkavy, *Zikron*, V, 155, top; comp. Malter, *JQR.*,
N. S., vol. III (1912-1913), p. 492.

CHAPTER VIII

LEGENDS ABOUT SAADIA

The Orient is *par excellence* the country of legends. Persons and events that in other parts of the world might have remained unnoticed because of their insignificance, have there been made the center of fanciful tales and traditions. It is therefore surprising that concerning the Geonim, whether of Sura or of Pumbedita, extremely little has come down to us that can properly be described as legend. I have undertaken no special enquiry as to Saadia, but I have no reason to think that he is an exception in this respect, or that there is much of a legendary character to be found about him in the works of mediæval authors. The few legends about the Gaon that have come to my notice may here be briefly recorded. The oldest anecdote, it seems, is the one reported by Judah Ḥasid of Ratisbon (12th century), which runs as follows:[651]

"A wealthy man set out on a journey to a foreign land, taking with him a slave and large sums of money. His wife he left at home in the state of pregnancy. It happened that the man died on the way and his slave, claiming to be his son, took possession of all his money and other property. In the meantime the widowed wife gave birth to a son. When the latter grew up he found out the whereabouts of the dishonest slave and betook himself thither to see whether he could not get back his inheritance. The slave had managed to marry into a very prominent family of the town, so that the cheated son was afraid to lodge his complaint publicly, lest the people do him harm. It so happened

---

[651] ספר חסידים, ed. Berlin, § 291. The object of Judah Ḥasid in relating this story was not exactly to glorify Saadia, but to emphasize the duty of a son to mourn for his father on the day of the anniversary of the latter's death.

that R. Saadia lived in that place, and the unhappy son stopped in his house. He was offered something to eat, but, like Eliezer of the Bible, he would not touch anything until he had revealed the secret of his mission. Saadia advised him to bring the matter before the king (or caliph), which he did. The king at once sent for Saadia to decide the case. Saadia ordered that each one of the two litigants should have some of his blood drawn into a vessel, whereupon he laid a bone from the body of the dead father into the blood taken from the slave, but the bone did not absorb any of the blood. He then placed the bone into the blood of the other man, and, lo, the bone eagerly absorbed the blood, because they both were one body. Saadia now decided that all the money in the possession of the former slave should revert to the real heir, who had come as a stranger to the town." [652]

Of somewhat later origin is the story found in a manuscript work of a fourteenth century author.[653] Considering the fact that the events told therein are obviously supposed to have taken place in a Christian country, we may even suspect that the Saadia who is the hero of the story, is not the Gaon, but his German namesake, Saadia b. Nahamāni, of the twelfth century.[654] However, the author repeatedly mentions " Saadia the Gaon," and we must take his word for it. Here is the story:

---

[652] For the origin and popularity of this blood-test story see Steinschneider, *HB.*, XIII, 133 f., who quotes numerous parallels from Jewish and general literature; comp. G. A. Kohut, *Blood-Test as Proof of Kinship in Jewish Folklore* (in *Journal of American Oriental Society*, XXIV, 133 ff) ; Davidson, ספר שעשועים, New York, 1914, p. lxii; Berliner, *Pletath Soferim*, Breslau, 1872, p. 50, n. 52.

[653] See Berliner, פליטת סופרים, Mayence, 1872, p. 30, no. 8; comp. *ibidem*, German part, p. 31, where it is suggested that the author is Nethanel Caspi, a Provençal scholar, who wrote a commentary on Judah ha-Levi's Kusari.

[654] See *JE.*, X, 578, 586.

"I heard that the priests (גלחים) of the city of לופייל
מדייאה (?)[656] had placed the penalty of death upon any Jew
venturing into the city. One day R Saadia Gaon, of blessed
memory, chanced into the forbidden city and was at once
seized by the priests for execution. They could not agree,
however, as to who should administer the first blow to the
Gaon, each one of them claiming the privilege for himself. At
last an old priest appeared on the scene, and, noticing the
dissension among his colleagues, advised them to defer the
matter until the arrival of the Bishop (הגמון), who would
punish the captive for his offence. Saadia was put into
prison, where he was given only bread and water, pending
the coming of the Bishop. When the latter came and was
told of the imprisoned Jew, he went to see him personally.
Upon beholding the prisoner he was awe-struck, for the
Gaon was of tall stature and fine appearance. The Bishop
now assumed a friendlier attitude, asking the prisoner who
he was. The latter answered, 'I am a Jew, and I beg you,
Sir, not to shed innocent blood. If you wish to try my case.
do it in a spirit of justice, and if I am found guilty, do with
me as you please, for it is written (Deuteronomy, 1 16):
Hear the causes between your brethren, and judge right-
eously' Thereupon the Bishop asked Saadia whether he
would be willing to engage in a disputation with the priests
and reply to their questions. The Gaon answered in the
affirmative, whereupon all the priests assembled in a certain
place, with the Bishop presiding over the assembly The
Gaon was brought from the prison and thus addressed:
'Say, Jew, why did your ancestors kill Jesus, who was quite
innocent? Was it not simply because he was God?'"

The author or reporter of the tale gives the reply of
Saadia, the burden of which is that Jesus was not God, as
God cannot be killed. He is evidently of the opinion that
the argument was strong enough to convince the priests,

---

[656] Berliner, l. c., p. 33, does not make any suggestion as to the
identity of this city. Perhaps it is Laval in the Department of May-
enne, which was the seat of the Order of Cordeliers (Franciscans).

for he informs us at the end that the Gaon was "at once dismissed in peace."

In a curious note [656] by some anonymous writer Saadia is credited with the discovery of a recipe for the making of a certain kind of cakes, by the eating of which one is assured of never forgetting his learning. The prescription, written in Aramaic, is as follows:

Recipe: "To prevent forgetfulness; tested and reliable; was used by R. Saadia b. Joseph, of blessed memory, who found it in the cave of R. Eleazar Ḳalir, and it is used also by all the scholars of Israel and their disciples with much success—here it is: On the first day of the month of Sivan take flour of wheat, knead it while you are standing, make it into a cake, bake it, write on it, ' He hath made His wonderful works to be remembered, the Lord is gracious and merciful ' (Psalms, 111. 4) ; then take an egg, boil it well, peel it, and write on it ...... (here follow five mysterious words, which are to be written on the egg). Eat that cake every day with the egg until the end of thirty days, and you will grasp every thing that you read [literally : *see*] without ever forgetting it again."

It is needless to say that Saadia had nothing to do with this "kitchen-wisdom." Nor was the story itself originally invented in honor of Saadia. The belief in the efficacy of cakes with certain mystical inscriptions as a means of strengthening the memory and for similar purposes was prevalent among the superstitious elements of various

---

[656] Published from Codex de Rossi, 327, by Ch. M. Horowitz, in בית נכות ההלכות, I, Frankfurt a/M., 1881, p. 58: לשכחה בדיק ומהימן ובו הוה עסיק רב סעריה בר יוסף ז"ל והוה אשכחיה במערתא דר' אלעזר קליר ובו מתעסקין כל חכמי ישראל ותלמידיהם ומצליחים וזו היא. בריש ירחא דסיון סב קמחא רחטי ולש יתה כדאת קאים ועבד יתה קורסין ואפות יתה וכתב בה זכר עשה לנפלאותיו חנון ורחום ה' וסב ביעתא ובשיל לה שפיר וקליף יתח וכתב עלה אספייים כיסתם תרמת אוזן דכווה. אכול ההיא קורסא כל יומא עם ביעא עד משלם ל' יום ותליף כל מה דאת חזי ולא תשכח.

peoples.[651] In Jewish history, the custom of eating cakes
inscribed with Biblical verses in order to gain wisdom is
known from times prior to Saadia; for the great liturgist
Eleazar Kalir, in whose cave Saadia is here reported to have
discovered the prescription, derives his name according to
some scholars,[652] from such a cake (קלר, Greek κολλύρα = a
small cake), which he was given to eat when he began to
go to school, that he might become wise. Hence the connection established in the foregoing story between Saadia and
Kalir.[653]

The preceding piece is well matched by a " Prescription "
(תקון) for frightening away highwaymen which is attributed
to Saadia in two Kabbalistic manuscript works. The direction is: Take a rod of almond, make a hole in it, write in a
spirit of contrition, while fasting, ten (eleven?) mystical
words on a piece of parchment made of the skin of a deer
that was killed ritually, insert the parchment in the hole and
swing the rod before the faces of the highwaymen, saying
" stop!" They will stop at once and, terrified, will be unable
to do you evil. Then smite the ground three times with the
rod, whereupon they will go their way. As a further pre-

[651] See Goldziher's admirable study *Muhammedanischer Aberglaube
über Gedächtnisskraft und Vergesslichkeit*, in Berliner's *Festschrift*,
pp. 150 f.

[652] Nathan b. Jehiel, *'Aruk*, s. v. קלר, 3; comp. *JE.*, VII, 418.

[653] Goldziher, *l. c.* The story of Saadia's imprisonment for thirteen
years as well as the report of Kabbalistic authors that he was buried
at the foot of Mount Sinai are both of a legendary nature; see
above, notes 278, 606. Abraham Ibn Daud's assertion, that Saadia
was a descendant of the Tanna Hanina b. Dosa (see above, p. 31),
though it may not be accepted as truth, cannot be classed among
legends, since Saadia himself traced his pedigree still further back, to
the Biblical Shelah, the third son of Judah; comp. above note 18. As
to mystical works attributed to Saadia by later ages see the *Bibliography*, section VIII, pp. 403 ff.; comp. also Poznański, רב דוסא
ברב סעדיה גאון (reprint from *Ha-Goren*, vol. VI), p. 26.

caution one should recite certain verses (Jer. 10, 10: Gen.
49, 18) and Psalm 121 before starting on his journey.[850a]

Finally there should be mentioned an anecdote reported
by the famous bibliographer Ḥayyim Joseph David Azulai
(died 1807), who found it in a manuscript which contained
Saadia's "Poem on the Number of Letters." The anecdote
runs as follows: "In a joking way the Gaon R. Saadia asked
a tailor who came to his house, 'How many stitches did you
make to-day'? to which the tailor retorted, 'May your
Highness please tell me how many letters there are in the
Torah.' The Gaon was very painfully impressed by this
reply, for until this time it had never happened to him that
anybody should ask him a question to which he knew no
answer. For several days he worried about the matter,
being unable to establish the exact number [of the letters].
He then used a mysterious name [of God] by which he

ללסטים תקון הר'ר סעריה ז''ל. קח מקל לוז או של שקרים[850a]
וכתוב אלו עשרה (!) השמות אדרמו''ן כסו''ס והגינ''א אברתי''א
איטמו''ן נור''א נוראו''ת י''ה צבאו''ת ויה''י ציב''א על קלף צבי
שחוט כשר בדקרוק אות לבדו בטחרה ובענוה ובצום ועשה חור
במקל והכניס הכתב בתוכו ובעת שתראה לסטים או אדם שתפחד
ממנו אז תכה במקל כנגרם ואמור עמדו ותבהלו והם יעמדו ויבהלו
ולא יוכלו לדבר אליך רע וכן תכה ג''פ בארין והם ילכו לדרכם
ואתה תלך בשלום. אך בעת שתצא מן העיר אמור בשם י''י אלקי
ישראל אלקים חיים ומלך עולם מקצפו תרעש הארץ ולא יכלו גוים
זעמו ושיר המעלות לדוד אשא עיני אל ההרים כו' לישועתך קויתי
י''י לי''ק קי''ל קל''י יל''ק יק''ל.

The text, as here given, is taken from the "Fountain of Wisdom"
(מעין החכמה) of Moses Botarel (MS. of the Jewish Theological
Seminary of New York, *fol.* 73), who is probably himself the author
of the תקון (see below, p. 404, no. 1). The same, with a few slight
variants, is found in another MS. of the Seminary. In place of the
last five abbreviations this MS. reads: י''י ולהפך לפורקנך סברית.
ובסוף אמור בשם סמוא''ל אוריא''ל ענא''ל אוריא''ל. The word
ולהפך directs the reading of the words לישועתך קויתי י''י in reverse order. I am indebted to Prof. Marx for having called my
attention to the two MSS.

conjured up an angel who to his great rejoicing revealed to
him the number asked for." [660]

This story is obviously fabricated to explain the reason
for the Gaon's composition of a poem on a subject which
seemed to be very trivial. [661]

The few anecdotes here reproduced do not contain any
historical element, nor do they add any particular feature to
the picture of Saadia's personality as conceived on the basis
of historical research. Their underlying idea, however, is
fully in accord with the general results brought out by our
investigation, that the Gaon was a wise and great man in
Israel, whose wisdom was admired by Jew and Gentile
and whose literary activity was a blessing to his nation.

[660] Azulai, שם הגדולים, ed. Benjacob, s. v. סעדיה. The same author,
a great believer in the teachings of the Kabalah, here informs us on
the authority of the famous Kabalist Hayyim Vital (died 1620.
Damascus), that Saadia was endowed with the soul which belonged
formerly to Hushai the Arkite (II Samuel, 15. 32) and subsequently
to the Tanna Phinehas b. Jair (second century). In view of Saadia's
bitter condemnation of the belief in the transmigration of souls (see
above, note 511), the honor here intended for Saadia by the Kabalists
is a great insult to his memory. For another story according to which
Saadia taught the secret of producing life by means of the alphabet
see above, note 622.

[661] See above, note 350.

PART III
BIBLIOGRAPHY

AN ACCOUNT, HISTORICAL AND CRITICAL,
OF MANUSCRIPT TEXTS, COMPLETE AND
FRAGMENTARY, EDITIONS, TRANSLATIONS,
AND CITATIONS OF SAADIA'S WRITINGS;
TOGETHER WITH A REVIEW OF THE ENTIRE
MODERN LITERATURE BEARING ON SAADIA

BIBLIOGRAPHY

PREFATORY NOTE

The intention in this Bibliography is not to register all the discussions on Saadia's life, or on one or another phase thereof, which occur in general works on Jewish history, or in historical studies of particular aspects of Judaism. For instance, a monograph on the attitude of Judaism toward superstition may contain a chapter relating especially to Saadia. Such works will be recorded as far as they have come to my notice, but completeness cannot be aimed at. The same restriction applies also to the innumerable notes and miscellaneous articles on Saadia scattered through the vast periodical literature of different countries and languages during a period of nearly a whole century. Most of these articles have been recorded in Moïse Schwab's *Répertoire*. Moreover, nearly everything that is of any significance for the present work has been referred to in the footnotes. My chief concern here is to give, in orderly arrangement, a complete and systematic bibliography of all the writings of the Gaon himself, whether these writings have been preserved or not. All the publications of Saadianic texts, either entire books or fragments, whether in the original language used by Saadia or in translation, will be minutely described. Naturally, all that has been written by later scholars, ancient and modern, in connection with one or the other of these writings, will have to be noted in the appropriate places. The whole may thus be expected to form a fairly complete history of the Saadia literature and to give the student the necessary information on any point he may be interested in, respecting the life and literary activity of the Gaon.

A bibliography of the numerous MSS. of Saadia's writings extant in various libraries is not included. New dis-

coveries of fragments in the Genizah collections are constantly being made, so that investigation of this field cannot yet be considered as concluded. Occasionally, however,
references to the Catalogues of MSS. in various European
libraries will be given.

I. PHILOLOGY

1. *'Agrōn* (אגרון), a Hebrew rhyming dictionary. Two
fragments, one Arabic and the other Hebrew, both forming
parts of Saadia's Introductions to the work, were discovered
in the Genizah in 1864 by the Karaite Abraham Firkovich.
The fragments were published completely for the first time
by Harkavy, *ZfalV.*, II, 73-94, 175 (also separately, 1881;
comp. Steinschneider, *H. B.*, XXI, 96; see also the Bibliography of Harkavy's writings by D. Maggid and S. Poznański, in Harkavy's *Festschrift* (also separately), nos. 81,
123, 238, 242, 246), and then in his *Zikron*, etc., V (1891),
pp. 40-57, with copious notes and an Introduction in which
everything pertaining, and many things not pertaining, to the
history of the work and its fragments were collected; see
Bacher's review of this publication in *RÉJ.*, XXIV, 307 ff.
(comp. also Bacher and Porges, *RÉJ.*, XXV, 143-151).
Independently of Harkavy, David Kohn (Kahana) published
the Hebrew fragment from a copy of H. J. Gurland with
lengthy notes and disquisitions under the peculiar title
כפר לתולדות רס"ג, Cracow, 1891 (reprint from the אוצר הספרות,
IV). At the end of the book a Hebrew translation of the
Arabic fragment is given without the text (see *RÉJ.*, XXVI,
140); comp. below, under כפר הגלוי, p. 394. An article on
the *'Agrōn* by Senior Sachs is found also in the Hebrew
monthly החוקר, I (1891), 5-9, 36-40; comp. also *ibidem*,
pp. 62-64 (Harkavy).

Aside from the two fragments of the Introductions here
discussed some additional portions of the *'Agrōn* itself were
found and partly edited by Harkavy, *Ha-Goren*, VI, 26-30.
For further details see Steinschneider, *AL.*, p. 61, no. 22;
see also Berliner, *Plêtath Sôferim*, Breslau 1872, pp. 29 f.;
above pp. 39 f.

2. *Kutub al-Lugah* (כתב אללגה), "Books on the (Hebrew) Language." Fragments of this work were found by Harkavy in the library of St. Petersburg, but only a few pages were published by him, together with a Hebrew translation, in *Ha-Goren*, VI (1906), 30-38. It will be remembered that portions of the work were incorporated by Saadia in his Commentary on the *Sēfer Yeẓirah* (Paris, 1891), pp. 45 f., 75-79. One of these (pp. 76, l. 2—78, l. 19) was published by Neubauer in the *Journal Asiatique*, 1862, pp. 261 f., and then republished, with a Hebrew translation, by Harkavy (*Zikron*, V, 61-65), who thought the passage to be part of the *'Agrōn* (see above, note 297). For various quotations in the works of later authors see Harkavy, *l. c.*, pp. 68 ff. A presentation of its content, so far as was possible on the basis of Saadia's Commentary on the *Sēfer Yeẓirah* and of citations found in works of later authors, was given by Bacher in *Die Anfänge der hebräischen Grammatik*, Leipzig, 1895, pp. 38-60; comp. also Bacher, *REJ.*, XXIV, 307 ff., and especially Steinschneider, *AL.*, p. 60.

3. *Tafsir al-sab'ina lafẓah* (תפסיר אלסבעין לפטה), "Explanation of the Seventy Hapaxlegomena." This booklet was published four times within one year, first by Dukes in the *Zeitschrift für die Kunde des Morgenlandes*, V (1844), 115-136, with numerous notes; then for a second time by the same writer with the omission of most of the notes and with some corrections, in Ewald and Dukes, *Beiträge zur Geschichte der ältesten Auslegung*, Stuttgart, 1844, II, pp. 110-115. These editions were followed by that of Benjacob in דברים עתיקים, part I, Leipzig, 1844, under the title: פתרון תשעים מלות בודדות לרב סעדיה גאון. In this edition the Arabic words which were used by Saadia in explanation of the Hebrew are translated into Hebrew, probably by Jellinek, though the editor does not say this clearly. The explanatory notes are also in Hebrew. Simultaneously it was published also with notes in Geiger's *Wissenschaftliche Zeitschrift*, V, 317-324. Finally a new edition was prepared by the indefatigable Buber (in Steinschneider's *AL.*, p. 339, l. 5. from below, erroneously: Bacher) in 1856 for the

periodical כרם חמד, but the latter having discontinued its appearance, the work did not see the light until over thirty years later in the periodical אוצר הספרות, I (1887), 33-52, under the title פירש דבר. Buber's edition is based, so far as the text is concerned, on that of Benjacob, the Arabic phrases being given in the same Hebrew translation, but the learned editor added very copious notes and parallels from rabbinic literature. A Genizah fragment containing the larger portion of the book is described in Neubauer and Cowley's *Catalogue*, II, no. 2862, 27c, with the title שרח אלסבעין לפטה מן מפרדאת אלקראן, the Bible being here designated as Korân; comp. Eppenstein, *Beiträge*, p. 85, n. 1; Poznański, *ZfhB*, X, 148; Bacher, MGWJ., 1901, p. 565.

4. *Bible Translations and Commentaries*

A. PENTATEUCH

According to Saadia's own statement at the end of his Introduction to the Pentateuch, he had originally prepared a translation of the Pentateuch, together with a very extensive commentary, in which, to judge from the description given by the author and from the fragments that have come to light recently, he did not confine himself to the exegesis of the Biblical text, but embodied excursuses on Hebrew grammar and syntax, lengthy philosophic disquisitions on the entire Pentateuchal law in its two aspects as *revealed* and *rational* (see above, p. 208), and numerous polemics against the Karaites and other sectaries. This was the work to which earlier mediæval authors referred. Except for a few fragments of the commentary the book is lost, and what we possess to-day is a second translation without the commentary, which, as the author tells us, he prepared at the request of certain persons, who desired to have a plain, intelligible version of the Hebrew text without the insertion of all the elements mentioned before.

This translation was first printed from a MS written in Hebrew characters, in the *Pentateuchus Hebraeo-Chaldaeo-Persico-Arabicus*, Constantinople, 1546 A century later (1645) it was published (from a Paris MS.) in the Paris polyglot with a Latin translation by Gabriel Sionita, and

then reprinted in the London polyglot (1657). Variants
from another MS. (see Neubauer, *Catalogue*, I, nos.
28, 29) and from the Constantinople edition were given by Edward
Pococke in the sixth volume of the London polyglot. For the
Paris edition the Hebrew characters of the *editio princeps*
were transliterated into Arabic, the cause of innumerable mistakes in the text. The Arabic text of the London polyglot was
reprinted in the Arabic Bible edited by J. D. Carlyle, New-
castle-upon-Tyne, 1811 ; see Paul Kahle, *Die arabischen Bibelübersetzungen*, Leipzig, 1904, p. IV. During the years 1894-
1901 there appeared in Jerusalem an edition of the Pentateuch
under the title תאג (crown), in Hebrew כתר תורה, which, in
the Orient, is the usual designation for all Bibles printed together with Targum and Masorah (see Bacher, *JQR.*, XIV,
584, n. 1 ; ספיר אבן, I, 12, overlooked by Bardowicz, *Die Abfassungszeit der Baraita der 32 Normen*, Berlin, 1913, p. 39,
n. 4, who misunderstands the meaning of תגי ספר, quoted by
Norzi, for which see above, notes 52, 452). In this edition
Saadia's Arabic translation, taken from MSS. in the possession of Yemenite Jews, was printed in addition to the
Targum between the lines of the Hebrew text (in Hebrew
characters). A modern critical edition with explanatory
Hebrew notes was prepared for the occasion of Saadia's
millennium by Joseph Derenbourg and published as the first
volume of the projected edition of Saadia's complete works
(*Œuvres complètes de R. Saadia*, Paris, 1893). Numerous corrections to Derenbourg's edition on the basis of a
careful comparison with the texts of the Constantinople and
London Polyglots were recently published by Josef Mieses,
MGWJ., 1919, pp. 269-290. Derenbourg's edition contains
also Saadia's Arabic Introduction previously mentioned,
with a Hebrew translation by Derenbourg, who gives also
some specimens in French of Saadia's renderings of Pentateuchal passages, especially in the poetic portions. The
Introduction was translated into German by W. Bacher,
in Winter und Wünsche, *Die jüdische Litteratur*, II (1897),
248 ff., and later by W. Engelkemper, *Theologische Quar-
talschrift*, 1901, pp. 529 ff. ; comp. Poznański, *Zur jüdisch-
arabischen Literatur*, Berlin, 1904, p. 43. Extracts from

Saadia's translation of the book of Genesis taken " from an edition (*sic*) of an authentic (*sic*) MS." in the Grand-Ducal Library at Karlsruhe, Germany, were published in German with some comments by J Schwarzstein, under the title *Targum Arwi. Die arabische Interpretation des Pentateuchs von R. Saadia Hagaon*, Frankfurt a. M., 1886 (82 pages). A lithograph of eight pages of the Arabic text is given at the end of the book, but the author does not say a word about the origin and nature of the MS., except what I have translated above from the title-page; see also *MGWJ.*, 1901, pp 185 f (Fried's review of an Arabic translation of the Pentateuch)

Saadia's Arabic translation of Deuteronomy, 32-34, was reprinted from the Walton Polyglot (together with the other ancient versions of these two chapters) by L. Bodenheimer in two small volumes containing a comparative study on the different translations under the title הֹאזינו, *Das Lied Mosis. Eine wissenschaftliche Vergleichung der auf diesen Pentateuch-Abschnitt in der Walton'schen Polyglotte enthaltenen Uebertragungen*, Crefeld, 1856, and וזאת הברכה, *Der Segen Mosis, etc.*, Crefeld 1860.

All the editions of Saadia's translations of the Pentateuch with the exception of Schwarzstein's extracts (?) and Bodenheimer's reprints were based on MSS written in Hebrew characters. In the library of Florence (codex Palatinus Orient. 112, xxi) there is, however, a MS., dating from the year 1245 (643 of the Hegirah), written in Arabic letters From this MS the first four chapters of Genesis (and Ex 4, 20-26) were edited by Paul Kahle in his *Die arabischen Bibelubersetzungen*, Leipzig, 1904. pp 13-26, but according to Bacher (*Rivista Israelitica*, II, 45-49 ; comp *Theologische Literaturzeitung*, 1905, no. 8, and *JE., s. v. Saadia*, end of the article) the MS. does not contain the original work of Saadia, but a revision thereof, approaching more closely to the Hebrew text of the Bible ; comp. Poznański, *ZfhB.*, IX, 13 f Another, and still older, MS. of the translation of Genesis and Exodus (dated 637 of the Hegirah= 1239, c. e.), written likewise in Arabic characters, is extant

in the library of Leyden. The text, which was published by
Lagarde in *Materialien zur Geschichte und Kritik des Pentateuchs,* Leipzig, 1867, I, 1-108, differs considerably from the
other recensions; comp. Poznański, *ZfhB.,* IX, 12; see also
Kahle, *l. c.,* pp. viii, xii, 24. A third MS. in Arabic characters (of the 14th century), a specimen of which (Exodus,
35, 29 to 36, 13) is given by E. Tisserant, *Specimina codicum
Orientalium,* p. 53, is found in the Vatican. For the MSS.
of Saadia's other Bible works extant in various libraries see
the references in Steinschneider's *AL.,* p. 56; see also Neubauer and Cowley, *Catalogue,* etc., I, 969, II, 495.

Of Saadia's Commentary on the Pentateuch the following
fragments and extracts occurring in the works of later
authors, partly in translation, are known:

a) A lengthy extract from Saadia's Introduction to the
Commentary on the Pentateuch is preserved in a Hebrew
translation in the פרוש ספר יצירה of Judah b. Barzillai
(1135), edited by Halberstam, Berlin 1885, pp. 89-92. For
a reference to the Introduction in another work see Steinschneider, *HB.,* VIII, 71.

b) A fragment of the Introduction, published by Hirschfeld, *JQR.,* XVIII (1906), 317-325. Hirschfeld assumes
that the fragment formed part of Saadia's Commentary on
Jeremiah, and this view is accepted also by Eppenstein,
Beiträge, p. 80, n. 1. There is not the least evidence for this
assumption, except that a few verses from Jeremiah are
quoted at the beginning. Saadia refers here to his discussion in preceding pages of the various qualities or dispositions of the soul, and then takes up the discussion of joy
and sadness as "an appropriate theme for the Introduction
to the book which he is about to explain" (Hirschfeld's
translation of this passage seems to me incorrect). Now in
the second recension of the seventh chapter of his *Kitâb al-
'Amânât* (ed. Bacher, Steinschneider's *Festschrift,* p. 105,
line 18; *Emūnōt,* ed. Slucki, p. 111, bottom) Saadia says
explicitly that he had discussed the *sixteen* qualities or dispositions of the soul in his Commentary on Genesis. The
fragment, it is true, refers to *eighteen,* but, in the first place,

not much reliance can be placed upon the reading of this
badly mutilated text, and for ר״ה we may read ר״ו. A similar
mistake is found in two other parallel passages. In the *Sefer
Yeẓirah*, ed. Lambert, p. 68, line 3, Saadia refers to an
" Explanation of the Construction of the Tabernacle "
(שרח מעשה מישכן), no doubt in his Commentary on Exodus,
25 ff., where, he says, he showed eighteen (י״ח) parallelisms
between the upper world, the Tabernacle, and the human
body (comp. above, p. 186), but in the corresponding passage
quoted by Steinschneider (*CB.*, 2207, bottom) from the work
of another author, who cites directly from the Commentary
on Exodus, we read in three places sixteen (י״ו) which, however, is incorrect as Abraham Ibn Ezra on Exodus, 25. 40,
also quotes eighteen.   Secondly, the number eighteen in
our fragment may include the two additional dispositions of
joy and sadness which he had previously mentioned (in the
missing part) in connection with the other sixteen, and
which he wanted to discuss here with more detail for the
reason given before. We should not wonder at this procedure, as Saadia's habit of playing with numbers is well-
known (see above, notes 473, 531).

That the number sixteen in the *Kitâb al-Amànât* is correct can be proved also by the recently discovered fragment
of Saadia's commentary on Exodus, 21 (see below, under
letter i), in which the author speaks of the five senses " and
the other sixteen faculties of man " (וסאיר אלי״ו אלקוה אלתי
פי אלאנסאן) ; see *JQR., N. S.*, vol. VI (1915-1916), pp. 367
(line 13), 377. It is therefore surprising that in the " Ethical
Treatise of Berachya," in the passage corresponding to that
of the *Amànât* (ed. Gollancz, p. 75), the number is *seventeen*, and the faculties are specified accordingly.

c) *Genesis*, 1, 2. Judah b. Barzillai, Commentary on the
Sefer Yeẓirah, p. 197, lines 4-30, quotes a passage from
Saadia's Commentary on Genesis, as it seems, ch. 1, 2.
Another short quotation, probably from the same chapter, is
found *ib.*, p. 193, lines 11-17. The same passage occurs with
some variations in Saadia's Commentary on the *Sefer
Yeẓirah*, p. 9, lines 14-19.

d) *Genesis,* 3, 20, by Harkavy, הקדם, I (1907), 160 f. (only a portion of the discovered fragment).

e) *Genesis,* 18, 1, a lengthy extract in Judah b. Barzillai's Commentary, p. 131, l. 9 from the bottom. Here the author does not state explicitly that he is citing from the Commentary on Genesis, but it is obvious from the content. It is not certain how far the extract extends, but in all probability up to p. 135, l. 18, where another extract from a work of Saadia is introduced with the words וכתב נמי רבנו סעריה "this, too, did R. Saadia write." The Midrashic style of the first extract at times makes Saadia's authorship doubtful, but it is known that Judah seldom quotes literally. He mostly paraphrases and often inserts phrases and entire sentences of his own (see below, pp. 356 f.). The same applies to the second extract just mentioned (overlooked by Halberstam in his index, p. xiii), which perhaps goes as far as p. 137, l. 6 from bottom. The work from which this is taken cannot be positively identified, but in all likelihood it is from the Commentary on the Pentateuch, if not from the Introduction thereto. The translation of בכאים by אגאיץ, Mishnaic אגסים = pears, or prunes (*ib.,* p. 136, l. 8, where the words והם בלע''ז פרונץ are certainly Judah's addition, פרונץ = *prunus*) agrees with that of Saadia to Psalms, 84, 7, ed. Galliner, Berlin 1903, pp. xx, 44, n. 12.

Among the quotations from the commentary on *Genesis* (28, 12) we should probably reckon also the passage cited by Abraham Bédersi (13th century) in his חותם תכנית Amsterdam, 1865, p. 149.

f) *Exodus,* 7, 16, Harkavy, הגרן, II (1900), 85 f.

g) *Exodus,* 12, 2, Hirschfeld, *JQR.,* XVI (1904), 298.

h) *Exodus,* parts of chapters 15, 28, 30, published by G. Margoliouth, *JQR.,* X (1898), 385-403, from a MS. in the British Museum containing an Arabic commentary on II Samuel by Isaac b. Samuel ha-Sefardi, whose date is not certain, Margoliouth placing him in the early part of the 12th century, while Steinschneider, *AL.,* 247, is inclined to place him as late as 1380.

i) *Exodus*, 21, 1-6, a fragment of four leaves (eight pages, 23-24 lines each) recently discovered and published by Hirschfeld with introduction and English translation, *JQR , N. S.*, vol VI (1915-1916), pp. 359-372, 374-382 This fragment is in all probability part of the תפסיר ואלה המשפטים, mentioned in a book list found in the Genizah, for which see below, *Bibliography*, VII, p 396, No 2, comp. also above, p 311, under letter *b*.

j) Two fragments from *Exodus*, sections תרומה and כי תשא, published with a Hebrew translation by Harkavy, *Semitic Studies in Memory of Dr. Alexander Kohut*, Berlin, 1897, pp 244 f The passages published by Harkavy are found also in the Bible commentary אמרי נעם (Exodus, 19, 9) by Jacob d'Illescas (14th century), and in the so-called *Tōsāfōt* הדר זקנים (same verse). In the latter work they are quoted from the unpublished ספר הגן of Aaron b. Jose ha-Kohen (13th century), for whom see Poznański, פרוש ע׳ יחזקאל ותרי עשר לר׳ אליעזר מבלגנצי, Warsaw 1913, pp. xcviii ff.

k) A long fragment, *Exodus*, chapters 25-40 (see Derenbourg, *MWJ.*, VII (1880), 133), of which only 30, 11-16, was published in German by Bacher, in Winter and Wünsche, *Die jüdische Litteratur*, II, 251-254.

l) A fragment of about four printed pages, *Exodus, 35, 3,* and part of 36, published by Hirschfeld with an English translation, *JQR., XVIII* (1906), 606-613. For another passage from Exodus, 35, 3, see *Oeuvres*, IX, 170, no. 135.

m) *Leviticus*, 11, 11-28, with an English translation by Hirschfeld, *JQR , XIX* (1907), 140-161 This is the largest fragment that has so far been published, covering 12 printed pages.

n) Fragment containing introduction to *Leviticus*, 16, and interpretation of verses 11-15, published with an English translation by Hirschfeld, *JQR., N S ,* vol. VI (1915-1916), pp. 372-374, 382 f. The fragment consists of two leaves, but only three pages (with 23 lines to each), the first page having been left blank for the title, which is missing Between leaves one and two the pages containing the

interpretation of verses 1-11 are missing. This fragment is
in all probability part of the anonymous תפסיר אחרי מות,
which seems to be identical with the תפסיר אלעריות; see
below, *Bibliography,* III, p. 346; VII, p. 396, no. 3.

o) Fragment, *Leviticus,* section קדשים, referred to by Harkavy, הגרן, I (1899), 90; I do not know whether he has subsequently published it or not. A passage from the same section
is quoted by Steinschneider, *CB.,* 2166 f. (comp. Poznański
JQR., X, 244, n. 1) from a work of Moses Ibn Ezra; comp.
also Bacher, *Abraham Ibn Esra's Einleitung zu seinem Pentateuch-Commentar,* p. 20, n. 2; Neubauer and Cowley,
Catalogue, II, No. 2862, 28; Poznański, *ZfhB.,* X, 148; *RÉJ.,*
XIV, 119. According to a very probable suggestion of
Steinschneider (*CB.,* 2205), the טעמי תקיעות, for which see
below under Liturgy, p. 335, no. 1, also formed a part of the
commentary on Leviticus, 23, 24.

p) *Leviticus,* 25, 36-46 (two pages) recently published
with introductory remarks and translation by H. Hirschfeld,
JQR., N. S., vol. VII (1916-1917), pp. 45-46; 54-55.

q) *Deuteronomy,* 1, 41, and 2, 9-12 (two leaves by the
same hand; after the first leaf there is a gap), published by
Hirschfeld, *ib.,* pp. 50-54; 56-60; comp. the editor's general
remarks, *ib.,* pp. 46-48, pointing out the similarity between
the contents of this fragment and some passages of Saadia's
'Emūnôt [but see *Postscript*]. For the עשר שירות, probably
also a fragment of the Commentary, see below, *Bibliography,*
p. 403.

Saadia quotes his commentary on the Pentateuch very
frequently, *e. g.* in his Commentary on the *Sēfer Yeẓirah,*
p. 12, l. 3 (comp. above, note 416); p. 44, l. 9 (comp.
Schwarzstein, *Die arabische Interpretation des Pentateuchs
von R. Saadia,* p. 1); p. 68, l. 3 (see above, p. 312, top);
Kitâb al-'Amânât, p. 20, l. 4 from bottom; 37, l. 5; 84,
l. 4; 106, l. 6, and in the second recension of chapter VII
(Steinschneider's *Festschrift,* p. 105, l. 18; see above, p. 311,
letter *b*); in the treatise on "Forbidden Marriages" (תפסיר
אלעריות), Hirschfeld, *JQR.,* XVII (1905), 716, l. 4 of the
Arabic text (see for details regarding this treatise below,
p. 346, no. 4); Commentary on Proverbs, *ed.* Derenbourg,

pp. 52. 56, 119, 182 (see Derenbourg, Introduction) ; in the *Siddūr*, see Steinschneider, *CB.*, 2205, where the passage is given in full.

For quotations of the Commentary in works of later authors, see Steinschneider, *HB.*, XX, 39, *AL.*, p. 66, nn. 27, 28 ; Hirschfeld, *JQR.*, XVIII (1906), 600 ff. (Jephet) ; Poznański, *The Karaite Literary Opponents of Saadiah*, London, 1908, *passim ;* Eppenstein, *Beiträge*, pp. 83, 216, last §. See also the two quotations from the יָרֵח כָּבִיר (Long Commentary) in G. Margoliouth's *Catalogue*, III, 586, no. 1160.

It is very probable that the Commentary on the Pentateuch had the special title *Kitâb al-Azhâr* (כתאב אלזאההאר), " Book of Splendor," just as Saadia's commentaries on other books of the Bible (Isaiah, Proverbs, Job) had each a separate title. It is hard to believe that this title, mentioned by some authors and in Genizah fragments, designates Saadia's *'Azharōt,* as these would hardly be called *Kitâb* (book). A passage quoted by Steinschneider, *CB.*, 2207 (to which I have referred above, p. 312) reads : וקאֹל רבני סעריה ז"ל פי כתאב אלזאאוההאר פי ירח ויקחו לי תרומה. Steinschneider, *ib.*, 2208, changes (פי ("ירח)) into (ופי ("ירח), so as to separate the *Kitâb al-'Azhâr* from the Commentary. This change seems to me unwarranted, and the whole refers to one and the same work, the Commentary ; see for the entire matter Steinschneider, *AL.*, p. 66, n. 27 ; Bacher, *REJ.*, XXXIX, p. 206, no. 9 ; Poznański, *Schechter's Saadyana*, p. 22 ; Eppenstein, *Beiträge*, p. 81.

B. PROPHETS

Nothing has been preserved of Saadia's works on *The Earlier Prophets.* As early as 1886 Harkavy announced the discovery of portions of Saadia's commentaries on the Earlier Prophets (see *REJ.*, XIV, 119), but, so far as I know, they have not been published. Several references to these commentaries are found in Abraham Ibn Ezra's שָׂפָה יָתֵר and David Kimhi's *Commentaries*, for which see Steinschneider, *CB.*, 2190. For an anonymous Arabic translation see Steinschneider, *AL.*, p. 286, no. 91 ; Neubauer, *Catalogue,* I, no. 180.

Of Saadia's works on the *Later Prophets* the following have been preserved or are known to have existed:

Isaiah, translation and commentary, called *Kitâb al-Istiṣâlḥ* (כתאב אלאסתצלאח) " Book of (Moral) Improvement." The *translation* was first edited from a Bodleian MS. by H. E. G. Paulus: *Rabbi Saadiae Phiumensis versio Jesaiae arabica* etc., two volumes, Jena, 1790-91. The editor trans-literated the Hebrew characters of the MS. into Arabic and, not knowing the language sufficiently, made numberless mis-takes, which render the edition worthless; comp. Gesenius, *Jesaia,* I, 88 ff. ; Munk *Notice sur Saadia,* pp. 29 f.; Deren-bourg, *Oeuvres,* III, Introduction. A *Commentatio in Saadianam versionem Jesaiae arabicam* by D. Chr. Breithaupt appeared in Rostock, 1819. Solomon Munk published chapter 17 with a French translation and notes in his *Notice sur Saadia,* pp. 29-62. A critical edition of the whole, with the use of a Paris MS., was published with French notes by J. Derenbourg, *ZfaW.,* IX (1889) and X (also separately), and then again by the same writer and his son Hartwig with Hebrew notes and a complete French translation as the third volume of the *Oeuvres complètes de Saadia,* Paris, 1896.

Of the *Commentary* on Isaiah considerable portions have been preserved. Most of them, eighteen in number and rang-ing from chapters 14 to 63, were published with a Hebrew translation by Derenbourg in the volume just mentioned (pp. 105-147). Two additional fragments, parts of chap-ters 20 and 40, were published in Harkavy's *Festschrift,* non-Hebrew part, pp. 91-94 (by S. Fraenkel), and Kauf-mann's *Gedenkbuch,* pp. 138-143 (by M. Lambert). A much mutilated fragment of the Introduction to the Commentary is found in Schechter's *Saadyana,* p. 55, which is the source for the title *Kitâb al-Istiṣlâḥ* mentioned before. In an ancient book-list from the Genizah, *Saadyana,* p. 79, a תפסיר ישעיה is registered, which probably refers to this Commen-tary : see Bacher, *RÉJ.,* XXXIX, p. 206, no. 8 ; Poznański, *Schechter's Saadyana,* p. 21, no. 3 [*JQR., N. S.,* XI, 425].

For an anonymous Arabic translation of Isaiah with short
glosses see Neubauer, *Catalogue*, I, no. 181 (comp. *ibid.*,
no. 180), and below, under *Minor Prophets*.

Jeremiah and Ezekiel. Quotations from Saadia's works
on these prophets occur in several works of later authors,
for which see Steinschneider, *CB.*, 2192. The fragment
published by Hirschfeld, *JQR.*, XVIII, 317 ff., as part of the
Commentary on Jeremiah is more likely part of Saadia's
Introduction to his Commentary on the Pentateuch, see
above, under *Pentateuch*, letter *b*.

The Minor Prophets. The translation and Commentary
to the Minor Prophets were in use as late as the 14th century (see Bacher, *Ein hebräisch-persisches Wörterbuch aus
dem vierzehnten Jahrhundert*, Budapest, 1900, p. 45), but
since then no trace of them has been found. References and
quotations in the works of earlier mediæval authors are not
infrequent. They were noted by Steinschneider, *CB.*, 2192,
AL., p. 67, n. 29, and Poznański, *Schechter's Saadyana*, p.
21, n. 1. [A recent fragment mentions מסאיל (?) מן תרי עשר;
see *Postscript*, below, p. 427].

It should not be left unmentioned that there exists an anonymous Arabic translation (accompanied by short explanatory
glosses) of all the Later Prophets (MS., Neubauer, *Catalogue*, I, no. 181, dated 1196), which, it is generally assumed,
is based on that of Saadia, who is cited in it. *Hosea* and
Joel were edited by R. Schröter, in Merx's *Archiv*, I (1867),
28 ff. *Joel* and *Amos* by Deszö Klein, Budapest, 1897;
Zephaniah, Haggai, and *Zechariah* by A. Heisz, Berlin, 1902;
comp. Steinschneider, *AL.*, p. 286, no. 92; Poznański, *ZfhB.*,
VII, 50.

C. HAGIOGRAPHA

Psalms: Psalms 1-5 and 11 (in full) and extracts from
nearly all other Psalms (except the following eighteen:
43, 70, 97, 106, 108, 111, 117, 121, 124, 125, 128, 134,
136, 145-149) were first published with partial German
translation and comment by Heinrich Ewald, in Ewald and
Dukes, *Beiträge zur Geschichte der ältesten Auslegung und
Spracherklärung des alten Testaments*, Stuttgart, 1844, I
9-74, with additions on pp. 154-160 (in Arabic characters).

The edition of the translation and Commentary of *groups* of consecutive Psalms was begun by S. H. Margulies, *Saadia Alfajûmî's arabische Psalmenübersetzung*, Breslau, 1884, containing the first twenty Psalms (Arabic characters) with a German translation and notes. Margulies' work was continued by S. Lehmann (Ps. 21-41), Berlin, 1901 (see *ZfhB., VI, 50*); Th. Hofmann, *Die korachitischen Psalmen* (in *Programm des Gymnasiums zu Ehingen*), Stuttgart, 1891 (Pss. 42-49, 84, 85, 87, 88); S. Baron (Ps. 50-72), Berlin, 1900 (comp. *ZfhB.*, V, 40; *MGWJ.*, 1901, pp. 183 f.); S. Galliner (Ps. 73-89), Berlin, 1903 (comp. Bacher, *Theologische Literaturzeitung*, 1904, pp. 677-79; Eppenstein, *ZfhB.*, VIII, 98); J. Z. Lauterbach (Ps. 107-124), Berlin, 1903 (Bacher, *Theologische Literaturzeitung*, 1904, no. 1; comp. *MGWJ.*, 1905, p. 503); B. Schreier (Ps. 125-150), Berlin, 1904—all these editions (except that of Hofmann), bearing the same title as the publication of Margulies, but giving the text in Hebrew characters.

Single disconnected Psalms were first published by Schnurrer in Eichhorn's *Allgemeine Bibliothek*, III (1790), 425 ff. (Psalms 16, 40, 110). The difficult Psalm 68 was published (in Arabic characters) by Dan. Haneberg, *Über die in einer Münchener Handschrift aufbehaltene arabische Psalmenübersetzung des Saadia Gaon* (in *Abhandlungen der philosophisch-philologischen Classe der königlich Bayerischen Akademie der Wissenschaften*, III, 354-410), München, 1840 (comp. *Literaturblatt des Orients*, II, 349 ff.); for Psalms 84, etc., which are also to be included here; see above, under Hofmann.

Saadia wrote a lengthy Arabic Introduction to his work on the Psalms, in which the scope, purpose, and form of the Psalter were discussed. This Introduction is followed by a commentary on the first four Psalms, which is considerably longer than the commentary on the same chapters which accompanies the translation. Upon this commentary follows another shorter Introduction, representing perhaps an earlier recension. Both Introduction and the commentary on Ps. 1-4 were published in a German translation, with

notes by J. Cohn, *MWJ.*, VIII (1881), 1-19, 61-91 (comp.
Steinschneider, *HB.*, XIV, 118, XXI, 53), while the Arabic
text was published by S. Eppenstein in Harkavy's *Festschrift*, pp. 135-160.

Saadia calls his work on the Psalms *Kitâb al-Tasbîḥ*
(כתאב אלתסביח), " Book of Praise." This is not meant as a
special title, as asserted by Eppenstein, *Beiträge*, p. 81, but
is merely the translation of the Hebrew ספר תהלים, or
תהלות.

Proverbs, translation and commentary with the special
title *Kitâb Ṭalab al-Ḥikmah* (כתאב טלב אלחכמה). " Book of
the Search for Wisdom," first identified by Steinschneider
in a Bodleian MS. (*HB.*, X (1870), 172, *JQR.*, XIII (1901),
446, n. 1). The work is preceded by an extended and very
valuable Introduction, in which a general characterization
of the Proverbs is given.

Extracts with a German introduction and notes were given
by Jonas Bondi, *Das Spruchbuch nach Saadja*, Halle, 1888
(from chapter 1-9) ; by J. Derenburg, in Geiger's *jüdische
Zeitschrift*, VI (1868), 309-315, and by R. Schröter, in
Merx's *Archiv.*, I, 156, 160, II, 36 ff. The entire work, with
a French and an abridged Hebrew translation, was edited
by J. Derenbourg and M. Lambert as the sixth volume of
Saadia's complete works (*Oeuvres.* etc., Paris, 1894) ; comp.
Bacher, *Abraham Ibn Esra's Einleitung zu seinem Pentateuch-Commentar*, pp. 25 ff.: Poznański, *Zur jüdisch-arabischen Literatur*, p. 45, top ; Steinschneider, *AL.*, pp. 57 f.
A full description of Saadia's method in his work on Proverbs and a detailed analysis of the content was given by
Bernard Heller, *REJ.*, XXXVII, 72-85, 226-251.

Judah b. Barzillai, פרוש ספר יצירה, pp. 93, 155, quotes two
passages from Saadia's Commentary on Proverbs, 8, 26-29,
and 30, 4. The latter passage is also found in Saadia's
Commentary on the *Sefer Yeẓirah*, ed. Lambert, pp. 15 f.
The same passage is quoted by Eliezer b. Nathan of Mayence (12th century) in his Decisions (ראב"ן), no. 119;
comp. Halberstam's Notes on the aforementioned Commentary of Judah b. Barzillai, p. 309, l. 13. Many passages are

quoted by Joseph Ibn Naḥmias in his Commentary on Proverbs, edited by M. L. Bamberger, Berlin, 1911; comp. *ib*. p.
xv. Variants to the Arabic text from a fragment in the
Munich library were published by Johannes Goettsberger,
in *Biblische Zeitschrift*, II, 53-55.

Job, with Introduction, translation, and Commentary,
called by Saadia *Kitâb al-Ta'dîl* (אלתעדיל כתאב), " Book of
Theodicy." Extracts from a compilation in which Saadia's
translation and Commentary, as well as those of two other
authors are reproduced promiscuously (comp. Bacher, in
Harkavy's *Festschrift*, pp. 221 ff.; *JQR.*, XX (1908), 31-49),
were published by Ewald, *Beiträge*, etc., I, 75-115. See also
Geiger, פרשנדתא, 7-16. J. Cohn published the whole book
with the omission only of some parts of the Introduction and
Commentary: *Das Buch Hiob übersetzt und erklärt vom
Gaon Saadia*, Altona, 1889. A critical edition with a Hebrew
translation, introduction, and notes by Bacher and a French
introduction and translation by J. and H. Derenbourg appeared as volume V of the *Oeuvres complètes*, Paris, 1899;
comp. Steinschneider, *AL.*, p. 58. The first two chapters of
Bacher's edition of Job were reproduced by Paul Kahle, *Die
arabischen Bibelübersetzungen*, Leipzig, 1904, pp. 27-29.

Saadia mentions his commentary on Job in the *Kitâb al-
'Amânât*, p. 15, and in several other of his works; comp.
Bacher's Introduction, p. x; see also Poznański, *Schechter's
Saadyana*, p. 22, no. 11.

THE FIVE SCROLLS

a) *Canticles*. There is no doubt that Saadia made a translation of the Book of Canticles, and wrote a Commentary
on it, though direct quotations from it are very scarce and
not fully authenticated. Abraham Ibn Ezra cites in his
שפת יתר (a defense of Saadia against Dûnâsh b. Librat),
nos. 60, 67, Saadia's interpretations of two words in Canticles; but citations in this book, which is not quite reliable
in other respects as well (see Steinschneider, *CB.*, 2201, *opus*
30), do not always prove the existence of a work by Saadia
on the Biblical book in question. They may refer to a passage occurring incidentally in one or the other of the lost

21

writings of the Gaon. In his Commentary on Canticles, I. 2,
Ibn Ezra refers more explicitly to the Commentary of Saadia
on the same book, but here, too, another recension of Ibn
Ezra's work omits the name of Saadia and reads " one of the
Geonim " (אחד הגאונים)   More reliable testimony, however, is found in the Introduction to an unpublished Arabic
Commentary on Canticles by Joseph Ibn 'Aknin, the famous
pupil of Maimonides, from which it is apparent that he had
the Commentary of Saadia before him, taking it in some
respect, as he says (see above, note 592), as a model for his
own , comp. Steinschneider, in Ersch and Gruber's *Encyclo-
pædie*, II, vol 31, p. 54, n. 75; *CB.*, 2188. Moreover, there
are anonymous Arabic translations and commentaries on
Canticles in several MSS. and editions, which, in form and
content, bear so much similarity to the exegetical works of
the Gaon that they have been ascribed to him even by careful investigators of recent times (comp. Steinschneider,
Encyclopædic, l. c ; Rapoport, בכה"ע, IX, 37, n. 50). From
one of these MSS. a translation and part of a commentary
were published by A. Merx, *Die Saadjanische Übersetzung
des Hohen Liedes in's Arabische,* Heidelberg, 1882, with a
very learned Introduction, in which the authorship of Saadia
is asserted. While later critics have, on various grounds,
disproved Saadia's authorship of the translation and Commentary edited by Merx (comp. Jacob Loevy, *MWJ*, X,
33-41, and Bacher, *ZfaW.*, III, 202-211 ; Poznański, *JQR.,*
III, 343), as well as of another Commentary still in MSS.
(see Salfeld, *MWJ.*, V, 125-131), it is generally admitted
that these productions are in fact reworkings and amplifications by others of Saadia's original work; comp. Bacher,
Leben und Werke des Abulwalid Merwân Ibn Ganâh, Leipzig, 1885, p. 93, n 21.

    The same seems to be true in the case of a Hebrew transla-
tion of an Arabic Commentary and of the so-called *Twelve
Homilies* (ב"י דרושים) on Canticles ascribed to Saadia.
Rapoport, בכה"ע, IX, 37, n 50, considered the *Perush* genuine, Dukes, *Beitrage,* II, 104-109 (comp. Luzzatto, *HB.,* V,
146), on the other hand denies Saadia's authorship; see in

particular Steinschneider, *CB.*, 2187-89, *opp.* 18-20; Salfeld,
HB., IX, 137 ff., nos. 47, 71; Bacher, *ZfhB.*, ix, 50 ff.;
Poznański, *MGWJ.*, 1907, pp. 718 ff. To my mind Saadia's
original authorship has not yet been disproved, but the matter
requires special treatment. The discussion of nine (actually
eight) " musical tones " in the introd. to the Commentary has
a parallel in *'Amânât*, p. 317 (see above, p. 259). *Homilies*
(דראשאת) are often mentioned among works of Saadia. See
Saadyana, p. 128; *REJ.*, XXXIX, 200, 203; below, p. 405
[and *Postscript*, below, p. 427].

There is still to be mentioned a work entitled: *Three
Scrolls . . . . Canticles, Ruth, and Ecclesiastes . . . . with
Targum Jonathan '. . . ., Rashi, and the Arabic translation
of Saadia . . . .,* Jerusalem, 1911 (שיר . . . . שלש מגלות
השירים רות וקהלת בלוית תרגום יונתן . . . . רש"י תפסיר ערבי
של ר' סעדיה גאון). The translation, based on a Yemenite
MS., is identical with that edited in Arabic characters by
Merx, mentioned in a preceding paragraph. Regarding the
MSS. of the anonymous translations and commentaries discussed above, see Steinschneider, *AL.*, 58, 287, nos. 100a,
100b.

b) *Ruth.* No quotation is known, Abraham Ibn Ezra, שפה
יתר, no. 120, mentioning only the view of Saadia's critic,
Dûnâsh. This silence does not prove anything, however, for
we know positively that Saadia translated and interpreted
others of the Five Scrolls and yet, as we shall see below,
quotations from these works are extremely rare, or entirely
lacking. Besides, here again we possess two anonymous
translations (with portions of commentaries), one of which
was subsequently recognized as that of the Karaite Jephet b.
'Ali (see N. Schorstein, *Der Kommentar des Karäers Jephet
b. Ali zum Buche Rûth.* Berlin, 1903, Introduction; comp.
Poznański, *ZfhB.*, VII, 134), while the other is considered
to be either a modification of that of Saadia or the genuine
work of the Gaon. Both translations were critically edited
by M. Peritz, *Zwei alte arabische Übersetzungen des Buches
Rûth*, Berlin, 1900 (reprint from *MGWJ.*, 1899, pp. 49 ff.;
comp. S. Fränkel, *Deutsche Litteraturzeitung*, 1901, no. 20).
I have not the least doubt that one of these translations,

namely that edited from a codex of the British Museum
(defective at the beginning until c. 2, 13), represents the
original work of Saadia, though I cannot here offer proofs
for the statement. Even the Arabic Appendix to that translation, discussing the genealogy of David (Peritz, pp. 56-59),
as, likewise, the Arabic portion communicated by Poznański
(ZfhB., IV, 168) from another MS., containing one of the
translations with a mixed Hebrew and Arabic commentary
on Ruth of a Midrashic character, impresses me as genuinely
Saadianic, though the latter commentary as a whole must be
the work of a later author; comp. the extract given by Poznański, l. c., with Amânât, p. 147, lines 5 ff., where the same
idea is expressed. It should be added that the translation
edited by Peritz from the incomplete MS. of the British
Museum is identical with the one published later (Jerusalem,
1911) from another MS. in the Three Scrolls mentioned
above under Canticles. In this latter edition the text is complete. A literal Arabic translation of Ruth is found also in
the book מנחת בכורים by Elia Benamosegh, Leghorn, 1856,
but, the translation differs entirely from those edited by
Peritz and is certainly not the work of Saadia; see Steinschneider, AL., p. 288, no. 101c.

c) *Lamentations.* That Saadia wrote a commentary on
Lamentations is established beyond a doubt. It is referred
to by R. Mubashshir, a contemporary critic of Saadia (see
Derenbourg, REJ., XX, 137; comp. S. Fuchs, *Studien über
. . . . Ibn Bal'am,* Berlin, 1893, p. xxxii, n. 17; Poznań-
ski, JQR., XIII, 340, n. 1, and above, note 82) and by David
Kimḥi, s. v. כסף (see Steinschneider, CB., 2189, op. 20, line 8
from below). It is also mentioned in an ancient book-list,
Schechter, *Saadyana,* p. 79 (comp. Poznański, *Schechter's
Saadyana,* p. 20, no. 4) [JQR., N. S., XI, 425]. So far, however, no MS. containing either Saadia's translation or com-
mentary has come to light.

d) *Ecclesiastes.* The only author who mentions Saadia's
commentary on this book is the grammarian Ibn Ǧanâḥ;
comp. Bacher, *Leben und Werke des Abulwalid Merwân
Ibn Ǧanâḥ,* Leipzig, 1885, p. 92, n. 15. No MS. is known;

comp. Steinschneider, *AL.*, pp. 59, 137, n. 3. The Hebrew
Commentary published by D. Fränkel as the translation of
Saadia's original Arabic (קהלת עם פרוש רבנו סעדיה גאון,
Husiatyn, 1903), has been shown by Bacher (*ZfhB.*, IX,
50 ff.) to be the work of another author; comp. Poznański,
MGWJ., 1907, pp. 718 ff., who proves it to be based entirely
on a commentary of the Karaite Salmon b. Jeroham.

e) *Esther.* The *translation* is printed in the Prayer-book
according to the Ritual (סדר תפלות) of the Jews at San'a,
Yemen, Vienna, 1896. For a full description see Poznański, *MGWJ.*, 1902, pp. 364-372. The *Commentary* on this
book is mentioned by Saadia himself in his Commentary on
Daniel (Bodleian MS., see Neubauer's *Catalogue*, 2486), as
well as by his Karaite opponent Salmon b. Jeroham, quoted
by Dukes, *Beiträge*, II, p. 100, n. 1, and Joseph Kimḥi (see
Poznański, *ibidem*, p. 364). It is probably also cited by Ibn
Nahmias (above, p. 321); for the objection of Poznański,
l. c., p. 365, that the passage quoted by the latter differs from
Saadia's interpretation of the same passage in his *Amânât*,
p. 112, has little weight, since it is well known that Saadia's
interpretations of Biblical verses in the latter work often
differ from those found in his commentaries on the Bible. In
the book-lists mentioned before under *Lamentations* [*JQR.*,
N. S., XI, 425] a תפסיר מגלת אסתר לפיומי is likewise mentioned, but it is doubtful whether *tafsir* refers to the translation or to the Commentary or to both, as the word is often
used indiscriminately; comp. Poznański, *Schechter's Saadyana*, p. 21, no. 14; Steinschneider, *AL.*, p. 59. For a fragment of the Commentary in a Genizah MS. see Hirschfeld,
JQR., XVII (1904), 66.

Daniel. The *translation* was edited by H. Spiegel, *Saadia
al-Fajjûmi's arabische Danielversion*, Berlin, 1906. The
Commentary is extant in MSS. only. For a detailed discussion of the latter see Poznański, *Ha-Goren*, II (1900), 92-
103, and *MGWJ.*, XLIV (1900), 400-416, 508-529, where
several passages of the Commentary are given and the literature on the subject is treated; comp. also Malter, in Neumark's *Journal of Jewish Lore and Philosophy*, Cincinnati,
1919, pp. 45-59. In this Commentary, Saadia quotes twice

his *Kitâb al-Amânât* (Poznański, *Ha-Goren*, II, 101, and *MGWJ.*, XLIV, 511); consequently the work on Daniel was composed or revised after 933; see also above, under *Esther*. The Hebrew Commentary printed in the מקראות גדולות under the name of Saadia has been proved long ago (Rapoport, *Bik-kure ha-'Ittim*, IX (1828), 34 f.) to belong to a later author; see Steinschneider, *Die hebräischen Übersetzungen des Mit-telalters*, p. 445, § 260; comp. also Poznański's article in *Ha-Goren, l. c.*; below, p. 404. A. F. Gallé, *Daniel avec com-mentaires de R. Saadia . . . . et variantes de versions arabe et syriaque*, Paris, 1900, is pseudo-Saadia.

Ezra and *Nehemiah* (usually counted by the ancients as one book). Three mediæval writers quote passages from a commentary on these books in the name of "R. Saadia"; see the references in Steinschneider's *CB.*, 2195, *s. v.* Esra. These passages, however, have since been found in a Hebrew commentary on Ezra and Nehemiah which in most MSS. is anonymous, while one (Munich) ascribes it to Benjamin b. Judah, an Italian exegete of the first half of the fourteenth century, and another one (Milan) to Saadia Gaon. The commentary was published by H. J. Mathews, *Commentary on Ezra and Nehemiah by Rabbi Saadiah*, Oxford, 1882. The editor in his learned introduction proves with sufficient reason that the author is not Saadia Gaon, but, if his name was Saadia at all, he was probably the writer who is known as pseudo-Saadia, author of the Commentary on Daniel (see above, under *Daniel*). The three quotations from a com-mentary on Ezra and Nehemiah by R. Saadia are accordingly to be considered as referring to the pseudo-Saadia edited by Mathews, and there is no direct proof that Saadia Gaon ever wrote a commentary on these books. On general grounds, however, it is considered certain that he translated and commented upon them, as well as upon the rest of the Bible. Abraham Ibn Ezra, *Sefat Yeter*, no. 138, quotes Nehemiah, 5, 4 (Steinschneider, *CB.*, 2202, line 34, erron-eously: IV, 22) without the name of Saadia, but see above, under *Canticles* regarding quotations in this book; comp. also Joel Müller, *Oeuvres*, IX, p. 160, no. 79; Eppenstein, *Beiträge*, p. 79, n. 4, who on p. 216 contradicts his own view

as to the quotation in שבלי הלקט. For completeness' sake it
may be added that the Commentary edited by Mathews was
published a second time (the editor says on the title-page:
zum ersten Male), Berlin, 1895 (reprint from קביץ על יד, VII;
see also *MWJ.*, XVI, 207 ff.), by Heinrich Berger, who
ascribes it to Benjamin b. Judah, though his authorship was
fully disproved by Mathews, pp. ii ff.; comp. Halberstam, קבץ,
על יד VII, 42; Poznański, *Ha-Goren*, II, 98; Steinschneider,
AL., p. 59, bottom.

From a curious misunderstanding of a passage in Saadia's
'Emūnōt (ed. Slucki, p. 129; Arabic original, p. 253) both
Grünhut (in the מאסף edited by L. Rabinowitz, St. Petersburg, 1902, I, 137) and Poznański (*Ha-Goren*, II, 101) derived the proof that Saadia had quoted his own Commentary
on Ezra and Nehemiah. As a matter of fact in the passage
under consideration Saadia does not refer to his Commentary
on these books, but to his explanation of the particular verse
in question (Ezra, 4, 24), which he had given in another
place of the *'Emūnōt* itself (p. 122; Arabic, p. 238).

Chronicles. No definite reference to a work of Saadia's
on this book is known. The only evidence that such ever
existed is afforded by an anonymous Hebrew Commentary edited by R. Kirchheim (פרוש על דברי הימים מיוחס לאחד
מתלמידי סעדיה הגאון, Frankfurt a/M., 1874), which is supposed to have been written in the tenth century by a pupil of
Saadia and to be in part Saadia's work; see Kirchheim's
Introduction, p. vi; L. Donath, *MWJ.*, I, nos. 21-24; S. Lan-
dau, *Ansichten des Talmuds*, etc., Halle, 1888, pp. 65 ff.
Saadia is mentioned by name several times (pp. 19, 27, 36,
bis); comp. Brüll, *Jahrbücher*, II, 191 ff.; Egers, *HB.*, XIV,
124 f.; Steinschneider, *HB.*, XIV, 130; XVI, 90. For a
supposed quotation of the Commentary of Saadia in a Geonic
Responsum see Ginzberg, *Geonica*, II, 16; Poznański, *JQR.*,
N. S., vol. II (1912-1913), p. 424. For details pertaining to
this Commentary and its relations to Saadia see the recent
work of L. Bardowicz, *Die Abfassungszeit der Baraita der
32 Normen*, Berlin, 1913; comp. *ibidem*, p. 43, n. 3; above,
note 606; Aptowitzer, in A. Schwarz's *Festschrift*, Berlin,
1917, pp. 121 ff.

For a general characterization of Saadia's Bible exegesis
see in particular the following authors (cited in chronological
order). Gesenius, *Jesaia*, Leipzig, 1821, I, 88-96, Munk,
Notice sur R. Saadia Gaon (1838), pp. 44-58; comp. also
Additions in his *Commentaire sur le livre de Habakkouk*,
1843, pp 104 ff. (comp. *Literaturblatt des Orients*, II,
349 ff.); Ewald und Dukes, *Beiträge zur Geschichte der
ältesten Auslegung* . . . . *des Alten Testaments* (1844), I,
5-115; II, 5-100; Geiger, *Wissenschaftliche Zeitschrift*, V
(1844), 281-316 (comp. also his *Jüdische Zeitschrift*, IV, 201
ff ; *Nachgelassene Schriften*, IV, 116 f.), L Bodenheimer,
Das Paraphrastische der arabischen übersetzung des Saadia,
in *Frankel's Monatsschrift*, IV (1854), 23-33; Graetz, *Geschichte* (4), V, 285 f.; Weiss, רד"י (ed Wilna, 1904),
pp. 127 f , idem in האסיף, 1885, pp 275-293; M. Wolff,
Zur Characteristik der Bibelexegese Saadia Alfajûmi's,
ZfaW., 1884, 1885; Bacher, *Die Anfange der hebräischen
Grammatik* (1895), chiefly with reference to grammar,
idem, in Winter und Wünsche, *Die jüdische Litteratur*, II
(1897), 138 f., 243 ff.; *JE*, X, 579-586, comp also his
*Abraham Ibn Esra's Einleitung zu seinem Pentateuch-Com-
mentar*, Wien, 1876, pp. 23-37; 61-63; W. Engelkemper, *De
Saadiae Gaonis vita*, etc., Münster, 1897; B. Heller, *La version arabe et le commentaire des Proverbes du Gaon Saadia*,
REJ., XXXVII (1898), 72-85; 226-251; A Schmiedl, *Rand-
bemerkungen zu Saadia's Pentateuchubersetzung, MGWJ.*,
1901, pp. 124 ff (comp. *ibidem*, pp. 565 f., the notes of
Bacher and J Cohn), 1902, pp. 84-88; 358-361, Steinschneider, *AL.* (1902), p 55; Eppenstein, *Beitrage* (1913),
pp 85-89.

Aside from these works and essays, the introductions and
notes to the editions of Saadia's Biblical works or fragments thereof, whether genuine or merely attributed to him,
contain, likewise, general characterizations of his exegetical
methods, especially the Introductions of Haneberg
(Psalms), Merx (Canticles), Cohn (Psalms, Job), Bondi
(Proverbs), and Hartwig Derenbourg (to Bacher's edition
of Job); comp. also Morris Jastrow, Jr., *Jewish Grammarians of the Middle Ages, Hebraica*, III (1886-1887), pp
171-174.

For Saadia's Bible exegesis in his philosophic works see the *Bibliography* under *Philosophy*. For miscellaneous subjects bearing on Saadia's Bible translation see S. Fraenkel, *Miscellen zu Saadias Bibelübersetzung, MGWJ.*, 1899, p. 471 ; J. Schwarzstein, *Zoologie der Bibel nach der arabischen Interpretation des Rabbi Saadia Hagaon,* in the *Actes* of the eleventh Congress of Orientalists, Paris, 1897, *Section musulmane,* pp. 159-170.

II. LITURGY

Saadia's liturgical productions are all embodied in his Ritual (סדור) as yet unpublished. This Ritual was very frequently quoted in the works of mediæval authors from the 12th century onward (see the references in Zunz, *Ritus,* p. 19; comp. Kohut, *Die Hoschanot des Gaon R. Saadia,* Breslau, 1893. reprint from *MGWJ.* of the same year, p. 1, n. 1), but no trace of it was known until the year 1851, when Steinschneider discovered it in a MS. of the Bodleian. The MS. though defective at the beginning and at the end, as well as in several parts in the middle, covers nevertheless 247 pages. With the exception of the incorporated prayers, hymns, etc., which are in the original Hebrew, the whole work is written in Arabic (in Hebrew characters). A minute description of the entire contents and numerous excerpts of the text were given by the discoverer in his Bodleian Catalogue, *coll.* 2203-2216, and later, with various additions, by Neubauer, in *Ben Chananja,* vol. VI (1863), 552 f., VII, 199. 234. Several scholars have since dealt with the Ritual of Saadia in part or as a whole, more recently J. Bondi, *Der Siddur des Rabbi Saadia Gaon* (reprint from *Rechenschafts-Bericht der jüdisch-literarischen Gesellschaft*), Frankfurt a/M., 1904 (comp. *ZfhB.,* IX, 104-107), who promised a critical edition of the entire work together with the numerous Genizah fragments of it that have of late come to light, partly supplying the missing portions of the *Siddūr* (comp. Neubauer-Cowley, *Catalogue,* II, no. 2701). As the beginning is lacking, the title is not positively ascertained, but from a passage occurring in the work it is assumed with great probability that its name was *Kitâb ğawâmi' al-Salawât wal-Tasâbîḥ* (אלצלואת גואמע כתאב ואלתסאביה), "A Book Comprising all the Prayers and Hymns" (comp. Steinschneider, *CB.*, 2204, and Neubauer, *Ben Chananja*, VI, 552, who, however, writes *ğâmî'*, the singular of *ğawâmî'*). It is also possible that Saadia himself designated it by the technical Hebrew name *Siddūr*, or *Sēder*, which was employed very early for prayer rituals (comp. Steinschneider, *CB.*, 2203). The title וגוב אלצלוה; in the ancient book-lists (*RÉJ.*, XXXIX, 200, no. 30; *Saadyana*, p. 128; *JQR.*, XIII, 330, no. 91; comp. also Graetz, *Geschichte* (4), V, 533, n. 2) refers either to the whole Introduction or to a chapter thereof [see below, p. 427].

A. Of Saadia's own liturgical compositions embodied in the *Siddūr* and described above (pp. 147, 149 ff.) the following have so far been published:

1. *'Abōdāh* (עבודה), or, as Saadia calls it, *Pasūk* (פסוק), a hymn for the Musaf Prayer of Yom Kippūr, arranged alphabetically in 22 strophes of 8 lines each. It appeared in קובץ מעשי ידי גאונים קדמונים, edited by J. Rosenberg, Berlin, 1856, part II, pp. 10-17, with explanatory Hebrew notes by the editor; comp. Elbogen, *Studien zur Geschichte des jüdischen Gottesdienstes*, Berlin, 1907, pp. 64, 82 ff.

2. תרי"ג מצות, a Didactic Poem on the 613 Precepts, published with notes by Rosenberg, *ibid.*, pp. 30-38. The portion printed on pp. 26-29 is erroneously taken by the editor as an introduction to this poem; it does not belong there, as it is Saadia's Preface (פתיחה) to the *'Azhārōt* discussed below. The superscription מנין תרי"ג is an invention of the editor, as in the MS. the poem has no title; see Steinschneider, *CB.*, 2206; *AL.*, p. 68, n. 48. The same poem was more correctly edited with introduction and notes by Joel Müller in *Oeuvres complètes*, IX, pp. xviii-xxii, 57-69.

Recently the poem has been made the subject of an Halakic Work of enormous proportions by J. F. Perl (פערלא) of Warsaw, a private scholar of means. The work, three parts in four volumes, covering no less than *2060* pages in *folio*, appeared under the title ספר המיצות לרס"ג, Warsaw, 1914-1917.

3. *'Azhārōt* (אזהרות), Exhortations, an extensive poem treating of the 613 precepts and their derivation from the Decalogue, edited by Rosenberg, *ibid.*, pp. 39-54. The introductory poem belonging to the *'Azhārōt* is found there, pp. 26-29 (see above, under no. 2, and the editor's note, p. ii). The *'Azhārōt* are quoted by Rashi to Exodus, 24, 12. A general essay by Michael Sachs on the *'Azhārōt* and other poems is published in the same volume, pp. 84-100; comp. Brody, *JE.*, II, 369*b*, 370*a*, bottom.

4. The two *Baḳḳāshōt* (בקשות), Supplications (see the description above, pp. 153 f.). Both found their way through unknown channels into the so-called " Romanian," that is, the Greco-Turkish Ritual (מחזור רומניא), which was first printed in Constantinople (1910; Berliner, *Aus meiner Bibliothek*, p. 3), and thence perhaps into several other Rituals (see *CB.*, 2211-2215, and especially L. Landshuth, עמודי העבודה, Berlin, 1862, p. 293), and into the work תפוחי זהב by Jehiel Melli, Mantua, 1623. In all the ritual editions and MSS. three liturgical pieces of later origin have been added to Saadia's בקשות, which were then erroneously attributed to the Gaon by some bibliographers. One, beginning תהלתך אין לה תחלה, is a hymn in rhymed prose by Solomon b. Elijah Sharbit ha-Zahab (14th century) and was prefixed to the second בקשה, beginning שפתי תפתח יי, while the two other pieces, which are anonymous, are found in the middle and at the end of the first בקשה, beginning אתה הוא יי and לבדך. A critical edition of the *Baḳḳāshōt,* based on the printed Rituals and on MSS. thereof, was published by Luzzatto in the *Literaturblatt des Orients,* 1851, pp. 387 ff.; comp. also Luzzatto, כרם חמד, IV, 36-39. By that time, however, Steinschneider had discovered the MS. of the סדור itself, and from a copy made by him the first בקשה was printed in the aforementioned קובץ of Rosenberg (pp. 74-77), while the second was reprinted there (pp. 78-83) from the edition of Luzzatto in the *Literaturblatt* *). In

---

* For the sake of bibliographic accuracy it should be stated here that except for this one *Baḳḳāshāh,* printed without indicating its source, all the liturgical compositions of Saadia, as also those of some others which he had embodied in his *Siddūr* (the עבודה

passing it should be mentioned that in the rituals and hence
in the edition of Luzzatto and in the קובץ, the second *Bakḳāshāh* is throughout in the plural, voicing the prayers of
the whole community of Israel   This is not its original form,
as it appears in the *Siddūr*.   Saadia intended it for the individual   The rituals adapted it for the public worship and
therefore changed all the singulars into plurals   Similar
changes were made by the congregations in a ידו referred to
by Harkavy, הגרן, II, 87 f.   Saadia's Arabic translation of
this *Bakḳāshāh* is also in the singular; comp. Schechter,
Saadyana, no. xxv, *verso,* Derenbourg, *Manuel du Lecteur* (in the *Journal Asiatique,* 1870), p 544, n. 5

Finally the two *Bakḳāshōt* were edited satisfactorily on the
basis of a careful collation of the MS. with the edition of
Luzzatto by L. Frumkin in his voluminous work, the סדר
עמרם השלם רב, Jerusalem, 1912, part I, pp ר"ס – ס"ז, II, pp.
קס"א – קנ"ח; comp. also Schechter, *Saadyana,* nos xix,
xx, xxv

It is highly interesting to note that Saadia's second *Bakḳāshāh* (יי שפתי תפתח) has been made use of by the author of
a Hebrew version of the Book of Tobit published by M.
Gaster under the title *Two Unknown Hebrew Versions of
Tobit,* London, 1897. The Hebrew text, which is considered
by the editor as the original version of Tobit, contains several
passages taken almost literally from Saadia's *Bakḳāshāh;*
comp *ib ,* p vii, and קובץ, II, 78 f.   A comparison of the two
texts makes it clear beyond a doubt that not Saadia, but the
author of the version was the borrower

It should also be noticed that most of the second *Bakḳāshāh* has crept into the Italian, German, and Polish Festi-

or פסוק of Jose b Jose and another '.1bōdāh, beginning אתה
כוננת) found in the קובץ of Rosenberg were published from a copy
furnished to the editor by Steinschneider together with an introductory description of the Bodleian MS For reasons that cannot be
discussed here the editor suppressed the introduction, as well as any
indication of the source of his publication   Subsequently a special
pamphlet was published by Steinschneider (*Der Siddur des Saadia
Gaon,* Berlin, 1856) giving the history of the matter   Comp also
J. N Epstein, *Der gaonaische Kommentar zur Ordnung Tohoroth,*
Berlin, 1915, p 132

val-rituals (מחזורים), where it has been quite variously treated, showing numerous changes, transpositions, and additions; the latter being in part older than Saadia In the Polish rituals extensive portions of this *Bakkāshāh* were incorporated into the Penitential Prayers (*Seliḥōt*) for the Eve of New-Year, beginning יהי . . . . זכו ברית אברהם רצון; this part of the poem, by reason of its content, is frequently designated as *Widdui* (Confession). Portions of Saadia's text are here interspersed among other pieces of different origin. The early incorporation of Saadia's composition into these liturgies in all probability led various mediæval authors to refer to a " *Widdui* of Saadia "; see for details on this matter Dukes, נחל קדומים, p. 26; Steinschneider, *CB.*, 2215; Landshuth, עמודי העבודה, pp. 294-297, with numerous references, and Zunz, *Literaturgeschichte der synagogalen Poesie*, p 96, no. 6; comp. also *Ha-Goren*, II, 86, *ZfhB.*, X, 148, top. There exists, however, another, short, composition, beginning אלהי נשמה, quoted by Dukes (*Zur Kenntniss der neuhebraischen religiösen Poesie*, p. 152) from a MS. of 1308, which is described as: וידוי דרב סעדיה, but Luzzatto (*Literaturblatt*, 1851, p 487) and Steinschneider (*CB*, 2215) deny the Gaon's authorship, assigning it to a later Saadia, and I am unable to reconcile their opinion with the fact that the same piece is now printed in the סדר רב עמרם השלם of Frumkin (II, p קנ"ח), who states explicitly that he copied it from the MS. of Saadia's *Siddūr*. It is true that the MS. contains also a few later additions, such as *'Adōn 'Olam* (comp. Frumkin, I, p כ"א), but this fact alone does not disprove Saadia's authorship in the case of other parts of the *Siddūr*, unless there is some other internal or external evidence against it.

5. *Hōsha'nōt* (הושענות). Hymns for the Feast of Tabernacles, especially the seventh day. Of these 21 were published by Kohut, *Die Hosha'not des Gaon R. Saadia*, Breslau, 1893, who gives also explanatory notes and numerous references to the literature on the subject. Kohut's publication is based on Yemenite MSS., but the same *Hōsha'nōt* are found also in the *Siddūr* and in the *Aleppo Mahzōr*, Venice. 1526: see Kohut, p 5; Neubauer, *Catalogue*, I, no. 1096, and in *Semitic Studies*

in Memory of Dr. Alexander Kohut, pp. 388 f.; Berliner,
Aus meiner Bibliothek, Frankfurt a/M., 1898, p. 7. For
additions and emendations to Kohut's edition, see Halber-
stam, *MGWJ*., 1895, pp. 111f.; comp. S. Sachs, אוצר הספרות,
IV, 109; Frumkin, *l. c.*, II, 384; Bondi, *Der Siddur des R.
Saadia*, p. 37.

6. *Selīḥōt* (סליחות) and *Teḥinnōt* (תחנות), Penitential and
Devotional Prayers, a large number of which are found in the
MS. of the *Siddūr*, as also in other MSS. (*CB.*, 2211), some
recently found in the Genizah (Bondi, p. 40). Steinschneider,
CB., 2210 f., quotes from the *Siddūr* the beginnings of 50
Selīḥōt, 23 of which were destined by Saadia for the Day of
Atonement; and 27 for other fast days. They have been
characterized by Zunz in his various works; see the references in Landshuth's עמודי העבודה, pp. 297-299. Part of a
Selīḥāh was metrically translated into German by Zunz,
Synagogale Poesie, p. 164. The *Teḥinnōt* (the beginnings of
some of which are likewise quoted in *CB.*, 2211), partly Aramaic, fill the last ten pages of the MS. of the *Siddūr*, which is
here defective. Nine additional pages of *Teḥinnōt* were later
found in the Genizah (Bondi, p. 40), and there are probably
many more of such productions among the Genizah fragments. It is not safe to assume that all the *Hōsha'nōt, Selīḥōt*
and *Teḥinnōt* in the *Siddūr* were composed by Saadia himself.
Some of them he probably took from older sources and incorporated in his work, just as he did with the עבודה of
Jose b. Jose and the so-called *French* אתה כוננת (comp.
Luzzatto in Rosenberg's קובץ, pp. 107-110). In the case of
the *Hōsha'nōt* he states explicitly that there existed a very
large number of them (*CB.*, 2209; Kohut, p. 2). The solution of this question does not belong here. Many of these
Piyyūṭim have found their way anonymously into nearly
all the festival and fast day rituals in MS. and in print. A
detailed enumeration and classification of the individual
pieces transcends the scope of this Bibliography and should
be undertaken by others (see Landshuth, p. 298).

The numerous *quotations* from the *Siddūr* in the works of
mediæval authors, often without explicit mention of the
source, were collected among citations of other works of

Saadia (a quotation in the בו כל, Zunz, *Zur Geschichte,* p.
549, seems to have been overlooked) by Müller, *Oeuvres,*
IX, 145-173; comp. *ib.,* pp. xxxviii-xl. The details relating
to these quotations cannot be taken up here; comp. Steinschneider, *AL.,* p. 67, n. 28.

Very numerous *extracts* from the MS. of the *Siddūr* are
given by Frumkin in his סדר רב עמרם referred to above (pp.
332 f.). Most of these extracts represent Saadia's text of the
traditional prayers, such as *Grace* after meals, the *Ḳiddūsh,
Ḳaddish, Ḳedūshāh, Shemōnēh-'esrēh, Passover Haggadah,*
and many others, showing numerous variants in the phraseology, which are of great importance for the history of Jewish
liturgy. There are, however, among the extracts *piyyūṭim*
of Saadia's own composition. Frumkin's index is rather
confused. The following is a list of the passages in consecutive order, omitting a few minor references: I, 154, 184,
194 f., קי״ט, 238, 242, קכ״ב, קמ״ה, 298, קנ״ט, 334, 360, 368,
382; II, ד״ג, כ״ג, נ״ד, ס״ז, 132. פ״בf., ק״ח, ק״טf., ק״ב, קל״ה,
286-288, 328, קס״ו, 352, 356, 384, קצ״ר, קצ״ה, קצ״ו, 414.

B. Within the last decades there have come to light
several liturgical compositions which are not in the extant
Siddūr, but have been otherwise identified as Saadia's. These
may be enumerated in the order of publication:

1. *Ta'ame Teki'ōt* (טעמי תקיעות), ten Reasons for the
Blowing of the Shofar on New-Year's Day, embodied in
numerous festival rituals in the name of Saadia, translated
into German by Dukes, *Zur Kenntniss der neuhebräischen
religiösen Poesie* (Frankf. a/M., 1842), pp. 53 f. It was also
put in German verse by S. L. Heilberg in his נטעי נעמנים,
Breslau, 1847, pp. xiv f. According to Steinschneider, *CB.,*
2205. it originally formed part of Saadia's Commentary on
Leviticus, 23, 24 (see above, under Bible, letter *o*). The
piece is printed also in Müller's לקוטים, *Oeuvres,* IX,
165 f., no. 106; comp. Rapoport, בכה״ע, IX, 28, n. 21.

2. *Reshūt* (רשות) to *'Azhārōt,* an introduction containing
a division into 24 or 25 classes (comp. *JQR., N. S.,* vol. IV
(1913-1914), p. 539, n. 59) of the 613 precepts, which are
treated in the *'Azhārōt.* It was written originally in Hebrew,
but only the Arabic translation of the first 20 classes is extant,

being embodied in a fragment of an anonymous Arabic work. It was published by Neubauer, *JQR.*, VI (1894), 705-7: comp. Schechter, *Saadyana*, no. xv; *JQR.*, 1913-1914, pp. 539 ff. Eppenstein, *Beiträge*, p. 122, is unaware of Neubauer's publication.

3. *Hakkāfōt* (הקפות), a number of hymns for recitation during the processional circuits around the *almemar* on the seventh day of the Feast of Tabernacles (Hosha'na Rabbah). They were edited by Neubauer in *Semitic Studies in Memory of A. Kohut*, Berlin, 1897. pp. 390 f., but Halberstam in a marginal note in his copy of the aforementioned work (now in the Library of the Jewish Theological Seminary of America, from which it was communicated to me by Professor Marx) called attention to the fact that of the seven *Hakkāfōt* edited by Neubauer only the first can claim the Gaon's authorship, the remaining six having been added by a later author, who shows familiarity with the Ten *Sefirōt*, a Kabalistic idea of subsequent centuries. These *Hakkāfōt*, Halberstam shows, are identical with the *Hōsha'nōt* in the Sefardic ritual.

4. Liturgy on the Ten Commandments for the Feast of Weeks (סדר לעצרת עלי עשר הדברות) in several sections, following the order of א"ב and ק"תשר alternately. This composition, too, was edited by Neubauer in *Semitic Studies* (see the preceding number), pp. 392-395. On the basis of the date 851 occurring in the text (p. 394, top) the editor assumes in a note *ad locum* that the liturgy was composed in the year 920, that is, 851 years after the destruction of the Second Temple, but Halberstam in the manuscript note on the margin of his copy (see the preceding no. 3) proved that the date does not refer to the destruction of the Temple; see for the interpretation of the passage Bacher, *REJ.*, XXXV, 200-201, who gives it as a private communication of Halberstam. The latter, Bacher further reports, made the ingenious suggestion that the words נבר חבם בעו at the beginning of the composition (p. 392, l. 20) contain an allusion to Saadia as the author; for their numerical value (352) is the same as that of כעיר בן יוסף; see above, note 332.

5. פומון לחתן, "Hymn for a Bridegroom" in four stanzas, each containing three lines with a double rhyme and ending

with the refrain ישמח (*sc.* חתן בכלה). It was published from
a MS. collection of old *piyyūṭim* by S. A. Wertheimer in
גנזי ירושלם, III (Jerusalem, 1902), 16 *b*; comp. *ib.*, Introduction, pp. 7 f. For the refrain see Saphir, אבן ספיר, I, 81 *b*;
מחזור ויטרי, pp. 599, 602.*

פזמון לחתן

אורך יאיר כאורו האצור ומכל רע תהיה נצור
כאחור וקדם נצרו¹ צור וקרא שמות לכל יצור
גם כלה תמליט זכר כהכה צור² כלא עצב ולא עצור
ישמח [וחתן בכלה].

ברכה תהיה בארץ ותנצל מכל פרץ
כנכלט משטיפת הארץ³ ומזרעו נפצה כל הארץ
גם כלה כחתן תירין וידגו לרוב בקרב הארץ
ישמח.

גילה וחדוה תערה נא מכל צד ומכל פנה
כעש נפשות בחרנהי⁴ וקרבם תחת כנפי השכינה
גם כלה כליותיה תעלוזנה כנתחדשה לה עדנה⁵
ישמח.

החתן במלבושים והכלה בקדושים
הוא יפה באנשים והיא יפה בנשים ושניהם מקודשים
זה בזה יבורכו כפרושים כאל נערין בסוד קדושים⁶
ישמח.

WEDDING SONG

From God's treasury of light may thy light shine forth and be thou
    guarded from all ill,
Like him whom God created aforetime, who gave names to all
    creatures.
Be the bride blessed with a son like him that smote the rock; nor
    suffer pain, nor grieve for barrenness.
        Rejoice, O bridegroom, in thy bride!

---

*Among the numerous poetic productions of Saadia this poem
is the only one known of a rather secular nature. The English translation was prepared by Dr. Solomon Solis Cohen of Philadelphia:

[1] Read יְצָרוֹ, allusion to Adam; see Ps. 139, 5, Gen. 2, 20.

[2] Allusion to Moses, Numbers, 20, 11; Ps. 78, 20.

[3] Allusion to Noah, Gen. 9, 19.

[4] Abraham, Gen. 12, 5; see *Bereshit rabbah, c.* 39, 14.

[5] Sarah, Gen. 18, 12.

[6] Ps. 89, 8.

Mayest thou be a blessing in the land, mayest thou be spared misfortune,

Like him that escaped the flood, and with his offspring peopled all
the earth.

May the bride delight in her husband ; may they grow to a multitude
in the land.

Rejoice, O bridegroom, in thy bride !

Mirth and happiness encompass thee, joys thronging from every
side,

As with him that made souls in Haran, and brought them under the
wings of the Shekinah

May thy bride be thrilled with thy caresses, and in age be her youth
renewed.

Rejoice, O bridegroom, in thy bride!

The bridegroom in his gay attire, the bride bedecked with rich wed-
ding gifts—

Is he not handsomest of men ? Is not she fairest among women ?
O beauteous twain made one !

May they be blessed with a special blessing by Him that is revered
in the council of the holy ones.

Rejoice, O bridegroom, in thy bride!

6. A few fragmentary *Piyyūtim* in Schechter's *Saadyana,*
nos. xvii, xxii, xxiii. The *Seliḥah* for the Fast of Gedaliah
(no. xviii), beginning אבלה נפשי וחישך תארי, is printed in
numerous rituals and is found also in the MS. of Saadia's
Siddūr, so also *Saadyana,* no. xxi, for which see Steinschneider, *CB.,* 2210; Neubauer and Cowley, *Catalogue,*
II, nos. 2720, 18; 2847, 11. In the מחזור אהלי יעקב לרה"ש,
the ritual for the New-Year Festival according to the *Sefar-
dim,* with a learned commentary by the editor, Jacob Izha-
kovitch, Jerusalem, 1908, the latter erroneously remarks
(p. קנ"ח) that the author of the aforementioned *Selihah* is
not known (לא נודע מחברו).

7. *'Abōdah,* beginning אלהים יה מקדם, in four א"ב, incomplete, ending with the first line of the letter צ, published by
Elbogen, *Studien zur Geschichte des judischen Gottesdienstes,* Berlin, 1907, pp. 122-125; comp. Elbogen's characterization of the *'Abōdah, ib*, p 83

8 *Tokchah* (תוכחה, Arabic מרתיה), an extensive poem
arranged according to the letters of the alphabet with four
lines to each letter It was published with introduction

and explanatory notes by H. Brody, *JQR.*, N. S., vol. III
(1912-1913), pp. 83-99, who had previously published part of
it in Berliner's *Festschrift*, pp. 9-11; comp. Bacher's notes
and corrections to Brody's edition, *JQR.*, N. S., Vol. IV
(1913-14), pp. 119 f. [For a couplet on Purim see *JQR.*,
N. S., XI, 465, n. 32.]

For a general characterization of Saadia as a liturgist see
Zunz, *Literaturgeschichte*, pp. 93-98, and lately Elbogen,
Der jüdische Gottesdienst, Leipzig, 1913, pp. 321-324.

There is one more composition to be accounted for here.
This is Saadia's "Poem on the Number of Letters" (see
above, pp. 154 ff.), which, not being liturgical, must be considered separately. The Poem appears under different titles.
The MSS. in Neubauer's *Catalogue*, I, nos. 79, 869, have
חרוזות על האותיות, the fragment in *Saadyana*, p. 52, has only
פיוט לר"ס, while some editions have שיר instead of חרוזות.
In Derenbourg's *Manuel du lecteur* the title is merely
מנין האותיות, while in Benjacob's *Thesaurus* it is recorded
as אותיות דרב סעדיה (see Harkavy, היקב, I, 46). From
Saadyana, no. xvi (l. 1 recto and l. 3 verso) it would appear
that the original title was, as in Derenbourg's *Manuel*, מנין
האותיות and that שיר or חרוזות על is a later modification.

The poem has been repeatedly published in connection with
other works; the first time in Elijah Levita's מסרת המסרת,
Venice, 1538, also with a Latin translation by the elder Bux-
torf in his work on the Masorah, *Tiberias*, Basle, 1620, p.
183 (second edition, Basle, 1665, p. 171; comp. Steinschneider, *ZfhB.*, II, 94), and by Fürst in his *Concordance*,
p. 1379. For other editions see Steinschneider, *Bibliographisches Handbuch*, Leipzig, 1859, p. 121, where no less
than twelve editions are enumerated. To these are still to be
added: (1) In Chr. D. Ginsburg's edition of Levita's מסרת
המסרת, London, 1867, pp. 269-278; (2) in his *The Massorah*,
vol. I, London, 1880, letter א, § 224 (from a MS. in the
British Museum, Or. 1379; comp. Blau, *JQR.*, VIII, 348,
n. 1), and (3) in J. Derenbourg's *Manuel du lecteur, Journal
Asiatique*, 1870, pp. 447-457 (separate edition, pp. 139-149);
comp. the general discussion *ib.*, pp. 542-549 (234-241).

In Samuel Ashkenazi's collection נובלות חכמה, Basle, 1629-1631, which contains our poem (fol. 196), the latter is for the first time ascribed to one Saadia b. Joseph, surnamed Bekor Shor, and the father of this Saadia is supposed to be identical with the famous French Bible exegete Joseph Bekor Shor of the 12th century. Zunz (*Zur Geschichte*, p. 75), Luzzatto (*Literaturblatt des Orients*, XII, 132), Steinschneider, (*Bibliographisches Handbuch*, p. 121, and *CB.*, 2225), and others, following the testimony of Ashkenazi, denied the Gaon's authorship of this poem and ascribed it likewise to this Saadia Bekor Shor, whose name does not occur elsewhere in Jewish literature (comp Azulai, שם הגדולים, ed Benjacob, I, 150). Derenbourg, *Manuel*, pp. 542 (234) ff., has shown on general grounds the untenability of this view and attributes the poem to the Gaon; comp. also *ib*, p. 449 (141), n. 13. He is followed by Bacher, *JE*, *II*, 649, who properly proposes to strike the name of Saadia Bekor Shor from the list of Jewish authors altogether. This view is now fully borne out and the Gaon's authorship positively established by the Genizah fragment in Schechter's *Saadyana* no. xxvi (comp. Poznański, *Schechter's Saadyana*, p. 10. n 2), which contains part of the poem and explicitly mentions the Gaon twice as its author: comp Neubauer, *Catalogue*, I, p. 969; Lambert, in Harkavy's *Festschrift*, p. 390, n. 4.*).

* The mistake, I believe, has the following origin The name of the Gaon is current in Hebrew literature merely as רבנו סעדיה, very often ר' סעדיה גאון, and sometimes ר' סעדיה הביתומי, but very rarely ר' סעדיה בן יוסף. The editor who probably found the title "Saadia b. Joseph" may have failed to identify the name with that of the Gaon and, as among the few Josephs of the earlier Middle Ages who dealt with Hebrew grammar and Bible exegesis (as Joseph Kimhi), Bekor Shor was one of the most prominent, he volunteered this unfounded addition to the name of Joseph. This lack of criticism should not surprise us in a sixteenth century author. Elijah Levita, otherwise an excellent scholar, who, as mentioned before, edited our poem, gives as a reason for attributing it to Saadia Gaon the fact that "difficult and strange words, like those occurring therein, have been used by Saadia in his *Sefer Emunot*" It shows that

S. Eppenstein (Beitrage, p. 123, n. 1), not knowing of the existence of the poem and the literature thereon, informs the reader that in the Genizah fragment in Schechter's *Saadyana* we have "one of the hitherto unknown liturgical poems of Saadia"(!). On the same page he attributes to Saadia an Arabic commentary on the daily *Shemōnēh-'Esrēh* ("eine Erklärung der Tefilla "), and counts this commentary among "the otherwise unknown poetical writings" of the Gaon. He was led to this curious mistake by the fragment in *Saadyana*, no. xxv, which bears the heading תפסיר י"י שפתי לר' סעדיה ז"ל, followed by three lines of the Arabic text. This text, however, is Saadia's Arabic translation of his own second *Bakkāshāh* (see above, p. 153), which is introduced by the verse י"י שפתי תפתח (Ps., 51, 17), as is the *Shemōneh-Esrēh*. Hence Eppenstein's error. A comparison of this fragment with that in *Saadyana, no.* xx, might have helped him out of the difficulty.

III. HALAKAH

A. METHODOLOGY

1. *Kitâb al-Madhal* [*'ila al-Talmûd*] (כתאב אלמדכל [אלי אלתלמוד]), "Book of Introduction [to the Talmud]." The earliest references to this work are found in an ancient book-list, coming from the Genizah, which was published by Bacher, *RÉJ., XXXIX* (1899), 200, no. 28, and in a fragment of a similar list in Schechter's *Saadyana, no.* xlvii (p. 128). Five passages from the Arabic original of

Levita thought Saadia, who wrote in Arabic, to be the author of the Hebrew translation (*i. e.* the anonymous *Paraphrase;* comp. Zunz, in Geiger's *Jüdische Zeitschrift*, X, 6); comp. Dukes, *Beiträge*, II, 102; Steinschneider, *CB.*, 2225; Derenbourg, *Manuel*, p. 548 (240); Ginsburg, *l. c.* p. 269.

It is, finally, worth noticing that the addition of Bekor Shor to Joseph (based on Deuter., 33, 17) was made in several other instances, either by the bearers of the name Joseph themselves, or by others (see Poznański, פרוש על יחזקאל ותרי עשר לר' אליעזר מבלגנצי, p. lviii, top), so that in our case it is not even necessary to assume that the real Joseph Bekor Shor was meant; comp. Rapoport בכה"ע, XI, 84, who, as I found later, proposes the same solution.

Saadia in a Hebrew translation are cited by the famous
sixteenth century Talmudist Bezalel Ashkenazi, Rabbi in
Egypt and later (1558) in Jerusalem The middle section
of Bezalel's work, called כללי התלמוד, in which the citations
occur, was recently published by Marx from a unique MS
of The Jewish Theological Seminary, in the *Festschrift* of
David Hoffmann, Berlin, 1914, Hebrew part, pp. 179-217; see
ib., pp. 196 f. (nos. 228, 229), 204 (no. 319), 210 (nos. 369,
372). The passages were partly reproduced from Bezalel's
work by Solomon Algâzi (17th century) and by Azulai and
thence by Muller, *Oeuvres*, ix, 168, nos. 119, 121, comp.
Marx, *ib*, German part, p. 375, n. 4; Steinschneider, *AL*,
p. 50, no. 10; Harkavy תשובות הגאונים, p. 399, note to p. 392;
Ginzberg, *Geonica*, I, 163. The fragment published in *JQR*,
XIII, 55, no. 92 (see also *ib.*, p. 330) is perhaps from our
work. It should be noted that the Arabic title does not ex-
pressly state that the work is an introduction to the *Talmud*,
though it doubtless was. Bezalel emphasizes the fact that
Saadia called the work דרכי התלמוד. For a possible identification of this work with the כתאב אלישראיע see below, *Bibliography*, section VII, p. 400, no. 13.

2. פרוש י"ג מדות, "Commentary on the 13 Hermeneutic
Rules" Derenbourg reported that he had seen the Arabic
original among the MSS. of the late Baron Gunzburg; see
Muller, *Oeuvres*, IX, p. xxiii. The Hebrew translation
was first published by Schechter, בית תלמוד, IV (1885),
235-244, and then by Müller, *Oeuvres*, IX, 73-83, comp *ib.*,
pp xxiii,-xxxiii, xlii; Steinschneider, *IL.*, p. 50, no. 11,
whose doubts as to Saadia's authorship can no longer be
justified, Ginzberg, *Geonica*, I, 162 f. As to the anti-
Karaite tendency of the work suspected by Schechter in his
Introduction to the edition, see Poznański, *JQR.*, X, 258 f.,
RÉJ, XLVII, 136; above, note 548.

B COMMENTARIES

1 פרוש רב סעדיה גאון על מסכת ברכות, "Commentary
on the Tractate *Berakōt*," published from a Genizah MS. in
the Arabic original with a Hebrew translation, Introduction,

and notes by S. A. Wertheimer, Jerusalem, 1908 (see *RÉJ.*,
LVIII, 150; above, note 360). Its authenticity is maintained
by Ginzberg, *Geonica,* I, 164, and Aptowitzer, *MGWJ.*, LII
(1908), 302, but doubted, respectively denied, by Eppenstein, *Beiträge,* p. 118, n. 3 (*MGWJ.*, 1911, p. 65, n. 4),
and Poznański, *JQR., N. S.,* vol. III (1912-1913), p. 410,
and more recently again by J. N. Epstein, *Der gaonäische
Kommentar zur Ordnung Tohoroth,* Berlin, 1915, pp. 29 ff.
There is no conclusive evidence for either side ; but so much
appears certain that in its present form the Commentary is
not the work of Saadia. On the other hand, the short passage
given in the MS. explicitly in the name of Saadia and placed
by the editor at the beginning of the Commentary (see his
Introduction, p. 11 ; Epstein, *l. c.,* p. 31) is admitted as genuine even by those who otherwise deny Saadia's authorship.
Several other passages in the Commentary make it also very
probable that the compiler made use of a commentary by
Saadia on the same tractate (see above, note 360). The
אלפאט ברכות (Vocabulary of *Berakōt*), mentioned in the
ancient list, *JQR.,* XIII, 54, no. 45 (comp. also תפסיר,
אלפאט אלתלמוד, *ib.,* no. 67, and Bacher, *REJ.,* XXXIX, 203),
may well refer to the work in question, for though it does
not bear Saadia's name, there are in the same list other books
which are positively known as Saadia's (see nos. 32, 59, 69,
77), and yet his name is not added (comp. this *Bibliography,*
below, section VII, p. 396, no. 3). There is, indeed, no more
reason to ascribe it, with Poznański (*JQR.,* XIII, 326, no
45, and Schechter's *Saadyana,* p. 21, no. 7), to Sherira or Hai
than to Saadia. For it is now certain that like Hai, Saadia too
wrote commentaries on the Mishnah, which he may have
extended also to some tractates of the Talmud. Thus, it
has recently been established that the so-called פרוש על,
סדר טהרות quoted by many mediæval authors as a work of
Hai and published under his name by J. Rosenberg in the
קובץ מעשי ידי גאונים קדמונים, Berlin, 1856, I, 1-55, is
essentially a work of Saadia redacted by a later author
(J. N. Epstein, *l. c.,* pp. 29-36; comp. above, note 387). Like
the פרוש on *Berakōt* so also the one on *Teharōt* is but a col-

lection of short glosses and lexical notes (see the detailed characterization of Epstein) and as in the case of the אלפאט ברכות so in that of the אלפאט אלמשנה, mentioned in the Genizah list (Saadyana, p. 79; Poznański, *Schechter's Saadyana,* p. 21, no. 7) it is a work of Saadia that is referred to; comp. also אלפאט זרעים ומועד משנה, *REJ.,* XXXIX, p 200, no. 33, for which again Bacher, *ib.,* p. 203, unnecessarily suggests Sherira or Hai as authors. See also above, notes 359, 590; Epstein, *l. c.,* pp. 152 f. To the class of Mishnah-commentaries by Saadia belongs also the תפסיר אבות מלאכות for which see above, note 366

C. CODIFICATION

1 *Kitâb al-Mawârît* (כתאב אלמוארית), "Book on the Laws of Inheritance," first discovered by Steinschneider in a Bodleian MS. (CB., 2160; *Bibliotheca Mathematica,* 1894, p. 102; *idem, Vorlesungen uber die Kunde hebräischer Handschriften,* Leipzig, 1897, p 34). In 1891 S. Fuchs first copied the MS, gave a survey of its contents, and translated a portion thereof into Hebrew (החוקר, I, 9-12, 41 f.). Joel Müller then edited the whole in *Oeuvres complètes de Saadia,* IX (Paris, 1897), 1-53 The Arabic text is accompanied by a Hebrew translation (prepared by S Horovitz under the title ספר הירושות), introduction, and notes with additions by Harkavy; comp. Goldziher, "*Observations,*" *RÉJ.,* XXXVIII, 270; Steinschneider, *Die hebräischen Uebersetzungen des Mittelalters,* p. xxiii; idem, *Arabische Mathematiker,* in Peiser's *Orientalistische Litteraturzeitung,* Berlin, 1904, no. 6, pp. 206 f., where the general character of the work in its relation to similar works of Muhammedan authors is minutely discussed; comp. also Steinschneider, *AL ,* p. 48, and Ginzberg, *Geonica,* I, 165 f. The work is mentioned in several Genizah lists. *REJ ,* XXXII, 127; *JQR ,* XIII, 54, no. 42; comp. Neubauer and Cowley, *Catalogue,* II, 2827, 3

---

*The works preserved entirely or in fragments come first, the others, known only from quotations, follow in alphabetical order

2. *Aḥkâm al-Wadî'a* (אהכאם אלודיעה), "Laws on Pledges." Two considerable Arabic fragments were published by Schechter, *Saadyana*, nos. xi-xii, where the above title occurs twice. The book is also mentioned, under a somewhat different title (which seems to refer to an abridged edition of the original, hence מכֿתצר אלודיעה), in an old Responsum (Harkavy, תשובות הגאונים, no. 454; comp. *ib.*, p. 393, top, reprinted in *Oeuvres*, IX, 146, no. 8), [and *JQR., N. S.*, XI, 425] ; comp. Steinschneider, *AL.*, p. 49, no. 5, where for 362 read 393 ; Ginzberg, *Geonica*, I, 166 ; Poznański, *Schechter's Saadyana*, p. 4 ; *JQR., N. S.*, vol. III (1912-1913), p. 410. Mediæval authors (see Dukes נחל קדומים, p. 25) quote the book also under the Hebrew title ספר הפקדון, see Steinschneider, *l. c.* The fragment recently edited by I. Friedländer under this title as the treatise of Saadia (Isr. Lewy's *Festschrift*, pp. 60-72) belongs to a work of a later author; see Friedländer, *MGWJ.*, 1911, p. 501 ; Pcznański, *JQR., N. S.*, vol. III (1912-1913), p. 410.

3. *Kitâb al-Shahâdah wal-Watâiḳ* (כתאב אלשהאדה ואלותׄאיק), "Book on Testimony and Contracts," quoted by Hebrew authors (see below) under the title ספר שטרות. A small Arabic Fragment containing the introductory lines of this treatise was published with an English translation by Hirschfeld, *JQR.*, XVI, 294, 299. The definition of *truth* given in this fragment is found, partly in the same words, in the *Kitâb al-Amânât*, p. 16, ll. 4 f. Saadia says here explicitly that this treatise is the first in a series of his writings on civil law, and that he chose the subject of testimony first, because the people had special need of its elucidation. Two passages from this treatise are reproduced in Arabic by Saadia's opponent R. Muḥashshir (מבשר), quoted by Harkavy, *Oeuvres*, IX, p. xxxvii, no. 2 (comp. also his חדשים גם ישנים, I, no. 9). The treatise is mentioned in the Genizah lists, *JQR.*, XIII, 55, no. 78; p. 329, no. 78 ; *Saadyana*, p. 128 (where read פי אלשהאראת for פילש הנראת) ; *RÉJ.*, XXXII, 200, no. 38 (comp. Bacher, *ad locum*, p. 203) ; [*JQR., N. S.*, XI, 425], perhaps also in no. 2760, 13, of Neubauer and Cowley's *Catalogue*, II ; comp. Poznański, *ZfhB.*.

X, 141. For quotations of the treatise in the works of
Hebrew authors see Rapoport, בכה"ע, xi, 83; *Oeuvres*, IX,
145, nos. 1, 4; p 150, no 22; Steinschneider, *AL.*, p. 49,
no. 6 (where for " Lese n. 40 " read Lese, nos. 1, 4, 22) ;
Harkavy, תשובות הגאונים, p. 362, bottom; Judah b. Barzillai,
השטרות 'ס, ed. Halberstam, Berlin, 1898, p. 55, n. 3

4 *Tafsir al-'Arāyōt* (תפסיר אלעריות), " Inteipretation of
the Laws of Incest," of which a lengthy Arabic fragment
(four leaves) was edited with an English translation and
introductory remarks by Hirschfeld, *JQR.*, XVII, 713-720.
Another portion of the same woik seems to be embodied in
an Arabic fragment edited by Schechter, *Saadyana,* no. xvi,
p. 44, ll. 17 ff.; comp. Poznański, *The Karaite Literary Opponents of Saadiah,* p. 7, n 3, and p. 99; *idem, Zur jüdisch-
arabischen Literatur,* p 42. A lengthy quotation in Hebrew
was published from a MS. work of the Ḳaraite Jeshu'ah b.
Judah (11th century) by Steinschneider, in מגד ירחים,
edited by Joseph Kohen-Zedek, Lemberg, 1856, III, 176,
partly also in *CB* , 2163, reprinted by Muller, *Oeuvres*, IX,
171 f , no. 136. The work of Jeshu'ah under the title ספר
העריות has since been edited by J. Markon, St. Petersburg,
1908, where the passage occurs on pp 151-152; comp. Poznański, *Karaite Literary Opponents,* p. 53. The arabic title
of Saadia's work is not preseived. The title given above is
based on the citation of Jeshu'ah, who has פתרון העריות. In
the body of the Arabic fragment Saadia repeatedly uses the
arabicized Hebrew term אלעריות and applies to it the verb
פסר (See Hirschfeld, *l. c* , p. 717, ll. 15, 29-32) Azulai,
שם הגדולים, ed Benjacob I, 150 f , mentions a book on
אסורי ביאה, which may refer to the work before us. I must
admit, however, that although, following the bibliographers
heie referred to, I have placed this treatise among those
dealing with the codification of the law. I am not at all convinced that it actually belongs here, or that a work of Saadia
under that title was composed separately. Neither the Arabic
fragments nor the Hebrew quotations and references furnish sufficient evidence for such assumption. I am rather
inclined to think that we have here an extract from Saadia's

commentary on Leviticus, 18, which, like some other sections
of his lengthy Pentateuch commentary, may have circulated separately and may thus be identical with the תפסיר
אחרי מות, in Schechter's *Saadyana*, no. xxxvii (p. 79,
l. 7) ; see below, section VII, p. 396, no. 3 ; comp. Steinschneider, *AL.*, p. 49, no. 8. That the passage in *Oeuvres*,
IX, p. 35, n. 1 (comp. Müller, end of the Introduction, p.
xvii) refers to the work, is not certain.

5. *Kitâb al- Terêfōt* (כתאב אלטרפות), " Book on Forbidden Food." A treatise with this title is mentioned twice
in a Genizah fragment, Schechter, *Saadyana*, no. xxvii, while
no. xlix represents a small portion of the treatise (in Arabic
characters, which is a very rare occurrence). Another
fragment in two different recensions, one covering four
and the other two leaves, is found in the Imperial Library
of St. Petersburg (see below, p. 349, no. 10). A short
extract from each of the two recensions was given by Harkavy, *Oeuvres*, IX, p. xxxvii (see *Ha-Goren*, I, 91). Both
MSS. bear the title הלכות שחיטה, under which title a fragment is found also in the Bodleian Library (Neubauer and
Cowley, *Catalogue*, no. 2854A, 7 ; comp. also *Saadyana*, no.
xxxvii, p. 79, l. 10). The title כתאב אלמניאה (Grünhut,
MGWJ., L. (1906), 88, quotes אלמניאיה?) referred to by
Poznański, *Schechter's Saadyana*, p. 18, perhaps misspelt
for מניה (maniyya=death), expresses the same idea as
כתאב אלטרפות or שחיטה. It is hard to decide which was the
original title; probably the former, which was replaced in
some texts by the more usual terms טרפות and שחיטה, since
all the laws designated by these terms were probably included
in the work. For further references see Steinschneider, *AL.*,
p. 49, no. 9. Eppenstein, *Beiträge*, pp. 121, 217, failing to
perceive the identity of the two works, speaks of two different treatises, on שחיטה and טרפות.

6. *Ḳawl fi'l-Ribâ* (קול פי אלרבא), " Treatise on Usury."
This is the heading of a fragment from the Genizah published by Hirschfeld, *JQR.*, XVIII, 119 f. No reference to
it elsewhere is known to me.

7. ספר טמאה וטהרה, "On Defilement and Purity," quoted
by several mediæval authors, see Rapoport, בכורי העתים,
IX, 28, n. 19; Steinschneider, CB., 2162, no. 8, AL., p. 49,
no. 7; Müller, Oeuvres, IX, 159, no. 74. The treatise is
mentioned also in the Genizah lists, REJ., XXXIX, 200,
no. 13 (comp. ib., p. 205, no. 2), and Saadyana, no.
xxxvii, in the latter place under the title מכתצר טמאה וטהרה
"Compendium on Defilement and Purity"; comp. Poznański, Zur jüdisch-arabischen Literatur, p. 41 f. According to Rapoport, l. c., p. 22, and Steinschneider, l. c., this
treatise and the one mentioned below, no. 10, formed one
work, a view which seems to be supported by the extant
quotations. Lately I found the book quoted by Meir ha-
Kohen (13th cent.) in הגהות מיימוניות, section אסורי ביאה
§ 7, letter א; comp. Azulai, שם הגדולים, ed. Benjacob, s. v.
Saadia, who mentions a book on טהרות.

8. ספר המתנות, i. e. a book on laws regulating the legal
acquisition of objects received by gift. The work is quoted
by Naḥmanides in his Novellæ on the tractate Kiddûshin, see
Benjacob, Thesaurus, p. 389, no. 2624; Harkavy, Ha-Goren,
II, 89. At the beginning of his "Book on Inheritance"
(Oeuvres, IX, 9: comp. ib., p. xv) Saadia states that "the
transfer of objects from one person to another takes place
in one of three ways, either by inheritance, by purchase,
or by gift. Each of these three has its own laws and
provisions, of which we will here explain first those concerning inheritance, which are the subject of the present
treatise." It is obvious from this passage that he intended
to treat also of the other two. We have, however, no quotation from a work by Saadia on Laws of Purchase. That
on Gifts was in existence as late as the 13th century; comp.
Steinschneider, AL., p. 48, no. 4; Rappoport, בכה"ע, XI, 83.

9. מתנות כהונה, "On the Priestly Gifts." A work under
this title is attributed to Saadia in a fragment in Schechter's
Saadyana, no. xxvii. It is also mentioned, but without
the name of Saadia, in the list, REJ., XXXIX, 200, no. 30,
and Saadyana, no. xlvii, p. 128; comp. Poznański, Schechter's
Saadyana, p. 18, no. 2.

10. הלכות נדה, "Laws on Menstruation," quoted by Saadia in his *Commentary* on the *Sefer Yeṣirah*, ed. Lambert, p. 43, l. 12 (כמא שרחנא פי אמר מצות נדה) and by several mediaeval authors; see *Oeuvres*, IX, 157, n. 5; *MCWJ.*, XVII, 276. Codex Antonini, 155, contains the end of הלכות נדה, followed by הלכות שחיטה (above, no. 5); see Harkavy, הקדם, I, 63 f. Eppenstein, *Beiträge*, p. 119, n. 1, asserts that the work is mentioned in the lists referred to above (no. 9), no doubt through confusing it with some other work. His assertion that it was written in Egypt is likewise groundless, see above, note 293. According to Rapoport and Steinschneider, it was not a separate work, but formed part of no. 7 (see above); comp. Wertheimer, פרוש רב סעדיה על ברכות, pp. 6 f., no. 5.

D. RESPONSA, תשובות.

Saadia's Responsa have been collected from various sources and reprinted with numerous literary notes by Joel Müller, in *Oeuvres*, IX, 87-142. Altogether there are fifty Responsa in this collection, but the differentiation of the editor between the Responsa and other pieces which are arranged in the same volume under the heading of *Quotations* (see below) is not always accurate. Thus no. 50 is not a Responsum, but Saadia's reply to a Karaite, probably Ibn Sâḳawaihi, against whom he wrote a polemic, whence the passage in question may have been taken (comp. Poznański, *JQR.*, X, 253; below, p. 383, letter *f*). On the other hand, no. 110 of the quotations bears the heading תשובה and belongs to the Responsa. Moreover, not all the Responsa bear the name of Saadia, and in several instances the authorship is not certain, see *e. g.* nos. 22, 23, 38, 46. One Responsum (27) is in Arabic, in another (42) the question is in Arabic, while the Gaon deliberately answers in Hebrew. At the head of ten Responsa (2, 4, 5, 9, 12, 13, 15-17, 21) we find the remark "translated from the Arabic"; the translations being anonymous. The original language of the rest of the Responsa is not always certain, see Müller's Introduction, pp. xxxiv ff. Two Responsa (4, 16) were translated into

German in a condensed form by Zacharias Frankel, in
*Entwurf einer Geschichte der Literatur der nachtalmud-
ischen Responsen*, Breslau, 1865, pp. 81-83; comp. Steinschneider, *AL.*, p. 48 (the passage is badly printed: line 12
for " N. 8, 14. 27 " read *N. 27, 42;* line 13 after " (Lese) "
read *darunter 8, 14 arabisch;* line 16 for "erstere" read
letztere; line 17 read " GA. 49, 50 (50 aus Abr. b. Chijja
über Kalender)." For additional Responsa of Saadia see
Harkavy, *Ha-Goren,* II, 89. The כיסאל in the list, *REJ.,*
XXXIX, p. 206, no. 6, may also belong here [but see *Postscript*, p. 427]. A Kaminka in Winter and Wünsche's *Die
jüdische Litteratur*, II, 39 f., published a German translation
of Responsum no. 16, without stating that it had previously
been translated by Frankel.

E. QUOTATIONS, לקוטים.

It was no small task to collect, from the vast mediæval
literature, all the passages quoted from Saadia's writings by
various authors. This work was undertaken by Müller, who
gathered 136 passages (*Oeuvres,* IX, 145-173), to which a
considerable number were added by Harkavy in the same
volume, pp. xxxvii-xliv. Over two-thirds of these quotations are taken from Saadia's *Siddūr,* the rest from works
mostly lost. I cannot take up each of the quotations for
separate discussion, but a few points may be briefly touched
upon. Nos. 8, 14. 134 (the last is from the Commentary on
Proverbs, 18, 17), 135, are Arabic. For no. 13 see Harkavy,
ib., p. xliv; Cowley, *Catalogue,* II, no. 2745, 23; for no. 46
comp. *Kitâb al-Amânât,* p. 183 (*Em.,* Cracow, p. 123), overlooked by Poznański. *JQR.,* X, 252; for no. 106 see this
Bibliography, II. p. 335, 1; for no. 135 comp. Poznański,
Moses Ibn Chiquitilla, Leipzig, 1895, p. 197, addition to p.
62; Steinschneider, *AL.,* § 168; Eppenstein, *Beiträge,* p. 216,
addition to p. 83.

It goes without saying that the collection of Müller and
Harkavy contains but a fraction of what is still to be
gathered from MSS. and printed works, a task which, as
Dr. Freimann of Holleschau, Moravia, has told me, he
began some years ago and has probably brought to com-

pletion. I should here note only that Schechter's *Saadyana*
contains (aside from the numerous fragments of the Gaon's
own works, which have been discussed) numerous *Quotations* by others from unidentified works of Saadia, see nos.
xiv, xxiv, xxxi-xxxiv, li. Judah b. Barzillai, *Commentary*
on *Sēfer Yeẓirah,* p. 166, quotes a passage from Saadia on a
liturgical question. In his ספר השטרות, edited by Halberstam, Berlin, 1898, he quotes Saadia several times; see the
editor's Index. Saadia's interpretation of Exodus, 6, 3, is
quoted by Solomon Ibn Gabirol, see Berliner's פלטת סופרים,
Mayence 1872, p. 28; comp. *ib.,* German part, pp. 28, 30.
Various passages, some of which are recorded also by Müller,
are quoted in the מחזור ויטרי, ed. Hurwitz, Berlin, 1896-7; see
the editor's Introduction, pp. 45-47, and Berliner's additions
at the end of the volume (השלמה למחזור ויטרי), p. 815 (separate edition, p. 15) ; comp. also below, under *Calendar,* no. 2.
Gedaliah Ibn Yaḥya, שלשלת הקבלה, ed. Amsterdam, p. 72,
top, quotes Saadia's explanation of the value of certain coins
mentioned in the Talmud; comp. *Oeuvres,* IX, 146, no. 7;
Zunz, *Zur Geschichte,* 542, 548-549; Steinschneider, *MIVJ.,*
III, 47, 151 (Mosconi) ; Ginzberg, *Geonica,* I, 167, n. 1. For
the numerous quotations by Moses Tachau see above, pp.
281-285. Saadia is quoted also by an Arabic commentator of
the Passover Haggadah; see W. H. Greenburg, *The Haggadah According to the Rite of Yemen,* Leipzig, 1896, p. 32.
The quoted passage is found, however, in תנחומא, section
פקודי, § 9. For quotations by Jacob b. Asher see above,
note 369; see also above, p. 348, end of no. 7.

For a general characterization of Saadia as a Talmudist
see Weiss, דור דור ודורשיו, Wilna, 1904, vol. 4, pp. 137-143;
Ginzberg, *Geonica,* I, 162-167. Halevy's דורות הראשנים,
III, 275 ff. does not serve our purpose.

IV. CALENDAR AND CHRONOLOGY

A. CALENDAR

Excepting incidental discussions of the calendar which
occur in all the anti-Ḳaraitic writings of Saadia, his works
in this field, so far as they are known, were all occasioned

by his controversy with Ben Meir. Great confusion exists
with regard to the identification and chronology of the
various documents relating to this controversy. I have
therefore treated the subject separately under the title
" Documents on the Ben Meir Controversy " which will be
found below, pp. 409 ff., as an appendix to chapter IV (see
JQR., N. S., vol. III (1912-1913), p. 500). As most of the
bibliographical details about Saadia's writings on the calendar are given there, I shall deal here only with the few additional works, while for the others reference is made to
" Documents."

1. ספר זכרון, see *Documents,* no. 9.

2. ארבעה שערים, " Four Gates." In the Genizah lists
published by Bacher, *RÉJ.*, XXXIX, 200, no. 28 (see also
no. 41, where a work under the same title appears anonymously) and Schechter, *Saadyana,* no. xlvii, Saadia is explicitly mentioned as the author of a work under this title,
as also in a work on the calendar by a later author; comp.
Bornstein, מחלקת רב סעדיה, p. 25, n. 2; Poznański, *RÉJ.*, XL,
87 f. For further details regarding the " Four Gates " see
above, p. 73, note 151.

Here should be added the סימנים, *i. e.,* mnemotechnical
" Signs " summarizing the rules for the four Postponements
(דחיות) as laid down in the "Four Gates." They were published by Berliner in his Supplement to the מחזור ויטרי (see
above, p. 351), pp. 815-816.

3. ספר המועדים, see *Documents,* no. 10. As to the real
title of the work see Malter, *JQR.*, N. S., vol. III (1912-
1913), pp. 490, n. 9.

4. Three Letters, see *Documents,* nos. 4, 5, 11; comp. also
no. 1.

5. סדר (סוד) העבור, " Order (or, Mysteries) of the Calendar," counted among the works of Saadia by the Muhammedan author Muhammed Ibn Isḥâk al-Nadim (987) in his
Fihrist al-'Ulûm, ed. Flügel-Rödiger, I, 320, who calls it
Kitâb al-'Ibbur and, as *'Ibbur* is a Hebrew word, adds the
explanation wahuwa al-Ta'rîḥ, " and this means Ta'rîḥ,"
i. e. calendar, or chronology. This explanation has led some
recent authors to identify the work with the *Kitâb al-Ta'rîḥ*

which is quoted by Judah Ibn Bal'am (see below under Chronology). Hebrew authors refer to a סוד or סדר העבוד of Saadia; see on the whole subject, Rapoport, בכה"ע, ix, 29, n. 23; Steinschneider, *CB.*, 2170 f., and *AL.*, p. 63, no. 26; Poznański, *JOR.*, X, 260 f. An Arabic Genizah fragment of three leaves dealing with the calendar (Schechter, *Saadyana,* no. ix) was thought to be part of the work, but more probably it belongs to the *Kitâb al-Tamyîz;* see this *Bibliography,* p. 380, letter *a.* In the List edited by Bacher, *RÉJ.*, XXXIX, 200, no. 20, a book אלעבור is mentioned, which, as Bacher, *ibidem,* p. 205, no. 3, thinks, refers to this work (*i. e.* the סדר העבור) [comp. also below, p. 427].

B. CHRONOLOGY

1. *Kitâb al-Ta'rîh* (כתאב אלתאריך), "Book of Chronology," published in Neubauer's *MJC.*, ii, 89-110. In the Introduction to the volume, p. xi, Neubauer calls attention to the fact that a passage quoted by the grammarian and exegete Judah Ibn Bal'am (11th century) in the name of Saadia is found literally in the work before us, and that the Arabic translation of geographical names in the Bible agrees mostly with Saadia's translation. Bacher in a thorough review of the work (*RÉJ.*, XXXII, 140-144) pointed out many more Saadianic elements and suggested Saadia's authorship, which was taken into consideration, but not positively affirmed, by Steinschneider, *AL.*, § 146. Subsequently the matter was again taken up by Bacher, *RÉJ.*, XLIX, 298 f., who tried to show that the *Kitâb al-Ta'rîh* had originally formed part (the second chapter) of the Arabic version of the *Sêfer ha-Galui,* but was later detached from the original work and circulated as a separate volume under the new title. In this form alone, Bacher thinks, it was known to Judah Ibn Bal'am. This view, however, is quite improbable, for, to judge from the existing fragments of both the Hebrew and Arabic *Sefer ha-Galui* (see this *Bibliography* below, p. 391, 393, letter *c*), the latter was written in a rhetorical style little in harmony with a dry Biblical chronology like the *Kitâb al-Ta'rîh.* Nor is it probable that an extensive work like this would have formed a chapter of the

23

Sêfer ha-Galui. Moreover, the latter was essentially a
polemic against the Exilarch and other adversaries of the
author; and although, as he states in the Introduction (see
JQR., N. S., vol. III (1912-1913), p. 491), the second chapter
of the work contained the discussion of the duration of prophecy in Israel and of the redaction of the Mishnah and the Talmud, that discussion, judging from the existing fragment (see
below, p. 391, letter *a*), is of an entirely different nature. Be
this as it may, Saadia's authorship of the latter work is now
established beyond dispute, for a small Genizah fragment
from the *Kitâb al-Ta'rîḫ,* published by Marx, *RÉJ.,* 1909, p.
299, which contains the beginning of the composition, mentions Saadia explicitly as the author. Moreover, a second
fragment of a work on the calendar (written in 1028), published by Marx, *ibidem,* p. 300, likewise quotes the *Kitâb
al-Tawâîḫ* (plural of *Ta'rîḫ*) as a work of Saadia; comp.
Steinschneider, *AL.,* p. 344, addition to § 146 (where for S.
Fränkel read W. Bacher and for " xl. 182 " read xlix, 298)
and especially his *Geschichtsliteratur der Juden.* Frankfurt
a. M., 1905, p. 19, and § 29*b;* see also Bacher, *MGWJ.,* 1911.
pp. 253 f. The List in Schechter's *Saadyana,* no. xxxvii,
mentions also a כתאב אלתאריך. though without the name of
the author.

2. סדר תנאים ואמוראים, " Chronological Order of the Tannaim and Amoraim," the discovery of which was announced
by Harkavy in his חדשים גם ישנים, no 1, published in
the periodical מיצפה, 1 (1886), 1-12 (see *RÉJ.,* XIV, 119 f).
To my knowledge it has never appeared, and some doubt may
be entertained as to its identity; see Steinschneider. *AL.,*
p. 50, no. 10 (where in line 10, 119 should be read for
" 110," so also in Steinschneider's *Geschichtsliteratur der
Juden,* p. 19, l. 14).

3. תולדות רבנו הקדוש, " Genealogy of Rabbi Judah the
Holy," redactor of the Mishnah. In a fragment published by Schechter. *Saadyana,* no. l. p. 135, Saadia reports
that while in Mosul he was asked in a letter (במגלת ספר)
to set forth R. Judah's genealogy and to explain the relationship between Rab and Hiyya (see b. Pesahim. 4a), which he
did, as it seems, in a letter ([במג]לה כמו וישב)); comp.
Bornstein. מחלקת רס"ג. p. 72.

4. מגלת בני חשמוני, "The Scroll of the Ḥasmoneans."
Much has been written about the time, country, and original
language of this Scroll (see in the main Harkavy, *Zikron,*
V, 205 ff.; Gaster, *Transactions of the Ninth International
Congress of Orientalists,* London, 1893, II, 3-32; Neubauer,
JQR., VI, 570 ff.; Ginzberg, *JE.,* I, 637; Lévi, *REJ.,* XLV,
171 ff.). It may now be considered certain that it is the work
of an author living either in Babylonia (Ginzberg) or in
Syria (Lévi) during the seventh or eighth century, and that
its original language was Aramaic. Very early it was translated into Arabic, Hebrew, and, later, Persian; while the
Hebrew version served as original for translations into
Latin, German, and Spanish. Gaster (*l. c.*) again translated
the Aramaic into English. We are here concerned only with
the Arabic version. It exists in numerous, mostly Yemenite,
MSS. None of them bears the name of Saadia as the author.
Hirschfeld who published this version, therefore, gives it as
an anonymous piece (*Arabic Chrestomathy,* London, 1892,
pp. 1-6). Later A. S. Wertheimer published the same version
with many different, often mistaken, readings from a Yemen
MS. (לקט מדרשים, Jerusalem, 1903), which, he asserts, is
700 years old. He was the first to suggest (p. 10) Saadia as
the author [and his view is now borne out by a Genizah fragment recently published by J. Mann, *JQR., N. S.,* XI,
425, which represents a catalogue of Saadia's writings compiled shortly after his death, and in which the מגלת בני
חשמוני is mentioned as one of the Gaon's works. From the
words . . . וצדר לה following upon the title of the Scroll it
appears that he wrote also an introduction to his translation,
of which, however, nothing has so far been recovered]. As
already noted (above, p. 173), Saadia referred to the Scroll
several times in his *Sefer ha-Galui* (Harkavy, *Zikron,* V,
150, 162. 180); comp. also Malter, *JQR., N. S.,* III, 489,
n. 6; Steinschneider, *AL.,* p. 277; *MGWJ.,* XLVII, 365 ff.

V. PHILOSOPHY

1. *Tafsîr Kitâb al-Mabâdî* (תפסיר כתאב אלמבאדי), "Commentary on the Book of Creation," of which only one complete MS. is preserved in the Bodleian Library. Short extracts therefrom were published by Steinschneider, *CB.,* 2220:

by Neubauer, with a French translation, *Journal Asiatique*, 1861, ii, p. 247 ; 1862, ii, pp. 261-267 (separate edition : *Notice sur la lexicographie hebräique*, Paris, 1863, pp. 7, 215-219), reprinted and translated into Hebrew by Harkavy, *Zikron*, V, 61-65 (comp. above, p. 307, no. 2) ; by Derenbourg, likewise with French translation, *Journal Asiatique*, 1870, pp. 496, 515 f. (separate edition : *Manuel du lecteur*, Paris 1870, pp. 188, 207) ; comp. Kaufmann's *Notes* on פס"י of Judah b. Barzillai, p. 347, *ad paginam* 229. A complete edition of the Arabic text with a French translation, introduction, and notes was prepared by M. Lambert, *Commentaire sur le Sefer Yesira par le Gaon Saadya*, Paris, 1891 (comp. Steinschneider, *Deutsche Literaturzeitung*, 1892, p. 148 ; A. Epstein, *MGWJ.*, 1893, pp. 119 f), Arabic characters being substituted by the editor for the Hebrew characters of the MS. The text together with the Hebrew paragraphs of the *Sefer Yezirah* itself, covers 105 pages. Since the appearance of this edition several fragments of the Arabic text, covering about 26 pages of the printed book (viz. 1-11, 10-12, 26-38, 100-102), were found in the *Genizah ;* see Neubauer and Cowley, *Catalogue*, II, nos. 2669, 23 ; 2787, 21 ; 2850, 7 ; 2860, 6. There may be more fragments which I have not seen. The portions published by Steinschneider, Neubauer, Harkavy, and Derenbourg are found in Lambert's edition, pp. 13 (ll. 4-7) ; 24 (ll. 1-5) ; 42 (l. 7)-43 (l. 12) ; 76 (l. 2)-78 (bottom) ; 79, ll. 5-13.

The work was translated into Hebrew by one Moses b. Joseph of Lucena, whose date is not certain, presumably the twelfth century. This translation is extant only in MSS. A short extract was given by Dukes, נחל קדומים, p. 3 (ed. Lambert, p. 21, l. 14 to 22, l. 15 ; comp. M. Sachs in Rosenberg's קובץ, II, 85, n. 2) ; comp. also *ib.*, pp. 23-25. Several pages were reproduced by Kaufmann in his *Notes* to Halberstam's edition of Judah b. Barzillai's פרוש ספר יצירה (Berlin, 1885), p. 338 (Lambert, p. 19, bottom—20, 17) ; 339, *ad paginam* 155 (Lambert, p. 15, l. 15—16, 5) ; 340-342 (Lambert, 60, 7—74, 3). Several shorter passages were reproduced by Jellinek, *Beiträge*, I, 73, note ; Epstein, *RÉJ.*, xxi, p. 93, n. 4, and Kaufmann, *Sinne*, p. 134, n. 20 ; p. 153, n. 16. For a detailed characterization of this Hebrew translation, see Steinschneider, *Die hebräischen Uebersetzungen*, pp. 443-445.

Prior to this translation there must have existed two, perhaps even three, other Hebrew translations, partial or complete. The aforementioned Judah b. Barzillai (1135) reproduces, at the end of his Commentary, pp. 268-278, a considerable portion of an earlier Hebrew translation by an unknown author, which contains the whole Introduction and most of the first paragraph of the first chapter of Saadia's work (Lambert, pp. 1-23, l. 7). To this translation he refers also on p. 184, complaining of its poor, unintelligible Hebrew style. He had, however, as appears from p. 255 (l. 19), two other versions—unless we assume that one of them is identical with that which he had designated as poor. Be that as it may, that translation which Judah considers the most correct, is cited extensively in various parts of his Commentary, the quotations covering nearly thirty pages of the book. Thus the Hebrew translation of about half of Saadia's Commentary is to be found in the Commentary of Judah. A careful comparison of the two texts, the Arabic and the Hebrew, would bring out many an interesting point, especially for the study of the mediæval Hebrew. To facilitate such a comparison I subjoin in parallel columns a table of the corresponding texts in the two Commentaries:

Saadia						*Judah b. Barzillai*		
Page	5, line	4—page	6, line	3	page	174, line	4-20	
"	31, "	16— "	32, "	9	"	209, "	5-13	
"	38, "	14— "	41, "	7	"	162, "	9-163, 17	
"	42, "	7— "	46, "	9	"	229, "	30-231, 23	
"	46, "	13— "	47, "	17	"	237, "	4-16+34+	
36-40+page 238, 1 (the rest being inserted by Judah)								
"	48, "	3— "	50, "	9	"	254, "	26-255, 19	
"	51, "	2— "	54, "	15	"	213, "	16-215, 3	
"	55, "	1— "	58, "	5	"	260, "	12-261, 22	
"	59, "	3— "	60, "	7	"	221, "	24-222, 13	
"	61, "	4— "	63, "	14	"	244, "	14-245, 15	
"	69, "	8— "	74, "	3	"	177, "	11-179, 12	

Kaufmann in his *Notes* on the Commentary (pp. 238, 347 f., *ad paginam* 229, 7-8 from below) assumes that Judah is himself the translator of some of these passages. He overlooked Judah's clear statement (p 237) that he did not possess the Arabic original. It is also doubtful whether any of his Hebrew translations was complete, see p. 245, l. 16. However, aside from the passages he quoted, he made extensive use of other portions of Saadia's Commentary, even where he does not mention it; comp. *e. g.* his interpretation of the Divine Names (pp. 126 f.) with that of Saadia, pp 19 f ; further, the lengthy exposition, p 240, with the Commentary of Saadia, pp. 59-62; see also Judah, p 209, bottom, and Saadia, p 80, with reference to the רל"א שערים ; Kaufmann, pp. 339, 345, *ad paginam* 209.

Aside from the translation of Moses of Lucena and those used by Judah b. Barzillai, there was another Hebrew translation from which Moses Tachau, or Tackau (1230, see for details above, pp 281 ff), quotes a lengthy passage in his כתב תמים, published by Kirchheim in אוצר נחמד, III (1860), 66. The corresponding Arabic text in ed. Lambert is p 70, 5-71, last line but one The same passage in an entirely different version is found in Judah's commentary, pp. 177 f. Another short passage from the same translation of Saadia's Commentary (ed. Lambert, p 47. 11 ff.) is quoted by Tachau, *ibidem*, p. 67, 10, which is found also in Judah's Commentary, p. 237, 4 from below; comp Steinschneider, *Die hebräischen Uebersetzungen,* p 444, n. 523.

Finally, there is still another translation to be mentioned, the existence of which has hitherto escaped notice. Berechiah ha-Nakdan (מצרף, ed. Gollancz, London, 1902) reproduces pp. 118, 5 (from below)—119, 23, the Hebrew translation of a passage from Saadia's Commentary (Lambert, p. 18, 17-20, 4), which does not agree either with that of Moses of Lucena (according to the copy made for Halberstam, which I have compared in the library of the Jewish Theological Seminary of America in New York), or with that reproduced by Judah b Barzillai, pp. 275 f. As Berechiah is not supposed to have known Arabic, it would follow that he drew upon some translation which is no

longer extant (see above, note 632). For further details
on Berechiah and his connection with the works of Saadia
see above, p. 288, and below, pp. 361 f. Another author of the
12th century, the mystic Eleazar of Worms, who also wrote
a Commentary on the *Sefer Yeẓirah* (published in Przemyśl,
1883), drew upon the Commentary of Saadia only indirectly,
making use of the Hebrew extracts of Judah b. Barzillai;
comp. Epstein, *MGWJ.*, 1893, pp. 117 f.; Halberstam,
MGWJ., 1893, p. 247, and the references there given.

The foregoing account shows sufficiently that Saadia's
Commentary on the *Sefer Yeẓirah* was very widely used by
earlier mediæval authors. In later centuries, as well as in
recent times, however, little attention has been given to it.

2. *Kitâb al-'Amânât wa-'l-'I'tiḳâdât* (כתאב אלאמאנאת
ואלאעתקאדאת), "Book of Philosophic Doctrines and Religious Beliefs."

A. ARABIC TEXT

The Arabic work under the title here given has been preserved in two MSS. only, one of which is in the Bodleian
Library at Oxford and the other in the Imperial Library of
St. Petersburg. The latter is not quite complete; several
pages are missing here and there, while many others have
been damaged by fire. Aside from these two MSS. there is
a Genizah fragment in the Bodleian Library (see Neubauer
and Cowley, *Catalogue*, II, no. 2753), of which I possess a
copy. The fragment covers nearly the whole sixth chapter
of the work, lacking only 14 lines at the begining and 4 lines
at the end (p. 189, l. 4-211, l. 1, of the printed edition, which
will be discussed below) and part of the seventh in the
edition of Bacher in Steinschneider's *Festschrift* (see below), p. 105, ll. 24-108, l. 10. Another Genizah fragment
in the collection of the Cambridge University Library (pp.
116, 15-119, 8 of the printed edition) was published with an
English translation by Hirschfeld (*JQR.*, XVII, 721-725),
who mistook it for part of another work, but subsequently
corrected his mistake (see *JQR.*, XVIII, 146). All the MSS.
extant are written in Hebrew characters.

As early as 1717 John Gagnier edited a specimen of the
Bodleian MS., then the only one known, side by side with the

corresponding section of the Hebrew translation of Judah
Ibn Tibbon (see below) and his own Latin translation. This
specimen is so rare that according to Steinschneider, *CB.*,
2172, not even the Bodleian Library possesses a copy. From
the same MS. the beginning of chapter VIII (pp. 229-233, 4
from below of the printed edition) was published with a
French translation by Salomon Munk, *Notice sur R. Saadia
Gaon*, Paris, 1858, pp. 20-29.

The entire work, transliterated into Arabic characters, was
critically edited on the basis of the Bodleian MS. by
S. Landauer (Leyden, 1880). The editor also made careful
use of the St. Petersburg MS., giving in footnotes all its important variants and sometimes, though not in an adequate
measure, incorporating them into the text instead of the
readings offered by the Bodleian MS. A minute review of
this edition was published by Goldziher in *ZDMG.*, XXXV
(1881), 773-783.

Pages 125, 4 from below—128, 2 of Landauer's edition
were reprinted (in Hebrew characters) by Hirschfeld in
his *Arabic Chrestomathy*, London, 1892, pp. 35 f.

As was stated above, p. 194, Saadia wrote the seventh
chapter of his work, dealing with the question of resurrection, in two entirely different recensions. One of these recensions, probably the older one, is found only in the Bodleian
MS. while the other is represented in the St. Petersburg
MS. Landauer's edition contains only the first, usually designated as the Oxford Recension; the recension of the St.
Petersburg MS. was edited in 1886 by Bacher, in the Steinschneider *Festschrift*, Hebrew part, pp. 98-112. Two passages of considerable length, at the beginning and toward the
end of the chapter, which are missing in the MS., were reproduced by Bacher on the basis of Ibn Tibbon's Hebrew translation. Saadia's authorship of this so-called St. Petersburg
Recension, which was denied by Landauer in his Introduction
to the *Kitab al-Amânât*, pp. x-xi, is proved beyond doubt by
Bacher, *ibidem*, German part, pp. 219-226. Recently another
fragment of this different recension of the seventh chapter
has been found among the MSS. of the Genizah, for which
see Neubauer and Cowler, *Catalogue*, II, no. 2642, 11a.

B. TRANSLATIONS

a) *Hebrew*

I. THE ANONYMOUS PARAPHRASE

The first attempt at rendering the *Kitâb al-'Amânât* into Hebrew was made by an anonymous author as to whose identity, time, and country much has been written. I am here not concerned with the details of this investigation, and shall merely state the facts. The work, entitled פתרון ספר האמונות, exists in several MSS. in various European libraries. One of the MSS. (Vatican, no. 269) has at the end the date 1095, which is probably that of the translator, not of the copyist (see above, p. 289). The contention of Dukes, *Beiträge*, II, 16, that the date is to be corrected to 1195, is entirely unwarranted. The translation, or, as it is usually and correctly designated, the " Paraphrase," is certainly older than the translation of Judah Ibn Tibbon (1186), and its author, I believe, was one of the Palestinian (Porges, *ZfhB.*, VII, 38: *Babylonian*) Payyetānim who flourished in the 11th century. The work is written in the most peculiar style, having no parallel in the entire Hebrew philosophic literature of the Middle Ages. The author is indefatigable in coining new and strange words and phrases to express philosophic ideas in the liturgical language of Eleazar Ḳalir! For textual criticism this work is of little use, as it never keeps to the original, but merely paraphrases its content. From a general linguistic point of view, however, it is of great interest. For a detailed characterization of this Paraphrase see Steinschneider, *HB.*, XIII, 82; *Die hebräischen Uebersetzungen*, pp. 440-443. For extracts from the MSS. that have occasionally been published by various scholars see the references *ibidem*, p. 440, n. 498, to which should be added several passages in Guttmann's *Die Religionsphilosophie des Saadia*, pp. 264, 266, 268, 270, 273, 276-279, 281, 283.

About three-quarters of a century after the appearance of the Paraphrase, Berechiah ha-Nakdan, the well-known author of Hebrew fables, set himself to the task of epitomising it, making additions to it from the works of other authors (Abraham Ibn Ezra, Abraham Ibn Daud, Solomon

Ibn Gabirol, Baḥya Ibn Baḳūda, Abraham b. Ḥiyya). His work has no special title. The same author compiled another work in fifteen chapters under the title ספר המצרף. Of this work chapter I is taken partly from the Paraphrase and partly from a translation of Saadia's Commentary on the *Sefer Yeẓirah* (see above, p. 358), while the last six chapters (X-XV), with the exception of a few insertions from other sources (as in chapter XI), are again taken entirely from the Paraphrase. Both compilations were published with an English introduction and translation by H. Gollancz under the title *The Ethical Treatises of Berachya*, London, 1902. This is not the place to discuss the merits or demerits of Gollancz's edition. I must say, however, that it in no way deserves the praise bestowed upon it by N. Porges, in *ZfhB.*, VII, 36-44. Much more reasonable is the review of Guttmann, *MGWJ.*, XLVI, 536-547; comp. also Israel Lévi, *RÉJ.*, XLVI, 285-288, and Steinschneider, *JQR.*, XVII, 581, top.

Much uncertainty prevails regarding the original text used by the anonymous paraphrast. It was noted above that the recension of the seventh chapter in the Oxford MS. differs entirely from that in the St. Petersburg MS. The Paraphrase follows partly the one and partly the other recension (see Landauer, Introduction to the *Kitâb al-'Amânât*, p. xi) and the epitomizer Berechiah naturally adheres to the same order. The question is now whether the anonymous paraphrast had both recensions before him and tried to combine them into one, or whether he had an Arabic text in which the two recensions had already beeen fused by some unknown editor. The question may here be left undecided. It is of more importance to note that the anonymous Paraphrase was the source not only of Berechiah, but of several other authors, who embodied parts thereof in their own works, or published them as separate books. These may be arranged as follows, according to the order of the chapters of the *Kitâb al-'Amânât* in which the excerpted materials occur:

1. ספר התשובה של רבנו סעדיה. Under this heading a por-

tion of Chapter V is reproduced by Judah he-Ḥasid (died 1217) in his ספר חסידים, Bologna, 1538, § 612-613; Berlin, 1891, § 36 (the texts in the two editions show many variations). The fifth chapter of Saadia's work must have circulated as a separate treatise under the above title before the time of Judah, who made extracts from it. A comparison of the text of the ספר חסידים with the corresponding passages in Berechiah's work (pp. 33, 38) shows convincingly that the translation is that of the Paraphrase and, so far as this extract is concerned, there is no ground for the assumption of H. Michael, אור החיים, p. 300 (see Steinschneider, *AL.*, p. 66, n. 18) that there existed a *third* translation of Saadia's work. Judah does not reproduce the text in its original order. Thus the greater part of one paragraph (ed. Berlin, p. 38, top, to וגם יש רשע, third line from below) corresponds to *Kitâb al-'Amânât,* pp. 180, 2-181, 5 from below (in Ibn Tibbon's translation, ed. Slucki, pp. 90, 21-91, 15; Berechiah, pp. 38 f.), while the end of the same paragraph corresponds to pp. 171, 14-172, 2 (Ibn Tibbon, pp. 86, 2 from below—87, 6; Berechiah, p. 33). Possibly Judah is not responsible for these changes, but gave the text as he found it in the separate ספר התשובה, which may have been a free recast of the fifth chapter, based on the Paraphrase. Eleazar of Worms used the same source, perhaps also Juda Ḥalâz; see note 491. The title מאמרים מספר התשובה, quoted by Steinschneider (*CB.*, 2178) and others, is based on a misunderstanding of Rapoport's words in בכורי העתים, IX, 30, bottom.

2. ספר התחיה והפרות, a condensed edition of chapter VII of Saadia's work as contained in the Paraphrase, but with considerable changes, transpositions, and amplifications by an anonymous author, published for the first time at Mantua, 1556, then with an addition from a work of Moses de Trani (see below), Wilna, 1799 (in *Literaturblatt des Orients,* 1847, p. 177, mistakenly identified with the work given below as no. 4), reprinted Sudzilkow, 1834; Warsaw, 1841. The exact title is ספר התחיה, but והפרות was added, because the publication was intended to cover also no. 4 (below, p. 367)

which, however, was published separately two months later;
see Steinschneider, *CB.,* 2179.

3. תשובות שאלות לרבנו סעדיה גאון, an anonymous compilation in the style of the Paraphrase, containing the *Ten
Questions* regarding resurrection which form the last portion
of chapter VII of the *Kitâb al-'Amânât,* printed first at the
end of מדרש שמואל, Constantinople, 1522 (see Buber's Introduction to his edition of this work, Cracow, 1893, p. 36).
The same recension of the Ten Questions, taken from a
Parma MS., showing numerous, though not essential variants, was edited under the title עשרה שאלות by Chaim M.
Horowitz, בית נכות ההלכות, I, Frankfurt a. M., 1881, pp.
59-62. It will be remembered that the seventh chapter
of the Paraphrase, and hence also of the compendium of
Berechiah, is a combination of both Arabic recensions (see
above, p. 362). Now we find that the number and order
of the *Questions* in the *Paraphrase* is exactly the same as in
the St. Petersburg MS., which agrees throughout with the
recension presented in the translation of Ibn Tibbon, while
the content and wording of the individual Questions and
answers agree fully with the recension of the St. Petersburg
MS. The same is true of the separate editions of the Ten
Questions, except that the text is here very much abridged,
rendering the comparison somewhat difficult. The only
compilation in which the order as well as the number of the
Questions is entirely different from that of both Arabic recensions is the ספר התחיה (above, no. 2), whose author, though
drawing upon the Paraphrase, perhaps through intermediary
sources, has disposed of the material in an altogether
arbitrary manner. The style and diction of all these compilations, however, is entirely similar and their common
source is the Paraphrase : comp. *e. g.* ספר התחיה, Question 7,
and עשרה שאלות, ed. Horowitz, Question 3 ; see also Guttmann, *Die Religionsphilosophie des Saadia,* p. 227, n. 5 (for
" siebente " read there (fourth line from below) *sechste.*
Bacher's assertion (Steinschneider's *Festschrift,* p. 223, n. 1)
that the Ten Questions, ed. Horowitz, agree with the recension of the St. Petersburg MS., is therefore correct only in so

far as the order is concerned; in style and content the compiler follows the Paraphrase or some of its later epitomizers,
but not the translation of Ibn Tibbon. It should be noted that
in ed. Horowitz and in שמואל מדרש the text begins with the
words תלמידי שאלוני סעדיה אמר, as if the Questions were
addressed to him by his pupils, which is of course an invention of the compiler.

The Paraphrase was also the source of the French
Tōsafist Samson b. Abraham of Sens (12th century), who
quotes two of the Questions (6, 7) in one of his epistles to
Meir b. Todros ha-Levi Abulafia (אלרסאיל כתאב, edited by
Jehiel Brill; Paris, 1871, pp. 136 f.). Apart from a few insignificant variants the text agrees literally with that of
Berechiah, p. 60. The editor, Brill, evidently did not know of
the existence of the Paraphrase, and is therefore surprised at
the differences between his text and that of Ibn Tibbon.
Samson calls the Questions סעדיה רבנו תשובות, and says that
he asked one of the scholars (חברים) to *copy* (להעתיק, see
Zunz, *Gesammelte Schriften,* III, 65 f.) them for him. The
text of Question 6 (Landauer, pp. 223, 5-19, and 224, 11-18)
is corrupt both here and in the work of Berechiah. Gollancz
in his edition of the latter, p. 119, translates blindly without
noticing the difficulty; comp. the corresponding passage in
התחיה ספר, Question 5, which offers here a more correct
text. For יאכלו (Brill, p. 137, 4) read יובלו, as in Berechiah,
p. 60; comp. also Steinschneider, *CB.,* 2224, bottom.

An altogether different recension of the Ten Questions is
that published from a Leipzig MS. by Jellinek in his *Bet ha-*
Midrasch, VI, 148 f., under the title אליעזר רבי שאלות. The
text here is much shorter than in any of the compilations
previously mentioned. Its anonymous author does not follow, so far as the wording of the text is concerned, any of
the Hebrew versions known, but merely gives the gist of the
Questions and the answers in his own language. The order
of the Questions is the same as in all other sources, except
the התחיה ספר. The " R. Eliezer," to whom the work is
here falsely attributed, represents, according to Delitzsch
and Jellinek (see the latter's introductory remarks, p. xxxv,

and Steinschneider, *AL.*, pp. 53 f.) either Eliezer b. Hyr-
canos or b. Jacob, both teachers of the Mishnah of the first
century. For the various MSS. in which the different recensions of the Ten Questions are found (sometimes anonymously and sometimes attributed to one of various mediaeval
authors) see Steinschneider, *CB.*, 2178, no. 6, and *AL.*, p. 53.

To dispose of all the material in connection with this subject I add here an account of some other complete or partial
editions of the Ten Questions, though the texts of these
editions are in no wise based upon that of the Paraphrase.
Thus, in a lengthy Responsum of the Gaon Hai (in the Hebrew periodical, כוכבי יצחק, V, 75, published more completely
in the collection טעם זקנים by Eliezer Ashkenazi, Frankfurt
a/M., 1854, pp. 59a-61a, who, however, omitted the entire
passage with which we are here concerned), the contents of
which is based entirely on chs. VII and VIII of the *'Amânât*,
the author gives, in the name of Saadia, the contents of
Questions 6, 7, 5 (this is his order) ; comp. Bacher, Steinschneider's *Festschrift*, p. 225, n. 1 ; above, notes 578, 614.
It should be noted that the passage corresponding to Question 7 contains elements which are not found in either of
the two Arabic recensions, and agrees almost verbally with
the recension in מדרש שמואל and in the edition of Horowitz.
It thus appears that Hai's Responsum or a derivate of it was
used by the Editor of the recension in question.

Moses de Trani (1505-1585) incorporated the Ten Questions into his ethico-ritualistic work בית אלהים (Venice, 1576 ;
Warsaw, 1872), part III, ch. 59. His text is that of Ibn
Tibbon. To each Question he adds a sort of commentary,
which in some instances is of very considerable proportions.
The extensive commentary on Question 3 was printed also
in the later editions of the ספר התחיה. This led an uninformed writer in the *JE.*, XII, 219, to make Moses the author
of the latter work, which he characterizes as a " commentary
and notes on ch. 7 and 8 of Saadia Gaon's Emûnōt we-
Dēōt."

The edition of the Ten Questions by M. L. Bisliches at
the end of his edition of Shem Tob Palquera's ספר הנפש,

Lemberg, 1835, is unveracious. The text is copied from Ben-
Seëb's edition of Ibn Tibbon's translation of the *'Amânât,*
but Bisliches introduces the Questions as "addressed to
the Gaon by his pupils" (an imitation of the edition in
מדרש שמואל; see above, p. 364) and pretends to have
drawn upon a MS. To Question 3 he adds a commentary
under the name חקר דעת which is that of Ben-Seëb, whose
name he suppresses. The "note" (הגה"ה) at the very end
is also copied from the edition in מדרש שמואל, end, which
is found also with some variations toward the end of the
ספר התחיה, but is not in any of the Arabic recensions.

4. ספר הפדות והפורקן, containing about two thirds of ch.
VIII of the *'Amânât* (Landauer, pp. 229-245, line 8; Ibn Tibbon, ed. Slucki, pp. 118-125, line 18) in the translation (Paraphrase) of the anonymous author (Berechiah, pp. 62-69, line
11, with variations). It appeared first in Mantua, 1556 (as
a continuation of the ספר התחיה, which appeared but two
months earlier) and has since been frequently reprinted. It
is reproduced with a German translation in the work שלישה
שושנים of the apostate Joh. Salomon of Posen (Danzig,
1675), who subsequently wrote a special book in refutation
of Saadia's views regarding the expected redemption of
Israel ("Zerteilte Finsterniss, oder Widerlegung des Buches
Fajjumi's von der Erlösung und befreiung Israels," Danzig, 1681). The ספר הפדות was edited also by Jacob Emden,
who wrote a short introduction to it (Altona, 1769). For
other editions see Steinschneider, *CB.,* 2180; Benjacob,
Thesaurus, p. 456, no. 20.

It would lead us too far to treat here in detail of the many
authors who, down to the 14th century, assiduously studied
the *Kitâb al-Amânât* in the Hebrew text of the Paraphrase
instead of the more accurate and scientific translation of
Judah Ibn Tibbon, and embodied lengthy excerpts therefrom
in their works in various fields of learning. The names of
these authors and their works, which for the most part
exist in MSS. only, have been pointed out by Zunz in Geiger's
Jüdische Zeitschrift, X, 4-10 (*Gesammelte Schriften,* III,
231 ff.) and many more could now be added (comp. Stein-

schneider, *MWJ.*, III, 151 · Judah Mosconi ; above, note 493 :
Judah Ḥalâz). Such an enumeration is not within the scope
of the present Bibliography I shall mention only a few
authors from whose works lengthy passages, taken from the
Paraphrase, have been occasionally published. Thus several
pages of the Paraphrase were published by Isidore Loeb,
RÉJ, XVIII, 46-52, from the work מלחמות ה', a polemic
against Christianity by Jacob b. Reuben (1170). Some of
the citations are embodied in chapter XII of the מלחמות,
which was published in part by Natan Amram, Amsterdam,
1842, reprinted at Stettin, 1860 ; comp Steinschneider, *CB*,
2032 ; HB., III, 44 Jacob b. Reuben's work contains many
more extensive quotations of Saadia's *Kitâb al-'Amânât* in
the text of the Paraphrase (see Loeb, *ib.*, p. 48), which a
future editor of the latter will have to consider The publication of the whole work on the basis of three MSS. was
begun by the late Dr. Adolf Posnanski, but was interrupted
by the untimely death of the author, so that only the first
three chapters (80 pages) were printed (Warsaw, 1912),
but not yet published

In the controversy between Aaron b Meshullam and the
aforementioned Meir ha-Levi Abulafia (see above, p. 365)
regarding certain views of Maimonides, especially those on
resurrection, both men, very well-known Talmudists of the
twelfth and the thirteenth centuries, refer often to Saadia's
opinion upon the question at issue Their source was again
the paraphrase, from which one passage is quoted directly
(כתאב אלרסאיל, p 57, comp *ib.*, pp 14, 36)

Numerous passages from Saadia's work under consideration were quoted from the Paraphrase also by Moses Tachau
(1230) in his fragmentary כתב תמים, published by Kirchheim in the אוצר נחמד, III, 58-99 ; comp above, pp 281 ff.,
and Zunz, in Geiger's *Judische Zeitschrift*, X, 4-10 To the
parallels from the שיר היחוד given there by Zunz several
more could be added ; comp *Emūnôt*, ed Slucki, p. 43, with
the end of that poem for the Fifth Day המדעים בעשר כלוליס,
וטבע כמיות וששת נדות (תנועות Ibn Tibbon) וטלש גזרות ועתות
ומדות

Hirschfeld, in his *Descriptive Catalogue of Hebrew MSS.
of the Montefiore Library*, no. 483, 9, records " Contents of
Saadyāh's ספר האמונות, copied from a MS. written 1540 by
a certain Isaac," without indicating whether they were taken
from the Paraphrase or from the translation of Ibn Tibbon.
They are probably taken from the latter.

In more recent times a few extracts from the Paraphrase
have been published by different scholars ; see the references
above, p. 361. The beginning of chapter VI appeared in the
periodical ציון, I, 79. An extract from chapter X (Landauer,
p. 117 ; *'Emūnōt,* ed. Slucki, Leipzig. 1864, p. 160; Berechiah,
pp. 98 f.), dealing with music, was published by Steinschneider together with two other pieces on the same subject,
under the title אוצר הספרות) לקוטים מחכמת המוסיקא, I, pp.
xxix ff.). The same passage was given there by Steinschneider in another version taken from an unpublished commentary on the *Kuzari* of Judah Halevi, called בית יעקב, by
Jacob b. Ḥayyim Ferussol (1422) : see Steinschneider, *Hebräische Uebersetzungen,* p. 404; *Renan, Écrivains,* p. 409
Jacob b. Ḥayyim gives as his source the work מגלת המגלה of
Abraham b. Ḥiyya (about 1130), which is likewise extant in
MSS. only (see Guttmann,*MGWJ.,*XLVI 446-468 ; XLVII,
545-569), but Steinschneider (*HB.,* XIII, 36) called attention
to the fact that the whole passage is only a verbal translation,
probably by Abraham b. Ḥiyya himself, of the Arabic text in
Saadia's *Kitâb al-'Amânât.* Aside from some variations in
terminology this translation agrees fully with that of Ibn
Tibbon. We thus possess three different recensions of
Saadia's theory of music, which has not yet been properly
explained ; comp. Steinschneider, *JQR.,* XVII, 559 f., 561,
no. 16, and above, note 543. According to Steinschneider,
HB., XIII, 36, the passage is found in the MSS. of two
other commentaries on the *Kuzari,* namely those of Menahem
b. Judah and Nethanel Caspi (both, like Jacob b. Ḥayyim,
pupils of Frat Maimon and writing in the year 1422), who
also quote it from Abraham b. Ḥiyya ; comp. Steinschneider,
Alfarabi, St. Petersburg, 1869, p. 79, n. 16.

24

II. THE TRANSLATION OF JUDAH IBN TIBBON

Though, as we have seen, the Paraphrase was more extensively used by mediæval authors than has been hitherto admitted (Steinschneider, *Hebräische Uebersetzungen*, p. 441,
n. 502), yet it was Judah Ibn Tibbon's translation through
which Saadia was studied by all non-Arabic speaking Jewry
from the Middle Ages to our time. Judah translated the
work in Lunel, Southern France, in the year 1186, under the
title ספר האמונות והדעות. So far no critical edition of this
standard work has been made. The following is a brief
enumeration and description of the various editions:

1. Constantinople, 1562, in 4to. in the so-called Rashi
script. In a colophon the dates of the composition (933)
and of the translation (1186) are given.

2. Amsterdam, 1647, 4to, a poor reprint of the Constantinople edition, to which an index of the subject matter
was added, covering 6 pages. For a characterization of
this edition see Guttmann, *Die Religionsphilosophie des
Saadia*, p. 27, n. 1.

3. Berlin, 1789, 4to, with a double commentary חקר דעת
and שומר אמונה by Judah Loeb Ben-Seëb. The text of
this edition, which is a reprint of the preceding ones, is
full of arbitrary, uncritical changes and of typographical
errors. A new feature of this edition is the division of the
text into comparatively short paragraphs to facilitate quotation. The division, too, is often quite arbitrary and unscien-
tific, but in the absence of a better one, writers on Saadia
often quote according to the paragraphs of this edition. The
commentaries contain many a valuable and learned remark.

4. Leipzig, 1859, 8vo, by Fischl Hirsch, who made use
also of the *editio princeps*, Guttmann's contention to the
contrary notwithstanding (*l. c.*); see *e. g.* p. 118, where the
reading מנופפים is found only in the first edition, while
the other editions have incorrectly מנפחים. The heading of
ch. VII (p. 132) likewise rests on the Constantinople edition,
as it was omitted in those of Amsterdam and Berlin. On
p. 23 there is an explanatory note in German by Jellinek
(the only one, not "several," as Steinschneider, *Hebräische*

Uebersetzungen, p. 439, has it). This edition has the merit
of giving the references to the Biblical books for the numerous verses quoted in the work. Unfortunately, however, the
references are often incorrect.

5. Leipzig, 1864, small 8ᵛᵒ, by D. Slucki with an introduction containing a sketch of Saadia's life and works (compiled
from Rapoport, Fürst, Graetz, and others) and explanatory
notes on the text, mostly taken from Ben-Seëb and Fürst.
They have no scientific value. The editor's notes extend only
to p. 87 (beginning of ch. V) and are then continued by
I. Dines; see the latter's remark on the last page of the book.

6. Cracow, 1880, 8ᵛᵒ, a reprint of No. 5 with the omission
of the Introduction and the suppression of the names of the
two annotators. In this edition numberless misprints are
added to those of the earlier editions.

7. Jósefów, 1885, 8ᵛᵒ, by Israel ha-Levi with a commentary, שביל האמונה. This is the only edition that appeared
after the publication of the Arabic original, but the editor, a
Russian Rabbi of the old school and neither in touch nor in
sympathy with modern research, is not at all aware of the
existence of an Arabic original. Nor does he take
cognizance of anything that was written on the subject by
Jewish scholars for the last hundred years, though he knows
of the existence of such writings, as is obvious from his
polemics against Slucki (see his Introduction, p. 7). His
appreciation of Saadia rests wholly on what he gathers from
mediæval sources, to which he refers in the Introduction.
As he here informs us, he made use of four previous editions,
of which he mentions explicitly the *editio princeps* and that
of Slucki (the other two are probably those of Amsterdam
and Berlin). His text, which he, too, divided into short paragraphs is on the whole more correct than that of the other
editions. In several passages, however, which contain
Saadia's polemic against Christianity (pp. 92, 183 f.), it was
mutilated by the Russian censor. His references to Bible
and Talmud are likewise correct; his commentary, written
in a lucid style, shows remarkable insight and keen pene-
tration into the real meaning of the difficult text, and his sug-

gestions as to eventual emendations are often supported
by the original. It goes without saying that due to the cor-
ruptions in the text and to other reasons he at times falls
into misinterpretations, but on the whole he understood
Saadia better than all previous commentators (Fürst not
excluded). Considering the nature of the author's re-
sources, as well as the public for which he wrote, his commentary must be recognized as a highly creditable production. The work is preceded by a dictionary of philosophic
terms in mediæval Hebrew literature (published also separately under the title באר ישראל, Jósefów, 1886). Most of
the terms are fairly well explained, while the explanation of
a few others (as תכלית בישלוח, מדברים, חלק) shows the
author's naïveté.

A critical edition based on all the existing MSS. and on a
careful comparison of the Arabic recensions, including the
Genizah fragments, has been prepared by the present writer
and will be published soon after the present work.

Ever since the Arabic original was made accessible,
first through copies from the MSS. and later through Landauer's edition, various scholars have repeatedly furnished
notes and emendations to Ibn Tibbon's text, which are scattered in several periodicals and other publications. They are
of considerable value and should therefore not be omitted
from this Bibliography:

L. Loewe, in the Hebrew weekly המגיד, 1867, p. 37.

M. Wolff, ZDMG., XXXII (1878), 694-707, continued
in MWJ., VII (1880), 73-100, VIII, 60 (to the whole work
with the exception of chapter VII).

D. Kaufmann, ZDMG., XXXVII (1883), 230-149 (to the
Introduction only, for which he compared also MSS. of the
Paraphrase; comp. also his article in Rahmer's Jüdisches
Literaturblatt, 1878, p. 65).

S. H. Margulies, MWJ., XV (1888), 123-133; 160-169;
XVII (1890), 280-288; Kaufmann's Gedenkbuch, Breslau
1900, pp. 210-220 (covering altogether the Introduction and
the first six chapters). It is rather strange that in his introductory remarks to the article in Kaufmann's Gedenkbuch

the author states that the latter is a continuation of two previous articles which he had published in *MWJ.*, XV, but omits the reference to his third article in *MWJ.*, XVII, from which about a third of the notes are here repeated. W. Bacher, Kaufmann's *Gedenkbuch*, pp. 188-207 (to the whole book), followed by a specimen of his intended edition of the whole text (taken from ch. 1, ed. Slucki, pp. 21 f.). I. Goldziher, *REJ.*, LX (1910), 32 f.

Aside from these separate articles on the subject numerous emendations of Ibn Tibbon's text were occasionally suggested by Bloch, Guttmann, Bacher, and Horovitz, in the works to be mentioned below.

For completeness' sake I mention here the work פתוחי חותם by the well-known Russian-Hebrew writer Isaac Baer Levinsohn, which was written in 1845, but published for the first time by his nephew B. Nathansohn, Warsaw, 1903 (see the latter's biography of Levinsohn under the title ספר הזכרונות, Warsaw, 1899, p. 156, n. 2). The work consists of seven literary pieces, the sixth of which (pp. 54-77) is an abridged and, as the author thought, emended edition of Ibn Tibbon's text of Saadia's Introduction, with a profuse commentary in which the author tries to justify his arbitrary changes. As he had no other sources than the corrupt Berlin edition, his emendations are mere guesswork and of no critical value. So far as I know no reference is found anywhere to this curious attempt of the so-called "Russian Mendelssohn."

b) *Latin*

1. Joh. Gagnier, *Specimen novae editionis libri* האמונות והדעות etc. Oxford, 1717, for which see Fürst, *Bibliotheca Judaica*, I, 268; Steinschneider, *Christliche Hebraisten*, in *ZfhB.*, III, 13; comp. above, p. 360.

2. Theodor Dassov, *Diatribe qua Judaeos de resurrectione mortuorum sententia crasse explicatur* etc., Wittenberg, 1675, containing the translation of most of the seventh chapter; see Fürst, *l. c.*, I, 197, 268. As regards the author see Steinschneider, *l. c.*, II, 124.

c) *German*

1. J. Salomon, translation of ch. VIII, see above, p. 367, no. 4.

2. Julius Fürst, *Emunot we-Deot, oder Glaubenslehre und Philosophie von Saadja Fajjumi,* Leipzig, 1845. This translation or rather paraphrase of the whole work of Ibn Tibbon with the exception of chapter X (ethics) has been justly designated as entirely inadequate, or as Steinschneider (*Hebräische Uebersetzungen,* p. 439) puts it, "not worth the trouble that scholars have taken in trying to correct some of its mistakes." Fürst is not to be blamed too much for these mistakes, for nobody could have correctly translated Ibn Tibbon's text without the aid of the Arabic original. It would have been better, however, not to have published a work of which a considerable part had to be based on vague conjectures.

3. Philipp Bloch, *Vom Glauben und Wissen, München,* 1879, containing the translation of the Introduction and of the first chapter (reprint from Rahmer's *Judisches Literaturblatt*) Bloch made use also of a MS. of the anonymous Paraphrase, and his translation, so far as it goes, is incomparably superior to that of Fürst. But as the original was at that time inaccessible in print, he likewise often misunderstood the text. While it was in the course of publication M. Wolff's notes and emendations of the Hebrew text, based on a comparison of a MS. of the Arabic original (see above, p. 372), appeared, following which Bloch appended additions to his work, wherein most of the mistakes were corrected; comp. also Bloch's article, *MGWJ.,* 1870, pp. 401-414, 449-456

4. A. Kaminka, *Die Litteratur der geonäischen Zeit,* in Winter and Wünsche's *Die jüdische Litteratur,* II (1897), 31-39, translated part of the Introduction (Landauer, pp 1-5, l 12; Hebrew text ed. Cracow, 1880, pp. 1-4, l 7) and nearly half of the sixth chapter (Landauer, pp. 188-198, l. 6: Hebrew text, pp 127-132, l. 18).

5 Wilhelm Engelkemper, *Die religionsphilosophische Lehre Saadja Gaons über die Heilige Schrift,* Munster, 1903,

containing the translation of chapter III with a general Introduction and copious notes. The author, who had previously published a learned biography of Saadia in Latin (see above, note 191), translates from the Arabic original with the aid of the Hebrew text of Ibn Tibbon, and on the whole acquits himself creditably; but not being sufficiently familiar with the ideas and sources of mediæval Jewish theology, which is the essential content of this chapter, he often misunderstands and misinterprets both texts. The Introduction, too, contains a number of misstatements, as for instance that Israëli's treatise (see Steinschneider's *Festschrift*, pp. 131 ff.; *JQR.*, XV, 689 ff.) exists only in Latin (p. 2, n. 2), that ch. V of the *Emūnōt* appeared in the ספר חסידים (p. 6, n. 2), while in fact only about one page is there reproduced (see above, p. 362, no. 1); comp. the reviews of Guttmann, *Theologische Literaturzeitung*, 1904, no. 2; Seybold, *Orientalistische Litteratur-Zeitung*, VII, 255. Chapter VIII was partly translated into French by Michel A. Weill, *L'Univers Israélite*, 1870, pp. 271 ff. For translations of other part into French (Munk) and English (Hirschfeld) see above, pp. 359 f.

In this connection it should also be recorded that in 1840 Steinschneider, in collaboration with Julius Barrasch, prepared a translation of and a commentary on the *Emunot,* but, as he explicitly states in his *CB.*, 2175, postponed publication until a more reliable Hebrew text should be available. This translation and commentary are now in my possession; the author, who, I am proud to say, was my beloved teacher and friend, having placed them at my disposal. The unequalled position of Steinschneider in the field of Jewish literature warrants a short description of his unpublished work. The MS., covering 578 pages in quarto, contains the translation of the whole text with the exception of ch. X. The Introduction (of Saadia) and the first four chapters (pp. 1-256) are translated by Julius Barrasch, a distinguished physician and writer who died at Bucharest in 1863. It is interesting to note that the first twenty pages are written in Judæo-German, the rest in German script. The margin shows numerous corrections by Steinschneider. Barrasch began the translation in Prague, "Friday, 24th of January, 1840" and finished it "Sunday the 17th of July" in the same year. The remaining five chapters are translated by Steinschneider. In the course of time he made various changes in the MS. so that the deciphering is sometimes difficult On the margin are numerous notes, partly in Judæo-German script by Barrasch, but mostly from the hand of Steinschneider. At the end of the volume is a complete index of the Biblical and Talmudic passages of the *Emunot*, but unfortunately the pagination refers to the edition of Ben-Seéb which to-day is worthless I hope to prepare the whole work for publication

The "Commentary" to which Steinschneider referred is a separate little volume of 70 pages. It does not really explain Ibn Tibbon's text, but is more in the form of a glossary, elucidating the peculiar words and phrases of the translator by references to analogous passages in the works of the same writer and in other philosophic treatises. The terminological material collected in this little volume by thousands of references is almost inexhaustible. Part of it was utilized by Delitzsch in his edition of the חיים עץ by the Karaite Aaron b Elijah (Leipzig, 1841 ; comp Delitzsch's Introduction to the edition, p. 14), and later by Steinschneider himself in his numerous writings, but much of it can only be used in connection with a critical edition of Ibn Tibbon's text

In conclusion mention should be made of two MSS. commentaries on the *'Emunōt* by mediæval authors (cod. De Rossi, nos. 769, 1283), for which see Steinschneider, *CB.*, 2175, no 4.

C. BIBLIOGRAPHY *

A Geiger, *Wissenschaftliche Zeitschrift*, V (1844), 291-314.

S. Munk, *Mélanges de philosophie juive et arabe*, Paris, 1859, pp. 477 ff.

* General works, monographs, essays, etc, in which characterizations of Saadia's philosophy, or of some particular branch thereof are to be found (in chronological order).

H. Graetz, *Geschichte der Juden,* V, fourth edition by
S. Eppenstein, Leipzig, 1909, pp. 296-312; Hebrew transla-
tion by S. P. Rabbinowicz with notes by Harkavy, vol. III,
Warsaw, 1893, pp. 292-306. In the English translation
(Philadelphia, 1894), vol. III, pp. 197 f., this most important
part of Saadia's scientific work was unwisely omitted.

A. Schmiedl, *Saadia Alfajûmi und die negativen Vorzüge
seiner Religionsphilosophie,* Vienna, 1870.

M. Eisler, *Vorlesungen über die jüdischen Philosophen des
Mittelalters,* Vienna, 1876, pp. 1-43 (with an appendix, containing Hebrew extracts from the *Emûnôt*), a very valuable
summary of Saadia's philosophy, though in some parts
antiquated.

D. Kaufmann, *Geschichte der Attributenlehre,* Gotha,
1877, pp. 1-77 (with an appendix entitled *Der schriftstel-
lerische Charakter des "Emunoth,"* pp. 78-90), a very important study; comp. Brüll, *Jahrbücher,* IV, 134-156; see also
Kaufmann, *Die Sinne,* Leipzig, 1884, index, *s. v.* Saadia.

M. Joel, *Beiträge zur Geschichte der Philosophie,* II, Breslau, 1878, *Anhang,* pp. 34-44 (reprint from Wertheimer's
Jahrbuch für Israeliten, 5626, Vienna, 1866).

Jacob Guttmann, *Die Religionsphilosophie des Saadia,*
Göttingen, 1882, the best work on Saadia's philosophy.
Following the order of the Hebrew text the author gives an
excellent translation of the most essential parts of the work
elucidating each of the translated portions by general discussions and by quoting numerous parallel passages from
Greek and Arabic writers, thus presenting the content of the
whole as a fairly complete system. The work is preceded
by a well-written general Introduction (p. 1-32); comp.
Steinschneider, *Deutsche Literaturzeitung,* 1883, p. 77; see
also Guttmann, *Die Beziehungen der maimonidischen Reli-
gions-philosophie zu der des Saadia,* in Israel Lewy's *Festschrift,* Breslau, 1911, pp. 308-326, also in *Moses b. Maimon,*
II (Leipzig, 1914), 201-216.

M. Wolff, *Ein Wort über Religion und Philosophie nach
Auffassung Saadjâ al-Fajjûmî's, ZDMG.,* XLIV (1890),
154-164.

W. Bacher, *Die Bibelexegese der jüdischen Religions-philosophen des Mittelalters vor Maimuni*, Strassburg, 1892, pp. 1-44, dealing exhaustively with Saadia's *philosophic* Bible exegesis, particularly in the *Kitâb al-'Amânât*.

M. Schreiner, *Der Kalâm in der jüdischen Literatur* (printed in the *Dreizehnter Bericht über die Lehranstalt für die Wissenschaft des Judenthums in Berlin*), Berlin, 1895, pp. 5-22. The author quotes extensively from the works of Muhammedan writers, showing in particular Saadia's relation to the philosophy of the Mutakallimûn.

G. H[enkel], *Religiozno-Filosofskoe Sochinenie Saadii Gaona, Voskhod*, 1895, II, 3-20; III, 51-62; IV, 3-20; VI, 3-31. See also above, note 191.

S. Bernfeld, דעת אלהים, Warsaw, 1897, pp. 113-139; see also above, note 191.

Ph. Bloch, *Die jüdische Religionsphilosophie* (reprint from Winter and Wünsche, *Die jüdische Litteratur*, II (1897), 704-715).

J. P. Muller, *De Godsleer der Middeleeuwsche Joden*, Groningen, 1898, pp. 59-89.

S. Horovitz, *Die Psychologie bei den jüdischen Religions-philosophen des Mittelalters von Saadia bis Maimuni* (in the "*Jahres-Bericht*" of the Jewish Theological Seminary of Breslau), Breslau, 1898, part I, pp. 1-75, a learned work with copious notes, in which numerous Greek sources are adduced. His emendations of the Arabic and Hebrew texts, however, are often far-fetched. See also Horovitz, *Über die Bekanntschaft Saadia's mit der griechischen Skepsis*, in Hermann Cohen's *Festschrift*, Berlin, 1912, pp. 235-252.

D. Neumark, *Geschichte der jüdischen Philosophie des Mittelalters* (I, Berlin, 1907, pp. 429-469; 536-551), a voluminous work showing great erudition, keen reasoning, and admirable industry. Owing to the author's extremely dogmatic conception of the history and development of Jewish philosophy, however, his conclusions will hardly find general acceptance.

David Rau, *Die Ethik R. Saadjas* in *MGWJ.*, 1911, pp. 385-399, 513-530, 713-728; 1912, pp. 65-79, 181-198, the most exhaustive study on this particular subject. The end of this work has not yet appeared. The author died before he had a chance to print his book; it was to be published by Brann, the editor of the *MGWJ*, who in the meantime has also passed away.

Isaac Husik, *A History of Mediæval Jewish Philosophy*, New York, 1916, pp. 23-47 (comp. Malter, *JQR.*, N. S., vol. VIII (1917-1918), pp. 233-244).

H. Malter, *Se'adiah*, in Hastings's Encyclopaedia of Religion and Ethics, XI (1920), 279-282.

In addition to the monographs on Saadia's philosophy here enumerated and the more comprehensive works which deal with the latter in its entirety or with some important branch thereof, there are numerous dissertations in which certain phases of Saadia's philosophy are more or less minutely discussed. Of these the following may be mentioned.

A. Schmiedl, *Studien über jüdische Religionsphilosophie*, Vienna, 1869, in which various theories of Saadia are unsystematically discussed. The work has no index; see, however, pp. 42, 59, 78, 88, 94, 100 ff., 134-138, 160, 165 f., 172-175, 185, 198, 223-225, 252 f.; comp. Geiger, *Jüdische Zeitschrift*, VIII, 171-177, and for a contrary view as to the merits of Schmiedl's work, see Steinschneider, *HB.*, XI, 139-141.

D. Rosin, *Die Ethik des Maimonides*, Breslau, 1876, p. 10.

L. Stein, *Die Willensfreiheit und ihr Verhältniss zur göttlichen Präscienz und Providenz bei den jüdischen Philosophen des Mittelalters*, Berlin, 1882, p. 1-14.

David Joël, *Der Aberglaube und die Stellung des Judenthums zu demselben*, II, Breslau, 1883, pp. 2-10 (discussing Saadia's attitude toward superstition).

L. Knoller, *Das Problem der Willensfreiheit in der älteren jüdischen Religionsphilosophie des Mittelalters*, Leipzig, 1884, pp. 17-29.

N. Sandler, *Das Problem der Prophetie in der jüdischen Religionsphilosophie von Saadia bis Maimûni*, Breslau, 1891, pp. 14-22.

B. Templer, *Die Unsterblichkeitslehre bei den jüdischen Philosophen des Mittelalters*, Leipzig, 1895, pp 21-34.

J Kramer, *Das Problem des Wunders im Zusammenhang mit dem der Providenz bei den jüdischen Religionsphilosophen des Mittelalters von Saadia bis Maimûni*, Strassburg, 1903, pp. 7-27. Kramer treats the subject very satisfactorily.

For various references to older works see Steinschneider, *CB.*, 2172 ff.: *idem, Hebräische Uebersetzungen*, pp. 439 ff.; *AL.*, pp 51 f.

VI POLEMICS

1 *Kitâb al-Radd 'alâ 'Anân* (כתאב אלרד עלי ענן), " Refutation of Anan." For details relating to this work, of which nothing but a few quotations has been preserved, see Poznański's exhaustive study, *The Anti-Karaite Writings of Saadiah Gaon*, *JQR.*, X, 240 ff., comp. also Poznański, *The Karaite Literary Opponents of Saadiah Gaon* (reprint from *JQR*, XVIII-XX, hereafter quoted by the initials *KLO*), London, 1908, p. 72, no 32. and p 94, *Addenda* to p. 242. The work is also mentioned in an ancient book-list (12th century). *JQR.*, XIII, 54, no. 69, comp. Steinschneider, *AL.*, pp 51, 339; Poznański, *JQR.*, XIII, 329, no. 69; *RÉJ.*, XLV, 192, no. 2, Hirschfeld, *JQR.*, XIX. 136 ff; see also *RÉJ.*, XXXIX, 208, lines 4 f., with reference to no. 19

2. *Kitâb al-Tamyîz* (כתאב אלתמייז, in Hebrew sources ספר ההכרה, or ספר המבחן), " Book of Distinction," *i e.* of critical analysis. Of this work against the Karaites, which is supposed to have been very voluminous (see Poznański, *KLO.*, p. 95, n. 1), several fragments of considerable length and extensive extracts in the MS. work of the Karaite Jephet b 'Ali (altogether about fifteen pages in print) have thus far become known. Not all of the fragments, however, have been positively identified as having formed part of the *Kitâb al-Tamyîz*

a) A fragment of a work by a certain Nathan b Isaac al-Sikili (of Sicili) which seems to have been a compilation from older sources in defence of Jewish tradition in general and the calendar in particular. Nearly the whole fragment, is according to the statement of the compiler, a verbal reproduction of the first chapter of Saadia's *Kitâb al-Tamyîz*. It was published by Schechter, *Saadyana*, no. ix, pp. 30-34; comp. Poznański *KLO.*, p. 96; *idem, Zur jüdisch-arabischen Literatur*, p. 42; Eppenstein, *Beiträge*, pp. 76, 113, n. 2, and above, under *Calendar*, p. 169, no. 5.

b) The concluding portion of the work, three printed pages, published by Hirschfeld, *JQR.*, XVI, 102-105. For a full description of the content see Hirschfeld's introductory remarks (*ibidem*, pp. 98 f.) and especially Poznański, *KLO.*, pp. 94-96.

c) Numerous passages reproduced verbally by Jephet b. 'Ali in his Commentaries on the Bible. These were collected by Poznański and published in *JQR.*, X, 246-251.

d) A fragment of nearly three pages containing a defence of the calendar and its authority, published with an English translation and annotations by Poznański, *JQR.*, X, 261-274. Poznański's arguments in favor of Saadia's authorship of this anonymous fragment seem to me fully convincing. The question is only to which work of Saadia it belonged, but as the כתאב אלעבור, suggested by Poznański (p. 274) is, for reasons given above (p. 169, no. 5; see also p. 352, no. 5), out of the question, the only work that can come seriously into consideration is the *Kitâb al-Tamyîz*, which is also suggested by Poznański. For another fragment, thought by Harkavy to have been part of the *Kitâb al-Tamyîz*, see below, no. 3c.

e) A passage quoted in Hebrew by Abraham b. Ḥiyya in his ספר העבור, London, 1851, p. 96, in which the date of the composition דתרֹפֹּ־פֹּ=926-7 is given; comp. Poznański, *JQR.*, X, 245. The passage is reproduced also among the לקוטים, given by Müller, *Oeuvres complètes*, IX, 149, no. 15; Rapoport, ערך מלין, pp. 85, 87. For references to the *Tamyîz* in the works of some other mediæval authors see Poznański, *l. c.*; comp. Steinschneider, *AL.*, p. 50, no. 12; Eppenstein, *Beiträge*, pp. 76 f.

In view of the comprehensive character of the *Kitâb al-Tamyîz* I am of the opinion that the passage (two pages in print) quoted by a Ḳaraite in his Arabic polemic against Saadia (Hirschfeld, *JQR.*, N. S., vol. VIII (1917-1918), pp. 183 ff) is likewise part of this work. That it was taken from a work against the admissibility of *kiyâs* (speculation) in matters of tradition (Hirschfeld, *ib.*, p 167) is without basis, as there is no evidence that such a work by Saadia ever existed (see this *Bibliography*, VII, p. 400, no 13). Saadia's views on Mishnah and Talmud (p. 170) agree with those found in some other works of his Unfortunately, the editor's translation of the passage is incorrect and unintelligible. In place of what is given there ll. 22-30 read as follows: "they betook themselves to the consideration of the *principles* (of the oral law) and fixed them, calling the whole Mishnah, but the details they left unfixed in the hope that these would be preserved by the fixing of the aforementioned principles. So it was The details thus left unfixed were preserved until we went into the second exile and were scattered even more than in the first. Then the scholars feared (read in Arabic · *faḥâfa*) that—as had happened previously (read: *kadîman*), before it (the Mishnah) was fixed—they might be forgotten ; they therefore betook themselves also to the consideration of the details and fixed these This they called Talmud."

3. *Kitâb al-Radd 'alâ Ibn Sâḳawaihi* (אבן עלי אלרד אלרד כתאב סאקויה), "Refutation of Ibn Sâḳawaihi." Of this work some extensive fragments, covering eleven pages in print, have latterly been recovered.

a) A fragment discovered by Harkavy, part of which he edited in the Russian periodical *Woskhod*, January, 1900, p. 83 The same portion was re-edited with a French translation by Poznański, *RÉJ.*, XL, 88-90 The entire fragment was published with an English translation and notes by Harkavy, *JQR*, XIII (1901), 662-667, and for a second time with a Hebrew translation by the same in the Hebrew periodical הקדם, I (1907), 124-128. A much-damaged portion of the same fragment was published from another Genizah MS by Hirschfeld, *JQR*, XVI, 112, no. x. The whole

fragment belongs, according to Hirschfeld (*ibidem*, p. 100,
bottom), to the earlier part of the work; comp. Poznański,
KLO., p. 6, n. 6.

b) Six leaves belonging to the middle part of the book,
published by Hirschfeld, *JQR.*, XVI, 105-112, who gives also
a summary of the contents (pp. 99-102).

c) A fragment edited by Harkavy with an English translation and notes as part of the *Kitâb al-Tamyîz* (JQR., XIII,
655-660), which is assigned, however, by Hirschfeld with
much more probability to the latter part of the work under
discussion; see Hirschfeld, *JQR.*, XVI, 100 f; comp. Poznański, *KLO.*, p. 7, n. 4. This fragment, like the one mentioned above (no. 3*a*), was published by Harkavy for a
second time with a Hebrew translation in הקדם, I (1907),
64-68.

d) A lengthy passage quoted in Hebrew translation by
Judah b. Barzillai of Barcelona (1135), in his פרוש ספר יצירה
published by Halberstam, Berlin, 1885, p. 20, line 19 to p. 22,
line 2 (comp. the notes of Halberstam and Kaufmann on
pp. 282, 334). The passage had been previously published
by Luzzatto in הליכות קדם, pp. 69 ff.; comp. also Luzzatto,
בית האוצר, I (Lemberg, 1847), 12. That the passage was
taken from the work against Ibn Sâḳawaihi, however, is only
a probable conjecture, but not positively established (see
above, p. 267, top; comp. Poznański, *JQR.*, VIII, 690; *KLO.*,
p. 6, n. 7; 9, n. 2, and p. 97, top.

e) Another shorter passage in Hebrew quoted by the
same author, p. 34, lines 3-16. Here too the origin is not
quite certain; see Poznański, *ll. cc.*

f) A passage quoted in Hebrew by Abraham b. Ḥiyya
(1136) in his ספר העבור, p. 94. which, as Poznański properly
suggests (*JQR.*, X, 253), is taken from our work. In
Oeuvre complètes de Saadia, IX, 141, no. 50, this passage is
placed among Saadia's Responsa, where it hardly belongs;
comp. Steinschneider, *AL.*, p. 48; above, p. 349. For other
quotations in the works of Rabbanite and Karaite authors see
Poznański, *JQR.*, X, 252-254; comp. Steinschneider, *AL.*,
p. 51, no. 15, where, however, the reference to a fragment,

edited by Lambert, *REJ.*, XL, 84, is a mistake, as that fragment is part of Saadia's ספר הגלוי; see Lambert, *l. c.*, p. 260.
Bacher (*REJ.*, XXXIX, 205 f., nos. 4 and 5) finds the book
mentioned in an ancient book-list of the *Genizah*.

4. *Kitâb al-Radd 'alâ al-Mutaḥâmil* כתאב אלרד עלי
אלמתחאמל (היום?), "Refutation of the Overbearing Ag-
gressor," perhaps again Ibn Sâḳawaihi. Only two leaves
have so far been found and published by Hirschfeld with an
English translation and notes, *JQR.*, XVIII, 113-119. For
quotations by Hebrew authors (under the title תשובה ע״ל
הטוען) see Poznański, *JQR.*, X, 254 f.; Steinschneider, AL.,
p. 51, no. 14. The quotations of Judah b. Barzillai, to which
both Steinschneider and Poznański refer, were later assigned
by Poznański to Saadia's work against Ibn Sâḳawaihi; see
the references above, no. 3, letters *d* and *e*. Regarding the
ספר היחוד (*i. e.* the second chapter of Saadia's *Kitâb al-
'Amânât*), mentioned there by Steinschneider, see especially
Poznański, *JQR.*, VIII, 691. The polemical work under consideration is mentioned also in two old book-lists from the
Genizah (12th century), printed in Schechter's *Saadyana*,
no. xxxvii (p. 79, line 16; comp. Poznański, *Schechter's
Saadyana*, p. 23, no. 24), and in *JQR.*, XIII, 54, no. 59;
p. 327, no. 59. The enigmatic word היום, which occurs as
part of the title in one of the sources (Nissim b. Jacob), is
perhaps the mutilated name of the Karaite against whom
the work was written. That it was Ibn Sâḳawaihi is only a
conjecture. In the aforementioned lists, the word is omitted,
comp. Hirschfeld, *JQR.*, XVIII, 113, n. 1; see also Eppenstein, *Beiträge*, p. 109, n. 4. For refutations of the Karaites
Ben Zuta and Daniel b. Moses al-Ḳumisi, supposed to have
been written by Saadia, see below, *Bibliography*, section
VII, p. 398, nos. 9, 10.

5. *Kitâb al-Radd 'alâ Ḥayawaihi al-Balḥi* (כתאב אלרד עלי
חַיַוַיְה אלבלֹבֹי), "Refutation of Ḥayawaihi (*vulgo* Hiwi)*

* The proper pronunciation of the name is, as suggested by Poznański, חיוי הבלֹבֹי, p. 6, n. 3, Ḥayawaihi (or Ḥaiwaihi), which
agrees with the spelling חיוֹיה in the St. Petersburg MS. of the *Kitâb
al-Amânât* (Landauer, p. 37) and in Ḳirḳisâni's *Kitâb al-'Anwâr*

of Balkh " (Persia). Under this title the work is referred
to by Saadia himself in his *Kitâb al-'Amânât,* p. 37, l. 6
(*Emūnōt,* ed. Slucki, p. 20). Saadia mentions the work
also in the ספר הגלוי, ed. Harkavy, *Zikrōn,* V, 177, and in
his Polemic against Ibn Sâḳawaihi (not in the כתאב אלתמייז,
as Davidson (see below), pp. 14, 82, following Graetz, has
it), in the passage reproduced from it by Judah b. Barzillai,
פרוש ספר יצירה, p. 21 (see above, p. 383, letter *d*). In this
passage one stanza of Saadia's original text is preserved,
which makes it evident that the work was written in Hebrew
and in rhymed prose. Various mediæval authors, both
among the Ḳaraites and the Rabbanites, refer to Ḥiwi as a
heretic, some of the latter pointing out the fact that Saadia
refuted his heresies; thus, the anonymous author of the
Kitâb ma'ânî al-nafs (12th century) ed. Goldziher, Berlin,
1907, p. 16, ll. 20-24; Abraham Ibn Daud, סדר הקבלה, ed.
Neubauer, p. 66; Simon Duran (15th c.), מגן אבות, Leghorn,
1785, *fol.* 31a; Saadia Ibn Danân (15th c.), חמדה גנוזה, ed.
Edelmann, Königsberg, 1856, pp. 16a, 28b, and others. In
more recent times (since the appearance in the בכה"ע, 1829,
of the *Biography* of Saadia by Rapoport, who first took up
the matter) the question of Ḥiwi's personality and writings,
as well as of the nature of Saadia's polemic against him,
has been the subject of minute study and investigation.
Among other things it was pointed out in particular that
numerous passages in Saadia's main philosophic work, the
Kitâb al-'Amânât, in which he argues against an unnamed
opponent, were directed against Ḥiwi; see Graetz, *Geschichte*
(4), V, *Note* 20, pp. 533 f. (Hebrew edition, III, 473 f.) ;
especially the extensive article of Guttmann, *MGWJ.,* 1879,

(Harkavy, *Zikrōn,* V, p. 147, n. 2). This pronunciation is supported
also by three MSS. of Ibn Tibbon's translation (Parma and the
Vatican) of which I possess copies and in which the name is vocal-
ized חִוְיִ (omitting the ה). The usual pronunciation Ḥiwi or
Ḥiwwi (Bacher; see Steinschneider, *AL.,* p. 65, n. 12) is based
on a wrong analogy to the Biblical name of a Cananite tribe
(Gen., 10, 17). The proper analogy is the Persian name Tatnai
(Ezra, 5, 3).

pp. 260-270, 289-300. An exhaustive study of the subject
was published by Poznański under the title חיי הבלכי, Berdyczew, 1908 (reprint from הגרן, VII, 112-137), in which
all the material then available was collected and presented in
a clear and systematic way.

Of the text of Saadia's polemic against Ḥiwi nothing was
known until recently except the stanza of four rhymes preserved by Judah b. Barzillai. It was therefore of great
interest to the scholarly world that a considerable portion
of this work was lately discovered by Israel Davidson among
the Genizah fragments in the Cambridge University Library,
containing 73 stanzas of four rhymes each, about one-sixth
of the whole work, which, as Davidson, p. 34, shows, consisted of about 460 stanzas. Davidson edited the fragment
with an English translation and explanatory notes under the
title *Saadia's Polemic against Ḥiwi Al-Balkhi*, New York,
1915 (vol. V of Texts and Studies of the Jewish Theological
Seminary of America). In a lucid introduction the editor
briefly reviews the literature of the subject, gives a minute
analysis and appreciation of the contents of the recovered
text, and brings out the points that are of either literary or
historical interest. Towards the end of the volume he reproduces all the passages relating to Ḥiwi in the works of Saadia
(numbering altogether 15), as well as all the passages occurring in the Arabic and Hebrew works of other mediæval authors, so that we have here the entire material bearing on
Saadia's polemic against Ḥiwi (comp. Gaster, *Journal of the
Royal Asiatic Society*, 1915, pp. 575-577; Poznański, *ZfhB*.
XIX, 2-8). Davidson's edition was made use of by Poznański, who has reedited the whole with Hebrew notes under
the title, תשובות רס״ג על שאלות חיי הבלכי. Warsaw, 1916
(see *ZfhB*. XX, 52 f.).

Of Ḥiwi's writings nothing has thus far become known.
In 1901 a remarkable Genizah fragment of twelve pages in
Hebrew verse was published in the *JQR*, XIII, 345-374, by
Schechter who thinks that it emanated from the school of
Ḥiwi. The fragment contains very vigorous attacks on the
Bible and was later made the subject of minute study by

Bacher (*JQR.*, XIII, 741-745), Poznański (*ib.*, 746-748),
Porges (*ib.*, XIV, 129-133), Seligsohn (*RÉJ.*, XLVI, 99-
122), who also translated it into French, and David Kohn
(הגרון, V, 5-42), who re-edited it with vowel-points and additional notes (comp. Poznański, *ZfhB.*, X, 68). Opinion on
the identity of the author and the specific object of his work
is still divided ; comp. Poznański, חיוי הבלכי, p. 27-30 ; Steinschneider, *AL.*, p. 65, n. 12, where for " XII., 329 " (line 31)
read : XIV, 129.

In an ancient book-list coming from the Genizah a כתאב חוי
בלכי is mentioned (*JQR.*, XIII, 54, no. 71), which in all
probability refers to Ḥiwi's work containing the 200 objections to the Bible, or to some other work of his. Poznański,
JQR., XIII, 329, no. 71, thinks that Saadia's polemic against
Ḥiwi is here meant, which is quite improbable, as in this
case the word *Radd* = Refutation, which is the main part of
the title, could hardly have been omitted by the cataloguer.

6. *Sēfer ha-Galui* (ספר הגלוי). Arabic *al-Kitâb al-Târid*
(אלכתאב אלטארד), usually translated " Book of the Exiled
One " (see below). The first intimation of the existence of
parts of this work, which had been known only from two
quotations in the works of Abraham b. Ḥiyya (ספר העבור
ed. Filipofski, p. x) and Abraham Ibn Daud (סדר הקבלה,
ed. Neubauer, I, 66), came, as in the case of the אגרון (see
above, p. 306), from the Ḳaraite Abraham Firkovich, who
discovered the MS. in 1864 in Egypt, and in an article in the
weekly המליץ, 1868, nos. 26, 27 (also separately under the
title מבוא להקדמות רמות etc., Odessa, 1868) gave some information as to its contents (comp. Geiger, *Jüdische Zeitschrift*, X, 262 ; XI, 155). Three years later, part of the text
appeared in Hebrew translation in the monthly periodical
הכרמל, 1871-1872, pp. 63-68. In 1891 the fragments which
were brought by Firkovich and acquired by the St. Petersburg Imperial Library, were critically edited by Harkavy,
who added a literal Hebrew translation, copious notes, and
an exhaustive Introduction, in which all the historical and
philological data relating to the work, as well as some important additional material, which he discovered subse-

quently, were minutely discussed. Harkavy's monograph on
the *Sêfer ha-Galui* forms the second part of his *Zikron*, vol.
V, Berlin, 1891, pp. 133-235 : see the reviews of this work by
Bacher, *Expository Times*, XI (1899-1900), 454-458; *REJ.*,
XXIV, 307-318, XXV, 143 f.; Porgès, *ib.*, XXV, 144-151,
and Neubauer, *JQR.*, IV, 490-494. The publication of Harkavy has aroused considerable controversy among scholars.
At first the meaning and correctness of both the Hebrew and
the Arabic title were doubted. It was pointed out that the
Hebrew *galui* does not mean " exiled," but " open," " manifest ; " while the Arabic *târid* can only mean " one who exiles,
banishes others," but not one who is himself exiled. Neubauer (*JQR.*, IV, 492) proposed to retain the meaning
" open " for the Hebrew and to read in Arabic correspondingly טאהר. Others proposed the reading *gillui*, " manifestation," and this reading is still maintained by Eppenstein
in his recent *Beiträge*, p. 129 (" *Das Buch der offenen Widerlegung* ") ; see, however, Harkavy, *l. c.*, pp. 142, 180, n. 7,
especially *JQR.*, XII, 550, where he defends the meaning
" exiled," and suggests the change of the Arabic טארד into
the passive form טריד, or טָרָד, admitting the possibility that
the Hebrew title contains an allusion to Jeremiah, 32, 14, in
the sense of an " Open Book." The question regarding the
title becomes still more complicated by the fact that R. Mubashshir, a contemporary of Saadia, refers to the work by the
title *Kitâb al-I'tibâr* (כתאב אלאעתבאר; Harkavy *l. c.*, 182),
which means " Book of Taking Example," *i. e.* an admonition
to the reader to derive moral lessons from the author's experiences as described in his work. This difficulty can be disposed of, however, by assuming that Mubashshir did not
quote the real title of the book, but referred to it in a general
descriptive way. His paraphrase does, indeed, cover the
contents of the book. The reason given by Harkavy (*l. c.*, p.
182, n. 2) for this form of R. Mubashshir's quotation is far
fetched and the interpretation of Neubauer (*JQR.*, IV, 492)
inadequate ; comp. Steinschneider, *AL.*, p. 68, n. 45. Harkavy's view (p. 146, followed by Eppenstein in his notes to
Graetz, *Geschichte*, V, 531, n. 1) that the title כתאב אלאמתתאל

quoted by the Muhammedan author Ibn al-Nadim (who wrote
in 987) as a work by Saadia divided into ten chapters, refers
to the work under consideration, is altogether improbable,
since the latter, contrary to the assertion of Harkavy
and Eppenstein, contains only seven chapters (see Bacher,
JQR., XII, 704; *JE.*, X, 585; Steinschneider, *AL.*, p. 68,
n. 45). אמתׂאל is merely a mistake for אמאנאת.

It must be admitted that none of the explanations is satisfactory. Aside from the linguistic difficulties, it would be
strange if Saadia, contrary to his wont, should have designated an important writing by a title which contains merely a
personal allusion (*i. e.*, to his exile), but does not indicate in
the least the contents of the work. Moreover, if we consider
the whole verse in which the title occurs, it becomes obvious
that the meaning *exiled* for *galui,* which is gained only by
making the latter an artificial substitute for *gōlēh,* is untenable. The verse reads: דברי ספר הגלוי הבמוס רָאֲוָה וחָסוּן
מוסר אמרי צחות הם אוצרו. The words כמוס (Deuter., 32,
34) and חסון (Isaiah, 23, 16) which mean *hidden, treasured,*
are clearly intended as a contrast to *galui=open, visible,* the
author wishing to say " this is the ' Open Book ' (Jeremiah,
32, 14), which contains hidden moral lessons and stored up
ethics; words of rhetoric are its treasure " (רָאֲוָה, Ez., 28,
17, is rendered in the immediately following Arabic verse by
אעתבאר, as quoted by Mubashshir (see above, p. 388), so that
ראוה receives the meaning of learning, that is, *beholding* the
truth; אוצרו is also suggestive of באוצרתי, Deuter., *ib.*). We
know from Saadia's general Introduction to the work that
these were, indeed, its main characteristics; see Malter, *JQR.*,
N. S., vol. III (1912-1913), pp. 489-495. The meaning *exiled* suggested itself only by the incidental fact that the work
was written during Saadia's retirement, and then the Arabic
târid was likewise given this unwarranted meaning. However, אלכתאב אלטארד, with the double article, which in the
meaning " Book of the Exiled " is grammatically impossible,
is not at all a translation of ספר הגלוי, but, as suggested
by Bacher (*Expository Times,*XI, 454-458, and *REJ.,*XXIV,
313; comp. Porgès, *ib.*, XXV, 150), means merely " The

Book that Refutes" and is used by Saadia as a descriptive
title to designate the aim and purpose of the work. It expresses the same thought as "Kitâb al-Radd," which is the
usual title of Saadia's polemical writings. It is true, all
other words in this Arabic line are a verbal translation of
the corresponding Hebrew; but the words ספר הגלוי, being
bodily taken over as a technical title from Jeremiah, did
not require any special translation, and the author replaced
them by two words which, for the Arabic reader, better indicate the character and content of the work.

Of far greater importance than the question of the title
seemed for a time the literary controversy that arose about
the origin and genuineness of the fragment. Some time after
the appearance of Harkavy's work, Professor D. S. Margoliouth came out with an ingenious article (*JQR.*, XII (1900),
502-532), in which he endeavored to prove with much detail
and acumen that the fragment is no fragment at all, but a fab-
rication by some Karaite, composed after the year 962, and intended to serve as a lampoon directed against Saadia, satir-
ically imitating and parodying the latter's philological method
and style, and inserting some of Saadia's opinions (see *ib.*,
p. 532). The article called forth rejoinders by Harkavy (*ib.*,
pp. 532-554) and Bacher (*ib.*, pp. 703-705), which were
followed by a reply by Margoliouth and another "Rejoinder" by Harkavy (*ib.*, pp. 705-707; the same controversy
was carried on between Margoliouth and Bacher in the
Expository Times, XI (1900), 46, 92, 192, 287, 521, 563).
Once more Margoliouth tried to defend his theory (*JQR.*,
XIII, 155-158), but it found no acceptance among scholars.
To-day, after the genuineness of the *Sēfer ha-Galui* has
been positively established by additional MS. material,
readers of Professor Margoliouth's articles may still admire
the ingenuity and art with which he succeeded in making an
entirely groundless theory appear tenable, but they will
otherwise dismiss the whole matter as a curious literary
episode in the history of our work.

As already noted, the *Sēfer ha-Galui* was written in Hebrew and about three years later an Arabic translation and

commentary, with an introduction, were added thereto by the author, who describes this work as " The Book that Refutes." There is no sufficient proof that the Arabic text was accompanied by a second enlarged edition of the original Hebrew text, as has been repeatedly asserted; though this may well have been so, as was the case with other writings of Saadia. At any rate the Arabic was not merely a repetition of the Hebrew content by way of translation, as hitherto assumed, but a new work, which, aside from the literal translation and the interpretation of the difficult rhetorical text of the *Sêfer ha-Galui,* contained much additional material of a controversial character (see below, p. 392, under *b, c*). Both texts must have circulated separately as well, for among the fragments we possess there are some that contain the Hebrew or the Arabic only, while others have both side by side. This is also obvious from two ancient book-lists, that come from the Genizah, the one of which records the " Sêfer ha-Galui " (Schechter, *Saady-ana,* p. 79), the other the " Tafsir Sêfer ha-Galui " (*JQR.,* XIII, 55, no. 77; comp. Lambert, *RÉJ.,* XL, 260). The latter refers to the Arabic text, Saadia using the word *tafsir* alike for translation and commentary; comp. Harkavy, p. 146, n. 6, and above, note 308. For the suggested identification of the *Sêfer ha-Galui* with a *Kitâb al-Kashf* see below, section VII, p. 402, no. 15.

To afford a better survey of the existing material I shall here arrange the Hebrew and Arabic fragments in two separate sections following in each group the order of publication.

A. HEBREW

a) Four pages (18 lines each) the first two of which represent the initial portion of the work, while the other two probably belong to the third chapter. The two fragments were edited together by Schechter (*JQR.,* XIV, 37 ff., reprinted in his *Saadyana,* pp. 4-7), who by way of introduction gives also a clear analysis of their contents. The first four lines of the first fragment (*Saadyana,* p. 4) had been previously published by Schechter from another Genizah MS. with some variations (*JQR.*, XII, 460).

b) A fragment consisting of two pages (19 lines each). The text is divided into verses and provided with vowel-points and accents like the books of the Bible. It was recently published with a French translation and notes by B. Chapira, *RÉJ*, LXVIII (1914), 3-8. In his introductory remarks Chapira still repeats the erroneous view of Harkavy that the *Sēfer ha-Galui* consisted of *ten* chapters three of which, he conjectures, were subsequently omitted by the Gaon This theory was refuted by Bacher long ago (*RÉJ*, XXIV, 314) ; see above, pp. 270 f , and Malter, *JQR.*, N. S , vol. III (1912-1913), p 492, nn. 20, 26.

B. ARABIC

a) A fragment covering sixteen pages (22-23 lines each), edited by Harkavy with an elaborate introduction, Hebrew translation, and copious notes (*Zikrōn*, V, 150-181). It contains nearly the whole Introduction of Saadia (lacking only a few lines of the beginning) and the first three Hebrew verses of the work itself. The first verse is followed by the Arabic translation, which is missing in the same portion published by Schechter from another Genizah fragment (see above, under *Hebrew,* letter *a*).

Another fragment of the same Introduction (four pages of 18 lines each) was published by Malter (from a MS. belonging to Dr. Cyrus Adler in the Library of the Dropsie College in Philadelphia) with an English translation and notes in the *JQR.*, N. S , vol. III (1912-1913), pp. 487-499. The text agrees on the whole with that published by Harkavy (pp. 151, l. 16-158, l. 1), but offers numerous, partly important, variants and also supplements some gaps in the text of Harkavy. For still another fragment of the Introduction, agreeing with Harkavy, p. 169, l 15; p. 173, l 12, see B Chapira, *RÉJ.*, LXVIII, 2.

b) Two leaves (four pages, 16-17 lines each), representing two different parts of the Arabic version, but edited as one by Harkavy (pp 187-193), who calls attention, however, to

the gap between the two leaves. Like the preceding fragment, this is translated by the editor into Hebrew and accompanied by explanatory notes. Both fragments contain
a denunciation of David ben Zakkai and a reply to the criticism of the *Sēfer ha-Galui* in its first edition; see above,
pp. 390 f.

c) Two leaves (four pages, 13 lines each), likewise belonging to two different parts of the work, edited with a French
translation by M. Lambert, *REJ.,* XL, 84-86, 260. It is
important to note that the first leaf of this fragment corresponds to the Hebrew text in Schechter's *Saadyana*, p. 6, leaf
2 *verso,* lines 10 ff.; for here we see clearly the relation of
the two texts to one another, namely, that the Arabic work
contained besides the translation also a commentary on the
Hebrew. The author quotes one or two catchwords from
the Hebrew text to indicate the verse or paragraph of the
Sēfer ha-Galui, which he is about to explain, and then comments upon the passage freely. It is furthermore to be noted
that the larger part of the second leaf is identical with
fragment *b* published by Harkavy (187, lines 1-12), so that
the latter is a continuation of the text edited by Lambert.
In this continuation we see the author interrupting his interpretation of the Hebrew text and suddenly beginning to
defend its style and grammar against the objections made by
his opponents. This, of course, could not have formed part
of the original *Sēfer ha-Galui.* It is thus clear beyond a
doubt that the Arabic *al-Kitâb al-Târid,* was not merely a
translation of the *Sēfer ha-Galui,* but an independent and
more comprehensive polemical work, the purpose of which
was to translate the original Hebrew text, to explain the
obscure passages occurring therein, and more particularly
to refute the attacks made upon it by its detractors.

d) Two fragments, four pages each (18-20 lines to the
page), were recently discovered in Cairo by Bernard Chapira, who published them with a French translation in the
REJ., LXVIII (1914), 9-14. In these two fragments each
Hebrew verse is followed by a literal Arabic translation, thus
evidently belonging to the Arabic edition of the work. Both

seem to have formed part of the sixth chapter, but the text, especially of the second fragment, is so badly mutilated that nothing definite can be said about the contents. We receive here the interesting information that the two opposing parties were designated by " right " (Saadia and his followers) and " left " (the Exilarch, Sarjâdah, etc.) ; see Chapira, *ib.*, pp 2, 7, n. 3; 11, ll. 2-4; B. Lewin, רב שרירא גאון, Jaffa, 1916, p. 2. To these fragments of the *Sēfer ha-Galui* itself may be added:

e) A fragment (43 lines) of a work of R. Mubashshir, in which the author criticizes certain portions of Saadia's *Kitâb al-'I'tibâr* (see above, p. 388), quoting the text of the latter, as it seems, literally (published by Harkavy, *Zikrōn*, V, 183-185). From the contents it appears that he quotes from *al-Kitâb al-Târid* and not from the *Sēfer ha-Galui,* for Saadia defends certain Hebrew expressions he used in the latter, to which Mubashshir objects Moreover, it is not probable that Mubashshir would have quoted the Hebrew original in Arabic translation The title, however, under which he quotes the work, may refer to both texts as a whole. For two other quotations from the work under consideration see Harkavy, pp. 196 ff.

For completeness' sake it should be noted that the text published by Harkavy was translated into Hebrew by Samuel Firkovich, a grandson of Abraham Firkovich, who sent the MS of his translation to H. J Gurland of Odessa. The latter placed it at the disposal of David Kohn (Kahana), who published it in the אוצר הספרות, IV (1892). 318 ff., also separately under the awkward title ספר לתולדות רס"ג, Cracow, 1892, pp 27 ff. He suppressed the name of the translator; see his note at the beginning of the translation; Harkavy, p. 149, n. 2, and above, p. 306 under *'Agrōn*

VII WORKS OF UNCERTAIN DESCRIPTION

Under this heading I propose to bring together a number of writings which, with only one or two exceptions (see nos. 2 and 3), are explicitly quoted in trustworthy sources as the products of the Gaon, so that there is no reason to doubt

their genuineness. The difficulty is that the titles under
which they are quoted, or, as the case may be, the general
terms in which they are referred to, leave it open to doubt
whether the reference is to separate works of Saadia, which,
like other of his writings, were subsequently lost, or to some
parts or chapters of more comprehensive books which
have been dealt with above under the various headings
of Saadia's literary activity. We know from other instances
that Saadia himself, after issuing short monographs on given
subjects, later combined them into one volume with a different, more general title, and that on the other hand he sometimes made excerpts from his larger works and, issued them
as monographs (see above, pp. 194, 267). There is also
sufficient evidence that later readers, who found some of
Saadia's works too extensive and were interested only in
particular sections, likewise made various excerpts for themselves and that these circulated as separate writings (see
below, no. 2). It is therefore unsafe to conclude from the
occurrence of such titles or references that there existed the
same number of separate and original works of Saadia. In
many instances they probably designate parts of works which
are otherwise known by some general title. Nor is the material at hand sufficient to enable us to ascertain in each case
whether we have before us a reference to an otherwise unknown work or merely a new title. As a matter of fact,
some of the writings which were enumerated above as separate works may well belong here. I shall indicate them by
a mere repetition of the titles and cross-references.

PHILOLOGY AND EXEGESIS

1. נקוד רב סעדיה, a grammatical work on *Punctuation* is
quoted by Rashi, Commentary on Psalms, 45, 10, but according to Berliner (see Steinschneider, *Vorlesungen über die
Kunde hebräischer Handschriften*, Leipzig, 1897, p. 15) the
passage is a later interpolation. Bacher (*Die Anfänge der
hebräischen Grammatik*, Leipzig, 1895. p. 60, n. 2), on the
other hand, thinks that it formed the sixth chapter of the

Kutub al-Lugah, which chapter was called by Saadia כתאב
אלדגיש ואלרפי ; comp. Steinschneider, *AL.,* p. 62, no. 23 ; see
also above, note 303.

2. תפסיר ואלה המישפטים, *Interpretation of the Section
Mishpāṭim* (Exodus, 21-24), mentioned in a book-list from
the Genizah, Schechter, *Saadyana,* p. 79 (no. xxxvii). The
name of the author is not given there, but in all probability
it is the treatise mentioned by Isaac Gaon, a preacher
of the 13th century (see Steinschneider, *AL.,* § 168) quoted
by Steinschneider, *CB.,* 2185, who remarks that various parts
of Saadia's commentaries on the Bible must have existed
as separate treatises with special introductions. Isaac Gaon
indeed quotes צדר תפסיר ואלה המישפטים, that is, *Introduction* to the Commentary on Mishpatim; comp. Bacher,
*Abraham Ibn Esra's Einleitung zu seinem Pentateuch-
Commentar,* p. 20, n. 2 [comp. below, p. 427].

3. תפסיר אחרי מות, *Interpretation of the Section Aharē
Mōt* (Leviticus, 16-18), mentioned in the list referred to
under no. 2. Here again no author is named, but in the same
list several other books are mentioned without the name of
Saadia, though his authorship of these books is definitely
established. Thus we find the *Sēfer ha-Galui,* the *Kitâb al-
Ta'riḫ* (see above, pp. 353 f.), and at least five other works
of Saadia mentioned anonymously. The compiler of the
list probably gave the name of Saadia whenever it was found
in the MSS. he catalogued ; where he did not add the name
it may have been missing also in his MSS. For another
explanation see below, p. 407. There is also a strong
probability that this *Tafsir* is identical with the ספר עריות
which was discussed above, p. 346, no. 4. It should be added
that nos. 2 and 3 are mentioned together in the same line
[see also below, *Postscript,* p. 427].

HALAKAH

4. שבועת היסת, *Treatise on the Oath of Inducement,*
referred to by Isaac b. Reuben of Barcelona (11th century)
at the end of the third chapter of his שערי שבועות (see
Steinschneider, *CB.,* 2161). The anonymous Arabic Genizah

fragment (Neubauer and Cowley, *Catalogue*, II, no. 2643, *opus* 23) which deals with the same subject is perhaps part of the treatise in question, as suggested by Cowley, *l. c.*

5. הלכות נדה, see above, *Bibliography*, pp. 348 f., nos. 7, 10. 6. *Tafsir al-ʾArāyōt*, see above, p. 346; 396, no. 3. For a treatise on charity (הלכות צדקה) see note 369. For תפסיר אבות מלאכות see note 366. A הלכות תפלין by Saadia is said to have recently been discovered and published by S. A. Wertheimer, Jerusalem.

CHRONOLOGY

7. *Seder Tannaim we-Amoraim*, see above, notes 357, 395, and *Bibliography*, p. 354, no. 2. For the "Four Gates" (ארבעה שערים) see above, p. 169, no. 2.

PHILOSOPHY

8. *Ḥadd al-ʾInsân* (חד אלאנסאן), "Definition of Man." I insert this work here (though it does not strictly belong to the class of writings here enumerated) as the authorship of Saadia is not fully established. A MS. in the Royal Library of Berlin (see Steinschneider, *Verzeichnis der hebräischen Handschriften der königlichen Bibliothek zu Berlin*, I, p. 48, no. 72,[1]) contains an anonymous Hebrew translation of the first chapter of the work in question, which is explicitly attributed to Saadia, the opening lines reading: בעזרת הבורא אתחיל זה הספר ששמו חד אלאנסאן כמו שפירש רבי סעדיה ראש ישיבה נ״ע . . . . ורבי סעדיה נ״ע חיבר זה הספר מספרי החכמים ותיקן אותו בה׳ שערים; see the rest of the quotation in Steinschneider's *HB.*, X, 25. Kaufmann (*Die Sinne*, p. 94, n. 23) nevertheless ascribes the work to Abraham b. Ḥiyya, because he is quoted by Jedaiah ha-Penini (about 1300) as the author of a work named גדר האדם, which, Kaufmann thinks, is merely the translation of the Arabic title of our work. This identification cannot be maintained, for Abraham b. Ḥiyya wrote all his works in Hebrew, not in Arabic, while the MS., as quoted before, plainly shows that the original was Arabic; comp. Steinschneider, *Abraham Ibn Esra* (in *Supplement zur historisch-literarischen Abtheilung der Zeitschrift*

für Mathematik und Physik, vol. XXV, pp. 59-128), p. 119.
From the contents of the extracts made by Steinschneider,
HB. X, 25, and Kaufmann, *l. c.,* pp. 95, 124, n. 6, dealing with
anatomy, nothing definite can be concluded. Various passages, showing Saadia's familiarity with the works on
medicine and anatomy of his day, are found also in Saadia's
genuine works, *e. g.* in his Commentary on the *Sefer
Yeẓiraḥ,* pp. 97 f., 103 (see above, note 454) ; *Kitâb al-
'Amânât,* pp. 196 (*' Emūnôt,* ed. Cracow, p. 131), 201 (134),
316 (205 f.) ; comp. above, pp. 182, 187 (n. 437), 193. The
topics noted in the outline of the contents of the other four
chapters—on the nature of the soul, mind, etc., on the four elements, on the parallelism between the microcosm and macrocosm, and on the definition or limits (חירוד = Arabic *ḥudûd,*
plural of *ḥadd*) of life and death and what follows thereafter—are all subjects treated by Saadia in his extant philosophic writings ; see above, pp. 187, 222 ff. I expect to arrive
at a definite conclusion by a future examination of the
Berlin MS. For the present we have no sufficient ground
to deny Saadia's authorship of this work against the explicit
testimony of the anonymous Hebrew translator. Steinschneider mentions the book in the index to his *Arabische
Literatur* (*Register* IV, p. 11, s. v. חר) as a work of Saadia,
but there is no trace of it in the paragraph dealing with the
works of the Gaon: see also Harkavy, *Zikron,* V, 162, n. 3.

POLEMICS

9. A *Refutation* of the Karaite Abu-l-Surri b. *Zuṭa* or
Ziṭa, twice referred to by Abraham Ibn Ezra in his Commentary on the Pentateuch (Exodus, 21, 24, and Leviticus,
23, 15, in the recension published by M. Friedlaender, *Essays,*
etc., Hebrew part, p. 70). It cannot be inferred, however,
from either of the passages that Saadia refuted the Karaite
in a special treatise. The latter, who is supposed to have
lived in Egypt, may have had oral controversies with Saadia
in that country, which were subsequently recorded by the
Gaon in his commentaries on the Bible, whence they were
then taken by Ibn Ezra : see for the whole matter Poznański,

JQR., X, 255, no. 5; *idem*, KLO., p. 4, and the references given there, n. 2; comp. Bacher, *JE.*, X, 582, col. 1, no. 5. 10. *Refutation of the Ḳaraite Daniel b. Moses al-Ḳumisi* or Ḳumsi (אלקומסי) of the ninth century, a small Hebrew fragment of which was published by Schechter, *Saadyana*, no. xiii. It is not quite certain that the fragment is part of a separate polemic of Saadia against the Ḳaraite, though the text seems to favor this assumption; comp. Poznański, *JQR.*, VIII, 681-684; *idem, J. E.*, IV, 432 f.; *Schechter's Saadyana*, p. 10, *s. v.* Daniel b. Moses; Eppenstein, *Beiträge*, p. 75; above, note 387.

11. *A Refutation of the Masorite Aaron b. Moses b. Asher*, whom Saadia knew personally. Dûnâsh b. Librât quotes a sentence (תלף תלף האותות) in which Saadia polemicizes against Ben Asher (see Baer and Strack, דקדוקי הטעמים, xi. n. 11). Here again it is not certain that the sentence was taken from a special polemic of Saadia; it may have occurred in one of his grammatical or exegetical works; comp. Steinschneider, *CB.*, 2200, no. 13; Bacher, *Anfänge*, p. 48; *JE.*, X, 582, no. 11; Eppenstein, *Beiträge*, p. 71, n. 1. Luzzatto's interpretation of the sentence (בית האוצר, I (1847), 11*b*) is far-fetched. It may perhaps not be a direct quotation of Saadia's words at all, but merely the information given by Dûnâsh, that according to Saadia the letters תלף are the radicals (האותות) of the noun תלפיות (Canticles, 4, 4), a view which Dûnâsh opposes. The second תלף is perhaps an erroneous dittography, or the first תלף is a corruption of the catchword תלפיות, which stood there originally.

12. *Maḳâlah fî sirâǵ al-Sabt* (מקאלה פי סראג אלסבת), "Treatise on the Light of Sabbath." The question whether or not it is permitted to have light in the house on the eve of Sabbath was an important point of controversy between Ḳaraites and Rabbanites. A work of Saadia under the above title is mentioned twice in an ancient book-list published from the Genizah by Elkan N. Adler and I. Broydé, *JQR.*, XIII, 55, nos. 78, 87. Abraham Ibn Ezra, Commentary on Exodus,

35, 3, says: והגאון רב סעדיה חבר ספר נכבד תשובות על החולקים
על קדמונינו על נר ישבת, which probably refers to the work
under consideration. Poznański, *JQR.*, XIII, 329, no. 78,
however, thinks that the *Maḳâlah* (meaning also paragraph,
chapter) was not a separate book, but formed part of the
Kitâb al-Tamyîz; see above, *Bibliography*, VI, p. 380;
Schechter, *Saadyana*, p. 44, ll. 10-15 [below, p. 427].

13. *Kitâb al-ḳiyâm 'alâ al-sharâï' al-sam'iyya* (כתאב
אלקיאם עלי אלשראיע אלסמעיה), "Book *in Support* of the
Ceremonial (literally: revealed) Laws." Under this title
a work of Saadia is quoted in a Bodleian MS. which contains
also Saadia's Commentary on the *Sêfer Yeçirah;* see Munk,
Notice sur R. Saadia, p. 14, n. 2. According to Steinschneider, *CB.*, 2166, the same work is referred to by Moses
Ibn Ezra under the title *Kitâb taḥṣîl al-sharâï' al-sam'iyya*
(כתאב התחציל אלשראיע אלסמעיה), "Book on the *Manifestation* of the Ceremonial Laws," while the Muhammedan
author Al-Nadim quotes it briefly as כתאב אלשראיע [see
Postscript]. Numerous theories, some rather strange, all of
them recorded by Steinschneider, *l. c.*, have been advanced as
to the identity of this work. Among these theories is worth
mentioning that of Dukes, *Beiträge*, p. 12 (noted by Steinschneider, *CB.*, 2163, no. 10), identifying it with the " Introduction to the Talmud," a view that greatly commends itself :
see above, pp. 159, 342. Later a suggestion of Haneberg
was taken up by Bacher (*Abraham Ibn Esra's Einleitung zu seinem Pentateuch-Commentar*, p. 20, n. 2) to the
effect that the work is identical with the *Kitâb al-Amânât*,
a view considered " plausible " also by Poznański, *REJ.*, XL.,
87, who had previously (*JQR.*, X, 259) adopted the opinion
of Munk, that it was some sort of a compendium of laws
comp. Wunderbar. *Literaturblatt des Orients*, 1847, pp. 487-
490. Recently again it was proposed by Hirschfeld (*JQR.*,
XVIII, 600, n. 3, repeated by him in the Cohen-*Festschrift*,
p. 265, and lately again in the *JQR.*, N. S., vol. VIII (1917-
1918), p. 167) to read the title: כתאב אבטאל אלקיאס
פי אלשראיע אלסמעיה, "Book on the *Rejection of Analogy in*
(the interpretation of) the Ceremonial Laws." These

changes in the title, as was pointed out by Poznański (*KLO.*, p. 97), have no justification whatever. Moreover, the reading אלקיאם (for אלקיאם = analogy, which had already been suggested by Steinschneider, *HB.* IV (1861), 46, n. 2) is supported by the title of the work given below, no. 14; comp. Eppenstein, *Beiträge*, p. 110, n. 1, where אלקיאם is a mistake for אלקיאם.

On the basis of the existing material no definite conclusion can be arrived at, but I am inclined to think, with Hirschfeld, Cohen's *Festschrift* (*Judaica*, Berlin, 1912, pp. 265 f.), that the *Kitâb al-Ḳiyâm*, or *Taḥṣil*, was originally a polemical treatise in defense of those religious laws that are not dictated by human reason, but are based on the doctrine of divine revelation (see above, p. 208). Subsequently Saadia made this treatise a part of his larger work, the *Kitâb al-'Amânât*, in which it forms the third chapter. We know that most of the chapters of this work, if not all of them, were originally circulated as separate writings, partly also under different titles (see above, note 456). It should be added that the title *Taḥṣil* under which it is quoted by Moses Ibn Ezra is found in the list, *JQR.*, XIII, 54, no. 59 (see Poznański, *JQR.*, XIII, 327, no. 59), so that Eppenstein's doubt (*Beiträge*, p. 110, n. 1) is not justified. For further references see Steinschneider, *AL.*, p. 50, no. 13; comp. Cowley, *Catalogue*, no. 2828,2.

14. *Kitâb kasr al-radd 'alâ al-ḳiyâm* (כתאב כסר אלרד עלי אלקיאם), "Rejoinder against the Refutation of the *Ḳiyâm*," *i. e.*, of the work under that title discussed in the preceding paragraph. This Rejoinder is recorded as a work of Saadia in the ancient book-list published by Bacher, *RÉJ.*, XXXIX, 200, no. 29; comp. Bacher's interpretation, *ibidem.*, p. 206, no. 5, who suggests that it may have been directed against the Ḳaraite Ibn Sâḳawaihi, the author of the *Kitâb al-Faḍâih*, in which attacks on Saadia's *Kitâb al-Ḳiyâm* (above, no. 13) may well have occurred (see above, p. 265). If Bacher's suggestion is correct, we may assume that this Rejoinder, too, was not a separate work, but that part of Saadia's polemic against Ibn Sâḳawaihi (see this *Bibliography*, VI,

26

pp. 382 f.) which dealt particularly with the latter's attacks on
the *Kitâb al-Ķiyâm*. Less probability attaches to the suggestion of Poznański (*RÉJ.*, XL, 87), that we have to read here
again קיאס=analogy, for קיאם. The word *ķiyâs* suggests
itself merely because of its frequency in the controversial
literature of the Karaites and the Rabbanites. This fact
should not mislead us to put it in place of קיאם everywhere.

15. *Kitâb al-Kashf* (כתאב אלכשׁף), " Book of Disclosure."
A work of this name is mentioned together with two other
polemical writings of Saadia (the כתאב אלרד עלי אלמתחאמל;
see above, pp. 266 f., and the one discussed in the preceding
paragraph, no. 14) in the list *JQR.*, XIII, 54, no. 59 (see
ibidem, p. 327, no. 59). It is in all probability the same as
quoted in a Genizah MS. recorded by Cowley, *Catalogue*, II,
no. 2668, 25. Cowley suggests its identity with the *Sêfer
ha-Galui* with a query. Indeed, the identification is quite
improbable. A *Kitâb al-Kashf* is mentioned also in Schechter's *Saadyana*, no. xxxvii, p. 79, but it is not obvious from
that passage whether it is to be attributed to Saadia or to his
pupil, a certain Abraham al-Sairafi, see above, p. 293; comp.
Poznański, *Zur jüdisch-arabischen Literatur*, p. 15; *Schechter's Saadyana*, pp. 8, 20, n. 1. The work was at all events
of polemical content.

16. *Kitâb al-'Iskât* (כתאב אלׂאסכאת), " The Book that Si-
lences " (*sc.* the opponent), mentioned as a work of Saadia
in the Genizah MS. (Cowley, *Catalogue*, II, no. 2668, 25;
comp. Poznański, *Schechter's Saadyana*, p. 20, n. 1) referred
to above, no. 15. As the title of the treatise indicates, it was
likewise of a polemical nature.

I place these last two works (15 and 16) in this section of
the *Bibliography*, because nothing further is known about
them. It is possible that they were separate parts of the
larger works previously described.

MISCELLANEOUS

17. מכתב סעדיה גאון (Epistle of Saadia Gaon), addressed to some unnamed community. The Epistle, covering
about three pages, is found in a manuscript volume which

was recently discovered by Dr. Nahum Slouschz on his travels in Morocco, in the house of a Jew by the name of Judah Perez. The volume which I had occasion to examine contains several mediæval writings, one of which bears the date 1438, but, if I remember rightly, is not written by the same hand that wrote the Epistle. The latter consists of a number of short moral exhortations, each one beginning with the words " Children of Israel! " (בני ישראל) and ending with some appropriate Biblical verse. A summary of the content with the facsimile of one page was given by B. Revel in the *Jewish Forum* (New York, 1918), pp 74-77, the writer promising to publish the text in full elsewhere.

18. עשר שירות (Ten Songs), a short fragment dealing with songs by Biblical personages, as the Song of Moses, etc., published by Harkavy in *Israelitische Monatsschrift (Beilage zur "Jüdischen Presse")*, Berlin, 1890, no 12 It was no doubt part of Saadia's Pentateuch Commentary, but perhaps existed also separately under the above title. For details see A. Epstein in the periodical ממזרח וממערב, I (1904), 85-89; Harkavy, *Oeuvres*, IX, p. lxiv; Neubauer-Cowley, *Catalogue*, no. 2745, 23; Steinschneider, *AL.*, p. 66, n. 24.

VIII. SPURIOUS WORKS

It is often as important to know what an author did not write, as it is to know what he wrote Many mediæval thinkers and dreamers, particularly the latter, had the peculiar habit of ascribing their own literary productions to some great name of ages gone by (pseudepigraphy). They were not inspired by evil motives; it was merely part of their system for the propaganda of thought. By hitching their book to the name of some famous personage they expected to secure adherents to the ideas expressed therein. Especially numerous were the pseudepigraphic writings in the field of the occult sciences and of all sorts of mysticism which did not appeal to reason and hence needed the sanction of a recognized authority. It is therefore quite natural that a man of Saadia's reputation should be credited with some such cryptic works, in order to assure their acceptance. They are here given in alphabetical order ·

1. אבן הפילוסופים, "The Philosophers' Stone" quoted by
Moses Botarel of Spain (about 1400) at the beginning of his
Commentary on the Sēfer Yeẓirah. Moses is known to have
been very liberal in the invention of authors and books; see
Rapoport, Tôledôt R. Saadia, n. 47; Steinschneider, CB.,
1780-1784, 2218; comp. Dukes, Beiträge, p. 103; Jellinek,
Beiträge zur Geschichte der Kabbala, I, 60.

2. גורלות (ספר ה), "Book of Lots," the superstitious con-
coction of an anonymous author of which there are several
MSS. and printed editions; see Dukes, Beiträge, p. 103;
Steinschneider, CB., 2218; idem, Zur pseudepigraphischen
Literatur .... des Mittelalters, Berlin, 1862, p. 80, n. 2;
idem, Hebräische Uebersetzungen, p. 868, no. 1; p. 869,
no. 5; Neubauer and Cowley, Catalogue, II, no. 2780, 2.

3. פרוש דניאל, Commentary on Daniel, printed in the Rabbinic Bible as a work of Saadia Gaon. Rapoport, Tôledôt
R. Saadia, n. 39, has proved beyond a doubt that the Gaon is
not the author thereof. Various arguments have since been
advanced by L. Grünhut (in L. Rabinowitz's הגן, St. Petersburg, 1899, pp. 178-188) to disprove Rapoport's view. They
were refuted by Poznański, Ha-Gorcn, II (1900), 101 ff.;
see, however, Grünhut's reply in L. Rabinowitz's מאסף, I
(St. Petersburg, 1902), pp. 137-154. As to the real or supposed author, whose name may also have been Saadia, see
Steinschneider, CB., 2195, and especially Poznański, Ha-
Gorcn, II, 92 ff.; Porges, MGWJ., XXXIV, 63 ff.

4. פרוש ספר יצירה. "Commentary on the Book of Creation," printed in several editions of the Sefer Yeẓirah, first
at Mantua in 1562. In discussing it, Munk (Notice sur
Saadia, p. 15) remarks that "it is the greatest insult one
could offer to Saadia to attribute to him a work which is
unworthy not only of a superior mind, but of any human
being capable of thinking." * For the literature of the subject see Steinschneider, Die hebräischen Uebersetzungen des
Mittelalters, § 260; see also Steinschneider, Pseudo-Saadia's

* C'est la plus grande injure qu'on ait pu faire à Saadia, que de lui
attribuer un écrit aussi peu digne, je ne dirai pas d'un esprit
supérieur, mais de tout homme capable de penser.

Commentar zum Buche Yezira, in *MWJ.,* 1892, pp. 79-85.
It may be added that even a recent obscurantist has made
the attempt to honor Saadia with a makeshift under the
title of מגיר עתידות (Future-Teller), or פתרון חלומות (Interpretation of Dreams), Lemberg, 1860 (?); see Steinschneider, *HB.,* VI, 134. For MSS. containing spurious and
dubious writings, nearly all of which have been treated above,
see the list of Steinschneider, *CB.,* 2222-2224. For *Twelve
Homilies* (י"ב דרושים) on Canticles by Saadia said to have
been translated from Arabic into Hebrew by Judah Saraval
(died 1617), see Steinschneider, *AL.,* p. 59, top; Poznański, *Zur jüdisch-arabischen Literatur,* p. 45; above, p. 322.

IX. WORKS ERRONEOUSLY ATTRIBUTED TO SAADIA
BY RECENT AUTHORS

It is not my intention to note here all the mistakes made
by various authors in attributing anonymous writings to
the Gaon. Thus, when a Commentary on Aristotle's *Ethics*
(פרוש ספר המדות) is ascribed to Saadia by Isaac Satanow,
because he confused it with the פרוש י"ג מדות discussed
above, p. 159 (see Steinschneider, *HB.,* XXI, 134; *idem.,
Hebräische Uebersetzungen,* p. 215, n. 778), or when even
scholars like Dukes (*Beiträge,* II, 38; comp. Steinschneider,
CB., 2198) and Harkavy (see Steinschneider, *HB.,* XXI,
96) credit him with a grammatical work under the title
מלאכת הדקדוק because they misunderstood a passage in the
'Emūnōt *, the matter needs no further discussion. The
proof offered by Kaufmann (*Notes* at the end of Judah b.
Barzillai's פרוש ספר יצירה, p. 335, bottom) for the existence
of a commentary on Chronicles by Saadia is likewise based
on an erroneous interpretation of a passage in the Commentary on Chronicles attributed to one of Saadia's pupils;
see above, p. 327, under *Chronicles;* Bardowicz, *Die Abfas-*

---

* Ed. Slucki, p. 126, ed. Cracow, p. 165. Saadia argues there
against those who claim that the Messianic promises of the prophets
referred to the time of the Second Temple (see above, pp. 239 f.) and
says that when he " subjected their theory to a minute examination "
(והבאתיה במלאכת הדקדוק), he found it all wrong.

sungszeit der Baraita der 32 Normen, p 86, n. 2, Poznański, *JQR.*, X, 248, n. 1.

For a number of other Bible commentaries as well as
translations that were erroneously attributed to Saadia by
various scholars and editors, see the *Bibliography*, above,
under *Minor Prophets and Five Scrolls* (*Canticles, Ecclesiastes*) For an anonymous commentary on the Pentateuch
noted by Deinard, see Steinschneider, *AL.*, p. 56 Special
mention, however, must be made here of the following
works, partly because of their resemblance to some of
Saadia's recognized writings and partly because their authenticity is here and there still maintained.

1. תפסיר אלעשר אלכלמאת, a rhetorical paraphrase of the
Ten Commandments, which exists in various recensions in
several MSS. and editions enumerated by Steinschneider,
AL., p 285, no. 87. To these are to be added the fragment
no. 2861, 12a in Neubauer and Cowley's *Catalogue*, and
another one in the collection of the British Museum In
both fragments the work is ascribed to one Eleazar b
Eleazar, who is otherwise unknown, while another MS in
the library of Paris ascribes it to the Karaite Kirḳisâni,
a younger contemporary of Saadia ; see Poznański, *ZfhB.*,
X, 148, *Zur jüdisch-arab. Liter.*, p. 48 The work has been
published under the name of Saadia also with a Hebrew and
German translation by W. Eisenstädter (Vienna, 1868), who
was deservedly criticized by Derenburg, in Geiger's *Jüdische
Zeitschrift*, VI, 314, and Steinschneider, *HB.*, XIX, 50,
comp Frankel's *Monatsschrift*, 1868, p 462 Zunz, who gave
a description of the contents (*Literaturgeschichte*, p 96),
expressed doubts as to the authorship of Saadia ; Steinschneider designated it as dubious in his Bodleian *Catalogue*,
2216, and later Saadia's authorship was positively denied by
Derenburg, *l. c.*, and Hirschfeld, in *Semitic Studies in
Memory of Dr. A. Kohut*, p. 248, n. 2. Somehow or other,
later authors claimed it again for Saadia ; thus Joel Müller.
Oeuvres, IX, p xix (corrected by Harkavy, *ib*, p xli) and,
as late as 1913, Elbogen, *Der Jüdische Gottesdienst*, p 321
The booklet was translated also into French with a few ex-

planatory notes by Isaac Morali (מרעלי) under the title *Dissertation homilétique sur le décalogue recitée dans les synagogues d'Algérie le premier jour de Pentecôte œuvre de R. Saadia Gaôn,* Algiers, 1913. The author used a manuscript; a comparison of the French translation with the Arabic text of Eisenstädter shows absolute identity of the contents though the text of Morali offered a few variants (see p. 12, n. 1). Morali takes no notice, and probably is unaware, of either Eisenstädter's or any of the other publications of the composition.

To the editions enumerated by Steinschneider, *AL.,* pp. 63, 285, and *JQR.,* XII, 484 (so read in *AL.,* p. 63) should be added the recensions printed in the liturgical collections ארבעה גביעים (Leghorn, 1877, pp. 74b-85b) and בכורים (Vienna, 1889) ; furthermore the three recensions reviewed by Bacher, *ZfhB.,* VII, 114, nos. 12-14, and the אגרת עשרת הדברות, Jerusalem, 1901 (a reprint of the edition noted by Bacher, *l. c.,* no. 14) ; see *ZfhB.,* VI, 104. Finally, it should be noted that while none of these recensions is attributable to Saadia, they are probably the further development and elaboration of a similar work on the Decalogue by Saadia himself, as suggested by Zunz, *Literaturgeschichte,* p. 96; for there does exist a Hebrew liturgical composition on the Decalogue, of which Saadia is unquestionably the author (see the *Bibliography,* II, p. 336, no. 3) and which proves that the Gaon cultivated this form of liturgical poetry. Moreover, in the ancient book-list published from a Genizah MS. (Schechter, *Saadyana,* p. 79) a תפסיר עשרת הדברות is mentioned, which, in all probability, is the work of Saadia, as are most of the anonymous works mentioned in that list. The compiler of the list seems to give the name of Saadia only in connection with the latter's complete commentaries on Biblical books (Isaiah, Lamentations, Job, and Esther) and to register all other works without the name of the Gaon. The commentary on the Minor Prophets mentioned there (l. 6) was fragmentary, as stated by the compiler (קטעתין), so that he may not have been sure about the author, and the same may have been the case with the כתאב אלאזהאר (l. 15),

if, as I assume, it refers to the commentary on the Pentateuch; see above, p. 316, and p. 396, no. 3; Poznański, *Schechter's Saadyana*, pp. 20-23.

One may judge of the popularity of this composition on
the Ten Commandments among the Jews of the Orient from
the fact that it is still being frequently published in various
forms wherever Arabic speaking Jews settle in larger numbers. Thus a תרגום עישרת הדברות ללישון ערבי was recently
published by a Society of Jewish Immigrants from the Orient
in New York (חברת עזרת אחים) as the work of "the ancient
Gaon Saadia (הגאון הקדמון סעאדיא) . . . . who has translated the whole Torah into Arabic " (New York, 1915; in
Hebrew characters). It is written in rhymed prose in the
latest Arabic vernacular, as it is spoken by the Jews in some
parts of the Orient, and is one of the first publications of
that kind in this country. For a more detailed description
of a similar publication in New York see Malter, *JQR.*, N. S.,
vol. VII, pp. 609 f. For some further details on Arabic
liturgies on the Ten Commandments see Steinschneider's
Arabische Predigten in Kayserling's *Bibliothek jüdischer
Kanzelredner*, II (1872), 1 f.

2. תקון, a rhymed composition in two parts, the one dealing
with legal monetary questions (שערי דיני ממונות) and the
other with laws regarding oaths (שערי שבועות). In the
Responsa of Meir b. Baruk and in the de Rossi MS. of the
Parma Library (codex 563, fols. 41-48) the composition is
erroneously ascribed to Saadia and hence also by Dukes,
נחל קדומים, p. 2, and *Beiträge*, II, 12, as also by Benjacob,
Thesaurus, p. 668, no. 869; see Steinschneider, *CB.*, 2161,
no. 7, where Saadia's authorship is denied. Halberstam,
who published the composition (*Jeschurun*, VI, 150 ff.),
proved that its author was the Gaon Hai; see Buber,
Introduction to מדריש שמואל, Cracow, 1893, p. 17, note. The
work was also published, under the name of Hai Gaon, in
the collection בית הבחירה, edited by S. Philipp, part II, Lemberg, 1899, pp 16-31.

3. מחברת התיגאן, a Hebrew treatise on the accentuation
and pronunciation of Hebrew, a MS. of which was dis-

covered in Yemen by the traveller Jacob Saphir of Jerusalem and published by Joseph Derenbourg under the title *Manuel du lecteur,* in the *Journal Asiatique,* 1870 (also separately; see above, p. 339). According to Saphir (אבן ספיר, I, 12*b*, 55*b*) the MS. contained also an Arabic text (published by Neubauer, *Petite grammaire hébraique provenant de Yemen,* Leipzig, 1891; comp. Bacher, *REJ.,* XXIII, 238 ff.), and the whole represents a work of Saadia on Hebrew Grammar; see Geiger, *Jüdische Zeitschrift, IV,* 202, note. Derenbourg, *l. c.,* p. 311 (separate edition, p. 3) dismisses the idea as untenable, since the author of the treatise embodied therein the " Poem on the number of letters " in the Bible (see above, pp. 154, 339), which he himself attributes to Saadia. Moreover, certain grammatical rules employed by the author were absolutely unknown in the time of Saadia, and are found first in the work of Judah Ḥayyûg. For further details on this matter see the references given by Steinschneider, *AL.,* p. 278, no. 36; p. 290, no. 110.

APPENDIX

Reprinted with changes and additional new material from *JOR.,* N. S.,* vol. III (1912-1913), pp. 500-509.

THE DOCUMENTS ON THE BEN MEIR CONTROVERSY

(See above, pp. 69-88; 351 ff.)

Altogether there exist at present twelve documents relating to the controversy of Babylonian authorities, particularly Saadia, on the one side and Ben Meir on the other. All these documents are more or less fragmentary. Some were patched together from separate leaves, partly doublets, found in different libraries, whither they had been brought from the Genizah, then published and republished sporadically by various scholars in several periodicals and separate editions, often with French or English translations and annotations, all within the last twenty years.

There is much uncertainty as to the chronological order or even the identity of these documents. This is due to their mutilated condition, as the beginnings and the ends, where the dates and the names of the authors are to be expected,

have suffered most or are missing altogether. Thus much,
however, seems certain: all but one (no. 12, perhaps also
no. 10) originated during the years 921-922 of the common
era. I shall try to give a brief description of each document
and to arrange them in their approximate chronological
order, using in particular the texts published in H. J. Bornstein's מחלקת רב סעדיה גאון ובן מאיר ספר (reprint from the
היובל in honor of N. Sokolow), Warsaw, 1904, pp. 45-102.

1. A letter of the Babylonian authorities, including Saadia,
addressed to Ben Meir at the beginning of the quarrel, subsequent to Saadia's return from Aleppo to Bagdad shortly
before the high Holy Days of the year 4682 (= 921). If it is
true that Ben Meir issued his first proclamation on the Mount
of Olives on Hosha'na Rabbah of that year, as is claimed
by Epstein, הגרן, V, 137, we might assume that this proclamation was the cause of the letter under consideration, and
that it was written as soon as the news of Ben Meir's procedure reached Babylon. However, Epstein's assumption is
subject to doubt, as such a proclamation by Ben Meir is not
clearly stated in the sources, and the various passages that
come into consideration may also be referred to the proclamation by one of Ben Meir's sons, which took place about
three months later. Moreover, to judge from the highly
respectful and friendly tone in which the writers of this
letter address themselves to their opponent, especially when
compared with the style of their subsequent letters to him,
it is hard to believe that Ben Meir had already taken his first
decisive step by officially proclaiming his reforms. I am
therefore of the opinion that if there was such a proclamation on Hosha'na Rabbah, as appears from the phrase הכרוז
הר הזיתים (Bornstein, p. 91, bottom, 92, top), this letter was
written prior to that event, after the first meeting between
Saadia and the authorities upon his return to Bagdad. This
finds some support in a passage of Saadia's second letter
to his pupils in Egypt, where he says (Bornstein, p. 70):
ושבתי אני וירדתי בגדד והייתי סבור כי קבל עד אשר באה
השמועה בבגדד כי הכריום חסרין. The wording indicates that
some time elapsed between his arrival in Bagdad and the

reaching there of the news of *Ben Meir's* proclamation. The word הכריזם, which occurs twice in that letter, as well as הכרותי (Bornstein, p. 62, l. 30; comp. p. 93, l. 15) is in favor of Epstein's view, though it is not impossible that the writers had in mind the proclamation of Ben Meir's *son*. At any rate the letter in question was written before the month of *Tebet* 4682, when the proclamation of the son took place, and is therefore the first and not, as Epstein (ib., p. 140) thinks, the third letter of the Babylonian Geonim to Ben Meir; comp. S. Eppenstein, *Beiträge,* p. 100, n. 3.

Of this letter, which is lacking at the beginning and the end, two defective leaves were first published by Schechter in the *JQR.,* XIV, 52, and in *Saadyana,* pp. 16-19, later reprinted by Bornstein, pp. 73-77. Quite recently another fragment of the same letter, consisting of one leaf, which agrees exactly with the first leaf published by Schechter and Bornstein, was discovered among the Genizah fragments of the Bodleian Library and edited by A. Guillaume in the *JQR.,* N. S., vol. V (1914-1915), pp. 546-547. In this fragment the portions missing in the publication of Schechter (about a third of the leaf on both sides) are restored to us, so that a better understanding of the contents is now possible. Why Mr. Guillaume has reprinted also the second leaf, which was edited by Schechter and Bornstein and to which he had nothing to add, is not clear to me.

2. The conclusion of a letter by the Babylonians addressed to Ben Meir, dated Tebet, 1233, of the Seleucidæan era (= 4682 Jewish era). The fragment counts but 10 lines, and contains only blessings and good wishes for the Palestinians. Eppenstein, *Beiträge,* p. 100, suggests that it might be the end of the preceding number. Whatever the case may be, this fragment, too, on account of its conciliatory tone, must be assigned to the time preceding the proclamation by the son of Ben Meir within the same month. It was first printed by Harkavy, *Zikrōn,* V, 213, then with variants by M. Friedlaender, *JQR.,* V, 197, by Epstein, *RÉJ.,* XLII (1901), 179, and by Bornstein, p. 45; comp. Epstein, הגרן, V, 137, n. 1. According to him it is the conclusion of the first letter of the

Geonim, which he considers lost, but, as we have seen above
(no. 1), without ground.

3 The reply of Ben Meir to the first letter of the Geonim,
written after the proclamation of his son, to which he refers
(Bornstein, p. 51, l. 10), thus either in the latter part of Tebet
or in Shebat 4682. It was published first by Harkavy,
Zikrōn, V, 213-220 from a Bodleian Genizah fragment
counting six leaves (copied for him by Neubauer), of which
the sixth offers only one legible line, and two additional
leaves which he found among the Genizah fragments in the
library of St. Petersburg and which continue the text of the
Bodleian fragment. Two years later M. Friedlaender re-
edited the Bodleian MS. with various omissions and corrections in the *JQR.*, V (1893), 197 ff. Subsequently two more
pages, partly corresponding with the text of Harkavy and
partly completing it (between leaf 2 and 4), were brought to
Cambridge by Schechter. One of these was published by
Israel Lévi, *RÉJ.* XL (1900), 262, the other by Schechter,
JQR. XIV (1901), 42, and in *Saadyana* (1903), p. 15 Very
recently another leaf containing part of the text published
both by Lévi and Schechter, was found by Elkan N Adler
among the Genizah fragments in his possession and published by him with a French translation in the *RÉJ.*, LXVII
(1914), 50. His text offers several better readings; comp.
Poznański in the same volume of the *RÉJ*, p. 290. In 1901
A. Epstein re-edited all the texts (with the exception of the
portion published by Schechter) with an elaborate Introduction and copious notes in the *RÉJ.*, XLII, 180-187 He also
added a French translation of nearly the whole text (*ib*, pp.
187-191). Finally, Bornstein, using all the material collected
by his predecessors, published the various fragments of the
letter in his work on the controversy (1904), pp. 45-56, with
partly different readings and interpretations. As there was
still a gap in the text of the letter, Bornstein, an authority
on the subject of the calendar, ventured to restore the missing portion (between leaf 5 and leaf 7) by conjectures: see
his introductory remarks, p. 45 His conjectural text was
recently borne out in all essentials by Elkan N Adler's dis-

covery among the Genizah fragments in his collection of the missing sixth leaf, which he published in the *RÉJ.*, LXVII (1914), 51. All these finds notwithstanding, the letter, which consisted originally of twelve leaves (Poznański, *RÉJ.*, LXVII, 290), is still incomplete, a fact overlooked by Eppenstein, *Beiträge*, p. 97, who, contrary to Bornstein's explicit statement (p. 45), and although at that time the leaf now published by Adler was also unknown, asserts that the letter "is preserved in its entirety"; comp. Poznański, *l. c.*, whose distribution of the individual leaves among the various collections, however, is not clear.

4. The letter of Saadia to his pupils in Egypt, which was translated and fully discussed above, pp. 55, 82 f. There is no reference in this letter to a proclamation of either Ben Meir or his son. I have shown, however, on other grounds (see above, p. 55) that it was written either in Tebet or in Shebat of the year 4682 (beginning of 922, common era), thus coinciding in time with the letter of Ben Meir discussed in the preceding number. The exact date cannot be determined, and the letter might perhaps as well be placed before that of Ben Meir. It was first published by Schechter from a MS. belonging to Mayer Sulzberger, *JQR.*, XIV (1901), 59 (*Saadyana*, pp. 24-26), and subsequently by Bornstein, pp. 67-69.

5. Saadia's second letter, written two months after his first letter to the same pupils, as he states explicitly. It was published by Neubauer, *JQR.*, IX (1897), 37; Harkavy, הגרן, II (1900), 98; with French translation and notes by Epstein, *RÉJ.*, XLII (1901), 200-203, and finally by Bornstein, pp. 69-71.

6. Ben Meir's second letter in refutation of the view of the Babylonian authorities. From the contents of this letter it is evident that things were running against him and that he had suffered some defeats, though he was not yet ready to give in. Contrary to his expectations even some of his former friends celebrated Passover of that year (4682) in accordance with the accepted calendar (comp. the passage

in the edition of Bornstein, p 92, l 9: ‏ואם עשיתם בנים‎
‏בשגגה אל תעישו בתישרי בזדון‎). Probably this was the case
with an overwhelming majority of the congregations It
is therefore safe to assume that the letter was written not
long after Passover

Two defective leaves (four pages) from the middle of
the letter were published by Schechter, *JQR*, XIV (1901),
56, *Saadyana*, pp. 20-22; Bornstein, pp 90-93. The same
portion of the letter was recently found on two other leaves
of the Genizah, which restore to us the parts missing in the
edition of Schechter and Bornstein (about the third of the
content). The fragment was published by A. Guillaume in
the *JQR.*, N. S., vol. V (1914-1915), pp. 552-555.

7. A fragment disputing the right of the Babylonians to
fix the calendar, published by Schechter, *JQR*, XIV (1902),
249, *Saadyana*, p. 131, Bornstein, p. 94. Bornstein suggests
that this fragment formed a part of Ben Meir's second letter
discussed before (no. 6). This is also the opinion of Epstein,
‏הגרן‎, V (1906), 139.

8 A letter against Ben Meir by some unnamed scholar,
who, as Bornstein (p 78, comp. Epstein, ‏הגרן‎, V, 141, n 2)
pointed out, was not a Babylonian. The author, addressing
himself to Ben Meir, uses a phrase that occurs in Ben Meir's
second letter (the passage quoted above in no 6), turning
the same against him and his followers, thus making it
certain that he wrote during the same summer, probably
soon after the appearance of Ben Meir's epistle It consists of three leaves, which were found and published at
different times, the third leaf by Israel Lévi, *RÉJ.*, XLI
(1000), 229-232, re-edited by Epstein, *RÉJ*, XLII (1901),
197-200; the second by Schechter, *JQR*, XIV (1901),
62-63 (reprinted in *Saadyana*, pp. 26-28); and the first by
the same author in *Saadyana* (1903), p 19 The three parts,
all badly mutilated and lacking about half of the original
contents, were then arranged in their consecutive order and
re-edited with explanatory notes by Bornstein (1904), pp
78-80 Lastly, here again another complete leaf corresponding to the first leaf edited in *Saadyana*, p. 19 was

recently found among the Genizah fragments of the Bodleian Library and published by A. Guillaume in the *JQR.,*
N. S., vol. V (1914-1915), pp. 550-551. This is a welcome
find, as the leaf contains more than double the contents of
the mutilated leaf previously published.

9. A fragment dealing with the differences between the
"Four Gates" of the accepted calendar and those introduced by Ben Meir. There is not the least doubt that
Saadia is the author of this fragment, as various phrases
and even a whole portion of it agree almost literally with
passages occurring in the remnants of the ספר המעדים; comp.
the phrase in Bornstein, p. 64, l. 18 and p. 102, l. 3, as also
the passages following there on pp. 65 and 102, respectively.
The question is only as to the chronological place of this
fragment within the controversial literature. Bornstein,
p. 99, suggests that it may have been part of the ספר המעדים
or an appendix thereto. Epstein, however, in הגרן, V, 140,
though recognizing the authorship of Saadia, is of the
opinion that it represents a letter of the Babylonian authorities to the Jewish communities. If that be the case we should
have to assume that Saadia was charged even with the composition of the official letters of the Geonim, which is not
very probable. Besides, the words (p. 102) : לכתוב את הספר
הזה להיותו לזכרון בתוך כל ישראל להודיעם מעשה בן מאיר הזה
מתחלה ועד סוף, do not seem to refer to a letter, but, like the
parallel passage (p. 65), to some memorial volume that was
intended for the Jewry in general. To such a ספר זכרון ומגלה
לדרות Saadia refers also in an Arabic letter published by
Hirschfeld, *JQR.,* XVI (1904), 296, *fol. 2 verso,* ll. 4-5, and
it is therefore probable that we have here a fragment of that
memorial volume. This is suggested also by Eppenstein,
Beiträge, p. 102, n. 3, but he overlooks the authorship of
Saadia. There is only this difficulty, that in the letter referred
to Saadia speaks of the book as having been written by
the Exilarch, while, as pointed out before, the fragment
indicates Saadia as the author. We may assume, however,
in this instance, that Saadia wrote the book by request of
the Exilarch and in his name, so as to give it more weight

and authority, and, therefore, in referring to it had to designate it as the work of the Exilarch. After all, it was not a
question who was the writer of a document, but what purpose it was intended to serve. The description Saadia gives
there of the ספר זכרון, as dealing with the *Four Gates* con-
trived by Ben Meir, tallies very well with the contents of
our fragment. I am therefore of the opinion, that the
ספר זכרון mentioned by Saadia in one of the fragments of the
ספר המעדים (Bornstein, p. 65) is not another name for the ספר
המעדים itself, as has been hitherto accepted (Epstein, הגרן
V, 140, Eppenstein, *Beiträge*, p. 101), but is the name of
another book, of which our fragment formed a part. Moreover, it was not the ספר המעדים, which was to be read in
public on the twentieth of Elūl, as generally assumed, but the
ספר זכרון mentioned therein. There is no basis for the assumption that the *Sēfer Zikkārōn* is identical with the *Sēfer
ha-Mō'adim*, or that the latter was intended for public recitation. Judging from the style of the extant fragments of
the *Sēfer ha-Mō'adim* it would, indeed, seem very strange,
that such a book should have been destined to be read in
public, as it could hardly serve the purpose. The passages
on which this view is based were simply misunderstood, because of the erroneous identification of the two books. It
should be noticed that in the fragment of the *Sēfer ha-
Mō'adim* (Bornstein, p. 65) Saadia reports that it was decided to write a *Sēfer Zikkārōn* for future generations
(נכתוב ספר זכרון לדורותינו אחרינו), which agrees with ספר
זכרון ומגלה לדורות in the letter published by Hirschfeld,
while in the fragment of the *Sēfer Zikkārōn* (Bornstein,
p. 102) he says that it was decided to write *this* book as a
memorial for all Israel (לכתוב את הספר הזה להיותו לזכרון
בתוך כל ישראל). This distinction between the two
books relieves us also of the difficulty that Saadia should
have repeated his report in nearly the same words in one and
the same book. The *Sēfer Zikkārōn* was written, first, at
the request of the Exilarch, when all other efforts against
Ben Meir had failed, and was finished before Elūl, 4682;
while the *Sēfer ha-Mō'adim*, which mentions the former,

may have been written at any subsequent time, but probably soon afterwards. As Saadia informs us in his ספר הגלוי (see Harkavy, *Zikrōn,* V, 151, l. 22; comp. *JQR., N. S.,* vol. III (1912-1913), p. 496, l. 6) he wrote the *Sēfer ha-Mō'adim* also by request of the Exilarch.

The fragment of the *Sēfer Zikkārōn* was published by Schechter, *JQR.,* XIV (1902), 498-500 (*Saadyana,* pp. 128-130), and by Bornstein, pp. 99-102.

It is rather surprising that Mr. Elkan N. Adler from whose unique Genizah MS. this fragment was first published by Schechter should have overlooked my discussion of the matter (*JQR., N. S.,* vol. III (1912-1913), p. 505-507) as well as the repeated editions of the fragment, and should have re-edited it in the *RÉJ.,* LXVII (1914), 44 ff., as a "new document" representing part of the *Sēfer ha-Mō'adim!* The new thing is the clear French translation which he contributed; comp. Poznański in the same volume of the *RÉJ.,* p. 290.

10. Three fragments of Saadia's ספר המועדים, written probably when the struggle, so far as we know it, was over, 4682-4683; see above, no. 9. One of the fragments (counted by Bornstein, p. 58, as no. II) was published with a French translation by Elkan N. Adler and I. Broyde, *RÉJ.,* XLI (1900), 224-229, later retranslated and re-edited with additional notes by A. Epstein, *RÉJ.,* XLII, 191-197. Subsequently the fragment was completed by two leaves discovered by Schechter, which partly overlap one another as well as the text previously published. The two additional leaves were published by Schechter, *JQR.,* XIV, 49-52 (reprinted in *Saadyana,* pp. 10-13).

Fragment no. I was published by Schechter, *JQR.,* XIV, 47-48 (*Saadyana,* pp. 8-9), and fragment no. III by Schechter, *ib.,* p. 52 (*Saadyana,* pp. 13-14). The whole was later re-edited by Bornstein, pp. 58-67. For another fragment of the *Sēfer ha-Mō'adim,* in which, however, the controversy is not explicitly mentioned, see Harkavy, *Zikrōn,* V, 220; comp. Hirschfeld, *JQR.,* XVI, 291, n. 1. A more recently

27

discovered fragment is described in Cowley's *Catalogue*, II, no. 2660, 27.

11. An Arabic letter of Saadia to three Rabbis in Egypt in answer to their inquiries regarding the calculations of Ben Meir, which they had accepted by mistake, celebrating the festivals accordingly. Saadia enlightened them on the situation and admonished them to read for themselves and to others the Letter of Reproof and Warning (כתאב תוכחה ואזהרה) of the Head of the Academy, copies of which he sent, together with copies of the *Sēfer Zikkārōn* of the Exilarch (see above, no. 9). This interesting letter is dated "Friday, the 11th of Tebet." The year is not given, but no doubt it is 4683. The letter was published with an English translation by Hirschfeld, *JQR.*, XVI (1904), 290-297; comp. D. Yellin's *Notes* thereon, *ib.* pp. 772-775.

12. A list of the differences between the respective calculations of Saadia and Ben Meir regarding the appointment of the festivals during the years 4682-4684. According to Epstein (הגרן, V, 141) the author of this list lived in Egypt after the death of Saadia, for he adds the eulogy זכרונו לברכה to Saadia's name. He also speaks of Saadia as "the Gaon" and "the Head of the Academy," which, as we know, he became only several years after the quarrel. The list was published first by Schechter, *JQR.*, XIV, 59 (*Saadyana*, pp. 22-23), later re-edited with a French translation by Epstein, *REJ.*, XLIV (1902), 235 f., and finally by Bornstein, p. 95.

In addition to the twelve documents here discussed there may be mentioned a fragment which was recently published by A. Guillaume (*JQR.*, N. S., vol. V (1914-1915), p. 556), and which seems likewise to bear on the Ben Meir controversy. The allusions are so veiled, however, that nothing definite can be said about the contents. My assumption (see Guillaume, *l. c.*, p. 545) that the fragment is part of Saadia's first letter to Ben Meir which he wrote in Aleppo (see above, pp. 82 f.) is not borne out by the passage (p. 557, l. 6): וישמא בישוב התלמיד הזה יישוב גם הראש, in which Ben Meir, if he is meant by "the Head," figures as the third person.

An epigram bearing the name of Ben Meir and supposed by Elkan N. Adler, who published it in the *RÉJ.*, LXVII, 52, to be intended against Saadia, is in all probability, as shown by Poznański (*RÉJ.*, LXVII, 291), to be ascribed to another Ben Meir, of a later period.

Of general articles on the controversy I wish to point out in particular that of Poznanski, *Ben Meir and the Origin of the Jewish Calendar, JQR.*, X, 152-160, as well as the elaborate essays of Epstein (*REJ.*, XLII, 173-210, XLIV, 230-236, הגרון, V, 118-142; comp. Poznański, *ZfhB.*, X, 67) and Bornstein, referred to repeatedly above.

The account here given of the chronological order and identity of the documents on the Ben Meir controversy differs essentially in several points from that of the various authors mentioned, but a careful examination of the sources will, I believe, justify this presentation.

While the present work was going through the press some
new Genizah material, bearing on Saadia, has been brought
to light by Dr. J. Mann, who has courteously sent me the
galley proofs of his article, which is to appear in the April
issue, 1921, of the *JQR*. It was too late to take full account
of that material in all the passages upon which it has a direct,
and often an important, bearing, without resorting to some
radical and extensive changes in our construction of Saadia's
biography. I have therefore thought it advisable to treat
the matter separately in the present *Postscript*.

The point that concerns us most is a new date for Saadia's
birth which is to be inferred from one of the recovered
fragments. The fragment in question contains the initial
portion of a Fihrist (list) of Saadia's writings compiled by
two of his sons (She'ërit and Dosa) eleven years after their
father's death, at the request of some person or persons whose
names are obliterated. The list was preceded by a few biographical data of which the following is all that remains
(the letters in brackets are supplied conjecturally) : פחות
מששים שנים מ . . [יו]ם מהן י"ד שנה בן[י]שי[בת] מחסיה
חסירות ד ימן[י]ס ו[נפ]טר בליל שני בסוף האשמורת התיכונה
בששה ועשרים בחדש אייר שלשנת [א]לף ורנ"ג היום לאסיפתו
[פ]חות מי"א שנה—"Sixty years less forty . . . . days of
which he (Saadia) was fourteen years less four days in the
academy of Sura. He died in the second night (*i. e.*, in the
night from Sunday to Monday) at the end of the middle
watch (about two o'clock) on the 26th of Iyyar of the year
1253 (of the Seleucidæan era = May 18, 942). It is now
nearly eleven years since his departure."

Judging from the exactness with which the date of Saadia's
death is here given, it seems quite certain that the missing
part at the beginning of this biographical sketch contained a

similarly exact information about the date of Saadia's birth
and that the words " sixty years less forty . . . . days " refer to some preceding verb indicating the total length of the
Gaon's life. Taking then the 18th of May, 942 as the day of
Saadia's death, we obtain the result that he was born between
the 30th of March and the 8th of April, 882 (the exact day
cannot be ascertained, as the units after " forty " are
missing).

The date 892, heretofore generally maintained, was based
exclusively on the testimony of Abraham Ibn Daûd, who
stated explicitly (see Neubauer, MJC., I, 66) that Saadia
died in 942 at the age of *about* fifty years (כב׳ חמישים,
or, as other MSS. have it, כב׳ נ; see below). Ibn Daûd's
statement is repeated in the works of all the following
mediæval chroniclers without exception. When, with the
appearance of Schechter's *Saadyana* (1903), the old mistaken
idea of Saadia's direct importation from Egypt in 928 to
assume the Gaonate of Sura, was corrected by a letter from
the Genizah from which we learned that as early as 921
Saadia had been sojourning in the East for at least six and
a half years (see above, p. 55), it was concluded that the
year 915 was that of his emigration from Egypt. For, taking
Ibn Daûd's date as a basis, Saadia was then 23 years old,
and it appeared quite improbable that even prior to this age
he should have left in Egypt, as is obvious from the letter in
question, not only a wife and several children, but also a
number of pupils, whom he now considered mature and influential enough to ask them for their support in his struggle
against Ben Meir. These conclusions tallied also with the
general assumption that the " Refutation of Anan," written,
as is well attested (see the references above, p. 380), at the
age of 23, was composed by Saadia in his native country ;
which may also account for his having emigrated soon after
(see pp. 58 f.), that is, in accordance with the chronology of
Ibn Daûd, in 915 !

Still more significant corroboration of these conclusions
was seen in a fragmentary diary, which was undoubtedly
written by Saadia and in which the latter was found travel-

ing in Babylonia and Syria at the age of "twenty . . . ."
years (here again the units are obliterated). Circumstantial
evidence made it appear very probable that these journeys
took place in 920-921, shortly before the outbreak of the
Ben Meir controversy (see above, note 107), and this again
was possible only on the basis of the old date, 892, given by
Ibn Daûd, as according to the date 882 of the recent Genizah
fragment Saadia must then have been 38-39 years old. It
should be added that the word עשרים (twenty) in the diary
is vocalized and accentuated, removing all doubt as to its
correctness (see above, p. 60).

If, then, the new date of 882 for Saadia's birth-year be
accepted as correct, most of the calculations concerning the
time of Saadia's departure from Egypt and his subsequent
travels in the East, as presented in the biographical portion
of this book, would have to be given up or essentially modified. We are thus placed before the alternative of rejecting
either the reading "fifty" (Ibn Daûd) or that of "sixty"
(recent Genizah fragment) as faulty. Ibn Daûd's text is
borne out by all the MSS. and editions of his work as well
as by those of the works of numerous later chroniclers, who
drew upon him. Hence a mistake in his text, if such it is,
would in all probability have to be traced back to the author
himself, who may have been misinformed. In the case of
the fragment, on the other hand, the mistake could only have
originated with some copyist (who had before him 'מנ (פחות)
which he read as 'מס, this reading being then given in full,
מששים, by another copyist), as it is inconceivable that
Saadia's own sons, the authors of the list, should have been
mistaken about the age of their father at the time of his
death.

Now, on general grounds, it might readily be admitted that
the mistake is Ibn Daûd's, who, as proved elsewhere, was not
always well informed (see above, note 86).* But then we
would ultimately be compelled to assume that even the
earlier source or sources relied upon by Ibn Daûd were like-

---

* Dr. Mann's suggestion that 'נ in Ibn Daûd's text is a copyist's
mistake for 'ס does not recommend itself for the reason stated above
that the reading is found in all extant manuscripts.

wise all incorrect or their authors misinformed with regard
to exactly one full decade of Saadia's life. Such an assumption, merely because a conflicting date is found in an otherwise badly mutilated Genizah fragment, seems to me
extremely hazardous. Genizah fragments are, after all, not
Masoretic texts, and, on the other hand, Saadia appeared
to the ancient writers, like Ibn Daûd and his predecessors,
important enough to make them treat his life with some care
and attention. Moreover, the expression כבן חמישים (*about
fifty*) used by Ibn Daûd, viewed in the light of the information we receive from the recent fragment, namely, that Saadia
lived " sixty years minus forty .   . days," suggests the
idea that the vagueness of Ibn Daûd was not due to his uncertainty as to the exact number of years, but that he too
was aware of the fact that the decades, which he took to have
been five, were lacking some days, the number of which he
either did not know or did not care to state.* If this be the
case, it would seem rather strange that while being correctly
informed with regard to a small fraction of a year, he should
have been misinformed as regards a whole decade of the
total of Saadia's life.

Finally, it should also be taken into consideration that,
while, as will be seen below, all the details contained in the
fragment can be borne out by other sources, nothing whatever can be found to support the new date of the year 882 as
that of Saadia's birth,** except perhaps the general reflec-

---

* Sherira, the chief historian of the Gaonate, who as Gaon and contemporary of Saadia, certainly was familiar with the details relating
to the latter, likewise gives only the fourteen years of Saadia's occupancy of the Gaonate, but omits the missing days mentioned in the
fragment.

** A passage in the אור זרוע (I 197, col 1, no 698) of Moses b.
Isaac of Vienna (1250) . ורב סעדיה גאון כריש בישם ר' היי גאון.
referring either to Hai b. Nahshon of Sura (died 896) or Hai b
David of Pumbedita (died 898), cannot be construed to prove a personal contact between the latter and Saadia, as in that case we should
have to assume that Saadia studied at the academy of Sura or Pumbedita prior to 896 or 898; for which assumption, even granting that
he was born in 882, there is as little reason as for its alternative,
that either of the two Hais ever was in Egypt.

tion that, having accomplished so much literary work he must have lived more than fifty years, which is hardly safe ground to build upon.

In view of the foregoing considerations it seems inadvisable to undertake a reconstruction of Saadia's biography on the basis of the new date. It may be suggested, however, that leaving Ibn Daûd aside, a harmonization of this date with the older Genizah material might, on the whole, be possible by placing Saadia's emigration from Egypt in the years 905-911, that is, when according to the new date, Saadia was 23-29 years old. He may at first have spent some time in Palestine, where he met Abû Kathir and other Palestinian scholars (see pp. 36, 65 f.), and then proceeded to the seats of the Gaonate, subsequently continuing his travels through Babylonian and Syrian cities. The diary (above, pp. 59-62), written during this period, would, contrary to our previous conclusions (see note 107), stand in no relation whatever to the letters of Saadia to his pupils in Egypt, written in 922 (see pp. 55 f.), that is, eleven or more years later. During the intervening years he must have lived again for some time in the Holy Land, for in one of the letters referred to, written somewhere in Babylonia, in which he complains to his pupils in Egypt of not having heard from them for six and a half years, he writes "you have probably thought that I am *still* in Palestine" (see p. 56).

While it would thus be possible to bring the various Genizah documents into harmony with the new date derived from the recent fragment, we have no explanation for the strange fact that Saadia should have lived for a period of seventeen years (905-922) in separation from his family— unless we assume that subsequent to his travels in Babylonia and Syria, as described in the diary, he returned to his native country; whence, for some unknown reason, he again emigrated to Palestine in the year 915. All this is quite problematical. Only new finds in the unexplored Genizah collections may eventually clear up this part of Saadia's biography. For the present, therefore, I deem it more desirable to leave the presentation of Saadia's life unchanged,

making allowance, however, for a possible need of readjust-
ment in the future. In the meantime I have inserted a reference to this *Postscript* wherever the results based on the older
material came in conflict with the data of the latest Genizah
fragment.

The new material, including the fragment in question, contains also a number of details which partly modify and partly
supplement or corroborate various statements made in the
course of our investigation They may here briefly be set
forth as follows:

1 Saadia's election to the Gaonate took place on the
22 of Iyyar = 15 of May, 928.

2 Saadia did not write a commentary on the whole Pentateuch, but only on Genesis from the beginning to the section
ויצא (28, 10), and on all of Exodus and Leviticus. Samuel
b Hophni continued the work by commenting upon Genesis
from ויצא to the end, all of Numbers, and Deuteronomy
from the beginning to the section שופטים (16, 18) ;* while
the rest of Deuteronomy was done by Saadia's famous
adversary Aaron Sarjâdah (see above, note 241). It is
interesting to note that of all the fragments of the Pentateuch commentary enumerated in our *Bibliography* (pp 311-
315) only the one under letter *q* may now have to be assigned
to Samuel b. Hophni.

3 Dosa actually became Gaon of Sura (see above, note
281), but not until 1013, when he was over eighty years old.
He died in 1017, four years after his succession to the Gaonate, at the age of about 87-89 years This fully substanti-
ates our suggestions above, notes 13-14, 290

4 Samuel b Hophni did not die in 1034, as, following
Abraham Ibn Daûd, has heretofore been maintained, but in
1013, when he was succeeded by Dosa. He was thus not the
last Gaon of Sura, as hitherto generally assumed. Samuel's
own son, Israel (see above, p. 29, note 13), succeeded Dosa
in 1017 He died in 1033, which may have been the cause of
Abraham Ibn Daûd's mistake in giving the year 1034 as that

---

* The part of Samuel's Commentary on Genesis published by I.
Israelsohn. St Petersburg, 1886 (see Steinschneider, *1L*, p 110, no
15), belongs to this work.

of the death of Samuel b. Hophni, through confusion of the
father with the son. Israel was succeeded in the Sura Gaonate by one Azariah, perhaps —— Israel's son, who died
shortly after, and was succeeded by Isaac, the last Gaon of
Sura. Israel survived Hai by some years. The Sura Gaonate accordingly lasted, contrary to previous assumptions,
longer than that of Pumbedita. The new material, it may be
added in passing, fully bears out my conclusion that owing to
Dosa's claims to the Sura Gaonate, there must have been
much strife and contention between Sura and Pumbedita
prior to the appointment of Samuel b. Hophni (see above,
note 281).

5. Dosa had an older brother by the name of Sheërit
(comp. above, pp. 29, 56). So far as I know this name does
not occur elsewhere in Jewish literature. The title *'allūf*
(see above, p. 64) is added to his name in the list of his
father's writings which he together with Dosa composed in
953. He must have been dead when Dosa became Gaon.

As to the works enumerated in the list, they will all be found
in the present book under their proper headings. Some titles
occurring only in the list remain obscure and require further
investigation. Thus it is not clear what is meant by מן מסאיל
תרי עשר ומן אלתוריה (comp. above, p. 318) or by כתאב
אבטאל (אלגמע)(?) . . . (comp. above, p. 400, below). The
אזהאר אלריאץֹ, *i. e.*, anthology, is probably the Arabic title of
the Poem on the 613 Precepts (see p. 330, no. 2). For this
Poem on the 613 Precepts (see p. 330, no. 2). For this
title see Steinschneider, *AL.*, p. 151. The כתאב וגוב אלצלאת
is not a new work, as thought by Dr. Mann, but the title of
the introduction to the *Siddūr,* which circulated also as a
separate work; comp. Neubauer, *Ben Chananja,* VI, 552;
Bacher, *REJ.,* XXXIX, 206, no. 7; above p. 330. The
אקאמה אלעבור כתאב גמע אלחגה לֹלסרוג, and כתאב גמע, the
אלשראיע are probably identical with the works mentioned
above, pp. 352, no. 5; 399 f., nos. 12, 13. The Commentary on
the *Sefer Yezirah* is here called תפסיר הלכות יצירה. For
the דראשאת see p. 323; for המשפטים ואלה and אחרי מות
see p. 396, nos. 2, 3. These sections of the commentary were
in circulation as separate books and hence the special titles.

It is therefore unnecessary to assume with Dr. Mann that
they were the titles of the entire second halves of Exodus
and Leviticus, respectively. Indeed, it is quite improbable,
as in that case there was no reason to mention them as
separate books immediately after having mentioned the commentaries to Exodus and Leviticus in their entirety.

PHILADELPHIA, January, 1921.

ADDENDA

Note 175: Comp. also Poznański in A. Schwarz's *Festschrift*, Berlin, 1917. p. 473.

Note 191: To the biographical sketches on Saadia should
be added that of A. Schwarz, *Jüdisches Literaturblatt*, XXII
(1893), pp. 17 ff.

Note 240: The name Sarjadah is probably not of Arabic
origin, but is to be derived from the Syriac סרג, to draw
straight lines on paper or parchment, hence סורגדא, a wooden
or metal ruler. The name may therefore have to be pronounced Sûrgada; comp. Krauss in Schwarz's *Festschrift*,
p. 575.

Note 645: For Dûnâsh b. Labrat's relation to Saadia see
Porges in Kaufmann's *Gedenkbuch*, pp. 245-259.

Pages 320, below (Eliezer b. Nathan), and 323 (Homilies): See Michael, *Jahrbuch der Jüdisch-Literarischen
Gesellschaft*, VI (1906), 32.

Pages 345, no. 3, and 348, nos. 7-8: See Michael, *ibidem*,
p. 31.

LIST OF ABBREVIATIONS

A. Initials

AIE. = Abraham Ibn Ezra.

AL. = Steinschneider, *Arabische Literatur*, Frankfurt a. M., 1902.

CB. = Steinschneider, *Catalogus librorum hebracorum in Bibliotheca Bodleiana.*

HB. = Steinschneider, *Hebraeische Bibliographie*, Berlin, 1858-1882.

JE. = *Jewish Encyclopedia.*

JQR. = *Jewish Quarterly Review*, London, 1889-1908.

JQR. N.S. = *Jewish Quarterly Review, New Series*, Philadelphia, 1910-1921.

KLO. = Poznański, *The Karaite Literary Opponents of Saadiah Gaon* (see p. 380).

MGWJ. = *Monatsschrift für Geschichte und Wissenschaft des Judentums*, Breslau, 1851-1921.

MJC. = Neubauer, *Medieval Jewish Chronicles*, Oxford, 1887-1895.

MWJ. = *Magazin für die Wissenschaft des Judenthums*, Berlin, 1874-1893.

REJ. = *Revue des Etudes Juives*, Paris, 1880-1921.

ZfaW. = *Die Zeitschrift für die alttestamentliche Wissenschaft*, Giessen, 1881-1921.

ZfhB. = *Zeitschrift für hebräische Bibliographie*, Frankfurt a. M., 1896-1921.

בכה"ע = בכורי העתים (see note 190).

רר"ו = דור דור ודורשיו (see note 32).

פס"י = פרוש ספר יצירה.

סתו"א = סדר תנאים ואמוראים.

B. Abbreviated Titles

Bacher, *Anfänge*, see note 22.

Bornstein, see note 4.

Dukes, *Beiträge*, see p. 328.

Eppenstein, *Beiträge*, see note 6.

Harkavy, *Zikron*, see note 3, beginning.

Jellinek, *Beiträge*, see note 405.

Lazarus, see note 194.

Nathan, see note 192.

Pinsker, *Likkūtē*, see note 3, near end.

Sherira, see note 192.

INDEX OF AUTHORS

[Numbers in heavy type refer to the pages of the *text*, all other numbers refer to the *notes*.]

431

INDEX OF TITLES

OF SAADIA'S ARABIC WRITINGS MENTIONED IN THE BOOK
(Mostly in Transliterated Form)

HEBREW TITLES

BIBLIOLIFE

Old Books Deserve a New Life
www.bibliolife.com

Did you know that you can get most of our titles in our trademark **EasyScript**™ print format? **EasyScript**™ provides readers with a larger than average typeface, for a reading experience that's easier on the eyes.

Did you know that we have an ever-growing collection of books in many languages?

Order online:
www.bibliolife.com/store

Or to exclusively browse our **EasyScript**™ collection:
www.bibliogrande.com

At BiblioLife, we aim to make knowledge more accessible by making thousands of titles available to you – quickly and affordably.

Contact us:
BiblioLife
PO Box 21206
Charleston, SC 29413

Made in the USA
Lexington, KY
31 January 2012